GENDER ON PLANET EARTH

Ann Oakley

polity

First published in 2002 by Polity Press in association with Blackwell Publishers Ltd, a Blackwell Publishing Company.

Editorial office:
Polity Press
65 Bridge Street
Cambridge CB2 1UR, UK

Marketing and production:
Blackwell Publishers Ltd
108 Cowley Road
Oxford OX4 1JF, UK

ISBN 0-7456-2963-6
ISBN 0-7456-2964-4 (pbk)

A catalogue record for this book is available from the British Library.

Typeset in 10 on 12 pt Times
by SNP Best-set Typesetter Ltd., Hong Kong
Printed in Great Britain by MPG Books Ltd, Bodmin, Cornwall

This book is printed on acid-free paper.

Contents

It is tempting to think that the problems that we face today, from the homeless on our streets and poverty in the Third World to ozone depletion and the greenhouse effect, can be solved by technology or technical expertise alone. But even to begin to solve these daunting problems . . . requires that we greatly improve our capacity to *think* about our institutions.

R. N. Bellah, R. Madsen, W. M. Sullivan, A. Swidler and S. M. Tipton,
The Good Society, 1992, p. 5 (my italics)

The emancipation of belief is the most formidable of the tasks of reform ... It is formidable because power that is based on belief is uniquely authoritarian; when fully effective, it excludes by its nature the thought that would weaken its grasp.

J. K. Galbraith, *Economics and the Public Purpose*, 1974, p. 223

Of all crippling hindrances in false ideas, we have none more universally mischievous than this root error about men and women.

C. P. Gilman, *The Man-Made World or Our Androcentric Culture*, 1911,
p. 268

A common interest unites us; it is one world, one life.

V. Woolf, *Three Guineas*, 1938, 1992 edition, pp. 364–5

Acknowledgements

For helping this book on its way, I'd especially like to thank André Schiffrin at the New Press, who believed in it when no one else seemed to, and my agent, Rachel Calder, who stoically put up with all my complaints about the horrors of the publication process. I'm also grateful to my long-suffering colleagues at the Social Science Research Unit, the University of London Institute of Education, who endured unreasonable mental absences, and some of the physical sort as well, and made a good job of pretending that they approved of my excursions into strange forms of authorship. Thanks especially to George Ellison and to Berry Mayall for introducing me to new ideas, and to Sandra Stone for help chasing references.

During the usual struggles which book-writing entails, I've been enormously supported by my family and friends: thanks to all of them, for all their various forms of help. For reading and commenting on the manuscript, I am particularly grateful to Jonathan Barker, Diana Elbourne, Adam Oakley, Robin Oakley, Sanja Oakley and Penrose Robertson. My discussions about gender with my daughters, Emily Caston and Laura Oakley, are a constant source of inspiration. Of course, I alone am responsible for the book's final form.

The book is dedicated to my grandchildren.

The author would like to thank the Equal Opportunities Commission for permission to reproduce the table on page 70 which is adapted from table 16.1, in 'Equal Opportunities Policies and Women's Labour Market Status in Indus-trialised Countries' by Shirley Dex and Roger Sewell, published in *The Economics of Equal Opportunities*, ed. Jane Humphries and Jill Rubery.

Every effort has been made to trace all relevant copyright holders, but if any have been inadvertently overlooked, the publishers will be pleased to make the necessary arrangements at the first opportunity.

1

The Self and
Other Dramas

Beyond the window the rain falls vertically out of a sombre, metallic sky. It makes multiple concentric circles in pools of gathered water on the flat tarmac of the roof. The monochrome images in the pools are framed by green: apples hanging heavy from full-leaved trees; willows sweeping long fringes over old stone walls; fields lying at rest in this hovering moment between summer and winter. Any minute now, without warning, the fields will be mauled by tractors pulling the rest of the harvest in; and then the grain silos will roar day and night in mechanical acts of preservation. Other mechanical acts wrap the scene through the window in an arc of twenty-first-century noise; the resurfacing of the road on the horizon has layered traffic sounds out over the countryside, which is now affected by these in much the same way as it offers a home to moles, squirrels, rabbits, spiders, rape beetles, thunderflies and their colleagues. But the latter infestations are seasonal, unlike that of the traffic, which drones on as a perpetual reminder of 'man's' despoilation of nature.

This is what I see and hear as I start to write this book. It's a very particular scene, and my eyes may not see it as other people would. Only I, for example, know about the white patches on the railings where the green paint's wearing thin, and I alone am familiar with the dip in the corner of the roof caused by a failed experiment with a pot of honeysuckle five or six summers ago.

In his book *Speaking from Memory*, Harold Rosen points out that:

A person's knowledge can only exist by virtue of a vast range of past experiences which have been lived through, often with the most intense feelings. These experiences, including textual experiences (books, lectures, lessons, conversations, etc.), we have been taught to disguise so that our utterances are made to seem as though they emerge from no particular place or time or person but from the fount of knowledge itself.[1]

Academics – Rosen used to be a professor of English – specialize in the crime of representing the personal as objective truth. Sometimes they're just deeply confused as to which is which; more often, they put the pursuit of knowledge through a sanitizing process which strips it of its most vital and interesting aspects – where it came from, just how it is mediated by the knower's own experience and rooting in the material social world.

This book is about what its title says: gender on planet earth. It's an attempt to think laterally, rather than compartmentally, about the relationships between many of the world's current social problems, on the one hand, and ideas and practices relating to femininity and masculinity, on the other. It's traditional in policy analysis to isolate social problems from one another: crime is treated in one box, environmental destruction in another; concern about The Family is the province of one set of 'experts', how we transport ourselves about the planet is the terrain of another. Gender – the way in which life on earth is divided into feminine and masculine experiences – is conceived as another separate topic and is considered mainly by academics.

In *Gender on Planet Earth* I argue that the following ideas and practices are closely and dangerously linked: women's continuing marginality as a minority group; feminism's 'failure' to transform society; masculinist power structures; violence towards people and the material and social environment; and various ideological systems, including psychoanalysis, the worship of economic growth and sociobiology, which provide an intellectual rationale for the current state of affairs. None of the book's themes is original on its own. For example, others have made the point about masculinist power structures and violence towards people and the planet,[2] about the sacrifice of the natural world for the sake of economic profit,[3] and about the alliance between economic addiction, commodification and the invisibility of certain forms of work, which turns caregiving, the exemplar of women's labour, into an economic problem;[4] and there are various elegant critiques of the 'expert' systems which support such mythologies.[5] But the synthesis of these ideas, their particular coalescence in the format offered here, is new. It's something I feel it's important to attempt for political, personal and scientific reasons.

The *political* reasons have to do with reactions against feminism and linked humanist movements, and with the allegation that we live in a post-feminist world. Like many revolutionary movements, feminism always had an importance much greater than itself. It may only be now, with the much-lauded wisdom of hindsight, that we can see how ideas about women's citizenship are also ideas about human social relations and our collective citizenship of the planet.

The *personal* reasons behind the writing of *Gender on Planet Earth* concern a search for meaning and integration; they also relate to being a survivor of a revolutionary movement. Why did our culture prove so inhospitable to feminism; why did it make it difficult for feminism to survive and achieve the transformation of the social order we saw as in our own and everyone's best interests? Feminism shares with women a victim status: it's feminism's fault that divorce rates are climbing, that boys underachieve at school, that young men turn into thugs and criminals, that women are a bunch of dissatisfied dykes and harpies. Simple, unicausal explanations with no firm evidence base are common in our culture, but this doesn't make them right. They have all the dignity and aesthetic appeal of garden weeds.

The *scientific* reasons for writing the book derive from the clash between the elegantly abstract and arrogant theorems of postmodernism, and people's everyday experience of the world and themselves. There's a great gulf between postmodernist dictates about the fluidity of social facts and personal identity even (or especially) as filtered by the mass media, on the one hand, and how people actually negotiate their way through daily existence, on the other. Postmodernist mythologies dangerously obscure our willingness to make connections, to imagine the links between how we see and treat each other, and forms of both personal and public violence towards people and the material world. Most seriously, they deny the possibility that some things are more true than others. Searching for unbiased, democratically accessible knowledge is an important scientific and moral project.

What I contend in this book about women and about men is that they are jointly locked in a culture which distorts the possibilities of humanness as an ethical project. Women are outsiders in a system which often appears to them to come from another planet. And so, indeed, it has been brought to them by men, whose alienation from the experiences of others is often so complete that they can't even see their own will to power. These dual positions of aliens and outsiders are the creation of a gendered division of labour inherited from the past. But that past, where men's domination was far more concretely manifested than it is now, lives in the present through men's understandable reluctance to give up their ownership and commodification of the world.

Gender on Planet Earth doesn't stick to the usual academic format of citing detailed evidence and then reaching what the author hopes is a credible conclusion. It doesn't do this for two reasons. The first is that I seem, at this stage in my life, to have developed an intolerance for anything other than plain speaking. In *Writing a Woman's Life*, the American writer Carolyn Heilbrun talks about women after fifty ceasing to be 'female impersonators', and being able to say what they think in a manner unbridled by conventional feminine constraints.[6] You have to stop 'holding back for fear of alienating some imaginary reader'.[7] However, the book does have notes so readers can see the sources for my arguments. Both the text and the notes stride through some disciplines and territories in which I'm not qualified as an expert; so I'm bound to have got some things wrong, although I believe I've also got some right. Straying into these 'expert' lands is something I'm convinced we all must do, because preserving the future of human beings and planet earth is a venture which is far too important to leave to the experts.

This is the second reason for departing from the usual academic format: the crisis facing human beings on planet earth at the start of the twenty-first century is simply too enormous for us *not* to say what we think. We urgently need to develop an understanding of our predicament that is sufficiently collective, accurate and sensitive to enable us to do something about it.

My own location as a white middle-class woman is necessarily reflected in the book. Although I have no sense of national identity, and 'class' and 'ethnicity' as applied to women are often seen as confusing concepts, these are the 'facts', and it's important for me to acknowledge them at the outset.

Gender on Planet Earth is a mixture of expert and non-expert opinion, personal narrative, statistical recitation and historical diversions. The trips into history (for example, the history of shopping in chapter 5; the story of the women's liberation movement in chapter 4) are there as examples of how the past has given birth to the present. As for the statistics, readers who don't like these should just skip them. Since the book is being published at the same time in the UK and the USA, there are twice as many statistics as there would otherwise have been – someone would have screamed had I left either set out.

The next chapter begins with a woman on a bicycle, ventures into the history of cycling as liberation for women and the working classes, and from there into the transport policy problems of modern urbanized nations. Its central point is that cars dominate public space in much the same way as men dominate public life, and both marginalize other kinds of planetary travellers. Extending either of these forms of domination won't result in a more hospitable or fairer world. The chapter that follows, 'Manslaughter', is all about crime and damage of various kinds: its linking theme is the institutionalization in our culture of a macho masculinity which is expressed in both individual and corporate forms. The next three chapters turn the spotlight on 'women's issues': the periodic demands of (some) women for equal rights with men, and what exactly *has* happened to women's position (chapter 4); gender divisions in housework and childcare (chapter 5); The Family in all its glory as practice and ideological value (chapter 6). In chapter 7 the frame changes to the more global scenario of environmental destruction, and its close relations, the killing of animals for food and the mutilation of female bodies for sex and reproduction. Since all of the above has to be sustained by some pretty powerful thought systems, chapter 8 offers a strong critique of psychoanalysis, neo-classical economics and sociobiology as major ideological supports for gender-divided power structures. A brief opinion about postmodernism saunters in at the end of the chapter. In the final two chapters of *Gender on*

Planet Earth, I look at cross-gender experiences and at different ways of organizing sex and gender for the light these may throw on what it feels like for an alien to become an outsider and vice versa (chapter 9); and then I try to bring it all together with some conclusions about the unfashionable subject of patriarchy (chapter 10).

Gender on Planet Earth isn't a book which offers simple policy solutions. There aren't any simple solutions to any of this, although the last chapter does suggest some ways forward. The most important way forward is a change of consciousness about the problems that confront us: a willingness to see that nothing will alter fundamentally without our understanding that gender isn't just something feminists get angry and write books about, that patriarchy isn't an ancestral disease but a living institution. *Gender on Planet Earth* also isn't a book which sets out to lambast men and blame them for the state that we and the world are in. The 'sex/gender system' is something with which both men and women actively collude: you and I support it in multiple, frequently unrecognized ways every day of our lives. But our positions in this aren't equal: men as a group do have more social and economic power than women. This includes the power both to damage and to heal; both to continue with the old oppressive ways and to dismantle the structures and practices which legitimate these as 'normal' behaviour.

I originally included in the last chapter of the book three fictional reviews of *Gender on Planet Earth* written by imaginary critics who were not entirely satisfied with whatever it is I've managed to accomplish in it.[8] I wrote these reviews to acknowledge the point that a book of this kind can only satisfy some of the people some of the time. Opinion was divided among those who read the manuscript about whether these reviews 'worked' or not. My publishers didn't like them, but everyone else did. So here they are:

1 Wayne Chauvin, in the *Daily News*

This is a peculiar book. Sharp-shooting Annie Oakley's war-cry is that we men, God help us (she won't), are quite deplorable creatures – violent to women, other animals, and the planet, far too interested in football, useless in the kitchen, emotionally incapable – like aliens from outer space, in other words. While women – you've guessed it – are gentle, caring people whose only problem is men. Men are The Patriarchy. We might not wear labels, but we're all guilty of a Great Plot Against Women.

A friend of mine who runs a big management consultancy sighed deeply the other day over a bottle of cabernet sauvignon and a nice rare New Zealand steak (meat-eating is another of Ms Oakley's *bêtes noires*). 'You know, Wayne,' she said, 'the biggest problem I have these days is all these young women who come to work for me all bright-eyed and buzzing with energy, and then off they go and have babies, and I'm landed with a whopping great bill for their maternity leave. I'm only going to hire blokes in future.'

The truth is it's us guys who are the real outsiders of Ms Oakley's title. Women really do Have It All. They pass the exams, they've got the jobs, they have the babies and then drop them in daycare (which Ms Oakley thinks is a good thing – she would). Feminism has left us men cowering on the sidelines while the Matriarchs blow the whistle.'

2 Maggie Twomey, in the *Sunday Record*

Gender on Planet Earth is a polemical tract against many evils of modern life – capitalism, violence, war, crime, cars, meat-eating, environmental destruction. Its author, a well-known academic feminist, sees all these as connected, and the guiding thread is how we construct what it means to be men and women. Professor Oakley's argument is sometimes very persuasive; I found the chapter called 'Delusional Systems', in which she attacks sociobiology, psychoanalysis and economics all at the same time, particularly plausible (as readers of these pages will know, I've never been very fond of economists or psychoanalysts, and some of the arguments about genes determining behaviour are far too simplistic to be believable, even for a woman who's notoriously bad at map-reading and crossword puzzles).

Sections of *Gender on Planet Earth* consist of personal narratives which engage the reader more directly. For example, the chapter on male violence starts with a tale about Oakley's own encounter with a rural flasher – an episode many women will identify with – and the chapter on family values has a nice account of taking her two grandchildren for a walk. But these personal stories are rather self-indulgent: Ann Oakley is hardly a typical woman.

The book is, in the main, engagingly written, and thoroughly researched – indeed, there are almost too many notes. But has Oakley got it right: do we live in a patriarchy? Several important questions are left unaddressed. One is why our world is patriarchal in the first place.

Oakley was herself part of the women's movement (chapter 4, 'Sick to Death of Women', gives an entertaining angle on this). She wants to know why it didn't achieve everything it set out to. I don't know the answer, but neither, it seems, does she. This is one of several loose ends that dangle in the air at the end of the book. But at least *Gender on Planet Earth* makes us think; questioning received wisdom is at the heart of the Oakley enterprise.

3 Grace Person, in *Feminism and Social Science*

Gender on Planet Earth advances an essentially unoriginal hypothesis: that the sex/gender system gives rise to particular identity formations – femininity and masculinity, or, better, femininities and masculinities – in which interlocking discourses 'explain' phenomena of gendered behaviour: men's predisposition to aggression, women's to maternal thinking; men's values-based, and women's more pragmatic, orientation to the family; the masculine predilection for technology and the feminine scepticism about its social and ethical uses; men's habit of 'penetrating' the secrets of 'Mother Nature' versus women's greater respect for ecological principles.

One would have hoped for more of a recognition of multiculturality and multivocality from a social scientist of Oakley's calibre. She also gives insufficient attention to the rooting of the politics of difference in master-narratives.[1] One question is to what extent the politics of difference can 'in fact' be disentangled from these. It is an ironic comment on the drift of the academic and policy debate since 1970s feminism that Oakley, who herself pioneered the use of the term 'gender' as a tool to clarify discourses about identity,[2] should find herself, thirty years on, returning to her original justification for this epistemological move. She performs a timely role in restating the parameters of her primary case and defending its relevance to a world torn by global, national, and domestic conflict. Her observations about the multitextured pathways according to which an emancipatory politics can (should?) be constructed are refreshing after recent waves of literature devoted to the deconstruction of gender and the politically unappealing postulate of fragmentary, rather than unitary, identities. The emancipatory politics of postmodernism have historically always had a deconstructive relationship with rationalism.[3] But how do we combine a recognition of this, and its corollary that truth is perpetually being made rather than merely there to be found, with positivism's outdated insistence on a world of demonstrable facts? *Gender on Planet Earth* fails to ask this question, despite the fact that it is one with which many academic readers of the book will identify.

[1]b. hooks (1996) Postmodern blackness. In W. T. Anderson (ed.) *The Fontana Postmodern Reader*. London: HarperCollins.

[2]D. H. J. Morgan (1986) Gender. In R. Burgess (ed.) *Key Variables in Social Research*. London: Routledge.

[3]A. Yeatman (1994) *Postmodern Revisionings of the Political*. London: Routledge.

■

The book's starting point is a personal one: the constant fracturing of personal identity by social values, customs and relations experienced by members of social minority groups.

When Virginia Woolf went to the British Museum in 1928 to find out the truth about women and fiction, she sent back all the books she'd ordered, having concluded one thing from them: the subject of women made people – mainly men – very angry. She went out to a restaurant for lunch, picked up a newspaper someone had left on a chair, and studied the headlines. 'Somebody had made a big score in South Africa . . . Sir Austen Chamberlain was at Geneva. A meat axe with human hair on it had been found in a cellar. Mr Justice – commented in the Divorce Courts upon the Shamelessness of Women.' Reading these headlines, Woolf decided that even 'The most transient visitor to the planet . . . could not fail to be aware . . . that England is under the rule of a patriarchy.'[9] The 'fact' of patriarchy explained the puzzle of women's attributed inferiority. 'Life for both sexes', she wrote, 'is arduous, difficult, a perpetual struggle. It calls for gigantic courage and strength.

More than anything, perhaps, creatures of illusion as we are, it calls for confidence in oneself.'[10] Ironically, Woolf's insight about the importance of self-
confidence failed to guarantee her own survival. Thirteen years after her epic
journey to the British Museum, having suffered from bouts of emotional
instability all her life, she put a large stone in her pocket and drowned herself
in the River Ouse at the age of fifty-nine.[11]

Patricia Williams, professor of law at Columbia University, learnt to think
of herself as Black at the age of three; but probably none of the little white
children who taught her this ever learned to see themselves as white. Little
girls, whether Black or white, may not appreciate their femininity by noticing
the lack of a phallus, as Freud, that arch phallus-worshipper, said, but gender
is, nonetheless, a pervasive early subject lesson. The question is about what
the membership of cultural minority groups means in terms of self-identity
throughout life. One exists within the ambit of a set of cultural conceptions:
Black people, or women, or children, or gays, have certain characteristics and
a particular social place. As Williams puts it, negotiating 'This distance
between the self and the drama of one's stereotyping . . . is an ethical project
of creating a livable space between the poles of other people's imagination
and the nice calm centre of oneself where dignity resides.'[12]

The concrete and the personal are always easier to grasp than generalities:

Scene 1

A smart French restaurant in London's Charlotte Street one summer
evening in 1999.

Players: A Swedish man and an English woman having dinner together;
various black-suited waiters; the restaurant owner; a certain ethos about
what restaurants ought to be; the agricultural and food production industries; the economies and governments of various implicated countries.

Food and drink: Leg of lamb with white beans, pommes dauphinois (him);
vegetables roasted with garlic, green salad (her); a bottle of Aligoté de
Bouzeron, two glasses of carbonated mineral water ('We don't do tap
water in this restaurant, sir').

The moment of truth:
'I'm paying this one, it's my turn' (her).
'Oh no, I can't allow that . . .' (him) (joint laughter, edged with slight
tension).
'You're going to have to, it's my treat, you're a visitor to London' (her,
placing a credit card in what she hopes is an authoritative gesture on a
plate on top of the leather folder containing the bill, in full sight of the
waiter, who's clearing away their dishes).
(What do you bet . . . she thinks to herself)

Five minutes later: The waiter reappears with the plate holding her credit card and slip of paper to sign, placing it neatly down in front of the man.

Scene 2

A March evening in a London street.

Players: Woman-on-a-bicycle and a lot of people in cars, including two policemen.

Action: Woman-on-a-bicycle is cycling in the cycle lane when a taxi ahead of her suddenly brakes, pulls into the cycling lane and then swings out, doing a U-turn in the road. Close behind her is a police van. Woman-on-a-bicycle, somewhat shocked, proceeds nervously to the next lights, making a quick getaway just as the lights are turning to amber.
 The two policemen materialize from their van.

One of the policemen: 'Excuse me, Madam, you went over a red light.'

Woman-on-a-bicycle: 'Did you see what that taxi just did?'

Policeman: 'You went over a red light, Madam.'

Woman-on-a-bicycle: 'Yes I did. But I just nearly had a collision with a taxi. Why didn't you stop the taxi-driver? Isn't it illegal to do a U-turn in the middle of a busy street? Isn't it illegal for cars to stop in cycle lanes?'

Policeman (staring hard at woman-on-a-bicycle): 'The taxi was only turning round. You admit that you went over a red light, then?'

Woman-on-a-bicycle: 'Yes I do. Are you going to report the taxi?'

Policeman (getting out notebook): 'Yes, yes' (irritated tone of voice). 'I need to take a few details. Name?' (she gives it) 'Is that Miss or Mrs?'

Woman-on-a-bicycle: 'Why is that relevant?'

Policeman: 'We need it for our paperwork.'

Woman-on-a-bicycle: 'It's professor, actually.'

Policeman raises his eyes to heaven in a gesture of God-save-me-from-nutty-women, looks at his colleague: both laugh: 'Is it Miss, or Mrs?'

Woman-on-a-bicycle: 'I told you, professor.'

Policeman repeats eyes-to-heaven gesture, and then looks down at note-book: 'How do you spell "professor"?'

■

The critical experience is that of marginality: of feeling, and being seen as, different from the human standard represented by men. In 1944 the Swedish

economist and public policy analyst Gunnar Myrdal published a classic work
on 'the Negro problem' in the United States. Myrdal's *An American Dilemma*
contains among its 1,542 pages appendix 5, 'A parallel to the Negro problem'.
This begins:

> In every society, there are at least two groups of people, besides the Negroes,
> who are characterized by high social visibility expressed in physical appearance,
> dress, and patterns of behaviour, and who have been 'suppressed'. We refer to
> women and children. Their present status, as well as their history and their
> problems in society, reveal striking similarities to those of the Negroes.[13]

In the ante-bellum South, the status of Black people was modelled on that
of women and children as non-citizens. Like second-wave feminism, the first
wave was started by activist women, such as Angelika Grimké, Lucretia Mott
and Susan B. Anthony, who defended Black rights first and then realized that
everything they were saying applied to women, too. Like Black people,
women have been seen as biologically and therefore socially inferior, and the
study of their intelligence and personality had until recently a history very
similar to that of Black people. 'In drawing a parallel between the position of,
and feeling toward, women and Negroes,' said Myrdal in the concluding para-
graph to his appendix 5:

> we are uncovering a fundamental basis of our culture . . . The similarities in the
> women's and the Negroes' problems are not accidental. They were . . . originally
> determined in a paternalistic order of society. The problems remain, even though
> paternalism is gradually declining as an ideal and is losing its economic basis.
> In the final analysis, women are still hindered in their competition by the func-
> tion of procreation; Negroes are laboring under the yoke of the doctrine of unas-
> similability which has remained although slavery is abolished. The second
> barrier is actually much stronger than the first in America today. But the first is
> more eternally inexorable.[14]

Here a footnote refers the reader to a book called *Nation and Family* by
Myrdal's wife, the renowned social scientist Alva Myrdal. The reference is to
chapter 22, 'One Sex a Social Problem', in which Alva Myrdal discusses the
'petty reforms' so far introduced in Sweden to solve what is seen as the
problem of married women working both in the home and out of it. 'In Sweden
as elsewhere,' she wrote, 'popular attitudes toward women's problems are still
chaotic in most groups. Traditional thinking is enmeshed in an accumulation
of vague interests, confused emotions, and pure nonsense.'[15]

An American Dilemma established the 'dogma of liberal social science'[16]
that Black people are Americans and nothing else. The work was commissioned by the Carnegie Corporation of New York in 1937. It was expected to
take two years, but lasted much longer. Like Virginia Woolf, Myrdal began

his work in the library, where he was amazed at how much had been written about the Negro problem – a complete bibliography would run to several hundred thousand titles. All this intellectual energy should, said Myrdal, rather as Woolf said about writings on women, have moved mountains, or at least have led to some collective enlightenment. The main reason it hadn't was because of the way the problem had been conceptualized: as belonging to Black people rather than white society. White Americans defined the economic and social position of Negroes and then wondered why they tended to behave differently. In just the same way, gender equality has been seen as a problem of, and for, women, not of, and for, men, or of the social system as a whole.

Black people and women constitute minority groups. A minority group isn't a statistical concept – it's a group of people who are treated unequally because of their physical or cultural characteristics, and who have some awareness of this differential treatment. Awareness is a tricky notion, because knowing one is discriminated against doesn't always follow the 'facts' of discrimination. The beholder's eye is often only half-open; acceptance of inferiority comes as part of the package, and there may be very little point in recognizing subjugation when there are few chances of escape.

Members of minority groups tend to exhibit certain kinds of behaviour; for example, they may place a low value on their own abilities, prefer to avoid conflict, dislike one another, use 'wiles' to get what they want, and appear helpless or overemotional (where too much emotion is definitely not counted as a good thing).[17] This is because the power relationships between dominants and subordinates identify self-importance, strength and rationality as human standards denied to those who are not quite human.[18]

■

I sit here looking out of my window, as I've done many times before; but each time is also the first, because the angle of vision changes, the sky alters its hue, discharging light differently, the seasons come and go, the paint on the railings and other surfaces of things wears and survives, and the perceiving self, the 'I' of the sentence, is differently comfortable or distressed, awake or fatigued, at peace or at war, sad or exultant. Since I started writing some days ago the apples at the top of the tree have reddened, but they're no nearer my grasp now than they were then. A wind has come from somewhere, battering the latches on the windows and diluting the drone of cars along the horizon. As predicted, a mechanical harvester now ploughs back and forth in my line of vision, converting a green field into a brown one, though in the more-or-less certain knowledge that what is temporarily fallow will soon be rendered fertile again.

In order to write this book I've had to deny relation in almost a masculine way. I've had to retreat to the countryside on my own, away from people and away from (too many) books. When I'm close to other people, sensitivity to their needs always encroaches on the hard task of finding out who I am and what I want to say. Books intrude differently by offering so many different and similar stories that telling one's own becomes a virtually impossible act.

Solitude is often the price that has to be paid for creativity. Books aren't written in the midst of parties, or paintings created *au famille*. History is littered with tales of female servitude in the interests of male creativity, and much less often by matching stories of masculine dedication to women's creative pursuits. The composer Gustav Mahler wrote much of his music in a hut surrounded by trees in the Austrian countryside. No one was allowed to visit this sacrosanct studio, because the mere sight of another human being was enough to put him off. The cook, taking his breakfast there, had to go by a steep and dangerous path to avoid the risk of being sighted by the great man.[19] Mahler was also hypersensitive to noise – except that of nature. He led a life of rigorous routines, dependent on his wife, Alma, for the orchestration of all practical details. A composer herself, Mahler forbade her to write music after their marriage: 'You must give yourself to me *unconditionally*, shape your future life . . . entirely in accordance with my needs.'[20] At the end of his life, Gustav Mahler was overcome with guilt at this suppression of his wife's creativity, seeking a consultation with Freud himself in order to understand and make amends for it.[21]

We don't all see the world in the same way, but we'll never be able to quantify the extent to which our perceptions differ, or are the same. We sense that our humanity is expressed in the existence of some common ground beneath the constantly shifting topsoil on which we mark out our individual postures and directions. This is why we go beyond ourselves when we decide just to be ourselves. Human liberation may be too much to ask for, but giving up the roles of aliens and outsiders in order to preserve the future of planet earth would be a good beginning.

2
On the Problem of Women and Bicycles

The first project is carrying the bicycle out to the street. The steps of the house weren't constructed for this purpose, and the pavement outside the gate is cluttered with the mush of fallen leaves. Piles of dog turds, explosive in their rank lubricity, cower under the leaves. Like all ordinary urban pavements, this one is lined with cars, nose to tail like bullets in a munitions factory. Many are oversized, with exotic names mythically suggesting the effortless exploration of space – Space Wagon, Freelander, Landcruiser, Scenic, Space Star, Galaxy. Super-glossy with their tinted windows and sleek seats high off the road, they give their occupants the appearance of hierarchy. Some have the polos of spare tyres tagged, like exaggerated fashion statements, onto their backs. These meretricious giants of the road cluster illegally on street corners these days, so desperate has the issue of parking in cities become.

I negotiate my bicycle between the cars, and set out on a journey to repeat the exercise undertaken by Virginia Woolf seventy-two years ago. I'm going to the library to look up 'women' in the catalogues. It's a somewhat disingenuous excursion, of course, since my house, the library, my head, and lots of other houses, libraries and heads are full of all the stuff about women that's been said and written since 1928.

I begin with the world of everyday experience, not the world of books. Everyday life is both trivial and sacred; these days many people feel a gap between 'the system' and the practical details of their existences.[1] The route to the library is part of *my* everyday experience, since I take it every day on my way to work. Getting out onto the main road is always a problem. The cars advance, growling beasts straining to go faster than the traffic lights and the flow – or non-flow – of the traffic allows; multiple feet pump accelerators against the restraint of brakes, pointlessly, but nonetheless making a point. In

Switzerland car-drivers have to turn their engines off when waiting at lights. It's surprising what a difference that makes to the whole ambience of the road (let alone the air quality). The car ahead of me, a great grey beast of a Ford Mondeo, is visibly racked by the bass thump-thump of its expensive stereo system, the driver bent over the wheel, rocking his head back and forth in a catatonic frenzy. It isn't the only car that's behaving like this – there's a whole orchestra here. It's a pity they're all playing only half the music. When I lie in bed at night, I can hear the insistent beat through the triple glazing, like the wild battering of drums in the jungle, except that it's hardly likely to be conveying a useful message.

There's no cycle lane here to offer even a fictional protection from the cars. Moreover, I want to turn right, which means moving from the left-hand side of the traffic out into the maelstrom of the middle of the road. Seventy per cent of accidents involving cyclists happen at junctions;[2] cycle lanes reduce accidents between junctions by 50 per cent,[3] but what happens at the moment of confrontation has apparently proved very resistant to change. I position myself in front of the lights, and thus the cars, in order to be able to make a speedy right turn before they catch up with me. It's a dodgy manoeuvre, and you have to get the timing right. The next problem is that I'm cycling down a road which is only wide enough for two streams of cars. With a cyclist there as well, the cars on one side have to slow down, the only alternative being to annihilate the cyclist. There are many days when I think, if killing people wasn't against the law, it'd be by far the most regular solution to the problem of bicycles on the roads. Amazingly, only 165 cyclists met their death on the roads in the UK in 1998 – 95 per cent of road deaths happened to other kinds of travellers. In the USA in the same year 761 cyclists were killed – 3 per cent of road deaths.[4]

The car behind me hoots angrily, indicating that I should get out of the way. But I can only do that by vacating the road altogether. It used to bother me, this angry what-right-have-you-got-to-be-here attitude, but after eight years of cycling in London I just smile and think of myself as another one of those mechanical speed stoppers, like bumps in the road or elongated pavements. I don't mind helping to slow the cars down, as long as I make it to the end of my journey.

The car that hooted is a red sports car, and now it shoots past with much dramaturgical acceleration, like a successful sperm, taking advantage of a space in the oncoming traffic. I am reminded of Desmond Morris's description of sports cars in *The Human Zoo* as 'Like a baboon's penis . . . long, smooth and shiny, they thrust forward with great vigour and they are frequently bright red in colour. A man sitting in his open sports car is like a piece of highly stylized phallic sculpture.'[5] Why are car manufacturers *allowed* to sell cars that can do more than the speed limit, when doing more than the speed limit is against the law?

Sometimes I try to see myself as other road-users might. I'm wearing a skirt today, so I'm obviously a woman; my helmet and yellow cycling belt mark me out as a routine, careful sort of cyclist, rather than the helmetless, risk-taking sort given to balancing all kinds of loads in funny places, or the lycra-shorted sort, doing it to develop hairy muscles, or to deliver mail to companies that can't possibly afford to wait. I'm riding a folding bike with small wheels and a large bag up front, so I'm hardly a speed maniac. Indeed, it seems likely that I'm not trying to prove anything, beyond my ability to get from A to B with as little fuss as possible.

There's another long queue of cars outside the swimming baths. If I do what I'm supposed to, and sidle up on the left of the cars, I have the familiar problem then of taking my life in my hands (or on my wheels) as I try to cut across the stream of cars turning left in order to go straight on. Many cyclists are simply not seen by motorists, despite their individual illumination with yellow fabric and flashing lights. 'I didn't see you', pleaded the motorist who knocked me down on the Euston Road some years ago (it was raining; he'd gone over a red light), as though not seeing is some kind of inherent justification for violence.

I can't help it, I go past sperm car again. The lights change just as I get to the head of the stream of traffic, and I'm away and round the corner before you can say 'bloody woman, what's she trying to prove?' This time the red car cuts in front of me in an overtly savage gesture, so that at the next T-junction where we wait for fast-moving traffic coming from the right in the one-way system, I am, indeed, forced to dismount and retreat to the pavement. 'Never have an argument with a car', I told my elder daughter when she considered taking to the roads as one of us rather than one of them. Happily, her new silver bicycle hangs unused on the wall like an art exhibit most of the time.

There's a cycle lane ahead. This, for a short stretch, offers real sanctuary, since the road is otherwise closed to moving traffic. I breathe more freely here, looking at the houses with their coloured front doors and their hanging baskets of wilted geraniums. But then the cycle lane comes out onto another very busy road, and the green strip with the stereotyped cycle image on it might as well not be there. Parked cars straddle it illegally; other cars swerve into it when it suits them; buses stop swaggeringly on it. The next lights have a green space for cyclists ahead of the cars, a growing phenomenon in these parts, and one that means cyclists don't in theory have to perform the kind of dodgy manoeuvre I did earlier in my ride. But the cars sit growling in this space, lordly as lions, oblivious to the assertion of greenness spread beneath their dirty undercarriages.

A little further on, past a canal stretched like a tight ribbon between rows of houses, is the graveyard of St Pancras church, where Mary Wollstonecraft was buried after dying from puerperal fever in 1797, leaving two little girls motherless.[6] She lived round here, in a street called The Polygon, which has since been demolished. She wrote her famous *Vindication of the Rights of Woman* a few minutes away in Store Street. Bloomsbury is full of signs and signifiers of disturbances in the waters of womanhood. The poet Christina Rossetti opened a school with her mother, writing poems for many years in Torrington Square. The novelist Dorothy Richardson worked in an attic in Endsleigh Street. In Great Coram Street, Emily Faithfull started a printing house in 1860 where she employed and trained women printers, against violent opposition from the male variety, producing Britain's first feminist periodical, the *Englishwoman's Journal*. The Pankhursts lived in Russell Square, where the Hotel Russell now stands. Millicent Fawcett campaigned for women's suffrage from Gower Street, where the actress Sarah Siddons once lived. Virginia Woolf lived in Gordon, Tavistock and Mecklenburgh Squares. The black plaque on the front of 50 Gordon Square mentions 'several members of the Bloomsbury Group', including Virginia Woolf, Clive Bell and the Stracheys, who included three Strachey women, active campaigners for the Cause;[7] next door, at number 51, lived Lytton Strachey.

Right, past the church, I launch myself onto another cycle path, a handy, raised one this time, just how they should be, running parallel to the pavement, clearly demarcated from the cars. But this is the land of the learner drivers – it's where the driving schools bring their pupils to practise three-point turns. There's much shuddering and stalling going on, and some of it is at the entrance to the cycle path. It also happens to be refuse-collecting day, and the bin-bags are out; black beetles of rubbish sleep soddenly in my path, the equation between domestic refuse and space for cyclists underscoring a number of other litanies in my head.

A group of veiled women are the next obstacle, out of place on the cycling path rather than the pavement. They're busy talking to one another, with much jangling of bracelets and spirited glances in the space between fabrics they are allowed for vision; one carries a chubby child, another wields a pushchair, the handles hung with Tesco shopping bags. I don't like ringing my bell – it seems too much like the motorists' aggression – but I would like politely to point out that they are in the wrong place. My indecision is intensified by the symbolism of their veils – I don't want to deprive them of any more freedom.

A feature of this part of the journey is the lavish decor of broken glass on the road. It sparkles like diamonds in the sunlight, but it's death to cycle tyres. Where does it all come from? It's always worse on Mondays, so I suppose it's a product of sociability – it's odd how some people's enjoyment punctures that of others. The man in the cycling shop advises regularly inspecting one's tyres and picking out the lumps of misplaced glass, but it isn't a very salubrious exercise.

It starts to rain lightly, and a man steps off the pavement between a parked Thames Water van and one of those Space Cruisers. He's used his ears and not his eyes to gauge that it's safe to cross. I ping my bell politely (no hesitation now), but have to swerve, as he stands unmoving in the middle of the road staring at me. He has dark greasy hair and cradles a can of lager in his arm. 'Fucking bitch', he screams suddenly, spitting a string of beer-laden saliva in my face. I wipe it away and wonder briefly about mechanisms of HIV transmission.

The new British Library looms on my left, an enormous red-railed excrescence, resembling a prison or a railway station. I wheel my bicycle through the gates and past the sculpture of Isaac Newton, a gigantic, muscular, crouched figure doing something suspect with a small piece of equipment. It's quite unlike the real Newton, born the size of a pint pot, and writing a million words on alchemy in coded Latin in an effete, closeted life devoted to the operations of the mind rather than the aggrandizement of the body.[8]

'After William Blake', says the plaque underneath the statuary Newton, 'By Eduardo Paolozzi.' And underneath that, 'Grant aided by The Foundation for Sports and the Arts. Funded by Subscription from The Football Pools. VERNON LITTLEWOODS ZETTERS.'

This isn't quite the notion of Edwardian scholarship Virginia Woolf and her co-readers would have brought with them to the old British Museum in the 1920s. The promotional leaflet for the new library, available for tourists at the Information Desk in the concourse inside, claims that the statue, which was inspired by Blake's vision of Newton measuring with a pair of dividers the immensity of the universe, expresses perfectly the purpose of the library, all twelve million books of it, 'bringing together arts and sciences in one place for posterity'. But it is rather a selective vision we're invited to look at – a man measuring what there is to know, not a woman thinking about it, in or outside a room of her own.

Virginia Woolf's journey to the old British Museum took her through streets of open coal holes and 'hoarse-voiced men' parading plants on barrows. At the British Museum, 'one took a slip of paper; one opened a volume of the catalogue'.[9] Today one sits in front of a computer terminal, enters one's card number and proceeds in electronic search mode to interrogate the three hundred kilometres of shelving lining the deepest basements in London. 'Have you any notion', asked Woolf, 'of how many books are written about women . . . ?' I type the word 'woman' and press a few keys: the answer, so far as the British Library in the year 2000 is concerned, is 39,301. Add 'women' and the total rises to 50,603. More than fifty thousand books, and that's only counting those with 'woman' or 'women' in the actual title, most of which are in English, and excluding those that haven't reached the British Library or haven't done so yet. Of the 50,603 titles, a mere 6,905 – 14 per cent – were published in or before 1928, the year of Woolf's own searches: the volume of literature in book form on women has increased sevenfold since then.

Out of interest – for the significance of these terms is entirely different – I enter 'man' and 'men': 69,355 titles, of which a much higher proportion – 34 per cent – already existed in 1928. The problem with the category 'man'/'men' is, of course, that it may well include women, masculinity being taken as synonymous with humanity (thus *Men, Motives and Markets, Man, Science and Humanism* or even *The Man-eater of Punami*); on the other hand, men may mean men (*Great Men of the Bible, A Few Every Day Hints Addressed to the Youths and Young Men of the Drapery Trade*). By contrast, one can be pretty sure that a book with women in the title isn't about men (unless men are in the title too). 'Gender', a modern invention in the domain of thinking about men and women, can be expected to yield a much lower 'hit'[10] rate, and so it does – 2,266 titles only, 99 per cent published since 1928. The 1 per cent of pre-1928 titles are overwhelmingly grammatical, for example, *A Complete Analytical Table of the Gender of all French Substantives in General Use.*

A little more fiddling with the keyboard and my calculator later I discover quantitatively what I already knew qualitatively – that the bulk of the growth in books about women has been since the last feminist movement: 87 per cent of the increase since 1928 dates from 1975.

■

One of the reasons Virginia Woolf was deemed 'mad' was because she had an 'undue' fear of being run down in the street. This is the view of her nephew and official biographer Quentin Bell.[11] The first volume of Woolf's diary and the first three volumes of her letters edited by Bell list fourteen traffic incidents. These include Woolf's mother's sister being killed by a car in 1916; her niece Angelica Bell being knocked over by one in 1924; and a woman being killed by a car in 1925 in Gordon Square, where the Woolfs and the Bells lived. Another episode involved a lady cyclist being run over by a cart in Gloucester Road at an hour and a place where Woolf's sister Vanessa might well have been on her bicycle returning from art school.[12]

Cycling was part of the 'Bloomsberries' world. Aside from cycling in London, both the Woolfs' country houses, Asham and Monk's House in Sussex, required cycle trips of several miles from the station. In 1914 Leonard bought Virginia her very own bicycle. Their friends George Bernard Shaw, Bertrand Russell and H. G. Wells were all regular cyclists. The painter Dora Carrington, lover of Lytton Strachey and friend of the Bells and Woolfs, regularly cycled up to forty miles a morning searching for a place to live while Lytton wrote *Eminent Victorians*. Tidmarsh in Berkshire, where they ended up, was twenty miles from Oxford, then regarded as an easy cycling distance. Beatrice and Sidney Webb learnt to ride bicycles at Beachey Head on the English coast in April 1895, cycling forty miles with Shaw from the Argoed to Cardiff for the TUC Conference in September.[13]

People in the early years of the twentieth century cycled because that was simply the best way of making many journeys; bicycles were the fastest, most economical and most convenient mode of private transport. The low, rear-wheel drive 'safety' bicycle, with adjustable handles and a sprung saddle, became standard in the UK and the USA in the 1890s. Bicycles were painted in individual colours and were sufficiently prized to be kept in the halls of great houses. In the 1890s they became widely affordable and were ridden by all social classes for all sorts of purposes. Cycling clubs and riding schools (including some for ladies) were formed, special maps produced, agitations started to make local authorities responsible for the deplorable state of the roads, magazines launched, and books written about how to cycle and how not to; bicycles entered fiction, with up-to-date detectives cycling round the country in Norfolk suits stuffed with automatics in hot pursuit of similarly transported criminals.[14] Dorothy Sayers' Lord Peter Wimsey was a cyclist; Sayers herself had been bicycling secretary of her Oxford women's college, in which capacity she was, apparently, extremely hard on stray bicycles.[15] Meetings on bicycles formed the stuff of romantic encounters. In H. G. Wells' *Wheels of Chance* Mr Hoopdriver, an assistant in a Putney drapery emporium, develops fantasies about a Young Lady in Grey whom he meets on a south coast cycling tour.[16]

When Flora Thompson wrote her classic autobiographical account of English rural working-class life, the trilogy *Lark Rise*, *Over to Candleford* and *Candleford Green*, at the age of nearly sixty, the details rescued from her incredible memory included those of the early cycling clubs in the late 1890s. These were composed of self-important, 'laughing, jostling' young men wearing uniforms of tight navy knickerbocker suits with red or yellow braided coats and small navy pill-box caps; the leaders carried bugles, like hunt-masters, and they used Flora's post office to telegraph proof of journeys actually made rather than merely boasted about.[17]

As an assistant Post Office clerk, Flora Thompson herself hired one of the new safety bicycles for 6d, left her petticoats behind on the post office bed, tucked her long skirt round her legs, and took off for her beloved country-side.[18] In France, around the same time, the Nobel prize-winning chemists Marie and Pierre Curie were given a wedding present of money to buy two bicycles when they married in 1895. They cycled on their honeymoon and everywhere together for years, with sums for bicycle maintenance cropping up regularly in the meticulous household accounts Marie kept in between her discoveries with the new wonder substance, radium.[19]

The peak of the cycling craze in the USA was in 1899, when 312 factories worked round the clock to turn out more than a million bicycles a day. Tiffany's made a jewelled model (silver frame, ivory and jade handles, ruby and emerald cut-crystal lights), which was bought by 'a titled Englishman'.[20] Bicycles were used in the public services; a special machine was provided for the Post Office in the UK in 1882, a quadricycle (two tandems joined together) invented for firemen; in 1897/8 the Americans pioneered the 'Police Patrol Tricycle', which had the front and rear seats for policemen, and one for a manacled prisoner in between. By 1885 the French and Austrian armies even had the forerunner of today's folding bicycle to carry on their backs – 28 pounds, with a folding/unfolding time of 30 seconds (compared to the 28.4 pounds and 20 seconds of the one on which I transported myself to the British Library).

Men tried to keep cycling to themselves, deeming it an unwomanly pursuit. Until the 1880s women rode only tricycles 'for decency'; around 220 different types of tricycle were in production, including 'Sociables' – tricycles for two riders side by side. These were especially recommended for women learning to ride.[21] Tandems were popular, too, for on these the expert rider could 'take a complete novice – his sister, his cousin or even in an emergency a lady who is not a relation'.[22] In England the Chaperon (*sic*) Cyclists' Association was formed to provide 'gentlewomen of good social position' to accompany ladies on bicycle excursions – the chaperone brought her own bicycle.

The women saw cycling differently. 'Men can't conceive', wrote one woman cyclist, 'what a thing this wheeling is to us poor women. How can a woman be strong and well without exercise? . . . Our grandfathers' ideas that a woman could get all the exercise she wants about the house are false, false, false!'[23] Eventually the men had to give in, resigning themselves to such mild thrusts as:

> Mother's out upon her bike, enjoying of the fun,
> Sister and her beau have gone to take a little run.
> The housemaid and the cook are both a-riding on their wheels;
> And Daddy's in the kitchen a-cooking of the meals.[24]

The presumption that greater independence for women means more domesticity for men is a recurrent theme in any library of books about women.

Cycling, associated with socialism and with feminism, did achieve a significant degree of practical liberation for women. When H. G. Wells' Mr Hoopdriver first spots his Young Lady in Grey, he speculates as to what kind of girl she might be. 'Probably she was one of these New Women. He had a persuasion the cult had been maligned . . . Rational dress didn't look a bit unwomanly.'[25] The disposal of endless petticoats and their replacement by 'rational' dress solved all those nasty problems about what lady cyclists ought to wear; it also laid down new standards for women's place in the public domain.

'Rational' dress consisted of stockings and knickerbockers or divided skirts. A doctor, writing in Paris in 1889, sought the advice of a cyclist, a Miss Violet Lorne, who had cured her own nervous troubles through cycling, on the costume to be worn on a bicycle. For hygiene and comfort the undergarments should be wholly woollen; the skirt should be 4 feet 8 inches in circumference and blue, brown or grey, and secured with elastic; a Norfolk jacket or Garibaldi bodice should be worn; a small fur cape was useful; and hats (obligatory) should omit floating ribbons, feathers and flowers.[26] Lady cyclists ought always to take with them a lamp, bread-and-butter sandwiches in waterproof paper, a notebook for jotting down things of interest, and a compass.[27]

But was it sensible for women to cycle in the first place? Dr Beresford Ryley considered that cycling had important health effects for women and children, as for men, but only healthy women aged between sixteen and forty ought to be allowed to cycle, provided, of course, they weren't pregnant or menstruating. Before sixteen, the bones weren't sufficiently ossified, and after forty women suffered from fatigue, becoming 'thin and wrinkled'.[28] Cycling during menstruation caused pain and sterility. Other doctors contended that cycling would especially benefit obese, apathetic or post-menopausal women.[29] Cycling was either the cause[30] or cure[31] of such common ailments as varicose veins, haemorrhoids, dyspepsia, constipation, nervous troubles and excessive menstrual bleeding. But some medical opinion was on the pro-cycling side: 'If such a thing were possible, it [cycling] is even better adapted to women and more beneficial to them than to men,' decided one doctor in 1895, 'for there is no other exercise whatever that is so gentle; so harmonious in its action; so pleasurably stimulating in its effects; so bracing in its character; so entirely free from violence or any strain upon any part, when taken rationally; so accessible; so safe; so practical; so inexpensive; and in such good taste.'[32]

Cycle use peaked in the interwar years but has declined since then. It continues to do so in many countries, including the UK, where cycles formed 37 per cent of all road traffic in 1949 and 1 per cent in 1995; less than 2 per cent of all journeys are now by bicycle.[33] On a typical day in London, only 1 per cent of women cycle – three times as many men do.[34] These figures are different in places with a more cycle-friendly road architecture, such as Cambridge, where cycle use is twenty times higher; in the Netherlands women make 32 per cent and men 25 per cent of their journeys on bicycles.[35] In the USA cycling is such a minority activity that it doesn't feature at all as a heading in the annual National Transportation Statistics.[36]

There are many reasons why people in industrialized countries don't cycle, but the low social status of bicycles and their association with childhood are at least as important as the perceived danger of being on the road.[37]

■

In 1993 Dr Robin Stott, a British hospital consultant living in London, was fined £10 for riding his bicycle through Kensington Gardens. He said, 'For those of us who take health and environmental responsibilities seriously, going to work on a bicycle is close to being a moral imperative.'[38] Whatever nineteenth-century doctors said, there's now a general medical consensus that cycling provides a range of benefits to health and fitness, including reducing coronary heart disease, high blood pressure, cancer, respiratory disease, obesity, osteoporosis, mental health problems and the risk of premature death.[39] Half an hour's cycling or walking a day halves the risk of heart disease and diabetes.[40] Regular cyclists are as fit as people ten years younger.[41] The health effects of cycling may well contribute to differences in life-expectancy between countries, for example, the notably enhanced longevity of men and women in the Netherlands.[42]

American studies of Harvard graduates show an astonishing 'dose' relationship between mortality and exercise; 35–49 year olds who cycled for 30–40 minutes a day had mortality rates 20 per cent lower than their non-cycling age-mates; for 70–84 year olds the reduction was 50 per cent.[43] This study, which is quoted in the British Medical Association's report *Cycling: Towards Health and Safety*, only included men, although it's presented as being a study of people. The BMA report's authors comment that, 'Most exercise-and-health research concentrates on men, though some attention has been paid to women.' They go on to describe a study of pregnant women showing that cycling improved their cardiovascular fitness and therefore might promote easy labour.[44] This is a well-known cultural device, of adding women in to some human project or other from which they've previously been omitted, but doing so only partially, within a limited vision of difference.

There may, however, be good reasons why *men* shouldn't be allowed to cycle: at the 1996 World Meeting on Impotence, findings presented by Boston urologist Dr Irwin Goldstein indicated that some 100,000 American men may have impotence problems because of cycling. Erectile dysfunction is twice as common in male cyclists as in male swimmers. Hard, narrow saddles can cause compression of the penile arteries and the dorsal nerve. 'Men should never ride bicycles', proclaimed Dr Goldstein,[45] in an interesting reversal of the old medical rule. An Austrian team reinforced Dr Goldstein's caution in 2000 by finding 'abnormalities of the scrotal contents' in 43 out of 45 mountain bikers.[46] These contraindications to cycling were anticipated, though entirely without evidence, by Dr Graeme Hammond of New York in 1895, but he said it was men's fault, as, when cycling, they should learn to sit on their gluteal muscles, not on their perinea.[47]

Cycling is good for health because the human body is designed for movement, not for sitting still. The demise of cycling is an aspect of a more general decline in exercise as part of everyday life. Most people in industrialized countries take very little exercise: in the UK, 96 per cent of women and 86 per cent of men don't take enough exercise to protect their hearts (physically speaking).[48] The substantial rise in childhood obesity over the last two decades in the UK, the USA and some other countries is associated with a marked reduction in the proportion of children who walk or cycle to school.[49]

The main reason why walking and cycling have both fallen out of fashion is the rise of the car. 'The hum of the motor is heard o'er the land', wrote 'Mrs Aria' in 1906 in a volume called *Woman and the Motor-Car: Being the auto-biography of an automobilist*:

> It is the siren's song of today . . . Nowhere can one escape from it; green pas-tures and Piccadilly alike are haunted by it; scaring the birds on the high moor-lands, it disturbs even the forest quiet; on desolate shores it obtrudes with sudden insolence upon the eternal sound of the sea . . . Scarcely more than a decade ago it was not; but now – ! . . . one hears always the assertive lamp-eyed monster rushing restlessly along, with its reverberant roar and tumble, its moan, its snort, its hoot, so that there is neither quiet nor silence anywhere.[50]

Many American communities today have few pavements, no provision for cycling, problems with safety in the streets, and shops, schools and workplaces that are many miles from homes, all of which make staying at home or driving cars the only attractive options. As recent reports on transport patterns in the USA put it, women with children, in particular, have little choice but to travel in cars. Travel patterns are among the most 'clearly gendered' aspects of American life; 85 per cent of women and 93 per cent of men had driving licences in 1995, and men drove some 6,000–7,000 miles more every year than women.[51] Women took more, shorter and more interrupted journeys than men by car in order to support household activities.[52] In Britain, men are twice as likely as women to have access to cars; in the early 1990s, five out of ten women and eight out of ten men had driving licences; men travel over 3,000 miles annually more than women, most of the excess by car.[53]

Car ownership in Europe is currently nearly one car for every two people.[54] In the USA 40 per cent of households owned two cars by 1995, and 91 per cent of all person miles are travelled by car.[55] Where I live in North London, my neighbours, well-informed and politically left-of-centre citizens, own two to four cars per household. They complain daily about the shortage of car parking spaces in the street; parents get their cars out every morning and after-noon for the briefest of school journeys (a quarter of all car journeys are less than two miles[56]). Three-quarters of delegates to a recent conference on the impact of the environment on health drove there. Senior people were most likely to arrive in cars, though there was no relationship between seniority and engine size.[57]

At first, in the early 1900s, cars were unpopular because of the clouds of dust they caused on the roads and the speed with which they tore through quiet villages. Again, women railed against the stereotype of a masculine sport: why *shouldn't* women drive cars? As with cycling, one burning question was what to wear; Mrs Aria counselled black satin knickerbockers lined with flannel, thick cashmere stockings and woollen socks, very high boots, long satin pet-ticoats lined with a substance called zenana; in the summer, a light black-and-white check tweed; hats, which were enormous, should be tied with 'motoring veils'.[58]

■

The first pedestrian to be killed by a car in Britain was a woman called Bridget Driscoll. She died of head injuries after being run down by a Roger-Benz demonstration car in the grounds of the Crystal Palace in London on a summer afternoon in 1896. At the inquest on her death, the coroner set a precedent for all coroners since in applying the term 'accident' to violence caused by motor vehicle speed.[59] The global toll of road deaths is some 30,000 annually:[60] about four in a thousand people living in the UK and about eight in a thousand in the USA are killed or injured on the roads every year. Ninety per cent of all road accidents involve a car.[61] Some 120,000 people die every year from car accidents in the fifty-one countries in the World Health Organization's European region.[62] In China, the annual toll of 'official' road deaths is more than three times that from infectious diseases.[63] Road accidents are fast becoming one of the most common causes of death worldwide; by 2020 only coronary heart disease and depression are predicted to kill more people.[64] In the UK the annual cost of injuries caused on the roads runs at over £10 billion – a quarter of the entire NHS budget.[65] Air pollution caused by traffic accounts for some 20,000 deaths and an additional 20,000 hospital admissions per year.[66] Aside from the global effects of health-damaging discharges from cars, the most seriously affected are the occupants of the cars themselves, who are exposed to pollutant levels two to three times higher than those which face cyclists or pedestrians.[67] Pollution caused by motorized traffic is greatest in urban areas, and for the socially disadvantaged who live there, and who are least likely to enjoy the 'benefits' of the private transport which causes the pollution.[68]

Like all statistics, those for road accidents can't simply be taken at face value. They probably seriously underestimate pedestrian and cycling casualties; cycling casualties may be under-reported by as much as two-thirds.[69] The second time in eight years I was knocked off my bicycle by a car, I telephoned the local police station to report the incident, but was told I had to visit the station in person to do so; as I was suffering from shock and badly bruised at the time, I never made it.

The International Classification of Diseases departs from the usual convention of associating deaths with their causes for the victims of road accidents, who are classified instead by their mode of travel at the time. This is interestingly twisted thinking, and rather like other victim-blaming epidemiology; walking or cycling are rarely *themselves* the cause of death. The result is that cycling appears to be an immensely hazardous activity. For example, London, with only 12 per cent of the national population, had 20 per cent of all national cycling casualties in 1995 – a disproportionately high rate.[70] Per kilometre travelled, cyclists are fourteen times more likely than car drivers to be killed or seriously injured in road accidents. Although cycle accidents are decreasing, the risk is going up since people are cycling less: between 1987 and 1998 cycle traffic fell by 37 per cent but the casualty rate rose by 17 per cent.[71] As 95 per cent of cycling accidents involve motorized vehicles,[72] cars rather than bicycles are the true hazard.

Even at prevailing UK road accident rates, cycling gains people more life-years than it loses them, because the health benefits achieved through regular cycling outweigh the risk of being killed or injured on the roads.[73] Only about 10 out of 3.5 million regular cyclists in Britain are killed every year; this compares with 350 people under 75 who are killed annually falling down steps or tripping: a mile of walking is much more dangerous than a mile of cycling.[74] The average British cyclist can cycle 330,000 kilometres before being seriously injured, and 17,000,000 before being killed.[75]

■

It's consoling to know how far I can cycle without being killed. Although I've got no intention of being killed in a traffic accident, I can think of no better way of dying in old age, infirmity or terminal illness than coming off a bicycle at thirty-five miles an hour down a hill in high summer in the English countryside.

Virginia Woolf wasn't mad to worry about road accidents, and I'm not mad to cycle in London. But as members of minority groups, we're both likely to be seen as the carriers, rather than recipients, of pathology. For much of their cultural history, women have seemed to specialize in madness; the links between madness and creativity allowed to men have mainly left women out of the loop. Mental instability in women has most often been associated with defiance of convention.[76] This is a complex relationship, since it seems to be the case both that protesting women get labelled as mad, and that the process of reacting against cultural norms can produce genuine psychological instability.

On my bicycle going to the British Library to find out about women, I'm a member of two minority groups: women and cyclists. The marginality I experience as a cyclist is quite literal: denied space in the centre of the road, I'm confined to its margins, where my relative invisibility then proceeds to confirm the principle that roads are for cars. But I'm also in a minority in my professional life: in the UK, 95 per cent of university professors are men. Moreover, since much of my work has been about questions of gender, I've occupied a minority space within academic social science. The Norwegian ethnographer Marianne Gullestad reflects on this issue of reinforcing marginalities – in her case the extra burden was that of doing ethnographic work on everyday life in her own country, rather than in the more usual fantastic, faraway places: 'When presenting my material to anthropological colleagues,' says Gullestad:

I have often felt like a sailor's wife who is insisting on the children's need for new shoes in front of a husband who is dreaming about the girls in exotic seaports . . . To put it bluntly, as a professional, my position is that I am marginal almost everywhere I go, but *these many marginalities add up to something which I see as very central and very important.*[77] [my italics]

Is it too far-fetched to see the psychological mechanisms underlying our cultural acceptance of cars as having a lot in common with those which hold patriarchy in place? I fancy that Virginia Woolf would have made this connection, had she walked into the kind of motorized world we now live in when she emerged from the restaurant where she took her lunch and deduced the fact of patriarchy from someone else's newspaper.

Most people leaving their homes in the morning expect to see a street full of cars; they find nothing remarkable about the way our urban and rural landscapes have so completely been given over to these 'lamp-eyed monsters'. They accept the governance of the air we breathe and the sounds we hear by traffic noise; everyday transportation would be unimaginable without cars. In the UK, tax relief is available for buying cars, but not for buying childcare services which enable parents to have paid jobs so their children don't have to live in poverty. Over time, social institutions such as the car mould their cultural habitat in precisely this manner, so that the time before they existed drops out of human memory. The hole closes, and there's nothing left.

In exactly the same way, the prevalence of men in public life is so accepted as scarcely to be commented on. We notice the dominance of men only when women creep in; a woman prime minister is remarkable, but the general rule of male prime ministers is not. The number of women MPs is charted, but the number of male MPs has habitually not been, because what is an MP, if not a man? Barbara Wootton, one of the first women life peers in that antiquated British institution, the House of Lords, noted that the queen's speech at the start of that historic session still began with the words, 'My Lords, pray be seated.' The House of Lords' signwriters, labelling lavatories to accommodate the new breed, got themselves into a dreadful tangle trying to differentiate between women peers and 'peeresses' – the wives of male peers: 'The concept of a woman peer must . . . have stuck in the throat of the signwriter because, when the revised notice appeared, the words "Women Peers" were enclosed in inverted commas, as though the description was something of a joke.'[78]

The American feminist Kate Millett was the first in second-wave feminism to invoke, in her *Sexual Politics*, a theory of patriarchy to explain the social relations of men and women. Millett's starting point was the horrific things men get up to in certain kinds of fiction: 'I bit the nape of her neck, the lobes of her ears, the sensitive spot on her shoulder, and as I pulled away I left the mark of my teeth on her beautiful white ass'[79] – and a good deal worse than that. At the time, linking the terms 'sex' and 'politics' was a revolutionary act;

it was unusual to see sex 'as a status category with political implications',[80] and even more out of line to read, as did Millett, the sexual exploits of men in novels by writers such as Norman Mailer, Henry Miller and D. H. Lawrence as accomplished within a system of political oppression.

Like Gunnar Myrdal and others, Millett called the relations between men and women those of dominance and subordination; most social, economic and political power belongs to men, where 'man' means 'human' and women behave as befits members of minority groups. She took the view that patriarchy is synonymous with culture itself, making it particularly hard even to see, for, 'When a system of power is thoroughly in command, it has scarcely need to speak itself aloud.'[81] The term 'patriarchy' was useful because it offered an overarching explanation for all instances of sexism. These could thereby be referred to the 'social and political power system' rather than to the errors of individual men. Men are surprisingly quick to take blame on themselves: when the writer Joan Smith published a book about woman-hating, she noted the 'unmissable irony' that this concern of hers to illuminate the many ways in which hostility to women is manifested, immediately turned her into a 'man-hater'.[82]

We obviously don't live in a patriarchal society in any 'pure' sense any longer. Production based on land-holding, primogeniture, the absolute power of men sanctioned by religious or official authority, women and children deprived of human status, the restriction of women's freedom to inherit property, be educated, have a public role and choose whom to marry – all these are things of the past, in the main, for most women in European and North American culture, though they still hold, or are being reinvented, in other parts of the world. In the culture which most of this book is about, the model of power implied by patriarchy – interpersonal domination – is not, in the main, what happens any longer; forms of discrimination can be subtle, sexual divisions are complex, the representational practices of women's oppression multiply imaginatively and incessantly. But none of this means that we no longer need the notion of patriarchy. As a system of social relations providing a material base for men's domination of women and children, patriarchy is the default mode: what's always there and will always happen unless it's actively contended. We are lost without it and lost within it. We need it to comprehend what goes on, and what goes on is a constant fracturing of our humanness into divisive and destructive ways of being and living.

3
Manslaughter

Snow coats the landscape with whiteness. It's the product of several days' faltering snowfalls, starting and stopping like an infant on the verge of walking. Then last night the snow suddenly got serious, and several inches fell. It crunches most satisfactorily underfoot, and my pioneer footprints join other smaller ones – birds, dogs, foxes, perhaps even those of the wild puma rumoured to be at a loose end in these parts. A full sun in a sapphire sky dazzles the snow into diamonds; every twig on every tree carries a snow-ruff, and tiny pendant icicles dangle far more magically than ornaments on any Christmas tree.

I cross the main road and take the hill down into the next village, feeling exhilaration and uncomplicated happiness at just being out here walking in the snow: 'Sometimes the unmeasured, the unlimited natural powers are what I need, what everyone needs', said the American writer and nature-worshipper May Sarton.[1] Being in this landscape is a multifaceted experience: not just what the eyes see, but what the ears hear and the nose senses and the skin feels: the sharp whack of the air; melted icicles dropping uninvited onto cheek or hand from skeletal conker trees; hearing the snow's silence.

About a mile before the village there's a turn on the right: a minor road, nothing of any great significance. There's a car parked a little way up the turn. My mind records the car's presence, a black wart on the entirely white and immobile landscape, as minds habitually pick up facts without knowing at the time what they mean. Then I see a man standing outside the car, his back to me: the car boot is open, I assume he's looking for something in it. Irrelevantly, I wonder whether he's looking for his fishing tackle – but the reservoir for fishing is several miles away, and you could hardly fish today, in all this snow.

I've been walking or cycling these roads for many years, and I've always felt perfectly safe on them (apart from the violence of passing cars), so I don't feel any sense of menace. But I am subliminally aware that I and the man-looking-in-his-car-boot are the only two visible human figures. The nearest houses and people are well over the horizon in the village beyond the fields. 'Excuse me,' says the man, and I turn towards him, down the side road, thinking he wants directions to somewhere or to know the time, 'would you like some of this?' My eyes drop from his face; his trousers, jogging pants, are round his knees, and his right hand is manhandling a semi-erect penis which can't compare to the snow in whiteness, being a distinctly off-white, dirty, sordid colour. It looks circumcised, I note, with that absurd attention to detail the mind can engage in at such moments. When I give the police that detail later, they don't flinch, but it doesn't help them to catch him.

'No', I say. No. I feel intense repugnance and a great gush of fear wrapped up in a cloud of unreality – can this really be happening to me? For some ridiculous reason I believed that one of the rewards of getting older was that women were spared such encounters. As I say 'no' I remember my mother telling me about a flasher she met on her way home when I was a baby. 'Put it away, young man', she'd apparently commanded. I find I can't quite manage this magisterial response.

'Wouldn't you like it between your tits?', continues 'my' flasher, relentlessly pursuing his own agenda. 'Or in your cunt?' The mouth moves, the hand pumps; the figure in the landscape has by now quite obliterated the whiteness of the snow. The man has dark hair and wears dark glasses, and his sweatshirt and trousers are dark, like his car: it's all darkness except for the bits of pallid, poking flesh he's forcing me to look at.

I 'know' that most flashers only flash, but this one . . . ? As I move away, he yanks his trousers up and follows me, he gets hold of my arm by the ditch at the turn of the road, and I scream, 'Leave me alone! Let go of me!' and other equally useless inanities, because nobody can hear me and he's certainly not listening. Everything – my past and future, all my experiences and thoughts and hopes, this life-giving natural world – is reduced to the menace of the man with the off-white penis who's picked on me for no obvious reason and is now using me for his own purposes with all sorts of consequences which are, even now, queuing up to be recognized in my head, while at the same time I try to figure out how to escape his clutches. It occurs to me I could die here, be raped and beaten and consigned to the ditch: no one would know.

It may have been his unsuitable shoes or his generally lower level of cardiovascular fitness, but I manage to tear myself away and then outrun him. I don't stop running until I reach the centre of the village where I can see people in their houses. All the time I'm running I never look behind me, never want to see if the man is there or if his car's following me.

There's no shop or post office or garage in the village, only a pub. I think about going into the pub (supposing it's open) and reporting what's happened and calling the police from there, but I don't want to make a fuss, and somehow regaling my story to strangers seems like repeating the experience. I want to be at home, safe behind my own bolted doors. Very irrationally, I decide to run all the way home – another two miles. There are houses some of the way, but also stretches without, and I run very fast in these, conscious of a manically beating heart and of how the chemicals of fear seem to be driving my leg muscles like pistons.

I drink some brandy and call the police. Two policemen come to the house, and they behave in an absolutely exemplary fashion, having clearly been through some relevant training programme. They tell me that it'll take me some time to get over my experience, that it shouldn't make me afraid to go out alone again, though I'd do well to equip myself with a strong walking stick, that I might like some victim support (they provide a leaflet), and do I have someone they can call to be with me? Their only slip from political correctness comes when they mention it's bad enough for something like this to happen to a woman of my age – just think how awful it'd be for an impressionable young girl! But I was an impressionable young girl once, and it did happen to me.

The policeman's comment was, though, right in a way, because women learn over their lives lessons about the prevalence and unpredictability of men's violence to them. It's almost an impersonal thing: a statement about masculinity rather than anything to do with us individually.

■

As a source of global human suffering, male violence probably outranks disease and famine.[2] Men commit 90 per cent of violent crime and over 80 per cent of all recorded offences.[3]

My encounter with the snow-flasher was one of 17,643 recorded indecent assaults on females in England and Wales in 1996.[4] These represented 5 per cent of all violent crimes, though for some bizarre reason they're classified as 'sexual' offences rather than crimes of 'violence against the person'.[5] Between 1996 and 31 March 2000 violent crime rose twofold, accounting for most of the increase in overall crime figures.[6] These figures for England and Wales are part of an international picture of rising crime rates – on average recorded crime rates rose by 5 per cent in 1997–8.[7] There are big geographical differences; Washington DC was the homicide capital of the world in one recent international comparison, with a rate 28 times that of London and 24 times that of Paris; next in line were Pretoria and Moscow (19 and 8 times the London rate respectively).[8]

These rising crime rates yielded the prediction in 1980 that 20–30 per cent of girls born in 1968 would suffer a violent sexual attack sometime in their lives.[9] Twenty-seven per cent of a large sample of American undergraduates questioned in the late 1980s had been the victims of rape or attempted rape since the age of fourteen,[10] a figure generally confirmed by other studies in the USA and the UK.[11] Very few of these acts of violence are reported to the police, and most involve men who aren't strangers. (Less than a third of homicides in the USA are stranger–stranger attacks.[12]) Rape and other sexual crimes are notoriously under-reported; in South Africa, for instance, fewer than one in twenty rapes are reported to the police;[13] in a Swiss study, 98 per cent of rape cases went unpunished, mainly because they were unreported.[14] A Home Office report published in 2000 calculated the true incidence of rape and indecent assault in England and Wales as between five and thirteen times the reported rate – some 118,000 to 295,000 'incidents' each year.[15] In another recent report, men were responsible for 90 per cent of stalking incidents involving women and 57 per cent of those involving men. Nearly one in five women aged between 16 and 19 reported 'persistent or unwanted attention' from another person; half of all stalking incidents involved violence, including forced sexual acts, or the threat of violence.[16] The global statistics are shocking: at least one in five women experience rape or attempted rape over their lifetime.[17]

Dutch architect Frans van Velden's first encounter with sexual violence was a woman falling off a balcony in a Rotterdam housing project: 'I could not make out if it was sexual violence or escape from it.'[18] Domestic violence, a quarter of all crime,[19] is the largest single type of violence against women. Thirty-three per cent of the 225 female homicide victims in England and Wales in 1998 were killed by a current or former partner.[20] In the UK someone rings the police for help for domestic violence every minute.[21] In British surveys a quarter of women report having been physically assaulted by a current or former partner at some time in their lives.[22] Worldwide, 20–60 per cent of women are beaten by their partners.[23] Domestic violence injuries include bruises, cuts, burns and scalds, concussions, broken bones, penetrating injuries from knives and other objects, permanent injuries such as damage to joints, loss of hearing or vision and physical disfigurement from burns, bites and knife wounds.[24]

Domestic violence is estimated to cause some 19 per cent of the total 'disease burden' of women aged 15–44.[25] In a study of the clinical histories of 4,500 women using the Yale-New Haven Hospital in the USA in the late 1970s and early 1980s, injuries caused by domestic violence were the main reason for women seeking medical treatment. Doctors significantly underestimated its importance: whereas they viewed 1 in every 35 of their patients as battered, the correct figure was close to 1 in 4; while they traced 1 presenting injury in 20 to partner assault, the actual figure was nearer 1 in 3.[26] Battered women are three times more likely than other women attending hospital for emergency injury treatment to be pregnant when injured; 20–25 per cent of all obstetrical patients have a history of being battered.[27] The health hazards of domestic violence in pregnancy include miscarriage, pre-term birth, low birthweight, fetal injury such as broken bones and stab wounds, and fetal death; battered pregnant women have higher rates of drug and alcohol use, smoking and attempted suicide.[28] Murder, most usually by the partner, is the commonest cause of death in pregnancy in the USA.[29] Despite its frequency, health professionals don't routinely ask about domestic violence. As one doctor has said, 'Although domestic violence is a taboo subject, if you don't look and ask, you won't find a problem.'[30]

Sexual assaults and domestic violence are part of a global picture of violence against women. This includes genital mutilation; gender-based torture and violence against women refugees and asylum-seekers; violence associated with prostitution and pornography; dowry-related murder; selective malnourishment of female children; sexual abuse of girls; and corporate crimes affecting women in their roles as childbearers and houseworkers.[31]

Male violence has been described as 'marvellously heterogeneous in form',[32] and it clearly is heterogeneous, manifesting itself in acts as apparently disparate as murder, robbery, assault, football hooliganism, terrorism, domestic violence, stalking, school bullying, pub brawls, rape and torture. The commonality of these crimes – the gender of their perpetrators – is rarely acknowledged. Each is studied on its own as though it's a separate subject: sex offences in one category; genital mutilation in another; the torture of civilians in warfare in a third, and so on; but when it comes to explanations, the logic of separation breaks down.

Of course, most men aren't criminal, and many eschew violence altogether, but the dominant form of masculinity in Western culture is both aggressive and misogynist – the latter in the sense of a phenomenon that begins with jokes and ends with murder.[33] Being a 'real man' still means being in control, and this implies a form of competition in interpersonal relationships which is very thinly divided from verbal or physical aggression. American studies of men's attitudes to masculinity have uncovered clusters of norms – 'avoidance of femininity', 'independence and self-confidence', 'achieving status' and 'aggressiveness' in one study; a 'need to achieve status and respect', 'mental, emotional and physical toughness' and 'avoidance of feminine activities and occupations' in another – as together making up what it means to be a man.[34]

Like everything else, masculine violence has a past. When children at school learn their national histories, these have traditionally consisted mainly of wars led and fought by men, interrupted by brief periods of peace in which more interesting things happen. The history of the earth as told in such narratives is largely one of aggression, domination and its commodification as packages of territory owned, and argued over, by warrior nation states. The other story is never told: of peace and who keeps it; or the earth as a common resource, rather than a commodity; of resistances to the warrior enterprise.

Men, it appears, have always fought; it's only their weaponry which changes. In the West, knife-fights and duelling with swords were for centuries accepted ways of settling disputes between men.[35] At their peak in the 1860s, Italian men's habit of duelling was running at the level of at least one a day, though with a low risk of death – less than 1 per cent in a series analysed by an Italian journalist around 1900.[36] This was highly stylized violence between men, offering the opportunity for a public display of courage as the embodiment of masculinity; women were excluded, though some of the fights were about them. What brought these types of stylized fighting to an end was the First World War, which provided a dramatic contrast between the 'metaphysics of courage and death' engaged in by the duellists and the actual wages of courage paid on the killing fields of a multinational conflict. In the twentieth and twenty-first centuries, technological developments in military weaponry have shut the door on close-quarters fighting – less than 0.5 per cent of all wounds were caused by bayonets in the two world wars[37] – but they've provided the technical means for a resurgence in the 'warrior values' of courage, endurance and 'honourable' combat.[38] Militariness, violence, technology and manliness have been tied in a new version of the old knot.

Men's fascination with machines and technology is well known.[39] Boys who play with machines rehearse future roles as technicians and fighters: one engineer, creating war simulations for jet aircraft using computers, explained: 'My work is just like playing computer games. The only difference is that this is reality and that nowadays I get paid for doing what I did in my room when I lived with my parents.'[40] Eric Harris and Dylan Klebold, who murdered twelve students and a teacher and wounded twenty-three others before shooting themselves at the Columbine High School in Littleton, Ohio, in 1999, were known to enjoy playing Doom, a video game licensed by the US military to train soldiers to kill.[41] Games such as Doom require the player to identify with the aggressor, reward players for killing people, and portray women either as helpless victims or as seductive sex objects. There's mounting evidence that access to violent video games of this kind is increasing aggression among children and young people, especially boys.[42]

In the US between 75 and 86 million people own some 200–240 million guns.[43] Most people believe they have the right to own one: 'it is simply the way things are'.[44] But the risk of homicide is increased three times and that of suicide five times for people living in homes with guns.[45] The typical handgun death occurs in arguments between people who know one another; for every stranger killed in self-defence by a handgun, 109 lives are lost in handgun homicides, suicides and unintentional shootings.[46]

'It is a cliché that the gun is a penis-symbol as well as a weapon . . . At both symbolic and practical levels, the defence of gun ownership is a defence of hegemonic masculinity.'[47] The attempt by the firearms industry in the USA to increase the sale of guns to women – 'firearms feminism' – only increases the risk of death for women, especially in homes already marked by domestic violence.[48]

Of course, women can be warlike too,[49] and, as in many other areas of life, their 'liberation' equates with the adaptation of masculine behaviours: so guns are replacing knives as the 'weapons of choice' in female-caused homicide.[50] But the different attitudes of men and women to aggression remain one of the biggest gender gaps ever to have been found by the blunt instrument of social research: so, for example, men, compared to women, support a resort to force in international conflicts by a margin of more than two to one.[51] Women may not be 'natural' pacificists, but they often exemplify a preference for words rather than weapons as strategies for resolving conflict.[52]

The chief activity of men in war is killing, not dying.[53] The direct and explicit focus of military strategy is human slaughter – the murder of men, women and children; the culpable, not intentional and definitely incorrectly named, 'manslaughter'. William Broyles, a former combat soldier, likened the 'sport' of war to the pleasure of small boys playing cowboys and Indians, considering slaughter 'an affair of great and seductive beauty'; the experience of using machine guns or napalm is 'orgasmic': war is the greatest turn-on of all. Broyles described what 'his' men did to a North Vietnamese soldier they'd recently killed: they propped the corpse up, put sunglasses on his eyes and a cigarette in his mouth and balanced a 'large and perfectly formed' piece of shit on his head. Broyles pretended to be outraged, but inside he was laughing at this obscene linkage of sex, excrement and death:[54] 'manslaughter' is also 'man's laughter'.

Joanna Bourke's *An Intimate History of Killing*, which recounts this incident, makes it very clear that men's exultation in the sport of desecration is a normal part of warfare. It isn't the only emotion, of course: guilt, remorse and mental breakdown because of the horrors of war are other sequelae. But what was most striking to observers in the two world wars and the Vietnam War, on which Bourke's book is based, was the ease with which most men killed; more men broke down because of not being allowed to kill than through the strain of killing.[55]

Military training instructed soldiers to treat their guns as they would treat women; in the words of the chant popular at the time, 'This is my rifle / This is my gun / This is for fighting / This is for fun.' In the Second World War a Home Guard Training Manual called *Rough Stuff* explicitly linked the masculinity of sex and fighting: successful lovers are men who give 'free rein' to their desires, and successful fighters are also men who hold nothing back.[56] Sexual intercourse and the murder of war are intimately linked. Killing is rape or 'the fuck of his life'; the earth moves and the appetite wants more.[57] At the massacre of My Lai in March 1968 US soldiers under orders from their superiors killed more than five hundred civilians; 'double veterans' were those who raped, then killed, their victims. These were divested of all humanity, becoming merely assemblages of enemy body parts. Trophy-hunting was a recognized ancillary sport, common in all three conflicts. Even the poet Wilfred Owen sent his brother a blood-stained handkerchief which he'd taken from the pocket of a dead German pilot. Japanese women had their breasts collected; in Vietnam, ears, teeth, fingers, heads, penises, hands and toes were all popular.[58] Sexual violence, including the enforced prostitution of women and children, in armed conflicts is a perversion with a long history.[59]

The sexual metaphors of warfare are peacetime occurrences, too. Serbian and Croatian women coined the term the 'post-TV news syndrome' to describe men's violence to their partners following watching TV news coverage of the war; during the Gulf War, Canadian women who retreated to women's refuges told stories of their husbands dressing in army uniforms before beating them.[60] Alex Comfort's well-known book *The Joy of Sex* contains detailed instructions on how to incorporate into 'normal' sex whips, beating, and tying partners.[61] Films, television, advertisements, magazines, newspapers, books and computer games all trade in images of violent, sexualized masculinity. The Internet is the latest to join this list, with multiple sites exhibiting violent pornographic sex, and men using its anonymity to dupe young girls and women into making sexual contact.[62] It's also the newest method of sexual harassment.[63]

Like rape, sexual harassment is a form of violence against people; rather than sidelined as a sexual act, most of it's an abuse of authority, the outcome of unequal power relations.[64] Airline pilot Sandra Valentine suffered from the wandering hands of a male colleague on a plane she was co-piloting from Birmingham to Portugal; his flying was 'appalling'; when she pointed out that he wasn't following standard operating procedures, he responded, 'Shut up, I am the captain and I will do as I please, you stupid bloody woman.'[65] Kazuo Matsuda, the deputy managing director of Fuji International Finance, kept a topless calendar on his desk and made it known that he was discouraging the recruitment of women because he wanted more men in the company; men were regularly promoted above more highly qualified women, one of whom sued for sex discrimination. When Lynn Goodall, an acting sergeant in the Royal Signals, attended a promotion course she was told, 'We do not want a fucking woman here.'[66] In one study, 40 per cent of women police had experienced low-level harassment and unwanted touching, while a further 6 per cent reported serious harassment, including sexual assault.[67] Most women experience some kind of embarrassment or discomfort because of the sexual behaviour of men at work.[68]

Sport – the prototypical metaphor for the 'fun' of war – is another culturally important vehicle for the expression of masculinity. Competitive team
sports for men exist in warfare-oriented societies, but not in other kinds.[69] In
one survey, 50 per cent of British men but only 8 per cent of women said that
sport was their favourite television programme.[70] Contact sports such as football, rugby, boxing, wrestling and ice hockey are all essentially forms of controlled violence.[71] There are lots of rules, but provided people stick to them,
it doesn't matter how many injuries are caused. Sport symbolizes 'free' activity, purposive bodily action, initiative and competition – all attributes of
masculinity in Western culture.

Association football (soccer) is the world's number one game; it's the
national sport in many countries; FIFA – the Fédération Internationale de
Football Association – founded in 1904, has more members than the United
Nations; the 1994 World Cup got an audience of more than 32 billion.[72]
Football is a sport created by men for men; sport, like cycling, higher education, writing and public affairs, was one of the many things nineteenth-century
doctors said women shouldn't do; the founder of the modern Olympics, Pierre
Coubertin, followed this line in decreeing women in sport to be against the
laws of nature.[73] In Britain, league grounds were formally closed to women
footballers from 1921 to 1969. Like many sports, football presumes qualities
of competitiveness, stamina and aggression – definitely unladylike qualities.
Studies of boys and young men show how aggression, sport and a commodified attitude to girls and sex combine in a 'macho' culture. In Mac an Ghaill's
study of a British state secondary school, the 'macho lads' substituted for
the conventional 3 Rs the equally conventional 3 Fs – fighting, fucking and
football.[74]

A footballer's worst insult is to be called a 'woman' or a 'tart' – the alternative 'black bastard' has mostly been banished for racist incorrectness.[75]
In 1979, conscious that they hadn't got very far in catching 'the Yorkshire
Ripper', a serial attacker of women in the Midlands and north of England, the
police played over loudspeakers at a Leeds United football match a tape sent
to the police in the hope that it would jog someone's memory. But Leeds fans
drowned out the voice with chants of 'Eleven–Nil' (eleven being the number
of known victims at the time).[76]

The first recorded women's football match was in 1895 between teams
representing the north and south of England (the north won 7–1). Women's
international football was promoted by the aptly named Nettie Honeyball,
the secretary of the British ladies team. The Women's Football Association,
launched in 1969 with a male secretary, was taken over by the (men's) Football Association in 1993 with a promise to promote women's participation, but
in its first full year of managing it the FA spent more than 130 times as much
on men's football.[77] Women's football lacks social and financial status, pay,
sponsorship and media attention compared to men's. There's no coverage of

women's football matches on terrestrial television, and they fail to make it into the national news. The marginalization of women's football (people rarely speak of 'men's football') reflects a basic principle of patriarchal systems – that they're organized in such a way that the belief in male supremacy 'comes true'.[78] When women's sport does hit the news, there's usually a gendered reason: 'The hot question in women's sport: how much is baring too much?' inquired a recent headline in a British newspaper, referring to the fashion for skimpy outfits among some women tennis players.[79] The executive director of the Women's Cricket Association claimed sex discrimination by Lancashire Cricket Board for not shortlisting her in its search for a new assistant secretary and development co-ordinator; she was told she wasn't suitable for the job, because she didn't know enough about the men's game.[80]

Like war, sport functions as an expression of national identity. In the 1969 war between El Salvador and Honduras, riots following World Cup qualifying games between the two countries escalated into large-scale fighting.[81] Football hooliganism has been an increasing problem in Britain and elsewhere since the mid-1950s, especially in international matches, when the pitch becomes quite literally the site of nationalist conflict. The 'feminization' of football audiences (some 10–15 per cent of fans are women) is seen as an appropriate policy solution, with 'family stands' promoted as areas where women and children can feel safe. But it's difficult for women to feel safe in this context, since the link between football and domestic violence has been known for a long time; violence to women increases after football matches, as supporters of losing teams go home and take it out on 'their' women.[82] Football comes close to arguments about housework as a precursor of domestic violence.[83] There's something about the emotions engendered by football that makes men spoil for a fight; the former chairman of Dundee Football Club was recently arrested for assaulting a television reporter in a post-match interview.[84]

Masculinity – a set of images, values, interests and activities held important to the successful achievement of male adulthood[85] – isn't a biologically given condition. Sociobiological explanations of masculine aggression and crime don't work, because these aren't universal,[86] because different cultures sanction and proscribe different patterns of behaviour,[87] and because male violence is systematically linked to sexual and economic power relations.[88] Masculinity is an achieved status; it's something men must actively campaign to acquire. Violence, crime, sport and war are all contexts for making masculinity happen.

As one (male) social scientist has put it: 'Explaining male violence towards women in terms of the gendered power relations in society as a whole is not the most obvious explanation to strike the non-feminist mind, which is more attuned to examining the characteristics of those men who are particularly violent. However, a persuasive argument can be made out for the power explanation.'[89] This would suggest that violence against women is particularly likely to happen when men feel their power is threatened. In one study of the relationship between gender, power and masculine violence in a number of US states, there was a U-shaped relationship between masculine violence and women's status. Violence was highest when women's status was both low and high.[90] Individual case histories suggest that domestic violence can be a response to women's greater freedom; such conflict often begins with arguments over women's employment, cooking, childcare, sex or money, and, although these conflicts are intensely personal, 'they are infused at every point with notions of female possibility and male power' which make them, often literally, a defence of traditional masculine authority.[91]

But crime and aggression are also linked to economic class. The men most likely to be convicted of crime are those at the economic margins of society – the unemployed, the poor, disadvantaged youth and ethnic minorities.[92] It's consoling for academics to note that only 0.05 per cent of UK prisoners have a university degree.[93] In the US, 50 per cent of prisoners (but only 11 per cent of the population) are Black[94] (the US has 25 per cent of the world's prisoners, but only 5 per cent of the world's population[95]). In England and Wales in 1997–8, the peak age for male offending was 18: 9 per cent of all 18-year-old young men were found guilty of, or cautioned for, an indictable offence (for women the peak age was 15, and 2 per cent of 15 year olds offended).[96] Judging from media reports, the age of criminal 'responsibility' is falling all the time; in Britain in 2000 two boys aged five and nine mugged and stole from an elderly woman,[97] and in Belgium three boys aged eight, nine and thirteen placed rocks and a concrete slab on a railway track and jammed a switching device with shards of concrete 'for fun', with the result that two trains collided, killing or injuring more than twenty people.[98]

Aggression is the hallmark of those whose positions are estranged or under threat, not those whose power is confirmed and institutionalized (who may exercise it in other ways). Gender and class inequality – the twin products of patriarchy and capitalism – underlie the statistics of crime and violence. The values of capitalism – competitiveness, profit and self-seeking materialism – interact with those of (white middle-class) men as the dominant group, for whom control and mastery are key, to create a literally no-win situation for those at the bottom of the pile. Missing from this whole picture are the pro-social human strategies of caring, empathy, compassion, altruism and forgiveness.

The British psychiatrist Anthony Clare commented thus in his recent book *On Men: Masculinity in crisis*: 'There is a truly awesome problem concerning male violence . . . and responding to it by desperately seeking to identify an equivalent amount of female violence . . . is a fairly predictable example of male projection and denial.'[99] Women play a greater part in the recorded statistics of crime and violence than they used to, but the typical female offender is still the non-violent 'petty' thief.[100] In the USA 17 per cent of homicides are committed by women, but most of these involve proactive or defensive strikes against male assailants; 40–70 per cent of women charged with murder or manslaughter were being abused by the man they killed.[101] Although women do abuse their male partners and their children – 8 per cent of domestic violence victims in a recent UK survey were men attacked by women[102] – women are twice as likely to have been severely injured in such attacks and to have suffered multiple assaults.[103] It's men who commit the bulk of serious cases of violence against people of both sexes and all ages.

Because male crime and violence are systematically linked to economic and social power relations, it doesn't make much sense to seek individualized explanations of male violence as exceptional acts. England's 'Yorkshire Ripper', Peter Sutcliffe, the mass murderer who savaged and killed thirteen women and attacked numerous others between 1975 and 1981, would have been caught much earlier than he was had the police not been looking for a monster, but instead been prepared to recognize as the perpetrator of such violence a 'calm, unremarkable' married man living an ordinary, suburban, semi-detached kind of life. When they first interviewed him, the West Yorkshire police ignored multiple clues; for example, Sutcliffe wore the same size boots as the murderer, was one of only 300 men who could have got in his pay packet the new £5 note found in the handbag of one of the victims, left prints of his car tyres at some of the murder scenes, and had a previous conviction for being in a woman's garden with a knife and a hammer – the same weapons used by the Ripper. What the police were looking for was an outsider, a man who stood out from the crowd, whereas Peter Sutcliffe was simply one of them, albeit one with a fragile sense of masculinity, whose wife had cheated on him with an Italian man who drove a sports car.[104]

Explaining rape or domestic violence in terms of differences between rapists and normal men doesn't work because men who rape or beat often *are* 'normal' men; 'Women's medical records', said Evan Stark and Anne Flitcraft in their study of domestic violence, 'are replete with instances of men who covet their wives at one moment as if they were unique and irreplaceable, then beat them the next as if they were disposable (and replaceable) objects.'[105]

Women are often pathologized in the debate about crime and violence. They're culpable for not having behaved properly: you shouldn't walk on your own in the country if you don't want to be attacked; if you don't catch buses late at night you won't be threatened by a drunk posse of lads at a bus stop; if you refrain from using your body for monetary reward you'll never deserve the frenzied loathing of Peter Sutcliffe and other Rippers; if you don't live with a battering man like Joel Steinberg you'll be able to be the good mother Hedda Nussbaum wasn't, and protect little Lisa from being murdered.[106]

As Hannah Arendt said in a much-quoted aphorism, 'Power and violence are opposites; where one rules absolutely the other is absent. Violence appears when power is in jeopardy.'[107] The apocryphal Moulay Ismail the Bloodthirsty, emperor of Morocco in the early eighteenth century, killed 30,000 men, had 888 children and kept a harem of 500 young women, each completely isolated and guarded by a eunuch and a female slave.[108] He presumably had a secure sense of his own masculinity – at least sufficiently secure not to kill and desecrate the bodies of women as well. Today, most men have fewer wives and children and less power, but as a group they still have greater power than women. The only explanations that fit the facts of masculine crime and aggression are that these behaviours have something to do with 'normal' gender relations, and 'normal' gender relations involve hierarchies of power in which men set the standards for what counts as human behaviour: 'I was violent with my first wife. She was my secretary. With my second wife such behaviour seemed to me somehow inappropriate. She is a faculty member like me.'[109]

■

But what is 'crime'? Legal categories and statistical definitions are created by particular social groups – middle-class professionals, bureaucrats, the agents of nation states. That's why rape was legal within marriage for many years after it had been rendered illegal outside it; it's why rape has, in law, to involve a penis – hammers, curling tongs or broom-handles[110] won't do, although they may actually inflict more injury: the key concern is not the damage done, but the power relations – the little matter of possible impregnation. Until 1828 in England the definition of rape required seminal emission to be proved. It's also why homicide and manslaughter are called what they are; it explains why thefts of property rather than personal injury were for a long time the major concern of English criminal law.[111] And the principle that crime is socially constructed underlies the anonymous poem, loved by A-level economic history teachers, about the law on theft as applying to 'the man or woman who steals the goose from the common, but leaves the greater villain loose, who steals the common from the goose'.[112]

What we think of as 'serious' crimes – individual acts of rape, terrorism, murder, housebreaking, mugging – aren't necessarily those which objectively cause the most suffering. There's another way to look at crime, and that's to see it as the outcome of power, not poverty. Crimes committed by large organizations, industries and governments are major killers and significant sources of damage to people's health and wellbeing. The key criminal here is 'the political economy of multinational corporate capitalism',[113] which supports powerful elites in their attempts to maintain the status quo. The following 'crimes' are regular occurrences: deaths due to employers' failures to maintain safe working conditions; deaths caused by drug manufacturers' failures to establish drug safety; murder caused by governments dropping bombs or chemical agents on civilian populations; theft from consumers due to manufacturers' malpractices, including misrepresentations in advertisements; deaths and injuries due to faulty consumer products; and financial injury to consumers through price fixing and monopoly pricing. Criminal prosecutions are few and far between in such cases, mainly because the criminals are high-status people whose social and business networks condone, if not actively foster, such actions. 'Elite deviance' is common, low-risk, socially sanctioned, 'normal' behaviour.

In terms of personal injury and death, the toll imposed by corporate crime is enormous; the number of people dying from avoidable industrial injuries and accidents is around six times the number who die from homicide as more conventionally defined,[114] and many millions are injured and thousands die because of faulty consumer products. Corporate crime deprives people of up to ten times more money and property than individual thefts.[115]

The largest transnational corporations are the worst offenders. But of course it isn't the corporation that offends: it's people within them. Women are notoriously scarce among top managers and executives: in the UK in 1998 they made up 18 per cent of executives and 4 per cent of directors.[116] Most corporate decision-making is in the hands of men recruited for their ability to put profit before ethics and act out a tough-minded, aggressive attitude to furthering the goals of the corporation above all else.[117] Corporate decisions are made in the context of male 'homosociability': ease of communication and discourse is promoted by restricting executive and managerial jobs to those who are socially homogenous, which men and women are not.[118] It's this social homogeneity which enables the value-systems driving decision-making to be regarded as impersonal and neutral, whereas they actually embody very particular attitudes to people, work and the environment.[119] Old/new boys' networks support the suppression of individual moral purpose among corporate executives and managers in the interests of corporate profit (there's usually a handsome salary pay-off as well); what would otherwise be acts of transgression become, simply, service to the company. As one corporate lawyer put it when asked why he'd produced bogus insurance policies: 'I didn't think of it; it was something the company needed done, that's all!'[120]

Behind the 'white-collar' crime committed by large private companies is the motive of profit maximization. This is a main reason why the privatization of state-owned or regulated industries is likely to compromise safety – a lesson currently being learnt the hard way by Britain's rail users in a series of derailments and collisions, due to neglect of infrastructure repair and safety standards by the private companies responsible for both tracks and trains.[121] We already know that privatization damages safety and impairs other standards of service. An experiment in the USA with contracting out to private firms the teaching of reading and mathematics in state schools in 1970–1 resulted in lower student performances in mathematics and academic work generally.[122] When the Airlines Deregulation Act phased out the Civil Aeronautics Board in 1978 in the USA, the regulation of airlines was turned into an 'experiment in free market economics' which dramatically decreased safety. PanAm flight 173, exploding in the air over Lockerbie, was only one of twenty-four aircraft explosions in the years 1980–9 which together killed or injured 1,406 people. More recently, the successful hijacking in September 2001 of four aeroplanes in the USA and the killing of thousands of people in New York, Washington and Pennsylvania followed a period in which airlines have put profit before security. The current level of security reflects cost-cutting, as does the fall in the number of mechanics employed by the major airlines, the use by some of less experienced pilots, the non-replacement of old aeroplanes and unsafe seats, the reduction in cabin air quality and the use of cabin materials which burn easily, emitting toxic fumes (the cause of most deaths in survivable crashes). Before deregulation, airlines' investment in safety could be priced into tickets, so this was not viewed as a potential drag on profits.[123]

Three of the best-known examples of profit-related damage caused by big corporations are the Ford Pinto, the Dalkon Shield and Love Canal; an ongoing example is the tobacco industry.

Ford produced the Pinto car in the 1970s as a competitor to the Volkswagen beetle. Before it was marketed, company officials knew it had a faulty petrol tank design which meant it would easily ignite even in low-speed, rear-end collisions. Ford carried out a cost-benefit analysis, on the basis of which they decided it'd be cheaper to pay the families of people who died because of the fault than the $11 per car it would cost to correct the fault. The company also lobbied in Washington to convince government regulatory agencies that crashes are caused by bad driving, not bad cars.[124] There were subsequently some 900 burn deaths due to exploding Pintos, which were eventually withdrawn.[125]

The Dalkon Shield, a contraceptive device, had already generated more than four hundred reports of damaging side effects, none of which was made public, before being put on the market in the US in 1971. The Shield was invented by Hugh Davis, a doctor and associate professor of gynaecology at Johns Hopkins University, and Davis' business partner, Irwin Lerner. Consciously exploiting current fears about the safety of the contraceptive pill, David and Lerner developed the device and initially marketed it themselves by forming a private corporation after Davis had 'tested' it on 640 mainly Black women in the hospital where he worked. In 1970 they sold the patent to the giant pharmaceutical company A. H. Robins, on the basis that Davis and Lerner would continue to earn royalties and consultancy fees from it. The Shield was inserted into the uteruses of some 2.86 million American women, and those of another 0.44 million overseas, including around 200,000 in Britain. The list of health problems attributable to the Shield included pelvic inflammatory disease, septicaemia, spontaneous abortions, ectopic pregnancies, perforations of the uterus, infertility and death. One of its major design faults, the 'wicking' effect of the string projecting from the Shield into the vagina, which enabled it to soak up bacteria, was spotted early on by a quality control supervisor working for A. H. Robins, but nothing was done about it.[126] The Shield also had a pregnancy rate considerably above the 1 per cent originally claimed by Davis.[127] In 1974 A. H. Robins suspended sales of the Shield at the request of the US Food and Drug Administration following reports of deaths and septic abortions; the FDA later ruled it unsafe, and hundreds of thousands of women filed claims against the company. A. H. Robins went on to dump 1.71 million shields in forty Third World countries, supported in this act by the US government in the guise of the Agency for International Development, which purchased hundreds of boxes of unsterilized Shields at a 48 per cent discount.[128] The story of the Dalkon Shield is only one of many examples of 'corporate dumping', in which unsafe products banned for domestic sale are disposed of to unsuspecting consumers in other countries.[129]

Love Canal, near Niagara Falls, was the dumping ground for more than 20,000 tons of toxic waste in the years from 1942 to 1953. The Hooker Chemical Company, which was responsible for this, then sold the site to the Board of Education for a dollar; the Board proceeded to erect a school, playground and housing development on it. In 1977 a toxic black sludge started to seep into the school cellars and some of the houses. Tests showed eighty-two chemicals present in the soil, water and air, including twelve known carcinogens. Hooker Chemicals had known about the problem since 1958, but had decided not to say anything because then they'd have to pay clean-up costs. As a result, people in the community experienced high rates of birth defects, miscarriages, liver disorders, respiratory and urinary diseases, epilepsy and suicide.[130]

The cost-cutting exercises induced by the motive of profit maximization are more likely to harm than protect the environment; Love Canal is only one of many episodes in which corporate decision-makers have chosen alternatives with negative impacts on the environment.[131] The chances of environmental damage are intensified by the economics of the private enterprise system – the drive is always towards the development of newer and more profitable, but not necessarily safer, technologies[132] – and by the legal logic, or rather lack of it, which fines individual citizens for dumping litter on the streets, but not corporations whose litter dumping is on a far greater scale.

Through the tax on cigarettes, governments are major economic beneficiaries of the health-damaging profits made by the tobacco industry. For example, in the UK, diseases caused by smoking cost the NHS some £1.7 billion annually, but revenue from tobacco brought in about six times that in 1997–8.[133] These profits continue to roll in, despite all that's known, and has been known for forty years, about the hazards of smoking. The tobacco industry is the 'only person out of step'[134] on the issue of smoking and health; even its strongest political allies are under no illusions that the industry is selling death for the sake of corporate profit. The global death toll runs into tens of millions. By 2030 there will be 10 million deaths a year worldwide from tobacco-related diseases, 70 per cent of these occurring in low-income countries.[135] One in three adults worldwide smoke; 4 million die annually from smoking. Out of 1,000 young British smokers, 1 will be murdered, 6 will die in road accidents, and 500 will be killed by tobacco.[136] The most recent evidence about the dangers of passive smoking – people exposed to cigarette smoke have a 16 per cent increase in lung cancer risk – produced a massive rearguard action by the tobacco industry. This was led by the top male management of Philip Morris, the world's largest cigarette manufacturer, which invested $6 million in attempts to discredit and distort the study data, prevent its conclusions from getting out, and stop any move of government policy towards further clean air legislation.[137] This move by Philip Morris was part of a long-lived company campaign to dispute the medical evidence that smoking is the largest single cause of premature and avoidable death.[138] Such behaviour is protected by what Peter Taylor has called 'the Smoke Ring' – the tight circle of political and economic interests supporting the continuing sale of tobacco products in the face of overwhelming medical and public health evidence.

Most national and international conflict and violence have a strongly gendered dimension; the use of interpersonal, state-sanctioned violence is a primary male preserve.[139] Crimes committed by governments are as 'marvellously heterogeneous' as other male-led crime. The most striking examples are those of international warfare, which subject millions of civilians to death and injury in conflicts concerned primarily with undemocratically decided national aggrandizement. Since 1945, more than 23 million people have been killed and 60 million injured in 150 major conflicts – 80 per cent of these casualties have been civilians, mainly women and children.[140] The conflicts in which they were killed – Cuba, Indonesia, Iraq, Vietnam, the Falklands, the Balkans – often violate internationally upheld laws for regulating the use of force in international affairs, and their effects on civilians are withheld from public attention unless they have some domestic impact. For example, the use of Agent Orange and dioxin in Vietnam affected US soldiers, but the bulk of their effects were felt by the Vietnamese, and stories about these health effects – including increases in fetal deaths, birth deformities and cancers – rarely made the headlines.[141]

Expenditure on war and national defence is itself a major threat to health. War accounts for more disease and disability than most of the major diseases combined, it destroys communities and environments, eliminates human rights, and contributes to the mindset which sees violence as the only way of resolving conflict. Investing in sound education, healthcare and welfare systems becomes an economic impossibility when the world's nations spend large amounts of their resources on arms. Military arms, including some three tons of TNT for every person on earth, are themselves a direct risk to health.[142] Health indicators such as infant death rates are directly correlated with the proportion of GNP devoted to military spending: the higher the amount spent on arms, the worse the infant death rate.[143] Between 1960 and 1990 public expenditure on arms more than doubled: from $322 to $676 billion (at 1987 dollar rates), with the greatest increases (more than fourfold) in developing countries, which can least afford them.[144] 'Every minute twenty children under the age of five die because they have not been immunized, because of malnutrition, or as a result of respiratory infections, diarrhoeal diseases, or other correctable conditions. During the same minute, the world's military machine absorbs in excess of $1,100,000.'[145]

The state is a masculine institution: men hold most of the top positions in government and its associated agencies, and the practices of state power subscribe to notions of secrecy, bureaucracy, autocratic decision-making and corporate aggrandizement. To say that the state is 'masculine', observes Australian academic Robert Connell:

> is not to imply that the personalities of top male office-holders somehow seep through and stain the institution. It is to say something much stronger ... The overwhelming majority of top office-holders are men because there is a gender configuration of recruitment and promotion, a gender configuration of the internal division of labour and systems of control, a gender configuration of policy-making, practical routines, and ways of mobilising pleasure and consent.

The top levels of business, government and the military form 'a fairly convincing corporate display of masculinity, still very little shaken by feminist women or dissenting men'.[146]

■

Our 'hegemonic' image of 'real' crime is all about acts committed by faceless, genderless, classless strangers on the streets. But facts are stranger than fiction, and a lot less comfortable. In America, as in the UK, we live in the midst of an epidemic of male violence. But we have difficulty naming it as such because of a deep-seated reluctance to admit that 'normal' ideas about gender and ordinary imbalances of power are both implicated as causes. People's relationships to power often go unrecognized – especially when they *have* power. A British study of young people in the late 1980s found that over half of young women felt powerless as women because of the threat of male violence or actual harassment or abuse, but the young men didn't explicitly recognize their potential to be violent to women as a source of feeling powerful at all.[147]

If women killed and damaged and expropriated others' property to the extent that men do, we'd be saying they'd all gone mad (or were caught in the grip of some gigantic plague of hormones). In the past we would have called them evil and burnt them as witches. But what we wouldn't do is accept and justify it as ordinary human behaviour. We may treat individual cases of male crime as news-grabbing pathologies, but still we accept these as a routine part of life, with little attempt to consider why men as a group should behave this way. The strange thing about crime and aggression as responses to poverty and gender inequality is that women ought to be the major criminals because they're poorer and less powerful than men. It isn't that women don't feel anger, but that they handle it differently; men talk about aggression as a public event, about the rules of fighting, about winning and losing; women talk about anger as a private experience, about the need for restraint, and about giving into displays of aggressive behaviour as defeat.[148]

Don't men as a group have some responsibility for all this? Isn't it time that male politicians ceased talking about the problem of violence, about strategies for 'getting tough' on 'brawling louts and yobs' as though they were talking about a species other than themselves that might as well inhabit another planet?[149]

Our not thinking about the everyday realities of crime and violence inhibits our ability to develop a sensible understanding of what's happening, and what we might do about it, but it's also, of course, the linchpin that keeps the whole sorry structure in place – not only manslaughter of all kinds and its associated practices, but the links between violence and other social problems. For instance, there's the link between exposure to domestic violence, on the one hand, and juvenile crime and antisocial behaviour,[150] on the other; there's the more basic cultural connection implied by the statement: 'As long as men have wars, so will boys do violence.'[151] It means, too, the way we focus on certain social problems and not others. For example, not only are most people more likely to be killed by people they know than by strangers, they're also ten times more likely to be killed by a car than a person[152] (though there is, of course, usually a person driving the car); this fits the hegemonic pattern, as owning and driving cars and being involved in car accidents are all more likely to be male than female activities.[153] Another example is that health professionals, health educators and policy-makers focus a lot of attention on smoking as a major cause of health problems, whereas a history of rape and/or assault may be a much stronger predictor of poor health for women.[154] Despite the fact that it probably blights the lives of more people than all genetic disorders put together, little attention has been paid to domestic violence as a social or public health issue, and it's certainly not seen as an acceptable topic for research.[155]

■

Flashing, whether in the snow or out of it, has two histories: as a criminal offence and as a medical condition. In England the Vagrancy Act of 1824 (section 4) made it an offence for anyone 'willfully, openly, lewdly and obscenely, to expose his person with intent to insult any female'; 'person' was subsequently clarified as meaning the penis.[156] Attempts to define flashing as a medical condition have centred on men's urge to exhibit their penises as a form of sexual perversion, as an attempt to dominate and control women, as a (very) disturbed attempt at courtship, as showing off the size of the penis or making up for a rather small one. It isn't true that flashers never assault their victims; in one study, one out of five convicted flashers confessed to sexual offences involving force.[157]

Sandra McNeill's survey of 100 women of different ages found that 63 had been flashed at, 43 more than once. Only 14 of the total 233 incidents had been reported to the police. Half the women were flashed at before they were sixteen, and most of the flashers were total strangers:

I was walking home from school. I was crossing the bridge. A bloke came towards me. Wanking. He had an erection. I have never been so scared in all my life. I thought . . . I thought I was going to have to hit him . . . He's going to murder me. He leered, wanking away, I thought he was going to grab me.[158]

The major fear women reported wasn't rape but death. Most of the women also said flashing had permanently affected their lives, usually by restricting their freedom to move around public spaces, especially walking in the country and going out after dark. In the British Crime Survey 18 per cent of women and 3 per cent of men reported feeling very unsafe when walking alone at night.[159] Women worry about their safety five times as often as men; they develop a whole range of strategies to deal with this (avoiding back alleys and poorly lit areas, controlling the speed of walking, staying at home).[160] Forty-two per cent of the urban women in an American study said they avoided going out alone and 40 per cent avoided going out at night (the figures for men were 8 per cent and 9 per cent).[161]

My encounter with the snow-flasher, a hugely insignificant episode in the context of violence against women in the world today, happened five years ago. In the last six months I've been able to walk in the country on my own again, but my heart, in that proverbial phrase, leaps into my mouth every time I see a car ahead (it may be another reason I don't like cars). Often I imagine that cars slow down when they've passed me, and always I think that's the flasher (him or another one) come to get me again.

In her book *Pornography and Silence*, Susan Griffin writes about our cultural familiarization with male violence:

We see a film in which a woman is murdered. Or a series of women are murdered, or beaten, or raped. The next day, we read in the newspaper that a woman has been shot to death by a stranger. We hear that the man next door has several times 'broken down' and threatened the life of his wife, his son. An advertisement for a novel depicts a woman's throat cut open and bleeding. And in our minds all this is woven into a fabric which we imagine is inevitable.

We begin to look on the violence of men towards women as a kind of natural phenomenon. And slowly, our own behaviour becomes part of this delusion which we have called reality. If we are women, we grow up with a fear which we come to believe is as common as hunger or thirst, or anger . . . If we are men, acts of violence toward women become part of a range of behaviour which we think of as human.[162]

Griffin's words, written in 1981, are even more true today, when media representations of violence are so commonplace that 'Most people can pass by any image, however brutal, with a single look of horror and then give just a quick shrug of forgetfulness.'[163]

But manslaughter and all its associated practices and perversions aren't human. It may be an everyday occurrence, but it can't be a behaviour anyone who prides themselves on their humanity would wish to claim.

4

Sick to Death of Women

In 1974, a group of twenty-eight 'informed and sensitive' men and women put together a picture of what they thought the situation of American women might look like in what was then the apocalyptic year 2000.[1]

Technology would, of course, be advanced: there would be coded front door pads, automated meal- and Martini-makers, house-cleaning, face-cleaning and pill-dispensing at the touch of a button, and Completecreditcards would have done away with burglaries altogether. It'd be hard to recall a time before gender-integrated sports teams, and a woman called Blossom was about to become the fastest long-distance runner in the world. Globally, nations will have given way to continental and subcontinental formations, and hypersonic travel will have made us truly transplanetary. On the health front, 50 per cent of doctors will be women, hormone replacement therapy will be routine for all women from their thirties on, and sex pre-selection will be accepted procedure; but the international scientific community voted in 1984 against the development of artificial wombs. A 1975 law allows children to carry only one name: thus, for example, somewhat painfully, 'Millenny'. Millenny and her peers are born in Natal Environment Centers, where women use videos and acupuncture for labour pain, but fathers still wear masks. 'Loyalty' marriages have replaced the old sort. Men's and women's earnings are equal, and so are their nurturant roles; everyone contributes 6 hours a month from the working week of 25 hours to socially useful volunteer work. Cots and playpens are banned as unwarrantably imprisoning; Millenny sleeps on a mat, with buttons to push if she wants to hear her parents' voices. The rest of childcare is done in 24-hour childcare centres. Millenny isn't allowed war toys, puts herself to bed when tired, in later childhood plays baseball, and as a teenager is taught by her mother and a friend the techniques of masturbation and menstrual extraction respectively. Education is more about life experience than the classroom, although every home has computerized teaching machines; in the universities female professors and administrators have multiplied, the chief justice of the United States wears a dress, a woman is president, and sexuality has become genderless, with physical attraction depending solely on authentic individual attributes (although vibrators are still used).

The more cynical contributions to *Woman in the Year 2000* saw little reason why things should change for the better. Twenty-six years on would, after all, only be another twenty-six years of brainwashing by television and the advertising industry. It would surely take a nuclear holocaust to shift this. Bella Abzug, lawyer, politician and women's rights activist, imagined surviving the holocaust only because she happened to be underground investigating women miners' complaints about unfair treatment at the time. The president and top Pentagon officials who started the war went off to the moon in their superjets, taking their secretaries with them (but not their wives and children, as this would look too much like nepotism). Earth survivors lived in geodesic radiation-proof domes eating synthetic food, which was rationed in socially equitable ways (just as food in Britain had been in the Second World War), but longing for the taste of sour pickles. A form of programmed socialization was introduced to replace the old sex roles, and one of the most popular class trips for children was to the Marilyn Monroe Wing of the New Smithsonian Institution, where there was a great collection of sexist artefacts (fake eyelashes, false breasts etc.), together with a continuous re-run of the *I Love Lucy* television series, subtitled to explain how mistakenly pre-holocaust humans lived.

It's a story with a mixed ending, but none of it's what really happened.

■

We grew up in the 1950s and 1960s, children of post-war retrenchment, returning heroes, and our mothers' retreat to the kitchen. We listened to the Beatles proclaiming 'All You Need Is Love', tried out high heels, impossible hairstyles and pale pink lipstick, and practised sex as our principal form of rebellion against parental norms.[2] In my childhood home, Betty Friedan's *The Feminine Mystique*,[3] the classic exposé of American women's dissatisfaction, sat on the bookshelf next to a rather different kind of book: *Modern Woman: The lost sex* by sociologist Ferdinand Lundberg and psychiatrist Marynia Farnham. Published in 1947, Lundberg and Farnham's tome argued that women were maladjusted to their proper feminine role, and were thus a problem to themselves, their families and society, being responsible for an incredible array of social problems, including juvenile delinquency, divorce, falling birth rates, 'the class struggle', alcoholism, homicide, modern art and 'political and business deceit'.[4] Lundberg and Farnham had carried out the usual library enquiries, noting that a lot had been written about women – in 1944 the New York Public Library stocked 10,625 volumes with 'woman' or 'women' in the title, compared to 22,677 containing 'man' or 'men'.[5] Others noted that there were more catalogue entries for rapeseed than for rape.[6] But Lundberg and Farnham didn't make much use of the scholarly literature on women in their book, preferring to rely on their own opinions. They thought that women were in the state they were because the Industrial Revolution (and most particularly, though obscurely, the steam engine) had displaced them from their homes. Most women in Europe and America were frigid, and both frigidity and infertility rise with education. Educated women make bad wives and awful mothers. The 'psychopathology' of feminism, said Lundberg and Farnham, is to regard the achievement of maleness by women as a goal worth pursuing. Actually feminism is an 'ego prop' for emotionally deprived women, stemming from a tremendously disturbed 'libidinal organisation': penis envy, in other words. The solutions to women's sorry state include mass re-education about women's needs, honorary degrees for good mothers, family allowances for children, financial incentives to get women out of employment and into the home, and more government-sponsored psychotherapy – around $100 million was suggested, the same amount as would be needed to treat war veterans.[7] 'Perhaps what is most distressing about *The Lost Sex*', remarked Kate Millett in her outspoken *Sexual Politics*, 'is its pervasive odor of commercialization. Psychoanalysis is . . . a business enterprise built on the grave of feminism.[8]

Modern Woman: The lost sex was a bestseller, a handbook for the backlash of the time, which was intent on opposing women's wartime freedom with the battlecry of refulgent domesticity. Betty Friedan attacked Lundberg and Farnham in her *The Feminine Mystique*, another bestseller: yes, women were having problems, but not because they'd lost their femininity. The 'problem with no name' – Friedan's phrase became indelibly stamped on twentieth-century cultural history – was that women wanted something more than they had. Of her own experience, moving to the suburbs to live out the nuclear family dream in 1947, she wrote:

> It was fine at first, shopping in those new supermarkets. And we bought barbecue grills, and made dips out of sour cream and dried onion soup to serve with potato chips, while our husbands made the martinis as dry as in the city and cooked hamburgers on the charcoal, and we sat in canvas chairs on our terrace and thought how beautiful our children looked, playing in the twilight, and how lucky we all were, and that it would last forever.[9]

Friedan lost one newspaper job to a returning veteran and another because of pregnancy.[10] At the time she wrote *The Feminine Mystique*, feminism meant the feminism of the past: the suffragettes and other brave fighters for women's most basic civil rights to legal personhood; the custody of children; financial independence and education. 'It is a strangely unquestioned perversion of history', declared Friedan, referring to those who espoused the debased Freudianism sponsored by Lundberg and Farnham, 'that the passion and fire of the feminist movement came from man-hating, embittered . . . castrating . . . non-women who burned with such envy for the male organ that they wanted to take it away from all men.' The real joke that history played on American women is 'twisting the memory of the feminists into the man-eating phantom of the feminine mystique'.[11]

'Women have very little idea of how much men hate them', pronounced Germaine Greer in Britain's equivalent to *The Feminine Mystique*, *The Female Eunuch*,[12] published in 1970. Of all the seventies feminists, Greer was the one the media most loved – that is to say, men liked her.[13] She certainly dressed better than her American sisters.[14] Greer's imagery in *The Female Eunuch* was of women as castrated human beings, having had their human essence removed by a masculine–feminine polarity in which masculinity was an aggressively imperialist thing and femininity passive and de-energized. Like many other women, Dale Spender, the Australian feminist and educationalist, read *The Female Eunuch* like a horror story: 'all those clues I had ignored, all those awful connections I'd never dared make, all the evidence I had not been brave enough to examine'.[15]

Philip Wylie's *Generation of Vipers* (1942)[16] is the arch woman-hating book of the pre-feminist post-war years. In it, the US is a matriarchy ruled by destructive mothers who are described in vituperative language reminiscent of that medieval witch-hunting manual, *The Malleus Maleficarum*, which was printed in a convenient pocket size so that men could easily refer to it when encountering women they suspected might be witches.[17] Wylie's own list of social problems to be blamed on women/'momism' included crime, trade unionist activity, civil corruption, homosexuality, alcoholism, economic depression and war. The rebuttal to Wylie was Elizabeth Hawes' *Why Women Cry* (1943). Hawes was a business woman who learnt at first hand about sexism and racism among both men and women by doing unskilled work in an aeronautical plant during the Second World War, later writing articles on racism, anti-semitism and fascism for the *Detroit Free Press*, working in the education department of United Automobile Workers, and developing a sophisticated interest in collective methods of childrearing. In *Why Women Cry*, she pointed out (twenty years before Friedan) that she'd never met a contented housewife, and most women wanted to combine homes and paid work, but weren't getting much help from anyone else to do so. She had her own dig at psychoanalysis:

> Some women who . . . cry often, are also rich, and they repair to psychoanalysts who try and get them in a condition to take what they get and like it. Most psychoanalysts apparently assume that the USA is a very backward country, and

the best solution is to adapt yourself to it and not wear yourself out trying to change anything.[18]

Hawes was an astute social critic, analysing women's magazines, films, radio and etiquette books in her *Anything But Love* to derive a compendium of rules for masculine and feminine behaviour:

Are you devastated when you see anyone defacing a library book? Male: no. Female: yes . . . Do you think it is disgusting for people to get drunk in public places? Male: no. Female: yes . . . Are you afraid to be alone at night? Male: no. Female: yes . . . Does your heart rebel when you realize the law does not prevent the shooting of deer for sport? Male: no. Female: yes . . . Do your feet hurt often? Male: no. Female: yes.[19]

We recognize our differences, some of which hurt more than others, and then we decide whether to accept or do something about them.

■

'I'm absolutely bored with hearing these series of accounts of the war in Vietnam,' complained one woman at the first National Women's Liberation Conference in Britain held at Ruskin College, Oxford, in February 1970.[20] In Britain, as in the US, what are conventionally regarded as radical politics were the breeding ground for second-wave feminism. For some reason feminism is often described in marine metaphors – the first wave, followed by the second; perhaps it's because the sea is feminine, or maybe it's to do with many people's worst fear – of the absolutely engulfing tidal wave.

The Oxford conference was the brainchild of a group of women historians who were tired of the way Oxford academics ignored the history of women. Treated to endless theories of class struggle in an uncompromisingly macho style of debate, left-wing women were progressively disillusioned with the displacement of their experiences to a place beyond politics. Of women in left politics in the US at the time, Robin Morgan, editor of the first collection of feminist writings, *Sisterhood is Powerful*,[21] wrote: 'it wasn't merely the mass epidemic of bursitis (from the continual cranking of mimeograph machines) which drove us all out, but the serious, ceaseless degrading and pervasive sexism we encountered there'.[22] The British feminist historian Sheila Rowbotham recalls sitting in a restaurant with a group of New Left men, including Perry Anderson, editor of *New Left Review*:

I was, as usual, out of the conversation. Irritated and bored, I noticed a man's silhouette through a lighted upstairs window. He was getting changed. I began a monologue on his state of undress. It took a while for the table to notice, they were so preoccupied with their intellectual debate. Perry regarded me with distaste. According to hearsay, he referred to me henceforth as 'that girl'.[23]

If women as a social group didn't exist, it was hard to see why anyone should be interested in what any individual woman had to say. However, Juliet Mitchell's essay, 'Women: the longest revolution',[24] which made this point, was published by Anderson, who was briefly married to Mitchell, in 1966; he'd earlier rejected a very similar but less theoretical article by historian Dorothy Thompson.[25]

The other circle in which radical young women moved in the 1960s was the peace movement. In Britain, the Campaign for Nuclear Disarmament grew out of the activities of the Women's Co-operative Guild in the early 1950s; there was a national women's anti-nuclear demonstration in 1957 and women formed two-thirds of the support for CND, officially launched in 1958.[26] The British peace movement provided my own entry to political activism in the late 1950s; it was a joyous, bold, creative time.[27] However, all I can recall now about gender in relation to it is the extensive mating rituals that took place over the fifty miles from Aldermaston to London, or as we blocked Whitehall by lying limply down in exciting acts of civil disobedience. I have particularly strong memories of a tall young man called Terry with golden Brylcreemed hair who played the trumpet in a Salvation Army band. Marching next to Terry was a strangely erotic experience, although we had nothing in common apart from our commitment to the peace movement, and I've never seen him since.

It was a culture which *seemed* androgynous but wasn't. Most women would have jumped a mile to detach themselves from the label 'feminist'. It would definitely have reduced our currency in the mating rituals, a point made by Sheila Rowbotham in her account of growing up in the 1950s and 1960s.[28] Both Sheila Rowbotham and I went to Oxford, attending women's colleges where a past of desiccated, spinsterish scholarship had been carefully preserved, floating like a strange atoll in a sea of cerebral male sexuality. Women like us didn't feel at home at Oxford. But, incipient feminists that we were, we did note and get very worked up about one particular double standard – it sounds today like some exotic tribal custom – according to which a young male and female student caught in bed with one another were punished quite differently: he was 'rusticated', which means sent away, for two weeks, while she was banished from the university forever. This was an era when pre-marital sex was unofficial, unmarried women couldn't get contraceptive advice, and abortion was illegal. I regularly watched my female friends taking trains to London for this purpose, and wondered if they'd ever come back.

The first women's consciousness-raising groups in Britain started in 1969 in north London and Essex. It was two years before I caught up with them, being very occupied with babies and my own version of suburban utopia at the time. Through a study I was doing of housework, I learnt about a local women's liberation group that was just starting up. I took the opportunity to ask the women I was interviewing what they thought of it:

'I'm afraid I don't take much notice. They're all a bit ridiculous as far as I'm concerned.'

'I don't go in for the extreme "take off your bra" type of thing, I think it's being silly, because women still want to be women.'

'I'm in favour of women's *equality*, but not to the extent that they're wanting it.'

'When the housewives in the present sample were asked for their opinions on the women's liberation movement,' I said officiously in my write-up of the study:

> the attitude revealed was a predominantly negative one. . . . Eight of the forty women simply had not heard of [it] . . . and many of the rest referred jokingly to the image portrayed by the mass media – of militant women angrily burning their bras. A few simply said that they knew about the movement, but were not personally interested in it. Of those who mentioned particular topics in this context, most cited equal pay . . . or other dimensions of job discrimination against women. Two women offered coherent descriptions of more basic ways in which women are trained to second-class citizenship. One gave an account of the processes involved in socializing little girls for domesticity . . . the other, who described herself as 'a bit of a Pankhurst', talked about the 'degrading' way in which men look at women, the indignities of the Miss World contest, and how 'even in hospital [having a baby], you're talked to as though you're rubbish'.[29]

At a time when women at the Oxford conference were still only discussing forming a movement, the National Organization of Women (NOW) in America organized a national women's strike. It was the largest women's rights rally in New York City since the suffrage movement: some twenty to fifty thousand women totally blocked Fifth Avenue; in Boston, women chained themselves to a huge typewriter; women in California marched with pots and pans on their backs.[30] Betty Friedan had written the manifesto for NOW on a paper napkin in the Washington Hilton Hotel in June 1966: 'to take the actions needed to bring women into the mainstream of American society, now, full equality for women, in fully equal participation with men'.[31] The ground in which NOW took root had already been prepared by earlier constitutional moves to take women seriously. When John F. Kennedy became president in 1960, Eleanor Roosevelt, still in her seventies very much a political mover, invited him to her house to take a closer look at his credentials, and he left so smitten that he asked her to be at his side for the inauguration ceremony. She declined, sitting in the open wrapped in mink and a blanket, but noted that only nine of his first 240 appointments were women. She sent a three-page list of suitable names to the White House, suggesting a Presidential Commission on the Status of Women.[32] Its report put women's issues back on the national policy agenda, documenting a degree and extent of discrimination against women in employment, the law and other public domains which shocked many people. JFK consequently ordered the federal Civil Service to hire on the basis of ability not sex, and Congress passed the Equal Rights Act of 1963, seven years ahead of the UK.[33]

In Britain, the celebrated four 'demands' of the women's liberation movement were formulated by the National Women's Co-ordinating Committee, the group set up in 1970 after the Oxford conference. Two of these 'demands' – free, 24-hour, state-provided childcare and free, universally available abortion and contraception – concerned women's reproductive responsibilities; the other two – equal pay now, and equal education and job opportunities – addressed their position in the public domain. In 1975, financial and legal independence, an end to discrimination against lesbians and women's right to determine their own sexuality were added; three years later, the net extended to 'freedom from intimidation by threat or use of violence or sexual coercion, regardless of marital status'; and 'an end to all laws, assumptions and institutions which perpetuate male dominance and men's aggression towards women'.[34] The formula arrived at by NOW in America was much more politely worded as a reasoned statement about the unacceptable face of American women's current position, which NOW said it would 'endeavour to change'.[35]

The mark of a vibrant social movement is often internal disagreement about correct theories and strategies. Second-wave feminism was more heterogeneous than most such movements, partly because of its resistance to leadership and hierarchy. People who wanted to hijack it for one purpose or another therefore tended either to get a headache or to get it wrong or both. In both the UK and the USA different factions and groups multiplied, as the complexities of women's interests bred on closer inspection, like microbes under a magnifying glass. 'We're lucky this is the women's movement', remarked Gloria Steinem, founder of the American magazine *Ms*, to Susan Brownmiller, author of the classic feminist work on rape, *Against Our Will*, on one memorably sparky occasion, 'In other movements they shoot each other.'[36]

New York feminists spawned Redstockings, whose Manifesto of July 1969 took a decisive turn in the interminable argument the New York women (and many others) had been having about the nature of the main enemy: men or capitalism? 'Women are an oppressed class', declared Redstockings. 'Our oppression is total . . . We are exploited as sex objects, breeders, domestic servants, and cheap labor . . . We identify the agents of our oppression as men.'[37] Other New York women went on to form WITCH, an acronym which stood alternatively for Women's International Terrorist Conspiracy from Hell, Women Inspired to tell Their Collective History, Women Incensed at Telephone Company Harassment, Women Inspired To Commit Herstory, Women's Independent Taxpayers, Consumers and Homemakers, Women Infuriated at

Taking Care of Hoodlums, Women Interested in Topping Consumer Holidays, and other troubling inventions.[38] WITCH women invaded a branch of the Chase Manhattan Bank on Hallowe'en 1968: the Dow-Jones index reportedly took a steep dive the next day.[39]

British feminism was less imaginative and more immediately practical, occupied with such issues as the strike for equal pay among women workers at the Ford factory in Dagenham, and the campaign for better wages and working conditions for women who cleaned offices and factories at night. But British feminists, like their American sisters, deployed the negative imagery of women to construct a positive politics: hence *Shrew*, the newsletter of the Women's Liberation Workshop, and the magazine *Spare Rib*.

Second-wave feminism did have a unifying strategy: consciousness-raising practised in small, non-hierarchical all-women groups. Taking part in such a process was exhilarating, insomnia-inducing, and quite literally radicalizing.[40] It broke women's customary silence about the commonality of their experiences, encouraged even the most silent to speak, and changed the way one saw oneself and the world forever. In America, the first consciousness-raising groups were held in Chicago and New York in 1967. The Chicago group included Naomi Weisstein, a Harvard psychology graduate who produced a germinal paper the following year called 'Kinder, Küche, Kirche as scientific law, or psychology constructs the female'.[41] She argued that most psychologists knew nothing about what women were really like because they'd never probed the surface of traditional gender roles and had therefore simply reproduced sexist views. When Weisstein read her paper at the University of California there was a silence as she finished, then a standing ovation.[42] Her allegations about academic psychology turned out to be true of an awful lot of what was conventionally regarded as science or knowledge. The New York consciousness-raising group contained Anne Koedt, a Danish artist and set designer, who wrote the equally conflagrationary 'The myth of the vaginal orgasm'. Koedt's paper was stapled together with other writings by New York Radical Women called 'Notes from the first year'; it sold for 50 cents to women and 1 dollar to men. Her argument was a straightforward statement of evidence that the clitoris, not the vagina, is the biological analogue of the penis, so women's alleged orgasmic deficiencies are likely to be due, not to their inherent deficiencies as women, but to men's mistakes in bed: hence, discordantly for men who value this organ, Koedt contended that 'a man without a penis can make a woman an excellent lover'.[43]

Penises are terribly prominent characters in literature concerning itself with women, and/or reasons for being sick of them. The other main currency in which anti-feminist ideas have been exchanged doesn't refer to a body part, but, appropriately for women, an artefact of femininity. 'Bra-burning' speedily became an epithet attached to feminism as a way of calling up a whole panoply of images of 'women's lib' – the media shortening of the term 'women's liberation movement', which intentionally designated 'embarrassing foolishness'.[44]

The date on which bra-burning didn't happen was 7 September 1968, when American feminists disrupted the Miss America contest in Atlantic City in an effort to prove to their sisters they could do more than just sit around raising consciousness. The Miss America contest was a perfect liberation target – sexist, racist (there'd never been a Black winner), militant (the winner went off to entertain the troops in Vietnam as a 'Murder Mascot') and capitalist (sponsored by big business), all rolled into one.[45] Robin Morgan had the idea of arranging a Freedom Bonfire in which girdles, bras, eyelash curlers, copies of the *Ladies' Home Journal* and *Playboy* and other items of sexist femininity would be consigned to flames on the Miss World Boardwalk. Morgan told a reporter about her plan, and the headline the next day in the *New York Post* was 'Bra burners and Miss America'. But they never got a police licence for the bonfire because of the fire laws in Atlantic City. Instead there was a Freedom Trash Can, and into it went dishcloths, mascara, high-heeled shoes, false breasts, tweezers, eyelash curlers, false lashes, steno pads, girdles *and* bras. Posters read: 'NO MORE MISS AMERICA. THE REAL MISS AMERICA LIVES IN HARLEM. CAN MAKEUP COVER THE WOUNDS OF OUR OPPRESSION? IF YOU WANT MEAT GO TO A BUTCHER.'[46] Someone rented a sheep and they crowned it Miss America with a blue rosette and yellow ribbons – there were no animal rights activists present at the time. The only two displays that ever came close to underwear burning were both organized later by men – a disc jockey and an architect – who tried to get women to fling their bras into a barrel and the Chicago river as media events; only three did so, paid for by the architect.[47]

The first Miss World contest was in 1951, part of the national celebration of post-war recovery in Britain, the profit-making invention of Mecca Ltd and chairman Eric Morley, who set the rules, which included banning married women because 'it might make a woman dissatisfied with her life as a housewife and mother'.[48] British feminists followed the American example in November 1970, throwing bags of flour, tomatoes and stink bombs at the Miss World event in London, causing Bob Hope, the compère, to flee the stage, the Mecca bouncers to spring into action, and a spate of arrests: the first militant confrontation with the law by women since the suffragettes.

In 2000, Miss World is alive and well; the 27 million[49] who watched it on television in 1970 have become 600 million.[50] Bodily measurements are no longer read out; the contestants, instead of parading in their bikinis in front of the judges, now do so as far away from home as possible, on the white sands of the Maldive Islands; the ninety-five putative Miss Worlds are Internet designers, violinists and medical students; Jerry Springer, of TV show fame, asks them questions such as 'What importance do you attach to the

nuclear family?' and 'What does a child need to grow up into a good person?';
but the formula of vacuous, plastic femininity is essentially unchanged.

In her book, *Backlash*, about responses to feminism, Susan Faludi argues
that it was the commodification of feminism which led to its ultimate demise
as a product. By 1971 the press, in America at least, was bored with feminism:
'All that "bra-burning"', the media perversely said of its own created myth,
had 'alienated ordinary women'.[51] Stories about women's liberation started to
be written in a deliberately anti-feminist tone. By the mid-1970s, the media
line was that women had got what they wanted and could now be exploited
as consumers of liberated lifestyles. Actually, the end of second-wave feminism had been predicted just as soon as it had begun – in 1968.[52] Since it
matured earlier in America, the backlash against it also arrived earlier and
in a more intense form. The greater political visibility of American feminism acted as a prompt to New Righters to include it in their agenda of
attacks.[53]

■

'Women – but are you not sick to death of the word?' asked Virginia Woolf
in her essay *A Room of One's Own*, 'I can assure you that I am.'[54] At this point,
she's 105 pages into an argument about the importance of women's writing
and how it's still hampered by poverty and oppression. A few pages earlier
she remarks that, 'No age can ever have been as stridently sex-conscious
as our own; those innumerable books by men about women in the British
Museum are a proof of it.'[55] The suffrage campaign was to blame, arousing in
men an 'extraordinary desire for self-assertion'. Woolf was tongue-in-cheek,
not about men's reactions, but about being sick of women. She was, perhaps,
considering her audience's sensitivities somewhat here; it was composed of
women in Cambridge colleges, so she may have thought her ideas a little too
radical for them. Woolf's lover, Vita Sackville-West, was present when she
read the original paper,[56] and the obscenity trial for the portrayal of lesbian
love in Radclyffe Hall's *The Well of Loneliness* was ongoing. Women (over
the age of thirty) had possessed the vote for a whole ten years, and most of
the professions had been open to them for only a little longer. Woolf, with all
her intellect, energy and cultural capital as a member of the British upper
middle classes, had been in receipt of a misogynist medical profession's
favourite prescription for worried professional women: go to bed and stay
there and never write or think ever again. One of Woolf's doctors, Sir Maurice
Craig, believed that the best way to define the insane is as people whose beliefs
are contrary to those of others.[57] Some years earlier, the writer and feminist
Charlotte Perkins Gilman had a similar experience in America, with that
country's top specialist in nervous diseases, Dr S. W. Mitchell. Gilman was

sent home at the age of twenty-six with a diagnosis of hysterical 'nervous pros-
tration', and the injunction to lead 'as domestic a life as possible' and 'never
touch pen, brush or pencil as long as you live'. Fortunately, she had always
noted that when she left her domestic life and went to stay with friends in
Pasadena she got better immediately, so she didn't follow Dr Mitchell's advice
for very long before realizing the error of his ways.[58]

■

When people start writing the history of something, it's because they think it's
over. The act of writing itself indicates closure; we put it down, because that's
the only way we're going to remember it. The history we have to write is the
history of these two biological groups, men and women, variously inserted
into different systems of social arrangements. It's a curiously repetitive
history: of the cases that are made, having been made before; of reaction and
counter-reaction, all of which rerun old waves, incessantly crashing onto our
tired cultural shores. Much of what was said in the so-called second wave of
feminism had been said before. Most critical responses to feminism reiterated
old themes – the themes of the masculinist arguments heard in the 1940s and
1950s and before, in reply to which it became necessary to produce even more
'new' texts. We're all guilty of this recycling of ideas, some of us knowingly,
more of us without recognizing the repeats, because nobody can read *all* those
books, and cultural memories are dishearteningly short in a world where
everything is supposedly moving so fast towards that utopia/dystopia of
globalization.

The cyclical affliction of being sick to death of women may be partly a case
of conversational fatigue: cultures, like people, need to change the subject
from time to time. This raises the interesting possibility that women may be
like the weather – a subject we always come back to. But there are obviously
a lot of other things going on. The first batch of these has to do with the line
that feminism came and then went. The reasons why it went are the obverse
of the reasons why it came: in either case what we're talking about is history.
'Feminism has served its purpose and should now eff off', as Germaine Greer
puts it.[59] The second group of reasons is a bit more complex: our tiredness with
women is a logical response to discovering that 'women' as a homogeneous
category don't exist; there is therefore, strictly, nothing to be tired of. A third
possible explanation is that only *some* people are sick of women, and these
are the ones who find women especially tiresome when they seem to be saying
something about equality, for which it's not too disingenuous to read power.
Of course all three explanations can apply at the same time. But a test of their
relevance requires evidence: looking at the facts, deemed by Woolf 'a very
inferior form of fiction'.[60]

■

Argument I: Feminism won the war

The habit of thinking in military terms is masculine, but some women would argue that our last bout of feminism was merely one battle in a protracted civil war over gender.[61] The litany of assaults on women that are classified as crimes of various kinds would certainly be called genocide if women constituted a religious, ethnic or racial group, observes Marilyn French in her book *The War Against Women*.[62]

Here are some examples of the non-persuasiveness of the argument that feminism has succeeded so that's why we don't need it any more. My starting point is the 'demands' of the women's movement thirty years ago, for equal pay, equal education and job opportunities, 24-hour childcare and access to abortion and contraception.

Equal pay?

In 1970, when the women's liberation movement was getting off the ground in Britain, women's average hourly earnings were 63 per cent those of men; by 1998 this figure had crept up to 80 per cent. Their weekly earnings were 63 per cent of men's in 1978 and 72 per cent in 1998, a bigger gender gap, reflecting women's shorter working week.[63] The hourly earnings of part-time women workers in Britain were 59 per cent of full-time men's hourly earnings in both 1978 and 1998.[64]

In 1996–7 around half of employed women in Britain, but one in five employed men, earned less than £100 a week (2 per cent of women and 10 per cent of men earned more than £500 a week); seven out of ten employees taking home less than the National Minimum Wage were women.[65]

The gender gap is bigger for income than for pay ('income' includes self-employment, occupational pensions, and investment and benefit income). In 1996–7, British women received 53 per cent of men's average weekly income: £153 versus £289. This had risen just 18 per cent (from 35 per cent) in 1975.[66] Access to bonus- and performance-related earnings and occupational pension schemes is greater in jobs done mainly by men than those in which women predominate.[67] Men and women are equally likely to work in jobs with pension schemes, but women are less likely to be included in them.[68]

The gender gap for lifetime earnings differs substantially by skill: 'low-skilled' childless women and 'low-skilled' women with two children earn 73 per cent and 34 per cent of men's wages respectively; for the 'mid-skilled' these figures are 73 per cent and 57 per cent and for the 'high-skilled' 89 per cent and 88 per cent.[69] The 'mid-skilled' childless woman in the

UK is estimated to earn £241,000 less over her lifetime than her male equivalent.[70]

Studies of the British labour market pre- and post-feminism show that the disadvantages of being female probably did weigh less heavily in the 1990s than they did at the end of the 1970s, but the evidence (taking into account all the factors that affect pay) isn't strong enough to exclude the possibility of no change at all. In the lowest pay and status categories of the labour market, the position of women has worsened.[71] In 2000 the British Equal Opportunities Commission said that at this rate of progress it would take another twenty years to close the gender gap in earnings.[72] Worldwide, women's earnings are lower than men's, on average by 30 to 40 per cent.[73]

In the USA women's median earnings were 62 per cent of men's in 1970 and 75 per cent in 1996.[74] Men and women with the same educational background are paid differently: in 1993, men with bachelor's degrees earned 27 per cent more and with professional degrees 38 per cent more than similarly qualified women.[75] This differential has changed little: in 1985 the mean annual earnings of women with bachelor's degrees were 59 per cent those of men: a decade later, they were 61 per cent.[76] Women's pay relative to men's has risen most in countries (Scandinavia, France, Belgium, Australia, New Zealand) with strong equal pay legislation and enforcement, centralized wage-bargaining, and stronger parental leave and childcare policies. It's risen least in countries which lack one or more of the above: Britain (lacking effective enforcement, parental leave and childcare); the US (lacking until recently parental leave and childcare); Germany (lacking childcare); and Switzerland (no equal pay legislation until 1981).[77]

The gender gap varies by occupational sector: British women's pay is highest (90p for every £1 earned by men) in education, and lowest in banking, insurance and pension services (55p for every £1 earned by men).[78] The reasons for the gap are gender segregation in employment (men and women doing different jobs); different work patterns (women doing more part-time work and taking breaks to have and raise children); discrimination within payment systems; and undervaluation of women's jobs.[79]

Gender-segregated occupations are the single most powerful explanation for the gender wage gap:[80] 'Occupational segregation by sex . . . is one of the most important and enduring aspects of labour markets around the world.'[81] About half the world's employed workers are in sex-stereotyped occupations (defined as those in which one sex predominates by at least 80 per cent); there are more than seven times as many male-dominated industrial occupations as female-dominated ones.[82] Men make up most of the employees in most of the high-earning occupations; women predominate in the lowest-earning ones.[83] Thus, in the US women nurses (92 per cent female) earn 95 per cent of what male nurses do; among physicians (31 per cent female), this figure is 58 per cent.[84] Having more women in the labour force doesn't decrease the size of the gender gap: the UK has a high female employment rate and the widest gender pay gap in the European Union.[85]

Despite this evidence, a survey of attitudes to equal pay conducted by the EOC in 1999 showed a high degree of confidence among employers that payment systems are free from gender bias. The most confident employers were those in the manufacturing sector, but these were also doing less than any other to ensure equal pay. Overall, 68 per cent of employers said they had an equal pay policy, but there was no difference in *actual practices* between those who had such a policy and those who didn't.[86]

One large High Street retail trade business in Britain, fond of its image as a trend-setter, established an equal opportunities initiative in response to the 1975 Sex Discrimination Act. The business developed a whole series of plans, including five-year targets for the proportions of Black and female employees, especially at management levels.[87] In the first few years of the initiative, some high-ranking white women were brought in, and a few were promoted; a Black senior male manager was also recruited. Middle management became more Black and female. But then progress appeared to stop. Women's low-paid part-time work increased, and part-time workers continued to be excluded from the company pension plan; most managerial jobs were specified as full-time. More temporary workers were hired, and a move to regrade women's manual and clerical work was deferred because of cost. Widespread annoyance was voiced by men at the implications of maternity leave. More store managers and management trainees were women, but attitudes to such jobs had changed: it was accepted that many people would stop at this level, and that the future of the industry lay with the computer specialists and the marketing, advertising and public relations men. When the equal opportunities manager proposed a meeting of female managers to discuss their position, she was told the meeting had to be held off site and out of office hours. After three years, she resigned, believing that she'd failed to achieve anything much.

When it comes to unpaid work, some 87 per cent of the time involved in looking after young children in Britain is provided by mothers.[88] Women in Britain provide two-thirds of all the informal care used by older people, 50 per cent more private household care than men.[89] A third of women carers spend more than 20 hours a week in unwaged caring work; this work has been valued at £39.1 billion a year.[90] In developing and industrialized countries alike, two-thirds of the work women do is unpaid; the corresponding figures for men are less than a quarter and about a third.[91]

The caring which is the hallmark of women's unpaid work is also expected of them in the paid employment sector. Secretaries are supposed to protect and support their bosses;[92] waitresses have to be kind and personable;[93] the job of para-legals is to mother lawyers;[94] airline attendants must cheerfully serve food and drink while also remembering to be heroic in crises.[95]

In Britain the two types of households most likely to be poor are older women living alone and lone mothers.[96] At all stages of the life cycle, women are in a worse position financially than men, whether they're employed, unemployed or not working because of sickness or disability.[97] In the USA, women are more likely to be poor than men at all ages, but the biggest gap is at and after 65, when 14 per cent of women and 6 per cent of men are living in poverty: on average older men have almost double the income of older women.[98] More than twice as many older women as men rely on income support; in Britain retired women's average incomes in 1996–7 were £94 a week, while men's were £174.[99] Worldwide, women account for 70 per cent of the 1.3 billion people who live in absolute poverty.[100]

Equal education?

In the USA in 1996, 21 per cent of women and 26 per cent of men earned bachelors' degrees or higher. The heavy over-representation of women undergraduates in the 'traditional' feminine fields of education, English and the health professions in 1973–4 was a pattern repeated twenty years later, though by then women had increased their presence in the biological sciences and engineering.[101] In the UK, 55 per cent of higher education students were women in 1999–2000.[102] At school, 51 per cent of girls and 41 per cent of boys gained five or more passes at grades A–C of GCSE (General Certificate of Secondary Education) or grades 1–3 of SCE (Scottish Certificate of Education) Standard, normally taken at age sixteen.[103] More girls than boys are now sitting and passing state Advanced level examinations (normally taken at eighteen); in 2000 for the first time girls overtook boys in the percentage of A grades at A-level.[104] These figures have prompted a widespread concern about the problem of male 'underachievement'. However, the gender gap is growing in physics, mathematics, computer studies and technology, with at least 30 per cent more boys than girls taking these subjects.[105] The gender gap in mathematics is wider in the UK than in any other country apart from Iran and Tunisia.[106]

At A-level in the UK all sciences, except for biology, are dominated by boys and arts by girls. The same pattern is repeated in further education and training. In 1998, 92 per cent of apprenticeships in hairdressing were held by women and 98 per cent of those in construction and electrical engineering by men.[107] In Britain in 1997–8, women were 15 per cent of full-time students in engineering and technology, 19 per cent in computer science, 54 per cent in humanities, 56 per cent in social, economic and political studies, and 77 per cent in education.[108]

Two-thirds of the 960 million non-literate adults in the world are women.[109] At the World Education Forum in Dakar in April 2000, the UN general secretary Kofi Annan pointed out that two-thirds of the more than 110 million children worldwide deprived of even elementary schooling are girls. He said that 'educating girls is not an option, but a necessity'. Moreover, it's 'the most cost effective form of defence spending', since educated women are tools for preventing global conflict.[110]

Equal job opportunities?

In 1970, 43 per cent of American women[111] and 56 per cent of British women[112] were in the paid labour force. In 1996 these figures had risen to 59 per cent and 72 per cent.[113]

In 1971, 34 per cent of British employed women worked part-time;[114] in 1998, 44 per cent did (the figure for men was 8 per cent).[115] In 1970, 60 per cent of employed women in America didn't work on a year-round, full-time basis; this figure had fallen to 48 per cent in 1995.[116] In the UK, 83 per cent of part-time employees are women;[117] in the USA, 67 per cent.[118] Doing 'piecework' at home is a particularly poor option financially; in Britain, 94 per cent of one million homeworkers are women and are paid on average 50p an hour.[119]

In 1971, 52 per cent of employed women in the UK worked in three service industries: sales, 'professional and scientific' (typists, secretaries, teachers, nurses); and miscellaneous services (catering, laundries, etc.);[120] the comparable figure for 1998 was 47 per cent.[121] In the US in 1983, 46 per cent of employed women worked in 'technical, sales and administrative support'; the figure for 1996 was 41 per cent.[122]

In America in 1983, women were more than 60 per cent of workers in the following occupations: dental assistants, librarians, nurses, social workers and elementary school teachers. In 1996, they were more than 60 per cent in the same occupations, plus 'managers, medicine and health' (up from 57 per cent to 75 per cent). Occupations with less than 10 per cent of women in 1983 were airplane pilots and navigators, auto mechanics, carpenters, clergy, data processing equipment repairers, dentists, firefighters, mechanical engineers, telephone installers, and repairers and welders. The picture in 1996 was the same except for the clergy (up from 6 per cent to 12 per cent), data equipment repairers (up from 9 per cent to 18 per cent), dentists (up from 7 per cent to 14 per cent) and telephone installers (up from less than 10 per cent to 14 per cent).[123]

Most professional women in most industrialized countries are nurses or teachers.[124] In 2000, women made up 18 per cent of managers and 4 per cent of company directors in the UK;[125] 51 per cent of Britain's top 100 companies have no women on their boards: 95 per cent of their directors are men.[126] Women hold 26 per cent of executive positions on the boards of non-departmental public bodies in the UK, and make up 24 per cent and 6 per cent respectively of members of boards of public corporations and nationalized industries.[127] In the USA women were 42 per cent of managers in 1992; women held 5 per cent of executive management positions and were 3 per cent of the highest-paid officers and directors; 21 per cent of companies in 1999 had no woman corporate officer.[128] In the UK, women make up 26 per cent of local council officials.[129] In the education sector, 25 per cent of senior staff are women, with 23 per cent of women and 43 per cent of men being at senior lecturer level or above; 17 per cent of chief education officers in the 172 local authorities in England and Wales are women.[130] In 1977, in the US, women were 10 per cent of all state-wide executive officials; this figure was 25 per cent in 1997.[131]

In 1978, 50 per cent of people surveyed in a study of race and gender attitudes in the USA said that women had to perform better than men to get ahead; 54 per cent said this in 1995. In 1978, 63 per cent, and in 1995, 50 per cent, complained that men excluded women from informal job networks.[132] In the UK, more than half of personal assistants have better qualifications than their bosses.[133] Two recent examples of 'job discrimination' are the biographies of a top BBC news presenter, Sue MacGregor, who had to get used to the fact that the major political interviews were all given to less experienced men,[134] and Dame Stella Rimington, the former director-general of MI5, whose memoirs are replete with accounts of men's patronizing ways.[135]

In the 1997 British general election, women gained 120 seats to become 18 per cent of MPs; in the House of Lords, 16 per cent of members are women. Before 1987, the maximum number of women elected at any general election was 29 (in 1964). Only seven women were in the Cabinet from 1924 to 1997; in December 1999, Blair's Cabinet contained 5 out of 22 women. The standard 'New Labour' line on women is, 'There might still be a bit of tidying up to do but, by and large, our house is in order. So please, can you stop whingeing.'[136] There've been increasing complaints about unsociable working hours and sexist behaviour; when Jane Griffiths MP made her maiden speech, Conservative backbenchers weighed melons in their hands.

In 1999, women were 24 per cent of Members of the European Parliament.[137] In the USA women were 4 per cent of Members of Congress in 1977, 11 per cent in 1997.[138] Both the UK and the USA do poorly compared with many other countries; in Sweden women were 43 per cent, in Denmark 37 per cent, in the Netherlands 36 per cent and in Spain 28 per cent of their respective national legislatures in 2000.[139] The world average for women as a percentage of representatives in national parliaments is 13 per cent.[140]

Childcare

In 1998, there were places in daycare or family centres for 4 per cent of children under the age of 8 in Britain. The proportions of children in state nurseries were 44 per cent of 3–4 year olds in 1987 and 56 per cent in 1997.[141] Between 1984 and 1998, the number of day nursery places provided by local authorities fell by 35 per cent.[142] Only 2 per cent of under threes are in publicly funded childcare services,[143] less than 1 per cent in local authority day nurseries.[144] Ninety-three per cent of rural areas lack any public nursery provision, 86 per cent have no private facilities, and 96 per cent lack any out-of-school facilities.[145] Only 1 per cent of British under fives are in a workplace nursery.[146]

In 1994, 60 per cent of Danish under threes and 79 per cent of Danish children aged from 3 to school age were in some kind of formal childcare, in France the figures were 33 per cent and 99 per cent.[147] In 1993 in the US, only 30 per cent of the 9,937,000 under fives of employed mothers were in organized childcare facilities;[148] most nursery provision is part-time.[149] The single most important type of childcare (used by 48 per cent) in the USA is relatives;[150] in Britain, 31 per cent of under fives of employed mothers are cared for by grandparents.[151]

Annual nursery bills for a two-parent family with two children in Britain average 77 per cent of families' total housing and food costs;[152] in the US, 319,000 families below poverty level (7 per cent of all families with children under five) spend 18 per cent of their income on childcare.[153] Federal childcare funding was vetoed by Nixon.[154] Of the three million British children currently living in households with no earner, less than 1 per cent have access to publicly funded childcare.[155]

In 1976, 34 per cent of British women who were at home looking after children said they'd go back to work if satisfactory childcare arrangements could be made.[156] Twenty years later, more than a third of British mothers not returning to work after taking maternity leave said they couldn't earn enough to pay for childcare, and a quarter said they were unable to find jobs with hours which would fit their childcare responsibilities.[157] In the USA, about a quarter of young mothers are prevented from taking paid work because of childcare problems.[158] A survey of British parents in March 2001 found that parents' top two priorities were more affordable provision (43 per cent) and more childcare places (38 per cent); 60 per cent saw helping with the costs of childcare as a government responsibility.[159]

Childcare workers are the lowest paid of all wage-earners, taking home less than zoo-keepers, janitors or car park attendants. In some US states, the training standards of childcare workers are less stringent than those for hairdressers.[160]

The United States is the only 'advanced' industrial country that doesn't have a national maternity policy. Around 60 per cent of American women have no right to any kind of leave when they have a baby.[161] The Family and Medical Leave Act passed in 1992 requires employers to provide twelve weeks' unpaid parental leave after birth, but there's a long list of exemptions, including workplaces employing fewer than 50 people, and the most highly paid 10 per cent of the workforce.[162]

The value of cash benefits paid to families with children, policies for parental leave and the percentage of children in formal childcare all vary enormously between countries. For example, the child benefit package available to parents in Luxembourg is 170 per cent of the European mean, the Greek version is 81 per cent less than the mean, and child benefits in the UK run at 6 per cent below the mean.[163] Parental leave was first introduced in Sweden in 1974; the country has the most financially generous provision, but very low take-up rates for men – in 1998, 69 per cent of Swedish fathers took no paternity leave.[164] Most parental leave schemes offer only unpaid leave, and are thus of no use to poor mothers. A seminar on father-friendly workplace policies in Britain in 1996 had to be cancelled because only six people applied to attend.[165]

Many public spaces and facilities don't welcome parents with children. Britain has a particularly poor record here. Hotels and restaurants are renowned for excluding small children, and making mothers breastfeed under the tablecloth or in toilets; 95 per cent of railway stations and 80 per cent of trains have no facilities for breastfeeding or nappy-changing.[166]

Abortion and contraception

Every minute 380 women worldwide get pregnant, and for 190 of these the pregnancy is unplanned.[167] Most of the women who have unplanned pregnancies are married or in stable relationships and already have several children. The most common reason for unplanned pregnancy, affecting at least 350 million women every year, is lack of access to contraceptive services.[168] The 'unmet' need for contraceptive services has been estimated as between a quarter and more than a third of childbearing women in countries such as Ecuador, Ghana and Tanzania.[169] Contraceptive and abortion services available on the National Health Service in the UK are patchy and inadequate.[170] In many areas, family planning services were actually cut in the late 1990s to reduce NHS expenditure.[171] Provision often involves little choice (of, among other elements, a female doctor),[172] lengthy waiting times, lack of confidentiality, and culturally inappropriate care for ethnic minority women.[173] A nationwide survey of birth control service use in Finland in 1994 found that 41 per cent of women using public health centres for birth control services complained about lack of time with health workers, and 36 per cent about problems with confidentiality; 9 per cent said their own views were ignored.[174] Shortcomings in the quality of contraceptive services in many countries include poor information about side effects, the promotion of client-inappropriate methods and poor clinical skills.[175]

In the USA in 1996, 1.2 million women had abortions;[176] 45 per cent of these were carried out after eight weeks' gestation; the proportion varied between states, with West Virginia having the highest rate of later abortions (74 per cent) and Maryland the lowest (26 per cent).[177] In the USA, 43 per cent

of women will have an abortion by the age of 45;[178] in the UK, the figure is
at least a third.[179]

Every minute worldwide, 40 women have unsafe abortions – 20 million
every year, 1 unsafe abortion for every 7 births. Ninety-five per cent of these
happen in developing countries, causing the deaths of at least 200 women each
day. The risk of dying after unsafe abortion is 1 in 150 in Africa, 1 in 1,900
in Europe.[180]

In 1987, 45 per cent of women asking for abortion in one British health
authority reported no use of contraception.[181] The UK has the highest unintended pregnancy rate among teenage girls in Europe: 8 in every 1,000 girls
under sixteen become pregnant; the pregnancies of 52 per cent of this age
group end in abortion.[182] Access to appropriate reproductive health services for
young women is a particular problem.[183] In the US, only 1.2 million out of an
estimated 5 million teenage women at risk for unintended pregnancy receive
services at publicly funded family planning clinics.[184]

In 1988 the proportion of abortions performed on the NHS varied from 1
per cent in South Birmingham to 99 per cent in North Devon, mainly because
of local gynaecologists' attitudes to abortion.[185] A report on abortion in
England and Wales in 2000 found continuing variation in NHS abortion rates,
with 48 out of 105 regions funding less than 75 per cent of abortions on the
NHS.[186] In developing countries, health workers' refusal to carry out abortions
because they personally don't support abortion is a reason why access to abortion, although legal, is often restricted.[187] Anti-abortion feeling is also reflected
in the fact that in the year from 1996 to 1997 the number of arsons doubled
and bombings tripled against abortion providers in the USA.[188]

Delays in carrying out abortions are routine, leading to unnecessary late
abortions; non-surgical abortion is underused,[189] despite this being women's
preferred method in 60–70 per cent of cases.[190] In the US, the 'abortion pill',
RU 486 (mifepristone), is covered by Medicaid only when a pregnancy results
from rape or incest or when the woman's life is endangered.[191] In the UK, NHS
provision of abortion services has declined since the late 1960s, and use of the
private sector is increasing.[192] Private sector abortions are twice as likely as
NHS abortions to be carried out before nine weeks.[193] The recent report on
abortion in England and Wales found that 67 per cent of units carrying out
abortions and providing audit data offered women no choice as to the method
used.[194]

Women lack access to any form of contraception that is 100 per cent reliable and safe. Between 8 million and 30 million pregnancies a year are the
result of contraceptive failure.[195] There are major concerns about the short- and
long-term effects of oral contraception, with 'third generation' pills being recognized as generally less safe than their second generation predecessors,[196]
and major questions about the safety of injectable methods. Depo Provera,
introduced in 1963, had been used by more than 30 million women worldwide

by the late 1990s, with established side effects of disturbed menstrual bleeding, weight gain and lowered bone density, and unknown long-term health consequences.[197] The coil is in disrepute for its safety and efficacy record, and mechanical methods such as the vaginal diaphragm and cervical cap are poorly promoted despite their relatively good record.[198]

A study by the International Planned Parenthood Federation found that 46 of 94 surveyed countries require the male partner's consent for contraception, abortion or sterilization. While 54 countries ask for the man's approval for female sterilization, only 20 require female consent for male sterilization.[199] Men's opposition to women's contraceptive use is one of the commonest reasons women worldwide give for unplanned pregnancies.[200]

■

It's not a brilliant record overall. That's one reason we now have a new rash of anti-backlash books which argue that, far from having it all, women actually don't have very much at all.[201]

It would be nice to have an easy way of summarizing the position of women in different countries, but cross-national comparisons suffer from a surfeit of idiosyncratic ways of counting and measuring. Table 1 is from a weighty (1.02 kg) tome produced by the Equal Opportunities Commission in the UK in 1995, called *The Economics of Equal Opportunities*. The table shows some status indicators for women in eight countries between 1988 and 1990.

Table I Women's status indicators by country, 1988–90

Country	Female/male earnings ratio	Top occupations, % women	'Dissimilarity index'	Low-paid, % women	% low-paid women
Sweden	90.0	41.3	37.9	68.0	16.0
France	79.5	18.2	38.3	51.0	20.0
New Zealand	75.3	18.2	41.9	–	–
Portugal	70.8	11.6	25.1	49.0	19.0
USA	70.3	27.6	37.4	–	–
UK	68.0	22.3	44.4	63.0	41.0
Switzerland	67.5	16.2	39.2	–	–
Japan	48.9	11.8	23.1	–	–

Source: S. Dex and R. Sewell (1995) Equal opportunities policies and women's labour market status in industrialised countries, p. 370. In Humphries and Rubery, *The Economics of Equal Opportunities*.

The first column in table 1, female/male earnings ratio, puts the USA fifth and the UK sixth on the list. The percentage of women in professional and managerial occupations (column two) has the USA second and the UK third; the 'dissimilarity index', a measure of occupational segregation (the higher the figure the greater the inequality in occupational distribution), places the USA third and the UK eighth; the UK is third in column four – the percentage of low-paid workers who are women – and fourth in column five – the percentage of women workers who are low-paid (no comparable figures were given in this source for the USA).

The United Nations has developed a gender empowerment measure as an index of gender equality in key areas of economic and political participation and decision-making. The top five countries are Norway, Sweden, Denmark, Canada and Germany, in that order. The USA comes eighth, the UK sixteenth. Some developing countries outperform the richer nations: for example, Ecuador, Slovakia, Costa Rica and Cuba are ahead of France and Japan.[202]

As of June 1993, 116 countries had ratified the United Nation's Convention on the Elimination of All Forms of Discrimination Against Women. Many countries attached reservations to their acceptance; for example, the UK, Austria, Brazil, Ireland, Jordan, Libya, Malta, Thailand, Tunisia and Turkey attached reservations to Article 15, which gives women full legal capacity. Among the 52 countries which hadn't signed the Convention were the United States, India, Pakistan and South Africa.[203]

The measures in table 1 are all about the public world of paid work in industrialized countries and are therefore an extremely limited way of conceptualizing women's status. Second-wave feminism hasn't been very much occupied with the global position of women. This is summed up in a recent, extraordinarily powerful newspaper photograph of a young Pakistani mother of twins; she's holding both her babies, the boy on the right, the girl on the left. One is breastfed, the other, a quarter of the size and about to die, sucks vainly at a bottle. There aren't any prizes for guessing which is which.[204]

Two other examples:

Seen from afar, the Antonio Bermudex Industrial Park presents a vision both compelling and contradictory, like a set by film-maker Luis Buñuel for a movie about the plight of the forsaken. In plant after plant, well-tended buildings house sophisticated manufacturing operations that produce high-tech items for consumption abroad. Behind these monuments to modernity lie shantytowns with names like Rebirth and Hope. These are the homes of a labour force of migrant women. This is the land of the *maquiladora*, the export-processing plants that are today's global sweatshops and a mainstay of Mexican–US economic relations.

... During the *maquiladora* boom of the early 1980s, women made up 80 per cent of the workforce. More men have been hired in recent years but the labour force remains overwhelmingly female. Companies such as Zenith, TRW and Delnosa (owned by General Motors) send trucks into residential neighbourhoods, advertising assembly-line jobs for 'women only' over loudspeakers.

As assemblers and line workers, women solder television circuit boards, assemble car radios, arrange medical kits, pack cables, sew garments, and perform a thousand similar tasks. They may never see the finished product or even know precisely what they are assembling. Typically, they work eight-hour or longer shifts, performing monotonous, repetitive movements at high speeds in conditions of intense noise, noxious fumes and suffocating heat.

. . . Women's massive presence in the border workforce has led to the institutionalization of discriminatory employment practices. Pregnancy testing as a condition of employment is routine; forced resignation if the worker becomes pregnant is commonplace.[205]

And:

Farmers Virginia Manyange, a 30-year-old mother of three, and her sisters-in-law are officially landless. They live in one of Zimbabwe's resettlement areas, Jompani, 250 km west of the capital, Harare, where government permits to land are usually not issued jointly to spouses but to men only. The women and other family members of the Manyange homestead labour on 123 acres of arable land where they grow cash crops. Working conditions are tough . . .

In addition, each woman cultivates a gandiwa, a one-acre plot traditionally granted by husbands for their wives' exclusive use. Here they grow crops for their families, some of which they sell locally to meet school fees, purchase school uniform and buy nappies for their babies . . .

The women's access to resettlement land is precarious. Should a husband die, a land permit does not automatically transfer to his widow . . . For a wife abandoned or forced to leave an abusive marriage, divorce usually spells economic ruin. It is she who must leave the resettlement land where she has laboured. She can try to apply for a land permit elsewhere; however, she may be sent packing . . .

The Zimbabwean government prides itself on its progress in implementing women's rights. . . . Progress on all fronts, however, has been overshadowed by a March 1999 Supreme Court decision stripping women of their legal adult status. . . . 'What is good in England and America does not . . . mean the same should apply to Zimbabwe,' MP Livingstone Manhombo objected.[206]

■

Argument 2: 'Women' don't really exist

One of the questions that fragmented the women's movement in Europe and North America in the late 1970s and 1980s is about whether the identity of women's interests as women over-rides the different allegiances they hold due to their different economic positions – because of family structures, ethnicity, disability or sexuality. It's almost as though women got tired of talking about themselves. So they got rid of the very *idea* of women in order to avoid having to do any more of it. In Britain, working-class women were particularly snooty about the feminist credentials of women from more advantaged backgrounds, ignoring the consensus they themselves otherwise subscribed to, that 'class' as a theoretical invention is based on men's, not women's, social position. Some of the backlash literature has made much of this point, arguing that the real pulls on the ground between 'work' and motherhood are hardly recognized at all in the concerns of professional middle-class feminists.[207] Black women, later 'women of colour', rightly pointed out how their particular oppression had been sidelined by a white middle-class vanguard with different models of both oppression and liberation in their heads.[208]

We stood connected, and then fell, as those antagonistic to feminism leapt on our dissensions and turned them into proof that women can't be trusted to agree about anything. It didn't help that those the media had learnt to see as feminist leaders blotted their copybooks: Friedan, proselytizer of mainstream 'family' feminism, got beaten by her husband and divorced; her husband called NOW a 'bunch of man-hating dykes',[209] and she was inclined to agree with him. She wrote a book substituting the 'feminist' mystique for the 'feminine' one, as another name for a nameless problem – the problem that feminism didn't seem to be working: 'The equality we fought for isn't livable, isn't workable, isn't comfortable',[210] Friedan declared; instead, we must throw off the old gender polarities and work together to recreate The Family. Shulamith Firestone, founder member of Redstockings, and author of that other early feminist classic, *The Dialectic of Sex*,[211] argued with lots of her 'sisters' about lots of things, and went on to have a breakdown,[212] as did Kate Millett, in the aftermath of the quite unanticipated success of her *Sexual Politics*. 'The whole bloody system is sick,' Millett concluded, after the media had gone to town on her lifestyle and conflated this with her scholarship: 'the very notion of leadership, a balloon with a face painted upon it . . . inflated by media's diabolical need to reduce ideas to personalities . . . the purpose of such barbarous adulation is ultimately the most savage type of social control.'[213] Germaine Greer wrote *Sex and Destiny*,[214] a book which raised important questions about equating women's liberation with sexual freedom, but which was widely hailed as yet another sample of feminist recantation. Ros Coward's *Our Treacherous Hearts* (1992),[215] subtitled *Why women let men get their way*, and Lynne Segal's *Is The Future Female? Troubled thoughts on contemporary feminism* (1987),[216] were both statements by British socialist feminists suggesting that the women's movement had, in several critical respects, got it wrong. Books such as Robin Morgan's *Going Too Far* (1978),[217] Kate Millett's *Flying* (1975)[218] and Gloria Steinem's *Revolution from Within* (1992)[219] were read as movements in a symphony of women's confessional writings, which have always tended to be demonized, compared with similar literature by men, which is more often received as brave and raw.[220] Once the feminist icons moved onto the menopause – Greer's *The Change*,[221] Friedan's *The Fountain of Age*[222] and sections of Steinem's *Moving Beyond Words*[223] – the choice of subject-matter decisively confirmed what the media already knew: that feminism had become a fractious, useless old woman. The parts that were not an old woman were simply insane – books such as Andrea Dworkin's *Intercourse*[224] and Mary Daly's *Outercourse*[225] confirmed the old suspicion that feminism in the beginning and the end is only about hating (hetero)sex and men.

Compared to the USA, feminism was never so flamboyant in England – or perhaps it just got less media attention. We also argued about whether we hated men or capitalism the most, but the truth was that most of us hated neither, particularly. There was much discussion in the UK and the US of something called 'men's liberation': men's alienation as human beings through being required to play the male role, or 'mask-ulinity'.[226] Around the same time, the misbehaviour of Erin Pizzey, founder of the battered women's movement, was much discussed in British women's liberation groups: Pizzey reported the Angry Brigade, a small violent faction, to the police, and gained the distinction of being the only woman formally to have been thrown out of the women's liberation movement.[227] This was probably just as well, as she later propounded the distinctly unfeminist idea that women have a tendency to bring violence on themselves.[228] She abandoned the refuge movement and emigrated to the Cayman Islands with a new husband, claiming she'd always at heart been only a good housewife, and writing lush romantic fiction as an alternative modus vivendi.[229]

None of this has a frontline presence in the minds of young women who weren't there at the time and who heard about it, if at all, second-hand from their mothers, whose perspectives on life they (understandably) have a principled disinclination to adopt. But Eva Figes, whose *Patriarchal Attitudes* (1970)[230] took an entertaining romp through religion, economics, Rousseau and Freud, did hand on her interest in feminism to her daughter Kate, who had to climb onto a chair at school to explain to her classmates what it was all about. Kate Figes' *Because of Her Sex: The myth of equality for women in Britain* (1994) (dedicated to *her* daughters) takes a cool look at what's happened to women, concluding that rampant discrimination still exists. She also interviewed women about their identification with feminism and, twenty-five years on from the answers I got in my study of housework, found that, while they all believed in equal opportunities, and thought women faced distinct problems as a result of their sex, 'feminism' had become such a loaded word that most of them didn't want anything to do with it.[231]

Katie Roiphe's mother, Anne, author of the feminist novel *Up the Sandbox*,[232] wouldn't let her watch *The Brady Bunch* on television because it was sexist. When Katie got to Harvard, she found such unexceptional practices dressed up in another language of anger about men and 'the colonialist appropriation of the female discourse'. There was such a lot, it seemed, you couldn't say; so many sentiments disallowed by political correctness that you might as well give up the effort of thinking for yourself. So she wrote *The Morning After*, as another kind of diatribe against the 'excesses' of feminism, and mainly in order to get back at those 'date rape-crisis feminists' who take all the fun out of sex by seeing women as victims of predatory men.[233]

For many young women, feminism and its achievements are simply their unacknowledged birthright. Some may not use the word, but this doesn't mean they haven't integrated feminist values into their own lives.[234] René Denfeld, a journalist and self-styled 'amateur boxer' living in Portland, Oregon, was born the year after NOW was created; like many others she can't remember a time when abortion was illegal, when 'work' and marriage were alternative trajectories for women, and when girls' education was overtly limited by stereotyped notions of what girls should be. Denfeld rejects the label 'feminist', contending that feminism got bogged down in an 'extremist moral and spiritual crusade' and has lost contact with the key ideas of individual empowerment and political activism. Worse than that, feminists have reinvented Victorianism, with its unhelpful tendency to put women on pedestals as chaste, morally superior creatures.

Christine Sommers, an associate professor of philosophy specializing in 'contemporary moral theory', thinks that 'gender feminists' have stolen feminism from the place where it rightfully belongs – with women like her who don't believe in the constraining power of social institutions, and who simply want to celebrate women's gains and achievements; or with those practical souls who labour in the trenches to help real victims of abuse and discrimination. To stop these fictions of male atrocity and beleaguered womankind, the gender feminists ought to be pushed over the ramparts.[235] Naomi Wolf's *Fire with Fire*[236] accuses the 'victim feminists' of switching women off feminism by losing sight of the old-fashioned notion that women simply deserve to be treated as human beings, irrespective of their gender.

It's either the 'date-rape' feminists or the 'victim' feminists or the 'gender' feminists who've got it all wrong. This strand of protests about feminist errors works by subdivision. It's a version of the straw man strategy: stick a lot of bits together, put her up and then knock her down. As the worst enemies of women in a patriarchal culture are other women, so the most vengeful examples of divisive anti-feminism come from women themselves. Camille Paglia is the star here, most famously for her observations on male erection and ejaculation being the prototypical cultural projects, on women as incapable of getting beyond the grass-huts stage of civilization, and on leaving gender to the feminists as being akin to consigning your dog to vacation at the taxidermists.[237]

But consider this: we don't get sick of party politics when trouble breaks out: on the contrary, our interest appears to be fuelled when leaders make asses of themselves or politicians with purportedly the same views disagree with one another. At least we watch it all avidly on television and read it in the newspapers: we don't say it spells the end of politics as we know it. But women's disputes are clearly a different matter altogether.

∎

When the sales of feminism as a commodity dropped, the product champions invented a new commodity called the crisis of masculinity, or the problem of men. *This* problem had a name right from the beginning. Hence:

Argument 3: Men, the real victims?

For some time now, men have been getting the headlines, not in their usual role as 'man' embracing humans, but as a gender of their own: 'Men teachers "are species in danger"';[238] 'Time we heard it for the boys';[239] 'Boys performing badly';[240] 'Men in crisis';[241] 'Fatherhood at crisis point';[242] 'Fathers seen as a nuisance at births';[243] 'The descent of man';[244] 'So, Germaine, since animals now have·rights, how about men?';[245] 'Official: men are the victims now';[246] 'US male wilts in charge of the in-your-face feminists',[247] and so on and so forth. The topic of the last headline in the list baldly asserts, 'Now, it is men who are the victims.' This is about masculine and feminine images in the advertising industry, which by 1993 had replaced the stereotypes we used to censor with stickers – 'this exploits women' – with 'new' images of strong, smart women alongside which men appear weak and foolish: 'While you don't necessarily dress for men,' said one such, portraying a woman in black lingerie, 'it doesn't hurt, on occasion, to see one drool like the pathetic dog that he is.'

The corporate masculinity of the advertising industry has turned in on itself, like some nasty auto-immune disease:

> We have seen the future and it belongs to women . . . They are better at school, more employable, stronger in body and mind, or so it seems. Male anxiety is all around; read it in the literature, see it in the dole queues, feel it in the sperm count. Men, for so long the winners, have not won the past quarter century. And it hurts.[248]

This isn't a mass revolt by men; they're not organizing a movement, writing manifestos or planning programmes of action. What we have is another media product dreamed up by an industry which has to have news to sell; the orchestration of an entertaining twist to the backlash saga: part 1, women make fools of themselves; part 2, feminism has failed; part 3, what about the men, then? Of course, the fate of men and children is tied to women's: we are all, definitionally, if not experientially, human. But implying that men's plight is both newsworthy and feminism's fault is to ignore the factual evidence about gender discrimination, and to give feminism/women a most unbelievable power – far greater than any they ever actually had. The whipped-up men's revolt is reminiscent of Bertolucci's film *The Last Emperor* with its image of hundreds of eunuchs filing out of the palace, each carrying his amputated testes in a jar (in the film a man did the castrating).[249]

In *The Failure of Feminism*, arch anti-feminist Nicholas Davidson is clear about the beginnings of men's present decline: the women's movement. 'Many was the man who came home from work to a sinkful of dirty dishes requiring his attention,' he postulates, 'who was about to initiate sex after dinner (probably cooked by him) when it was suggested he should clean the toilet. If the two of them made it into bed with any energy left, he could then stimulate her clitoris and eventually ejaculate in her vagina . . . after being sure she had climaxed first.'[250] If cleaning the toilet and cooking the dinner uses so much energy, perhaps it's not surprising that women have been called frigid.

Robert Bly, propounder of a fantasy about the Iron Man, a reworking of a Grimm's 'fairy' tale, looks like Santa Claus with his tangled white mane and rounded belly.[251] Bly first came to public attention as a sixties peace activist, going on to hold 'Great Mother' conferences in the 1970s which promoted a feminine, peace-loving spirit. By the 1980s, audiences had dropped and Bly was feeling less than manly. Deciding men had gone too far in their identification with women, and had now gone 'soft', he started leading the wilderness weekend retreats for which he gained his second bout of fame. On these occasions, he encouraged men to experience 'the beast within' by dressing up in tribal masks and behaving like the wild animals they really are. Sam Keen, another proponent of fantasies about archetypal men, is much taken with the penis as the majestic site of primal mystery 'deserving of hymns of praise', but also given, like men, to appalling weaknesses and lack of control.[252]

Perhaps the root problem of civilization is that men *are* barbarous; to leash man's energy to the pro-social service of the family involves 'a traumatic act of giving up his most profound yearning, his bent for the hunt and the chase, the motorbike and the open road'.[253] George Gilder, the intellectual New Rightist whose *Men and Marriage* (1986) promoted this image of men as yearning brutes, developed qualms about his own virility when he avoided being drafted to Cambodia in 1970. He took up jogging to give himself a manly kick, and determined on a career as 'America's number-one anti-feminist'.[254] *Men and Marriage* was an updated version of Gilder's earlier *Sexual Suicide* and was published in the hope of capitalizing on the 1980s backlash.

What Warren Farrell calls the 'wound' of men's disposability is the central character in all this melodrama. Farrell taught 'men's issues' in California and drove a leather-upholstered Maserati with the number plate Y Men R when Susan Faludi interviewed him for her book *Backlash*.[255] Farrell used to be a 'male feminist', serving out a three-year term on the board of NOW, creating numerous 'men's liberation' chapters of NOW, and generally enjoying the spectacle of himself as New Age sensitive man. Then, as audiences for feminism, including male feminism, waned, he decided to stand up for men instead. Having made this decision, he was able to find numerous examples of women executing power over men – a whole cosmos of oppressive women, mainly independent, middle-class women with careers, like his own wife, a vice-president of IBM, who left him for another IBM manager. And on top of all this American men have to put up with the draft, circumcision and aggressive sports: wounds all round.

In *The Whole Woman*, Germaine Greer's update of *The Female Eunuch*, she concludes that in the year 2000 more men hate more women more bitterly than they did in 1970.[256] Young men growing up today 'carry more than a residue of patriarchal and sexist attitudes and behaviour'.[257] What we're seeing is new forms of masculinity rising like a phallic phoenix from the ashes of the old: a new kind of macho man, confident in his right to treat women as sexually combative non-equals.[258]

There's a good case – put by Susan Jeffords in *The Remasculinization of America*[259] – for agreeing with Farrell about the appalling nature of what happens to men in war. It's for this reason that the Vietnam War probably had a significance in the gender war which escaped most people. The American men who fought in that war were victims, not only because some of them were killed, but because it was a pointless, immoral, globally damaging war, and the first America didn't win. The Vietnam War discredited old-style aggressive masculinity; its enemies were often pitiably weak and powerless – pregnant women, old people, children, malnourished youth – and the masculine bravado meted out to such victims was hardly 'just' in terms of either ends or means. By the time of the Gulf War in 1991, and now in the anti-terrorism war of 2001–2, militant masculinity has moved into a depersonalized, high-technology mode in which all the talk is of automated, high-precision targeting.

But this doesn't stop – perhaps it encourages – other men going back to basics in an attempt to revitalize the old metaphors. Sperm is 'the stuff on which our survival depends'[260] – though presumably it wouldn't be an awful lot of use without eggs. The ultimate crisis of masculinity is that supplies of this biological essence seem to be running out; mean sperm concentrations worldwide fell by half between 1940 and 1990,[261] with a continuing decline of about 2 per cent a year.[262] Testes are shrinking as well, and are more likely now not to be there at all – the incidence of cryptorchidism (undescended testicles) and other malformations of the male genital tract shows a sustained rising trend.[263] Consonant with the general picture, sperm deficiency is blamed on too many oestrogens in women and/or the water supply, though other environmental pollutants such as DDT may be to blame: there are an alarming 3,000 chemicals in food or the environment which mimic oestrogenic properties.[264]

Men's anger is alternatively cast as fear, a 'secret terror' which reveals itself figuratively and literally as impotence. This is an interesting word meaning lack of power, but the male referent is unmistakably the penis. The militant lobby for guns, 'western culture's quintessential, if clichéd, phallic symbol',[265] signals just this sense of threatened masculinity. Lynne Segal, survivor of the British feminist movement, believes that 'straight' sex has been given up as false consciousness, thus liberating no one from anything. The limp, post-modern penis is horribly emblematic of sickness, waste and disease all round.[266] Images of the failing phallus haunt contemporary images of man, says social critic Christopher Lasch in *The Culture of Narcissism*,[267] a book which challenges the contemporary moral ethic of self-absorption and personal relations as damaging a good deal more than the penis.

■

Backlash is the title of a 1947 Hollywood film in which a man frames his wife for a murder he himself has committed. It's essentially a 'counter-assault on women's rights',[268] both banal and sophisticated, a medleyed muddle of attacks, assertions, pleas, opinions, complaints, fears, fantasies and postures . . . but, like everything else in this narrative, it's not a conspiracy. Contending the backlash calls for more than just pointing a wagging finger of blame.

In *The Politics of Unreason*, political scientists Seymour Lipset and Earl Raab, Jews of the Holocaust generation, civil rights activists and democratic leftists, discuss the phenomenon of right-wing extremism. 'Extremist politics', they say 'are the politics of despair' and disaffection. Backlash politics, whatever their ostensible topic, have a number of common features. One, they go for overwhelmingly simple diagnoses, fastening on single causes for complex, multifaceted phenomena. Two, they're the reaction of groups which feel themselves to be in a position of declining power in moments of incipient change, when the rising aspirations of other groups tell them they have been deprived of something important they now want. Three, any backlash has a population group as its target: 'If the ideological project defines . . . that which it is to be preserved, the targeting defines those from whom it has to be preserved.'[269] Four, extremist movements aren't made up of evil types called 'extremists', but rather of ordinary people experiencing stress, who consequently develop a nostalgia for a disappearing way of life which they imagine holds arcane comfort and belongingness at its centre.

It's an explanation that fits McCarthyism, the Ku Klux Klan, the John Birch Society – and the backlash against feminism, although Lipset and Raab, being children of their time, don't mention gender as a potential site for a backlash movement. This is strange, since every episode of feminism has been followed by a backlash of a kind. In America, feminism has replaced communism in right-wing rhetoric: in Britain, feminism is more simply the enemy of Family Values. These counter-discourses have been enormously fertilized by the mood of party politics in both countries: the culture of individualism marked by Thatcher's precept about 'society' not existing; the pre-emptive dedication to 'market' forces and the postmodern mindset against state intervention. Whatever happens to women in these conservative times, feminism gets this contradictory construction: both as powerful enemy and as weak outsider.[270]

What makes such endings possible is a decisive turn in relation to gender, the word we brought into the language in the early 1970s[271] so we'd be able to talk about what men and women do that isn't in their genes. In the 1970s, gender was everything; now it's been returned to sex, as the new sociobiology deems culture only the icing on the cake. 'Gender is irrelevant', proclaimed a male student at a gender studies seminar attended by Imelda Whelehan, going on to 'extol the virtues of the playful postmodern-ironic approach to images of women which, both sexually explicit and nostalgically pre-feminist in their presentation, would have previously been denounced as self-evidently offensive . . . these days we were all far too sophisticated as cultural consumers to read images in such two-dimensional terms'.[272] Whelehan's book, *Overloaded: Popular culture and the future of feminism*,[273] coins the term 'retrosexism' to describe the cultural flavour of the 1990s, besieged by nostalgia for a golden age of traditional gender relations before feminism turned up to distract and contaminate.

■

In the year 2000, for which some people had such high expectations before everyone got tired of everything to do with women, the USA has twice as many shelters for mistreated animals as for mistreated women, no national health insurance plan for women, and no federal funding for daycare. In the UK the House of Commons has a shooting gallery but no nursery, and male MPs are still pretending that breasts are feminine ornaments, and preventing women MPs from breastfeeding on the job. As Germaine Greer put it with her usual incisiveness: 'Thirty years on femininity is still compulsory for women and has become an option for men, while genuine femaleness remains grotesque to the point of obscenity.'[274] As she says, 'The second-wave of feminism, rather than having crashed onto the shore, is still far out to sea.'[275]

In the 1970s the personal became the political, now the political's become personal again. Bra-burning is alive and well.[276] Because gender hasn't been challenged as a social structure, and patriarchy lingers on as more than an echoing mnemonic in old feminists' heads, it's the easiest way to reinvoke hierarchy in such moments of cultural confusion. These always send the fearful spinning off to the right. The rest of them stay just where they were, which is what many feminists have done; we haven't given up our now post-millennial visions of a reasonable society which understands there are more important things to do than argue about gender all the time.

Whether one is sick to death of women or not and for whatever reasons is really rather beside the point. The point is, it's time to move on.

5
Angels in the House

'It's amazing how you always end up in the kitchen, isn't it?', she said conspiratorially, as we both loaded up a tray with the previous people's dirty dishes. We made a good job of it, and then the waitress, whose face I can't remember because you don't really look at the faces of waitresses, removed the tray and wiped the table so we could put our own trays down on it and eat our lunch in the Coffee Shoppe in the Kingsgate Shopping Centre in a town in the middle of the flat, rain-sodden English fens two weeks before Christmas.

I didn't know her – she was just another woman who was making for the same table. I wanted to sit there because it had a good view of the concourse below, a shiny, pale-brown, fake-marble area interrupted by ramps for wheelchairs, circular plastic wooden benches for collapsed shoppers, and even a small pool dressed up as a lake – all covered up from the elements so no one would be in danger of remembering shopping's original function as a gatherer-hunter activity. The pool has a nativity scene perched on it, the whole image vastly incongruous and even slightly worrying, as the lamb with its pink lipsticked mouth by Jesus's crib looks as though it's about to topple over the edge into the water. A young couple sit to one side of the crib, the lad on his mobile phone, the girl sidling up to him, coquettishly. The only thing to be said in the floating nativity's favour is that it must look like a home away from home to many local shoppers, with much of England currently under water due to the highest rainfall since records began.

The woman who made the remark about being in the kitchen is joined by another. They both have white hair, and suitcases and raincoats. This is just a refuelling stop in a long and complicated cross-country travail of some 170 miles which the two women are having to make on three coaches over a six-

and-three-quarter-hour period because of the problems with the trains conse-
quent on the infrastructure neglect associated with privatization. They've just
been visiting one of their sisters, Daphne, who's had a stroke; she's married
to a man called Ted who's too mean to get her a wheelchair. 'It's a good thing
you don't know what's ahead of you, isn't it?', postulates Daphne's sister. I
nod mentally, but, somewhat bored with one another, they start to include me
in their conversation anyway.

'The lights are nice, aren't they? It really makes you feel like Christmas.'
Does it? Do I want to feel like Christmas? A tall Christmas tree on the
concourse below, supposedly the piéce de resistance, looks as plastically
unconvincing as everything else. The lights are awful: a glaring mix of primary
colours with turquoise and orange; flashing red, green and blue lights inter-
spersed with banners of turquoise and orange stars, and green segments of
Christmas trees with revolving silver balls – a terrible jumble of tones and
motifs.

The two women finish their chocolate tart and prawn open sandwich respectively, having treated me to further confidences about their plans for the festive
season, and got me involved in a conversation about the sex of grandchildren
and the gendering of their clothes – 'it's so difficult to find nice clothes for
boys, isn't it?' They saunter off to find their next coach, and I plunge into the
shopping melée below. A detail of the lighting display which isn't obvious
from the Coffee Shoppe is a circular yellow and blue image projected from
hidden cameras of three teddy bears holding hands; they dance haphazardly
around the shiny floor, drawing the bemused attention of small children who
are much nearer to it than I am. Round the corner is Santa's Grotto: £2.50 a
go, including a present. It's housed in a white nylon igloo, and, inside the flap
at the front, Santa's sitting on a sofa reading a paper having his lunch break.
Outside the nylon igloo, little silver creatures dressed as astronauts frolic with
jerky robotic movements in piles of synthetic snow; quite what the moon and
Santa or snow and the moon have to do with one another isn't clear.

When I've walked to the end and sussed out the shops, I come back again
and sit on one of the plastic wooden benches in the circular seating area
provided for those temporarily too tired to shop any more, or permanently
incapable of doing it. I count twenty-eight men and twelve women. Four of
the men are perched on the outer rim of the seating area, looking down over
the mall. They're in their sixties and seventies, with half-bald heads and beige
raincoats, and they remind me of the ageing rascals in the British television
series *Last of the Summer's Wine*. Like Compo and his mates, these four are
here to soak up the ambience, not to do anything; from time to time they hail
and chat with other similarly garbed men of similar ages. One imagines them
sitting here for hours and hours long after the shutters have come down, sealing
off the shopping centre from the rest of the town, which is aesthetically a different project altogether. The cathedral, so titled by Henry VIII in 1541, is a

splendid example of medieval architecture, and was once full of paintings and tapestries with a wonderful carved stone high altar under a gilded and painted roof. There was a ladies' chapel with two chambers above inhabited by a devout lady called Agnes, whose reason for being there is lost in the quagmire of history. One of Henry's wives was buried in the cathedral and so was Mary Queen of Scots. Later things went downhill, and Cromwell's soldiers ransacked the place, including breaking into the Queens' tombs, and destroying much of the building and its contents.[1]

The silver balls oscillate, the yellow and blue teddy bears dance, the polished escalators chug and squeak, and over it all lies a custard of children's cries and exclamations mixed with the unyielding beat of pop music flowing like raw sewage out of the shop-fronts into the flatland of shoppers' paradise. The shoppers in Kingsgate Shopping Centre are unaware of all this history lying just a few metres away from Argos, Our Price, the Disney Shop, C and A ('Buy Now Before We Close') and the Officers' Store ('All Stock Must Go'). Some of the men in the sitting area have obviously been left there by their wives and girlfriends who've long given up on their attempts to make shopping an occasion for heterosexual intimacy. One picks his nose, another reads the *Daily Mail*; several guard rising mounds of shopping bags. There are groups of women with babies in pushchairs, feeding them out of Heinz toddler jars. Two smartly dressed young Asian women are having a highly animated conversation, their looped silver earrings flashing in sympathy with the revolving Christmas lights. A large denimed man arrives next to me pulling a fussy, navy-and-white-fabric pram, from which he extracts a pale-faced baby dressed in blue with a dummy and red mock trainers. He settles the child in the crook of his arm, takes the dummy out of its mouth and a bottle of milk out of one of the other apertures in the pram. Testing the temperature of the milk on the back of his hand with a self-conscious new father gesture, he offers it to the baby, who's only mildly interested in it. The baby strains to sit up to see what's going on. But there's nothing very interesting to see. The women's faces wear a look of tiredness, of lists made, lost and unending, of expeditions thwarted or troubling, desired more in anticipation than in fact. At this time of year the strain of Christmas really tells, a mass consumption event involving, in the UK in 2000, the expenditure of a massive £12.5 billion on gifts and food and drink;[2] some 83 per cent of British adults expect to take part in a family gathering at Christmas,[3] and all of these have to be catered for, orchestrated and managed, largely by women.

■

When I was a little girl, I used to go shopping in London with my mother. It was the only thing she and I ever did together on our own outside the house. If it was a small shopping trip, we'd take the bus along the Uxbridge Road

either one way to Acton High Street or the other way to the rather more pros
perous Ealing Broadway: my early understanding of social class was fixed
visually by these contrasting geographies. Bigger trips involving the underground to central London were always called by my mother 'going up to
town', which perplexed me, as even I with my spatial affliction could see that
it was more a question of going sideways. We went to the big department stores
– Swan and Edgar's in Piccadilly, Selfridges and Dickens and Jones and John
Lewis: sometimes we went to Harrods, though more for the aromas in the food
hall and for me to look at the animals in the pet department than actually to
buy. I remember these shopping trips with affection, for there was a real sense
of being in it together, of being slightly naughty spending my father's money
– she had none of her own – and of participating in the grand shopping illusion, that the right purchases will make people love one another and be happy.
As a teenager I developed a more strategic streak, trying to persuade my
mother to buy me what I wanted rather than what she did, and rows would
therefore erupt, causing her to get her cigarettes out and then cough loudly all
the way home, which embarrassed me, so I sulked and looked the other way,
stuck deeply into mother-hatred, that not-inevitable sequitur of being female
in a patriarchal culture.

Now, when I shop with my daughters, my daughter-in-law or my grand-
daughters, I'm aware of being in this same shared female place: a psychological corral of gazing and imagining, of measuring and scrutinizing, of lusting
and detesting, of acquiring and abandoning. Actually I think shopping, not
childbirth, is the female equivalent of warfare: the Bad Buy is analogous
to the Bad Guy as the enemy to be overcome. Of all the cultural baggages
of femininity, I find it hardest to detach myself from this one. I like to think
it's the loving complicity that surrounds it, but the chances are this is just
self-deception.

Angels are everywhere at Christmas, and a lot of the rest of the time as
well; they've become a slick cipher for that very other-worldliness suspended
by the act of shopping and other popular modern occupations. We hang angels
on our Christmas cards and over our shopping malls, inscribing their painted
pudgy faces on biscuit tins and T-shirts with all the deceitful zeal of the genuinely spiritually lost.[4] The declamatory importance of angels in the Bible
makes them male, but in our cultural iconography angelic faces, behaviours
and accommodations are definitely female. The phrase 'angel in the house' is
said to come originally from the title of a poem written in octosyllabic quat-
rains by the Victorian poet Coventry Patmore, who in it described in much
inordinate detail the intimacies of a rectory courtship.[5] Patmore was married
to his own angel, Emily, who bore him six children before dying of tubercu-
losis while he wrote poems in the British Museum.[6] Angels are epitomes of
sacrificial femininity, always thinking about other people: 'If there was a
chicken, she took the leg; if there was a draught she sat in it.'[7] Anthropologist

ughter, Mary Catherine Bateson, married another aca-
enty years, whenever I interrupted my husband when
.ed what he was doing before he responded. When he
would drop what I was doing to respond to him . . . we have
.rom my peripheral vision.'[8] Virginia Woolf considered the Angel
.use syndrome not only an explanation as to what went on between
and women inside houses but a much more global impediment to
women's sense of realism, particularly about men. The American writer Pearl
Buck, whose multicultural upbringing (in China and the USA) produced some
fascinating speculations about culture and gender, talked about 'the halo
problem': women, given halos by men when they stay at home, often find it
difficult in practice to live up to this angelic image: 'She smiles at him the
way she has learned he thinks is most angelic. But the moment he is gone she
stops being an angel. She yawns, saunters about the house, does what she has
to do when she has to, for being an angel has demoralized her.'[9]

The iconography of family life remains firmly welded to these angelic
images and wares. It's one reason why it's so difficult to see the hard labour
that goes on there. Out of conviction, habit, fear, or all three, we clutch desperately onto the misty image of the home as a fine and private place within
which no one's an outsider and everyone plays the great twenty-first-century
game of The Equal Division of Labour. But the game is a form of cultural
warfare and its battles and secessions explain a lot of other politics as well.

■

The era of modern shopping started in London with Elizabeth I, when mer-
chants began to specialize in selling different types of wares to a socially
top-heavy society which had developed a high demand for luxury goods.
'Standing shops', as opposed to the movable feasts of market stalls, emerged
in Cheapside, London Bridge, Fleet Street and the Strand, and in the smartest
of these, tradesmen's wives, themselves debarred from selling, sat in specially
constructed doorway seats encouraging people to come in and buy. By 1850,
the prestige of retailing as an occupation had fallen – so much so that
'shopman' had become a term of abuse, and women were replacing men as
the main sellers.[10] In the US, Catharine Beecher added a chapter on marketing to the 1873 edition of her *Housekeeper and Healthkeeper*,[11] the new scientific engineers of housework argued that women had to train themselves to
be efficient purchasing agents, and the embryonic advertising industry created
'the consumer housewife' when it settled its internal debate about whether to
target men as the main earners or women as the main spenders by coming
down decisively in favour of women.[12]

'Women's relationship with consumption may be contradictory, troubling
and at times traumatic, but one thing is certain: it is unavoidable', say Maggie

Andrews and Mary Talbot at the beginning of their book on women in twentieth-century consumer culture.[13] Women do an awful lot of shopping. Some 80 per cent of everything that's sold is bought by women.[14] In one study of women's work in China, Japan and Britain, shopping was entirely or mainly female in 92 per cent of Japanese, 77 per cent of British and 38 per cent of Chinese families, and entirely or mainly male in 1 per cent, 4 per cent and 15 per cent.[15] A study of women and food in the north of England some years ago provided the following easily recognizable narrative about gender and shopping: 'even when men participated in food shopping their involvement tended to be tangential rather than central. Typically, they provided the transport and helped carry the shopping; they pushed the trolley or helped to look after the children; and occasionally they made individual forays down supermarket aisles for items already decided upon by their partners.'[16]

Men do buy things, usually quickly, but they don't shop. Not looking at price tags is 'a measure of virility'.[17] The language bursts with jovial references to women's need for shopping and shopping's need for women: retail therapy is a second cousin of psychotherapy, sharing a good portion of its genes. In his book *Why We Buy*, American economist Paco Underhill calls the study of shopping 'a science'. He runs 'Envirosell', a private business which helps stores to sell, and refers with a glib authority to women's 'affinity' for shopping:

> Most purchasing traditionally falls to women, and they usually do it willingly – even when shopping for the mundane necessities, even when the experience brings no particular pleasure, women tend to do it in dependable, agreeable fashion . . . Women can go into a kind of reverie when they shop – they become absorbed in the ritual of seeing and comparing, of imagining and envisioning.[18]

Small children are a handicap to efficient shopping, but shopping is a way of getting out of the house, not only to consume, but to imagine the other worlds conjured up by the visions in shop windows. Window-shopping is gazing through the glass lightly, playing with the possibility of purchases which are unlikely to make anyone except retail traders happy. In France, when the Paris arcades came into existence in the 1840s, they devised a special word for window-shopper, '*flâneur*'.[19] The meaning is somewhat less exotic when applied to shopping malls as 'temples of mass consumption' where a kind of panoptic surveillance is exercised over all who come there – Compo and his mates, the poor and homeless looking for a warm dry place, young people just hanging out in a postmodern version of street-corner society.[20]

And this is, of course, overwhelmingly a business in which women sell to women. Almost two-thirds of the retail workforce in the UK are women, though many of them work part-time and there are few in management positions. The retail workforce is the 'new proletariat' – selling is poorly paid, low-status work, despite the superficial glamour of handling so much desirable stuff. Women shopworkers earn two-thirds of what the men do.[21] The retail industry is highly casualized, with high proportions of temporary and part-time workers, as though shopping is simply a passing nightmare.

Shopping is part of housework, and housework is very ill-defined. A 'tacit consensus'[22] that everyone knows what it is hides its most important aspect – that most housework is done by women within the context of intimate personal relations: normatively the heterosexual nuclear family. It's for this reason that housework is always a theme in feminist movements; in backlashes against feminism, on the other hand, it tends to get swallowed up by something else; work mysteriously disappears, and the subject is changed to one about love, caring and altruism. 'There will be no true liberation of women until we get rid of the assumption that it will always be women who do housework and look after children', said Ellen Malos in a 1970s pamphlet called *Housework and the Politics of Women's Liberation*.[23] The most popular feminist critique of housework in that era was 'The politics of housework' by Pat Mainardi, a member of Redstockings, who described the high points of the debate that ensued between herself and her husband when she suggested they should share the housework: 'I don't mind sharing the housework, but I don't do it very well'; 'We have different standards and why should I have to work to yours?' and 'We used to be so happy.' Since men aren't conditioned to be housewives, argued Mainardi, they know the truth when they see it, which is that housework stinks. 'Participatory democracy begins at home', she declared. 'The measure of your oppression is his resistance.'[24] It was a point many of us took personally.

One reason why housework may be said to stink is that it's unpaid work. When almost everything else has a cost and a price, the concept of 'value' becomes wholly economic; terms such as 'value', 'labour', 'production', 'reproduction' and 'work' have all been hijacked into the service of economics.[25] Activities that are paid are socially valued and assumed to create wealth, yet they often do the opposite, destroying material and social resources and generating waste and environmental damage. Housework may be excluded from national accounts, but military activities and others which damage the environment as well as people are recorded as 'growth'.

National accounting systems such as the GNP and the United Nations System of National Accounts (UNSNA), used for measuring production and growth throughout most of the world, exclude household activities from their calculations. UNSNA was developed by five men in the early 1950s, following the tradition laid down by Adam Smith in *The Wealth of Nations*, according to which domestic services add nothing of value. The UNSNA Committee was headed by Sir Richard Stone, who won the Nobel prize for economics in 1984 largely for this work. The basic building blocks of the national accounting system were developed by Stone and by John Maynard Keynes during the

Second World War; their object was to work out how to pay for the war. As New Zealand economist Marilyn Waring observes, this means that the national accounting systems in use today are tailored to provide data on warring nations which must be very unclean, as apparently almost no housework is done in them.[26]

The real function of women and shopping is disguised in such accounting systems. Women's decisive economic contribution in modern industrial societies is, 'overwhelmingly, to make possible a continuing and more or less unlimited increase in the sale and use of consumer goods'.[27] The 'managerial effectiveness' of women shoppers is essential to the health of the GNP; but this is disguised in a rhetoric of 'curiously trouble free enjoyment', with all forms of consumer persuasion affirming that buying goods is the greatest source of pleasure, 'the highest measure of human achievement'.[28] Stripped of this ideological construction, the privatization of domestic work in households is, from a rational cost-benefit viewpoint, a very inefficient way to get it done. This point was made most cogently by early twentieth-century feminists such as Charlotte Perkins Gilman and Olive Schreiner, who took apart the myth of the congruence between housework and family relationships. 'Follow the hours in the day of the housewife,' admonished Gilman in a famous passage:

> count the minutes spent in the care and service of the child, as compared with those given to the planning of meals, the purchase of supplies, the labour either of personally cleaning things or of seeing that other persons do it . . .
> 'But,' we protest, 'all this is for the child – the meals, the well-kept house, the clothes – the whole thing!'
> Yes? And in what way do the meals we so elaborately order and prepare, the daintily furnished home, the much-trimmed clothing, contribute to the body-growth, mind-growth, and soul-growth of the child?[29]

In 1970 the Chase Manhattan Bank conducted a survey of families of Wall Street employees to determine 'what a wife was worth'. They divided housework into its component roles (cook, dishwasher, chauffeur, dietician, etc.), counted the average number of hours per week each took, applied the commercial rate per hour and derived a 'value' of $257.53 per week. Multiplying this figure by the number of weeks in the year and the number of housewives in the US gave a figure of between $500 billion and $650 billion per year – more than half the GNP of approximately $1 trillion, twice the total governmental budget, and five to six times the military budget at that time.[30] These figures would rise 272 per cent were the value of being 'on call' for childcare added in.[31] Canadian estimates around the same time produced a figure of 27 per cent of the GNP;[32] nine earlier studies dating from 1919 to 1973 yielded figures of 34–9 per cent.[33] In the UK, some 6 per cent of the GNP is accounted for by unpaid childcare alone.[34] In her book *Unpaid Work in the Household*

Luisella Goldschmidt-Clermont cites seventy-five different estimates of the contribution the household sector would make to the GNP if it was counted in rather than out. These estimates yield values of from 25 per cent to 40 per cent of the GNP accounted for by household work, estimates which would be 26 per cent higher if based on male instead of female wages.[35] In Britain in 1993 the Legal and General Insurance Company repeated the Chase Manhattan exercise with a larger and more representative sample, arriving at a value of £348.75, which gives a 'price tag' for a wife of £18,135 annually.[36]

Waged labourers are inside the social contract; the unwaged are outside it. The unwaged condition of housework powerfully reinforces the notion that housework isn't real work: the people who do it are thus unreal outsiders. Women's own status as outsiders has a lot to do with this primary division. The feminization of housework means that complaining housewives like Pat Mainardi are seen as nagging bitches, rather than workers struggling for more equitable working conditions.[37] Turning housework into paid work is one solution that offers itself cyclically in the history of gender and public policy. Wages for housework were proposed by Selma James, a New Yorker with a background in Trotskyite politics and anti-racism activism,[38] at the National Women's Liberation Conference in Britain in 1972. James envisaged paying women for housework as a 'revolutionary' demand which would change the structuring of capitalist social relations.[39] Construed alternately as radical and reactionary demand, wages for housework never gained widespread approval in either Europe or America as a strategy for unlocking the gendering of domestic work, although the argument that women's household work should be financially rewarded in one way or another has a long and interesting history.

The domestic division of labour is as much a context and a means for 'doing gender' as war or sport. In one study of eight European Union countries, there were considerable variations in childcare services, wages, levels of employment and the share of leadership positions held by women, but in all eight countries women did most of the domestic work.[40] In Italy, a recent supreme court judgement ruled that a wife's failure to clean the marital home is grounds for divorce.[41] In Vienna, home of psychoanalysis, a (male) psychotherapist believes that a failure to do housework properly is a sign of deep-seated psychological problems. He and his wife visit their (mainly female) patients' homes with a box of cleaning tools and psychiatric adjustment strategies.[42] Multinational studies show a 'pronounced gender segregation' in the division of most domestic labour tasks. Cooking, laundry, cleaning and washing dishes are feminine, and outdoor tasks and automobile maintenance are masculine.[43] In a Norwegian experiment, fourteen families had their work-lives rearranged so that both partners worked half-time outside the home and were instructed to share domestic work equally; the experiment had some impact on cooking and childcare, which became more egalitarian, but very little on car and house maintenance, and on shopping and housework, which retained the usual gender coding.[44] A survey of shopping carried out by Mass Observation in 1952 found that British housewives spent on average an hour shopping on weekdays and nearly two hours on Saturdays; any shopping men did wasn't worth mentioning.[45] In another study, middle-class housewives spent an average of 16 minutes a day shopping in 1937 and 55 in 1974–5; the figures for working-class housewives were 40 and 53.[46] In 1995 women in households with dependent children devoted an average of 46 minutes a day and men 24 minutes to shopping.[47] The women spent 2 hours 59 minutes daily on cooking and routine housework, and 1 hour 56 minutes on the care of children and adults, the corresponding figures for men being 41 and 54 minutes.

We can't answer the question 'do men do more housework than they used to?' definitively, because the requisite scientific data haven't been collected, so instead we have to cobble together what bits of data we can from different sources. An American study using information on time use from two datasets found no change in men's share of housework in the decade from 1965 to 1975. In 1965–6 men spent an average of 81 and women 290 minutes a day on housework; in 1975–6 these figures were 83 and 235 minutes.[48] According to the British Social Attitudes Survey, it was mainly women who did the shopping in 51 per cent of households in 1983 and 50 per cent in 1987; the figures for households in which mainly women made the evening meal were 77 per cent in both years, for cleaning 72 per cent in both years, for washing and ironing 89 per cent in 1983 and 88 per cent in 1987.[49] In my own study of women's experiences of housework, carried out in 1971,[50] 15 per cent of men 'helped' their partners a lot, 60 per cent not very much, and the rest fell in between. A very similar pattern was found in a small study using the same methods reported in 2000.[51]

Time-budget studies show a complex picture in which women's involvement in housework has declined somewhat over the years (by some 10 per cent between 1974–5 and 1984–5) as they've done more paid work outside the home, and men's housework time has increased, but from a very low base, and not sufficiently to take up the slack created by their 10 per cent decline in paid work hours.[52] Of course, this conjunction between decreases in women's and increases in men's housework time suggests a causal relationship, but mistaking correlation for cause is a well-known error. Most of the change in the male–female sex ratio for housework is accounted for by women doing less, not men doing more.[53] Children in many households do as much domestic work as men.[54]

The consensus of many studies is that women do some 70 per cent of total household work, and that their time commitment is affected by such factors as whether or not they're employed and the number of children in the household; men's input, on the other hand, is much more stable, running at some 15 per cent of total household work.[55] Contrary to received wisdom, 'women's entry into employment has made little difference to men's contribution to the domestic sphere'.[56] A review of sixty-five studies covering the period from 1970 to 1992 concluded that husbands' contribution averages about ten hours a week.[57] In dual-earner households where men and women are employed for the same number of hours, women do some nine hours more housework than men.[58] Men don't increase their household hours when their partners work longer hours.[59] When both partners are unemployed, women do 14 hours more; in households with non-employed women and employed men, the women do 22 more hours housework every week than their partners.[60] 'We discover – or rather rediscover, since this is found wherever we look in Europe and North America', say the authors of this report of British couples' behaviour, 'that the resemblance between husbands' and wives' work is only superficial'.[61] 'Traditional' patterns of household gender roles are liable to be accentuated when women have babies[62] and when men are unemployed – the latter situation can provoke a response of defensive undomesticated masculinity in some men.[63] The 'solution', increasingly common in middle-class households, of employing waged labour to take over some household tasks, acts to confirm gender patterns, since it creates more low-paid jobs for working-class women.[64]

One problem with statistics on gender and domestic work is that people may be saying what they think other people want them to say rather than what they actually believe or practice. Since most of us don't study what we actually do, we're free to invent estimates consistent with our gender ideologies. What we have here is a 'negotiated consensual myth',[65] according to which housework and childcare *ought* to be shared. Subscribing to the notion of domestic togetherness in household tasks is part of a long-term secular change in heterosexual relationships. Love no longer means respect based on difference but an economy of togetherness; the sharing of everything as a kind of cement binding the sexes together.[66] In 1987, the British Social Attitudes survey found that 43 per cent of women and 52 per cent of men agreed with the statement 'A husband's job is to earn the money; a wife's is to look after the home and family.' By 1994, these figures had dropped to 22 per cent for women and 27 per cent for men.[67] Younger people are more egalitarian: only 7 per cent of young women and 14 per cent of young men aged 12–19 agreed with the traditionalist view.[68] There's a gendering of 'shareworthy' tasks: grocery shopping is the most shareworthy and household repairs the least. On all these indices of who should do what, men come out as more traditional and less egalitarian than women.

This is tacitly recognized in the conflict between values and reported practices. The French magazine *Femme Pratique* published a survey in 1983 showing that 48 per cent of men thought housework should be shared, but only 32 per cent actually helped with shopping, 30 per cent with childcare, 20 per

cent with cooking and 17 per cent with cleaning.[69] Men consistently overesti-
mate the extent of their input to domestic work. When the American social
scientists Sarah Fenstermaker Berk and Anthony Shih looked at what men and
women in a large study of urban North American households said about who
did what with respect to forty-five household tasks, they found that agreement
was lowest for telephoning repair services and highest for changing children's
nappies: there was more agreement for tasks typically considered feminine
than for masculine ones. Women said that men did 9 per cent of the work
involved in cleaning bathrooms, 9 per cent of kitchen sink-cleaning, 5 per cent
of ironing and 16 per cent of vacuuming; the men's figures for these tasks were
21 per cent, 24 per cent, 10 per cent and 30 per cent.[70] The counter-argument
here, that women underestimate the male contribution, is unpersuasive in the
light of methodological studies which show substantial discrepancies between
men's estimates of domestic work time and the evidence of their own time-
diaries: in one such study, men estimated their childcare time as on average
11.3 hours per week, whereas their own diary entries gave a figure of 1.7
hours.[71]

When Rosalind Coward interviewed 150 women for her book *Our
Treacherous Hearts*, she thought they must all be married to the same man,
so uniformly did they describe their husbands as more stable, kinder and nicer
than the women themselves – they were lucky to be married to such helpful
and supportive men.[72] In her book *The Second Shift* Arlie Hochschild notes in
her interview data the same attribution of luck by women; the men, on the
other hand, didn't see themselves as lucky to have wives who do a lot of housework and childcare and/or work outside the home.[73]

■

The modern domestic washing machine was developed in Britain in 1792 and
in America in 1805; the first electricity-driven machine came onto the
American market in 1908, but its exposed belt-drive gave users the unwanted
extra of frequent electric shocks.[74] By 1918 only 6 per cent of British homes
had electricity, and as late as 1942 three-quarters of working-class households
lacked hot running water.[75] Washing machines only became commonplace
after the Second World War, with 29 per cent of British families owning one
in 1958 and 77 per cent in 1981.[76] Disposable nappies were a much later
technology, arriving in the 1960s after Procter and Gamble's director of
exploratory development spent time caring for his newborn grandchild and
decided there had to be some better system than washing cloth nappies.[77] Mr
Bissell of Grand Rapids, Michigan, invented the carpet sweeper in 1876 as a
solution to the problem of his own dust allergy. By 1900 there were vacuum
cleaners for domestic use, but their modern form originated in the work of

James Murray Spangler, an asthmatic school janitor from New Berlin, Ohio, who put together an assemblage of tin, wood, a broom handle, a motor, a fan disc, a cylindrical brush, and a pillowcase to catch the dust.[78]

Gas-cooked dinners in gas-heated dining rooms were possible in the early 1800s, but gas cookers didn't catch on until the end of the nineteenth century, at which point cooking with electricity had also become a viable alternative for the rich to the traditional coal range. At the Chicago Electrical Fair in 1893 the all-electric kitchen was a marvel, but people were very suspicious of this new, invisible energy source and the damage it might be doing to food as well as people.[79] Microwave ovens, about which the same suspicions continue to be voiced, were produced in Japan in the 1950s. There was rapid 'penetration' (an interesting word) of the UK market, with 50–60 per cent of households owning one by 1992.[80] These appliances, based on the military radar technology of the 1940s, are one of several examples – obstetric ultrasound is another[81] – of military technology being developed for domestic uses. Domestic refrigerators were first developed in the USA to deal with the long hot summers. Commercial freezing systems were extended to domestic deep freezers after Clarence Birdseye noticed on a visit to Labrador in the early 1920s how well the flesh of fish and reindeer kept in the Arctic air.[82] Throughout the nineteenth century a plethora of kitchen gadgets – mincing machines, coffee-grinders, food-mixers, knife-cleaners, biscuit-breakers, bread-slicers, apple-parers – you name it, someone has probably thought of it – arrived in the shops, but were of dubious value to most housewives, whose labour was performed in households which lacked facilities of the most basic kind.

Contemporary images of housework depict men and machines as the two factors freeing women from their classic burden. But household technology has had an effect on women's household work very like that of men. Both men and machines do some housework, but both call on women's time to service them. The very presence of an adult man in the household adds to the burden of women's work,[83] according to one estimate by eight hours a week;[84] this 'man effect' helps to explain why women with husbands but without children are less likely than unmarried women to be in paid work. The presence of technology requires similar attention to care and maintenance. It's also a dialectical process, with the technology inviting a change in housework standards, so that tasks are done more often and/or to higher specifications, thus filling freed time with more housework. A comparison of time-budget data for two similar American samples in 1965 and 1974 showed less time spent on cleaning, repairs/gardening/bills, childcare and shopping (minus 14, 6, 2 and 4 minutes per day respectively), whereas time spent on cooking had gone up (by 4 minutes).[85] Factoring in ownership of household technology to the data analysis suggested marginal impacts of technology on housework time: microwaves, dryers and vacuum cleaners slightly reduced it (by a daily average of 16 minutes), while dishwashers, washers, freezers and sewing machines increased it (by 12 minutes); the overall difference was thus an enormous reduction of 4 minutes per day over the ten-year period.

This is hardly surprising, when you consider that the prime purpose of new machines is not to reduce housework time, but rather to make as much money as possible for the businesses which sell them. The advertising of domestic technologies focuses on enhancing the activity the appliance is for, rather than simplifying it or making it quicker; undoing the conventional gendering of household work is certainly not the main aim.[86] Charlotte Perkins Gilman made this point about domestic technology in 1903:

> The domestic hearth, with its undying flame, has given way to the gilded pipes of the steam heater and the flickering evanescence of the gas range. But the sentiment about the domestic hearth is still in play. The original necessity for the ceaseless presence of the woman to maintain that altar fire . . . has passed with the means of prompt ignition; the matchbox has freed the housewife from that incessant service, but the feeling that women should stay at home is with us yet.[87]

WHY DONT MEN CONTRIBUTE

The affinity between men and machines is a recurring theme in the history of domestic labour. In an Australian study of the domestic division of labour:

> men preferred jobs that involved working with machines. A number of men were willing to do the vacuuming because they enjoyed playing with the vacuum cleaner. One woman described how her husband had refused to cook until they purchased a food processor. . . . Several women noted that their husbands had increased their participation in meal preparation after they bought microwave ovens.[88]

A Finnish study[89] provided a quantitative estimate: men did 10–15 per cent more vacuum cleaning when a new appliance was introduced. Much of the technology found in homes today is colour-coded for gender: white for housework items and black or grey for music systems, TVs, videos and other more interesting objects. Microwaves began life with an ambiguous gender, but were then later slipped into the 'white' category.[90]

Much the same observations as have been made about men and household equipment have been made of men's presence in prenatal clinics and labour rooms, where a change in mores (the 'masculinization' of birth) since the 1960s has been fostered by men's fascination with ultrasound scanners and automated fetal heart-rate and uterine contraction monitoring. The machines provide a focus for their gaze, diverting attention from the human beings who are really having the babies, and from mothers' needs for care and support.[91] The mechanization of birth and housework may encourage male participation, but this relationship also works the other way; the initial emergence of technology is often intimately shaped by gender relations. For example, it was

women's use of the early telephone for sociability, rather than conducting business, that originally persuaded a reluctant telephone company to think about
installing telephone services in homes.[92] Detailed case studies, such as Cynthia
Cockburn and Susan Ormrod's history of microwave ovens, show how men
are the 'technically informed actors', drawing women into the product development process only at particular points, as home economists, testers and sales
assistants. Whatever the actual status of men's and women's skills, the attributes of technical competence (him) and being hopeless with machines (her)
form a mutually reinforcing system of gender relations.[93]

The response Cockburn and Ormrod got when they told people they were
writing a history of microwave ovens was that such a project can't possibly
be serious social science. It's the same reaction as I encountered when I started
my own study of housework in the late 1960s, and is one of the reasons why
any attempt to ground speculations about gender and domesticity in firm evidence is such a difficult enterprise. The cultural trivialization of housework
seeps into its science, rendering the two ultimately indistinguishable. A small
example of this is that diaries kept by paid workers and people doing housework define work differently – houseworkers, but not employed workers, note
breaks for a drink or a smoke as non-work time.[94]

■

Christopher Robin Milne, the 'most famous boy in all of children's literature',[95] spent all his adult life trying to get away from his father and the world
of Winnie the Pooh, Eeyore and Piglet that A. A. Milne had created from the
material impedimenta of his son's childhood. 'People sometimes say to me',
Christopher Robin reflected in one of four volumes of autobiography published after his father's death, ' "How lucky you were to have had such a wonderful father", imagining that because he wrote about me with such affection
and understanding, he must have played with me with equal affection and
understanding.'[96] But it wasn't so. His father wrote about Christopher Robin
because he couldn't play with him – not because he could. Milne senior was
an essayist and playwright, a reserved, unfriendly man; his wife was 'well to
do' and used to servants. Christopher Robin was their only child; he was reared
in the manner of their class and times largely by a nanny in a nursery and then,
from the age of nine, at a boarding school, at which point nanny departed to
live in a bungalow, which she naughtily named 'Vespers', after the most
embarrassing of Milne's uses of his son's childhood, a poem about a small
boy kneeling at the foot of his bed reluctantly praying.

As a small child Christopher Robin met his parents briefly three times a
day, after breakfast, after tea and before bed. He later commented that, if
anything had happened to them, he might not have missed his mother and he
certainly wouldn't have missed his father – 'A teddy bear may be worth more

than a father.'[97] When he grew up, he married the daughter of a relative to whom his parents hadn't spoken for twenty-five years, went to run a bookshop in a 'backwater', and was estranged from both parents. Of the legendary Poohsticks Bridge, which is in Posingford Wood, south of Tunbridge Wells in Kent, he wrote: 'It is difficult to be sure which came first. Did I do something, and did my father then write a story around it? Or was it the other way about, and did the story come first?'[98]

The story of A. A. Milne and Christopher Robin is emblematic of a particular type of father–child relationship – one in which the British upper classes have specialized. But it's also part of a much bigger story of childhood as a socially constructed and idolized state which has very little to do with the rights of children as human beings, and a great deal to do with the way adults in a certain cultural setting see themselves.[99] Writers such as Milne, Lewis Carroll, Kenneth Grahame, Edward Lear and J. M. Barrie created a fiction about, and for, children in which it's the children, for a change, who are both aliens and outsiders. They live lives of comfortable hedonism outside the frame of normal social relations, often without the supports of family life. The writers of *Alice in Wonderland*, the Pooh stories, *The Wind in the Willows*, *Peter Pan*, and Lear's curious nonsense rhymes were all solitary, eccentric men who refused to grow up, and who remained fixated on a version of gender and generation from which women as sexually mature people were notably missing. As adults, Carroll and Grahame lived in rooms packed with toys, and Carroll took seaside holidays to meet little girls, armed with a supply of safety pins to hitch up the skirts of those who agreed to paddle with him, and sought to capture their 'innocence' in a collection of nude photos he ordered to be destroyed after his death. Barrie searched out little boys among the prams and nannies of Kensington Gardens, and Lear went for small girls in French and Italian hotels, and, like Grahame and Barrie, used a special baby language for conversing with his friends.[100] Only Grahame and Milne became fathers. They had one son each, the estranged Christopher Robin and Alastair Grahame, who killed himself at twenty by lying down on the rails adjoining Port Meadow in Oxford.[101]

One should not, of course, read too much into the fact that a bunch of strange men wrote books for children but didn't get on with them too well themselves – or at least not in the standard adult way. The parenthood credentials of female writers for children may also leave something to be desired.[102] But there *is* something unnerving in these parables of childhood. Amidst the enchantments of Alice's upside-down world, of Barrie's lost boys, of the riverbanks where Toad inhabited his Hall, of Pooh's Hundred Acre Wood, the labour of women – not just mothers but sisters, aunts, grandmothers, nannies, and servants of all kinds – producing and bringing up children have been written out in a cultural drama of family life which is all about patriarchal authority and paternal absence. Fathers are there symbolically but not actually; their presence in children's lives governs the conditions under which children live, but not children's psychology or social relations directly. There's something demeaning about being too closely involved with children and what has been called 'childwork';[103] children, like women, constitute a minority group, and too much association with minority groups risks contamination.

This is the sense of fatherhood implied by the term 'patriarchal', as in 'patriarchal family'. The rule of the father – the obeisance of wives, children, other family members and servants to the authority of the male head of the household, their disappearance as individuals within this mini-social system which tags them as male property – describes a family form that existed in pre-modern Europe and America. But it's also a more general representational system for social relations, for the hierarchical ordering of status, rights and responsibilities.

Inside the New Man of modern, putatively non-patriarchal families hides the New Father, 'in touch' physically and psychologically with his children, interactive, sensitive, watchful, protective, nurturing – all the things mothers are, and more. 'The figure of the New Father', says Anthony McMahon in *Taking Care of Men*, 'combines the narcissistic consumer and the male nurturer in a way which flirts with the feminisation of men . . . Superficially the appearance is one of sharing and gender convergence, but the underlying story is rather different.'[104]

In the American study of parental time use cited earlier[105] men spent 15 minutes a day involved in childcare in 1965–6 and 14 minutes in 1975–6; the figures for women were 54 and 51 minutes. 'Care of children and adults' took 54 minutes a day for fathers and 1 hour 56 minutes a day for mothers in the British Omnibus Survey in 1995.[106] In one study of 500 British families tracked from the mid-1980s for seven years, the percentage of fathers 'never' or 'rarely' engaging in routine tasks was considerable: 51 per cent for nappy-changing; 57 per cent for getting up at night; 70 per cent for taking seven year olds to school and 58 per cent for looking after them when they were ill.[107] In this study, the 'never/rarely' category was 8 per cent for playing with one year olds; there's a large amount of evidence from different sources demonstrating the tendency of fathers to involve themselves most in the easiest and more pleasurable aspects of childcare.[108] In her study of the domestic division of labour in a Canadian mining town, Meg Luxton reported that:

> The trend has been for men to take on those tasks that are the most clearly defined, or sociable and pleasant ones, while leaving the more ill-defined or unpleasant ones to the women. Repeatedly women noted that their husbands had taken on reading the children a bedtime story and staying with them until they fell asleep, thus 'freeing' the women to wash the dishes and tidy the kitchen.[109]

Fathers can play with their children regularly and often, but absent themselves from the day-to-day work needed to care for young children.[110] The 'negotiated consensual myth' of shared domesticity is considerably stronger for childcare than for housework; over 90 per cent of men and women think childcare should be shared, but only 68 per cent of women and 51 per cent of men think housework ought to be.[111] Good scientific data on fathers' domestic work over time is even harder to come by for childcare than for housework; one particular problem has been how to assess and measure fathers' interaction with their children. One group of researchers gave up and decided to count as 'involved time' all the time fathers and children were in the same room, on the (possibly false) presumption that this would mean they were interacting with one another.[112] Being in the same room has certainly become de rigueur for fathers at childbirth; the 1 per cent of Australian fathers who made it to childbirth in 1962 had become 80 per cent by 1980.[113] However, notably, being present at the birth doesn't mean that fathers do more childcare afterwards.[114]

One reason men do less than the New Fatherhood rhetorics suggest is that fatherhood still means breadwinning; in one British study, two-thirds of fathers worked in the evenings, six out of ten at weekends and nearly one in three at night.[115] Having children means that men work harder, earning on average some 5 per cent more with the birth of each child, a premium that's mysteriously higher when sons (8 per cent) rather than daughters (3 per cent) are born. The birth of boys increases work hours for men by 84 a year, 31 for girls. The sex of children makes no difference to mothers' earnings, which go down anyway. The more children a woman has, the less she earns, even if she works the same amount of time and remains with one employer for the same time as a childless woman.[116] Male children also increase by 7 per cent the likelihood of marriage lasting. 'We can only guess that having a son increases the value of marriage and family for men', said the (female) professor of economics who co-authored the study which produced these findings.[117]

These statistics of what fathers do with, and for, their children have to be set in the broader context of men's attachment to families. The demographics of family life in many countries mean that the biggest single change has been the huge increase in lone parenthood; but this is almost all a rise in lone motherhood. In Britain, for example, the numbers of lone mothers tripled between 1971 and 1995 to become 22 per cent of all families with dependent children, but the figures for lone fathers remained constant over this period.[118] About 8 per cent of all birth certificates in Britain (51,000 births in 1996) don't name the father.[119] More than 10 per cent of all men aged 16–65 in the UK are 'non-resident' fathers – fathers living apart from their children.[120] Between half and two-thirds of these don't support their children financially, and those that do contribute an average of 14 per cent of their net income to this cause – though, as with the data on who does what in the home, it seems that fathers say they pay more for children than mothers say they do.[121] In a large US study of fathers after separation and divorce, nearly 30 per cent of children hadn't seen their fathers in the previous year, and nearly half didn't see their fathers at all:

after ten years, two-thirds had lost all contact.[122] In Australia, a third of all separated men lose all contact with their children, and a further third have very little.[123] Whereas children who don't live with their mothers are almost as likely as those that do to say they have good relationships with them, boys not living with their fathers are twice as likely to report a poor relationship.[124] The physical and sexual abuse of children is another unhealthy change in family life. Fathers are prime abusers.[125]

■

Images of nurturing fathers – a 1980s favourite was a black-and-white post-card photo of a dishy young man naked (from the waist up) holding and kissing an infant – coexist with an uncompromising, cynical recognition that fathers remain marginal: 'Mummy, what are Daddies for?', inquires one toddler of her harassed mother in another postcard cartoon. Both men and women may value men's involvement in the family, but this doesn't guarantee a shared division of labour. The incentive to change, to create a matching fabric of prac-tices for the wallpaper of the New Man groundplan, simply isn't strong enough for most men, and the reason is straightforward: the conversation about gender and social change is one which takes care primarily of men's interests, through the fascinating sleight of hand of denying that these exist. When homes ceased to be the prime manufacturing sites in a money-based economy and system of social relations, it wasn't only housework and childcare that underwent a process of privatization, but the whole domain of personal life as well. This created the opportunity for a perpetual confusion, with women at its centre, between domestic work and personal life. A domestic division of labour which drains men far less than women and reserves to them the pleasurable fringes of house- and child-work is worth preserving (for men). But it can only be preserved because men have the power to ensure that it is.

No major policy developments or gender revolution in attitudes since second-wave feminism have carried this particular oceanic disturbance further forward onto the shore of land-dwelling mammals in most countries. Public policy has kept the domestic division of labour at home where it belongs, in closets of skeletons and/or closely guarded secrets. What is, in this sense, personal never really became political at all.

Homes aren't havens for the people who work in them, as they are for those who come back to them at the end of a working day spent elsewhere. The material effects of housework on mind and body seem like bragging or nagging when housework doesn't really exist as work. It's difficult then to see that public health, like participatory democracy, begins at home, and that most of the housework women do is primary public health work – an effective way of improving the health of populations.[126] Whenever women's accounts of their household work are studied, what stands out is this material experience of labour and responsibility: the 'compulsory' nature of housework and child-care, the unremitting obligation to do it or see that it gets done, the physical effects of heavy manual labour, the psychological effects of social isolation, fragmentation, and trying to stretch scarce resources.[127]

West African women interviewed for a study of work and health used the single term 'tukara' to embrace all these demands of daily life, their multiple responsibilities and heavy workloads:

> The 'tukara' in women's lives is that, you wake up, you sweep, you go to fetch water, you see to the children, you make fire, you cook for them. Then you prepare and go to the farm, you get to the farm. You work until you are tired, you close, and then you set off for home. When you return, you go and fetch water. After that you go to the market, and then you come and cook supper. By the end of the day, you are tired.[128]

The list of duties is different in settings where women's daily work doesn't include subsistence agriculture, and where water comes out of a tap instead of having to be fetched, but there's exactly the same note of fatigue.[129] This is one reason why, in carefully done scientific studies, full-time housewives experience higher levels of physical and psychological symptoms than women doing part-time or full-time paid work.[130]

But the activities involved in taking care of people and their health have a hugely important impact on the psychology of what it means to be an adult. We learn about this from those who care for us, so we need healthy models to emulate. When Virginia Woolf argued that fascism has its roots in the patri-archal family,[131] she wasn't joking, but few people took her seriously. These are the self-same family structures which have produced the New Man and the New Father – fabled creatures whose role is to signify the inability of such structures to unify men and women as human beings. Families are the basic unit of division, not coalition: hence the need for an ethic of intimacy – 'togetherness' – whose floridly seductive scents can mislead men and women into thinking they stand united, at last. But the division of labour in the home splits the men from the boys by shaping masculinity as the *denial* of relation; this is the counterpoint against which the theme of the New Man/Father strug-gles to be heard. Meanwhile, the endless chant of the women goes on; serv-icing households, men and children, women care selflessly in a theatrical dance of femininity which does nobody any good. The sexual division of labour goes hand in hand with male dominance, and male dominance makes men who can't really love and women who can't achieve selfhood.[132] The distortions of gender infiltrate the minds and souls of little children, turning them into aliens and outsiders of the future.

6

Family Values

Tabitha is one year old. She's an absolutely tiny figure on the muddy path leading to the ponds, where the coloured ducks and the white seagulls congregate in overfed hordes, dreading the next few dozen offerings of stale Mother's Pride or, more likely in this part of the world, great sinking globs of organic wholemeal bread. The birds have an interesting distraction just now, since the cold weather has brought frozen stretches of water. The ducks walk cautiously with their stick-like legs over the thin grey ice.

Tabitha's legs aren't stick-like, and she's only been on them for a few weeks, so walking's quite the greatest thing since any form of bread. She wears a wide grin under her bright pink tasselled hat, and mutters engagingly to herself as her very first pair of dark blue Startrite shoes stamp minute footprints in the mud. She's so small she's below most people's line of vision, and, when they do notice her, most of them laugh protectively, though a few pass with stony anti-child faces, as though they themselves never stumbled out into the world like this.

Little children rarely walk straight, and Tabitha is no exception. We constantly have to pull her back from the worse mud of the grass, from the edges of murky pools of water, away from the steep sloping bank down which her cousin Zoe, aged four, has cascaded, clutching our very own plastic bag of stale wholemeal slices. The overfed birds come soaring or swimming over, the ivory seagulls arguing in mid-air over bread none of them really wants. Tabitha flaps her arms and giggles; consternation at the birds' raucous noises shows on Zoe's face. They share 12.5 per cent of their genes,[1] these two, and one parent each brought up in the same household, but their differences are more remarkable (or remarked on by us) than their similarities.

I am a very privileged grandmother. Zoe and Tabitha are an enormous bless-
ing – beautiful, happy, healthy, intelligent, much-loved children, whose parents
are content for me to have an active relationship with them. When Zoe was
born in the middle of a snowstorm in a north London hospital, her parents
were too occupied to hold her, so the midwife gave her to me. Fortunately this
was a hospital which 'allowed' me to be at the birth – some, apparently, forbid
the presence of grandmothers as disturbing influences.[2] I sat with her in the
corner of the delivery room while she stared intensely at, and past, me with
those deeply searching, primordially blue eyes of the newly born, and I looked
at her, thinking, now it begins all over again. I meant the joy and amazement
of caring for new life, as well as its anxieties and responsibilities. Of course,
the wonderful thing about grandparenthood is that one has more of the first
than the second, but that seems only fair, given the huge input of worry and
24-hour-a-day care the first time round.

Becoming a grandmother, like becoming a mother, means entry into a world
of stereotypes. In children's literature, grannies have round bodies, white hair
and John Lennon glasses, and they sit comfortably in armchairs knitting with
a cat at their feet. Even more than mothers in this wishful saga of family life,
grannies are always there, in a fixed, selfless place, permanently available
for grandmotherly duties. It wouldn't do for granny to be off with hennaed
hair, nightclubbing, being entertained to candlelit dinners by lustful men, or
trekking through the Andes.

By the 1980s, research on grandparenthood was marked by this new
concern – of hedonistic habits among grandparents causing them to 'abandon'
their grandchildren.[3] A more prosaic reason for 'abandonment' is being out at
work full-time, which many grandparents are these days: greater youth, health
and economic security compete with employment, of grandmothers especially,
to reduce the time available for active grandparenting.[4] And we shouldn't be
surprised to learn from the literature on grandparenthood, a genre of its own
since the late 1940s, that grandfathers are the 'forgotten men' of the family,
in part because the flow of emotional and practical support comes mainly from
grandmothers, with the men giving mainly financial help.[5] Where is the New
Grandpa?

But, while grandparents are mostly good things to have, our cultural
perceptions struggle between benevolence – grandparents as endlessly kind,
indulgent, playful, helpful and knowledgeable – on the one hand, and suspicion, on the other. There are those who observe that the alliance between
grandparents and grandchildren is formed over a common enemy.[6] Parents and
grandparents can be doomed to fight over methods of childrearing, such arguments representing merely the tip of the iceberg of their own unresolved relations with one another. Mothers and their mothers, and especially mothers and
mothers-in-law, may use the child as a site of contestation. Grandmothers can
be sources of corruption, or irritatingly false wisdom. Australian writer Sally

Morgan's childhood home was sprinkled with cut-up onions by her grand-mother, who fondly thought this would get rid of germs.[7]

A smelly childhood with an extended family grouping is different from the fragrance-free zone of the pared-down nuclear family. But what is different isn't necessarily either worse or better. We all have our individual preferences, views, ideas, experiences and values – and never more so than in relation to The Family. Everyday life is permeated by The Family; our habits, choices, and traditions are steeped in it; we can scarcely consider who we are apart from it, and certainly our cultural practices of psychology and psycho-analysis demand that we constantly interrogate what our childhood families did to us in order to explain why we behave the way we do. This is one of the ways in which The Family has acquired a quite extraordinary importance in professional and policy rhetoric.

The Family isn't the same thing as housework, or the duties and cares of bringing up children; those who speak about it rarely concern themselves with such earthy details, preferring the higher plane of abstract concepts and values. Mirrored in popular thinking, through the usual media routes, these abstractions about family life are often completely out of step with the texture and meaning of our ordinary everyday experiences. It's as though our knowledge about the importance of family life operates on two disconnected levels: the level of dominant discourse, which includes 'expert' opinion and theory; and the altogether different world of how families, in all their amazing diversity, are lived and experienced, including on such mundane occasions as Sunday walks in the park.

When the ducks' stale bread is finished, the last of it, to Zoe's expressed dismay, eaten by Tabitha, who has, as yet, no concept of bread belonging uniquely to ducks, we ascend the path on our slow route to the playground the other side of the hill. To Zoe the word 'park' is synonymous with 'playground', so that, when you're in the park, she fiercely demands to know where it is. This question, I always think, is quite as sophisticated as many of those raised by Oxford philosophers.

Today the playground, touched by frost, is half-empty. Zoe rushes to the roundabout, where she immediately relates to a group of older children and embarks on an energetic, collaborative game of rapid roundabout-swinging. She's been at primary school for a term now, but her two and a half years in a day nursery before that taught her the skills and rewards of sociability. Tabitha, exhausted from the longest walk of her short life, is asleep in her pushchair. Laura, Tabitha's mother, and I sit on a bench talking. Every now and then Zoe, proceeding from one bit of equipment to the next, looks round quizzically for our faces, and we wave and cheer and off she goes again. Adults call this 'touching base'. Then she wants me to push her on the big swing. 'Faster, faster', she implores, putting her head back and laughing, open-mouthed, at the astonishingly blue sky. I am reminded of being pushed on a swing by my father as a child, of the mixed feeling of sickness and exhilaration, of entry into a world of risk with splendidly unknown outcomes. What would happen if you swung too fast and the swing went over the top and you fell off? The child on the next swing does fall off, and his father, a solid Hampstead type, congratulates his son on coping really well with the trauma of the experience. Zoe watches them interrogatively, with that focused, self-interested curiosity of the young.

There are plenty of fathers here, and even a few grandparents. One grandfather sports a baby in a fluffy pink suit tied to him in a baby sling. We bring our grandchildren to the park because we ourselves were taken there as children: the overfeeding of ducks – in other seasons the search for conkers, flowers or butterflies – and the scampering round unimaginative playground equipment are cultural rituals laden with emotional intensity.

Last on the list is the obligatory stop at the café for drinks and snacks. Restored by her power nap, Tabitha is on her feet again. En route she's assailed by a small dog; she sits down, with a plonk, nearly, but not quite, weeping. When we recite this story later, Zoe, experimenting with sibling jealousy at one remove, is quick to point out that she was frightened by the dog as well (although we didn't notice). Finally Tabitha falls headlong in the mud and has to be thoroughly changed before we can go into the café, where she sips something organic through a straw, and Zoe, whose tastes are now more articulately commercial, tangles with something blue and icy which she claims tastes of raspberries.

When we get home most of our clothes go into the washing machine, and the two girls play with an assortment of aged toys retrieved from the attic, and before that from three 1960s and 1970s childhoods: headless Barbies and brownskinned Sasha dolls with crudely cropped hair; scraps of ill-matching dolls' clothes; brown plastic horses; disused purses; a brightly coloured abacus; beads; paisley tins; a strange plastic sofa; scratched matchbox cars; a fumefree garage; and a large box of lego containing half-dismantled aeroplanes and hospitals, which Zoe, with some help, transforms into a café both like, and unlike, the one which disgorges oddly coloured drinks. Each of these items has a history, and it's surprising how many such histories their adult owners remember. It's sacrilege to give or throw these objects away; the artefacts stand for the experiences. Everything about The Family has to be constantly taken out and inspected, because The Family is the source of everything, the cause of all our happinesses and our social ills, the obstinate problem and the bright, facile solution on every policy-maker's lips.

Artefacts of childhood span the often conjoined terrains of domestic labour and Family Values, but housework and childcare – the focus of the last chapter – are not the same as the subject of this one: how we idolize, think and complain about The Family.

■

The Hollywood film *Fatal Attraction* starred actress Glenn Close as Alex, an embittered, sex-hungry, suicidal career woman who uses a one-night stand with a married man to launch a nearly fatal attack, involving knives, bloody baths and a boiled white rabbit, on his immaculate, well-heeled family. The film, released in 1987, raked in over $100 million in its first four months, and provoked a high level of audience 'participation'. *Fatal Attraction* was based on a story by the British screenwriter James Dearden, who, left on his own for the weekend while his wife was out of town, wondered what would happen if he picked up his address book and called a 'girl' he'd met at a party. In the original plot, which was made into a forty-five-minute film called *Diversion*, the man does exactly that, the two of them go out to dinner and to bed, and for him that's the end of it. But she rings the next day and he goes to see her, and that evening she freaks out and cuts her wrists. When his wife gets back, she finds out about the affair, and the man is left trying to sort out the mess.

The original story was one with a moral message about men's responsibility for causing suffering, about the penalties to be paid for human transgression. But in the Hollywood version all that's changed. It's the woman who takes the initiative, and the man is culpable only for being soft and responsive. The wife, a minor character in the original story, becomes central to the plot, and an icon of good wifery, modelled on director Adrian Lyne's own – even her job as a teacher in the original script is removed to make the transformation into a house angel complete. At the end of the film the wife shoots Alex and the camera passes to a slow shot of a framed family portrait.

Both Lyne and Michael Douglas, who played the film's main male character, easily confess to being sick of feminists and convinced that men are having a bad time because of them.[8] *Fatal Attraction* is one of a group of films made around this time (*9½ Weeks* and *Disclosure* are others) which vilify the image of single career women. The strategy, as Imelda Whelehan notes in her book about feminism and popular culture, is to suggest 'that feminism is the preserve of only the unstable, mannish, unattractive woman who has a naturally difficult relationship to her own femininity; such people only want to spoil "normal" women's lives by making them uncomfortable about their "natural" life choices'.[9]

Pitting women against one another is a well-known method for proving abnormality. Such films and texts demonize feminism and champion 'ordinary' women in a divisive and demanding rhetoric which assumes that ordinary women can't be feminists and that feminists must always be extraordinary. Feminists are outsiders but other women, provided they conform to what's expected of them, are rewarded with the badge of insiders.

The first strategy here is occupation of the moral high ground. Who could possibly disagree with such an empty, sanctimonious statement as the value of putting The Family first? Secondly, there's the huge appeal of nostalgia – in its very meaning, *nostos*, the return home – proposing a golden way of living in the past which we should all aspire to in the present. Thirdly, nostalgia's bedfellow is the little matter of rewriting history so as to prop the door unwaveringly open on that golden past. Fourthly, there's the presumption that women's freedom-seeking is responsible for the drop in Family Values; like some mechanistic stock-exchange operation, flooding the market with women's cheap, part-time labour has caused the value of shares in The Family to fall through the floor. This piece of victimization is part of a broader strategy, which is to base contentions about what's happened to The Family, who caused it, and with what consequences on deviously clever constructions of the evidence, thus creating what Amitai Etzioni calls 'factoids'.[10] Finally, there's an equally clever appeal to something which falls midway between sociobiology and real evidence – the demonstrable differences between the genders in their orientation to altruistic labour, for which The Family stands as our clearest and dearest prototype.

In all these manoeuvres, the genders stand unutterably divided. But the usual map is reversed. Men are the angels here, and women the demons. The argument about Family Values takes women's ordinary struggles to be good mothers and provide for their children, and condemns them for misreading the plot, or for writing it in the first place. But women never had that much power. Neither gender did, on its own. So it's even more remarkable that men are the saintly ones, the hurt, the victimized, the abandoned. The politics of Family Values makes men the outsiders, an experience which, if it were true, should enable them to understand better what it's like for women the rest of the time.

■

In European social history, families have always empirically been places of labour, but their competing theoretical representation as safe and harmonious havens of retreat from the harshness of the external world gained credence from the late eighteenth century on. The little family in its little (or big) home promised organic community on a small scale, which could compensate for the perceived disappearance of these kinds of ties from the industrial landscape.[11] Families were made up of biologically related parents and children, but other family members and servants were included, all bound together in a well-differentiated hierarchy.[12] Central to the domestic idyll was the image of the master's return to the home; windows with lamps lit, hearths with fires burning, welcoming doors to be opened on scenes of love, acceptance and security. Women were creators of community within the home, guardians of its physical and moral space. This static, middle-class ideal always failed to capture the diversity and poverty of working-class life, but Victorian sentiment was enormously successful in disseminating an idealized culture of feminine domesticity. Home and Family became synonyms, giving rise to the modern clash between homes as sites of hard labour and exalted moral and personal relations. New opportunities for blasphemy were created; as the American analyst of domestic life Charlotte Perkins Gilman noted poetically in 1935, the sanctity of the home gets in the way of any reasoned social discourse about it:

> You may talk about religion with a free and open mind,
> For ten dollars you may criticise a judge;
> You may discuss in politics the newest thing you find;
> And open scientific truth to the reluctant mind,
> But there's one place where the brain must never budge!
>
> Oh! the Home is utterly perfect!
> And all its working within,
> To say a word about it –
> To criticise or doubt it –
> To seek to mend or move it –
> To venture to improve it –
> Is the unpardonable sin![13]

Christopher Lasch's *Haven in a Heartless World*, published in 1977, gave us a memorable phrase with which to reinvigorate the Victorian ideal. The book's first sentence could almost have come straight out of a Victorian text: 'As business, politics and diplomacy grow more savage and warlike, men [*sic*] seek a haven in private life, in personal relations, above all in the family – the last refuge of love and decency.' Whether Lasch meant men or whether he meant human beings is unclear (and a reason for being careful to say what you mean). Later he recalled his own ambitions as a young man for an ideal family life; children brought up in an extended family or a community of friends: 'A house full of people; a crowded table ranging across the generations; four-hand music at the piano; nonstop conversation and cooking; baseball games and swimming in the afternoon; long walks after dinner; a poker game or Diplomacy or charades in the evening.'[14]

Haven in a Heartless World argues that a number of processes have acted to undermine The Family's role as the moral foundation of social relations: capitalism's extraction of work – or certain forms of it – from the home; the rise of armies of 'experts' on The Family – doctors, psychiatrists, teachers, social workers and so forth; an ethic, caught from the wider society, of competition, individualism and immediate gratification; feminism and the struggle for women's emancipation. Most of the book focuses on the theft of family functions by experts and its contamination by capitalist ethics – two very reasonable points – but feminism comes in for some strong words:

The trouble with the feminist program is not that economic self-sufficiency for women is an unworthy goal but that its realization, under existing economic conditions, would undermine equally important values associated with the family . . . feminists . . . need to acknowledge the deterioration of care for the young and the justice of the demand that something be done to arrest it.

Feminists have not answered the argument that day care provides no substitute for the family. They have not answered the argument that indifference to the needs of the young has become one of the distinguishing characteristics of a society that lives for the moment, defines the consumption of commodities as the highest form of personal satisfaction, and exploits existing resources with criminal disregard for the future. Feminists have mindlessly denounced every such argument as an expression of blind prejudice, but in its own heedless disregard of the family and of the needs of future generations, the feminist movement, like the cultural radicalism of the sixties that gave rise to it, merely echoes the culture it claims to criticize.[15]

Women's equality with men threatens The Family; feminists don't care about children; feminists are thoughtless and selfish. These themes are developed in Lasch's later books, *The Culture of Narcissism* (1979) (which sat, appropriately, for a while on the *New York Times* bestseller list between two self-help books about the joy of jogging and *How to Get Everything You Want Out of Life*[16]), *The True and Only Heaven* (1991) and *The Revolt of the Elites* (1995). In *The Culture of Narcissism*, self-absorption, one of the main themes of American society, isn't just the province of feminists but of all women, and especially mothers, whose narcissistic domination of their children makes them 'seductive and aloof, devouring and indifferent'.[17] It's hardly surprising that children come out wrong. The bitter tone of such allegations is reminiscent of others, notably Philip Wylie's *Generation of Vipers* (see chapter 4 above): one almost senses the rage of small boys against their mothers telling them what to do. In the feminized, expert-dependent family, where selfish mothers have their eyes on the world outside the home, the door is firmly closed on the golden past of paternal authority. Women are insecure, children are traumatized, and men are trapped in impotence and fear of what women have done, and might yet do, to them.

Lasch's psychodramas are part of a distinct genre of 'Family Values' literature which variously relates modern problems with, and in, The Family to changes in men's and women's roles. For Francis Fukuyama in *The Great Disruption* (1999),[18] crime and fatherless families are consequences of the moral corrosion of 'the information age'; women's increasing employment is the original sin. According to the American right-wing theorist Charles Murray,[19] it's the growing fashion for illegitimacy which turns children into hooligans: marriage is the main force civilizing men, by forcing them to focus on breadwinning rather than on less desirable forms of masculine behaviour;

without wives, men simply relapse into barbarism. Amitai Etzioni is kinder to women by discussing what he politely terms 'the parenting deficit', though what he *actually* means is mothers going out to work. His analogy, perhaps inappropriately for one who shares with other Family Values theorists an opposition to the social evils of market capitalism, is of parenting as an industry:

> If this were any other business, say, shoemaking, and more than half of the labor force had been lost and replaced with fewer, less qualified hands and still we asked the shoemakers to produce the same number of shoes of the same quality (with basically no changes in technology), we would be considered crazy. But this is what happened to parenting. As first men and then women left to work outside the home, they were replaced by some child care services, a relatively small increase in baby-sitters and nannies, and some additional service by grandparents – leaving parenting woefully shorthanded. The millions of latchkey children, who are left alone for long stretches of time, are but the most visible result of the parenting deficit.[20]

This understaffed industry produces gang warfare on the streets, drug abuse, lack of work commitment, and welfare dependency.[21]

The rhetoric of Family Values became a central plank of American and British party politics in the late 1980s and early 1990s. British 'experts' such as sociologist A. H. Halsey[22] became part of a cross-party chorus blaming ever-longer lists of social problems on The Family's failure to produce stable parenting. The bulk of this literature, and most of the Family Values agenda in party politics, has come from men, but it'd be wrong to repeat *their* gender errors and blame them for all of it. Women, too, have discovered the cardinal errors of feminism vis-à-vis The Family: expecting women to do it all in order selfishly to have it all; paying scant attention to the realities of motherhood; downplaying the importance of children. Even the early days of women's liberation produced notable pro-family, New Right activists such as Phyllis Schlafly, who adopted anti-feminism when anti-communism had ceased to sell. She called feminists 'Typhoid Marys' for carrying the fatal germ which would kill the 'marvellous' rights of women to be full-time wives and mothers, supported by breadwinning husbands.[23]

When American academic Sylvia Hewlett had her first baby in 1977 she was teaching at Barnard College, Columbia University, which offered no maternity leave; she was back at work within ten days, after which her milk dried up, and an undermining search of the childrearing manuals left her with pervasive guilt about her failure as a mother, and a decision to employ only part-time childcare help, thus further complicating her Barnard schedule. Two years later when she was pregnant again, the exhaustion multiplied; she gave birth prematurely to twins, who died, and was once more back at work in two weeks. Her departmental chairman advised her not to jeopardize her chances of tenure by getting pregnant again. These events taught her how hostile the world of academic employment is to 'working mothers', but also, à la Lasch, the 'gigantic mistake' modern feminists had made: 'They assumed that modern women wanted nothing to do with children. As a result, they have consistently failed to incorporate the bearing and rearing of children into their vision of a liberated life.'[24]

Discovering that full-time employment and motherhood require tiring juggling acts, a point well made in the social science literature,[25] has provoked a genre of conversional literature. In this women, self-labelled as feminists, admit to making politically incorrect choices, or having failed to understand just how anti-motherhood feminism apparently is. The challenge to British journalist Rosalind Coward's youthful 'confident, utopian feminism' occurred when she had her first child:

> when it came to a choice between a daily motorway drive to a job which did not fire my enthusiasm, and a small child to look after at home, the decision was easy. I gave up my university job and went freelance, cutting my hours of work, thereby pushing my partner and myself into a conventional division of labour that neither of us had ever anticipated.[26]

Seven years on, by the time of her book *Sacred Cows*,[27] Coward has to all intents and purposes given up calling herself a feminist. The political problem of the 1990s is men, and feminism's 'extraordinary' success has rendered it blind to the social changes, centred on both Family Values and family practices, that have turned men into the new victims.

One of Coward's main points sits high on the pedestal of pro-family anti-feminism: that the prize of a paid job outside the home fails to acknowledge the experiences and desires of many 'ordinary' women. 'Mummy, I *want* to be a housewife' said a headline in the *Times Higher Education Supplement* in 1996,[28] over a picture of a 1950s mother and daughter wearing identical heart-shaped aprons and engaged in something that looked suspiciously like cake-making. The writer was Catherine Hakim, a researcher at the London School of Economics. Hakim had published an academic paper the previous year called, 'Five feminist myths about women's employment',[29] which got an amazing amount of public interest, considering that it appeared in the relatively obscure *British Journal of Sociology*. The paper's contention, that some women *choose* to stay at home and that many people actually *prefer* traditional gender roles, was based on a reading of the literature on gender differences in employment in Western Europe; the real question, said Hakim, is why social scientists have been so dim about the evidence, preferring the 'feminist' myth that women don't want to be full-time homemakers. Gender differences in employment, according to this viewpoint, aren't the result of discriminatory employment practices, but the outcome of freely made choices. What holds women back from occupying the same positions as men in the labour market isn't lack of childcare and other support for their domestic labour, whether from men, grandparents, the state or the private sector, but their own inner reluctance to sacrifice The Family.

Hakim may not have liked what the media did with her sociological words of wisdom,[30] but she did set herself up as an anti-feminist feminist, forced against her will, as it were, to abandon the canons of feminism in the uncompromising light of counter-evidence. Whether it's the practical side of motherhood feminism is supposed to ignore, as Maureen Freely[31] alleges, or women's preference for 'straight sex', as Lynne Segal[32] puts it, or women's commitment to The Family, as in Elizabeth Fox-Genovese's *'Feminism is Not the Story of My Life'*,[33] the plain fact is that women collude in keeping conventional structures in place. Why they do so is, of course, another matter. Avoiding conflict with men is part of the answer. Women 'let men get away with it', thus creating more pressures for themselves, because rocking the boat could be personally uncomfortable (if not actually dangerous in the light of the statistics of male violence – see chapter 3 above).

An extreme version of the anti-feminism Family Values position in the British pro-family policy literature comes from another journalist: Melanie Phillips. In her *The Sex-Change Society* (1999), monogamous marriage with breadwinning fathers and supported mothers is again portrayed as the linchpin of a moral society, and its disappearance as an institution and key value is again seen as the cause of much anti-social behaviour, including boys' 'underachievement' at school, and men's laddishness and criminality. Phillips' diagnosis slips women into the role of plotting harridans, deciding to do without men, refusing to let men help with childcare, and using them as sperm banks, 'virtual reality' fathers and/or domestic drones. She sees this 'systematic' attack on the traditional family as happening for two reasons: because feminism regards men as an awkward and disposable commodity; and because 'our governing class of intellectuals, politicians, civil servants, lawyers and journalists' refuse to say that marriage and traditional gender arrangements are quite simply the right way to live: 'Non-judgmentalism and feminism thus joined forces to promote the feminised state based on women's independence from men, the destruction of the traditional family, the redistribution of labour from men to women and the decanting of children into substitute care.'[34]

Single motherhood and daycare are especially bad for children. The fecklessness and aggressiveness of men is created by women, either in reality or in myth; thus, for example, the 'evidence is overwhelming'[35] that women are just as aggressive as men, and they pose the main threat of physical violence to both men and children.

■

As Katha Pollitt has observed, 'When left, right and centre agree, watch out. They probably don't know what they're talking about.'[36] In a sense, everyone knows what they're talking about: we all come from, and belong, to families of some sort; we therefore all have an undisputed role as experts. The problem is that our knowledge is internally inconsistent, since family practices are heterogeneous and culturally diverse. The old divisions of class, ethnicity and gender mark out the terrain of Family Life and Family Values in a series of both parallel and cross-cutting strips: ours and theirs; his and hers. When we till this soil we're bound to dig up different sorts of weeds, and the soil itself will nourish many different varieties of seeds, plants and flowers; but you can be certain of one thing: in one way or another we'll all feed off it in one gigantic, long-running picnic.

When I was in Sweden for several months in 1997, I learnt what it was like to live in a culture which had a different attitude to family life and the position of women: one that on the whole accepted as non-contentious women's place in the labour market and children's place in high-quality, state-provided daycare. Everyday life and debate in Sweden have, in the main, consigned these arguments about feminism, women and family life to the past. It's not that all the problems have been solved – far from it; but the policy debate has moved from the realm of rhetoric and ideology to that of practical issues: how can social policy encourage men to be more active fathers, ensure reasonable incomes for lone-parent households, or finance further extensions of daycare?[37] One trivial example was that the academic institution I was working in celebrated the end of the working week with a drink on Friday afternoons at 3.15; this was a tricky disruption for those of us trying to get through an afternoon's work, but any later would have been inconvenient for parents who had to fetch children from daycare. Never mind there was only one parent with a child in local daycare among us: the policy was a *principled* and *consensual* one of promoting parent-friendly workplaces.

One of my brief trips home during this time coincided with a television programme called *Missing Mum*, which presented unpublished results from a study by a social scientist, Margaret O'Brien, on maternal employment and children's educational achievement. The study was of 600 two-parent families in north-east London, and the Panorama television programme cited the 'finding' that 25 per cent of the children of mothers with full-time jobs, but only 11 per cent of those whose mothers were employed part-time, got no GCSEs (General Certificate of Secondary Education). 'Emotive scenes'[38] were used to make the unoriginal suggestion that there's something inherently damaging to children about maternal employment. I reported all this to my colleagues in Sweden when I went back. Their mouths dropped open, literally, in amazement. 'We haven't had that kind of argument about working mothers for decades here', they said.

Like Hakim, O'Brien complained about the media's distortion of her research findings,[39] not least for omitting the fact that the examination fates of children of mothers who were not employed at all were the worst of the lot – 36 per cent of *them* didn't get any GCSEs – but also for generalizing from a

very specific sample of British manual and lower-grade clerical workers to
'working mothers' as a global group of anti-family women.

■

Nobody doubts that there are problems – indeed, quite a few of them are discussed in this book. The discourse of Family Values is partly a reaction to
family practices, and the statistics of family life show long-term trends away
from the model of enduring, multi-child, married-couple parenting. In 1972,
7 per cent of dependent children in Britain lived in lone-parent households;
in 1995–6, 20 per cent did so.[40] In the USA, 12 per cent of children lived in
lone-parent households in 1970, 27 per cent in 1995.[41] Lone-parent families
form 22 per cent of all families with dependent children in the UK[42] – the
highest figure of all countries in the European Union.[43] Until the mid-1980s,
most of the growth in lone parenthood was a consequence of divorce; since
then never-married lone parents have become proportionately more important, as long-term cohabitation has become a more acceptable alternative to
marriage.[44] More children are born outside marriage: 34 per cent of all live
births were outside marriage in the UK in 1995, compared with 8 per cent in
1970; in Sweden the majority of live births, 53 per cent, in 1995 fell into this
category (up from 19 per cent in 1970).[45] Marriage rates are falling and
have been in Europe since 1970. Marriage rates were 8.5 per 1,000 population in 1970 in the UK and 5.5 in 1995; 5.4 and 3.8 in Sweden; 7.8 and 4.4
in France.[46] Between 1969 and 1994 the number of divorces in the UK trebled;
some seven out of ten divorcing couples in England and Wales in 1994 had
children.[47]

There's also long-term decline in fertility rates, which began in the late
1960s. In all European Union countries the fertility rate is now below replacement level. Spain and Italy have the lowest fertility rates in the industrialized
world.[48] Italy is now on course for zero population growth. The reasons for
this are not understood.[49] Roman Catholic leaders argue that young Italians
are choosing material possessions over children, but studies of Italian mothers
suggest that they're reluctant to have more children when childcare and family
life already seem such a struggle.[50] 'No one wants to say the truth – that Italian
women don't want to be mothers. In this country, there is no help for a mother
with a child.'[51]

But most of the argument about Family Values doesn't tangle with the
details of statistics and how to interpret them. It's a stirring, blaming discourse
– a raging invective, rather than a reasoned look at the evidence. The Family
is symbol, not actuality; rarely is the story about real families; instead its language is that of fairy tales, horror stories or science fiction. The contrast was
neatly represented in the picture of a happy family accompanying an article
by Cardinal Hume, the archbishop of Westminster, in a British national news-

paper a few years ago. The article bemoaned the collapse of Family Life, arguing the need for a Royal Commission on The Family to find out what's gone wrong and why. The photograph showed a smiling couple sitting on a chintzy sofa with two little girls, reading to them from a book called *Alice in Wonderland*.[52] As a letter to the paper subsequently observed, this particular family was an unfortunate choice to illustrate the moral point, since one of the children belonged to the mother's earlier marriage, which ended in divorce, the couple employed a full-time nanny, and both worked full-time building the Brook Street Bureau into the first publicly quoted employment agency on the Stock Exchange; they later divorced.[53]

The unarticulated shift from families to The Family and Family Values is more than convenient shorthand: right-wing pro-family anti-feminism relies on just this conceptual shift to ignore the material realities of family life. Take children, for example, as many people do – for they have a signal role in most pro-family ideology. What is clearly not in children's best interests is whatever's happening now that's responsible for so many of them living in poverty. The UK has the highest child poverty rate in Europe: 25 per cent of British children live in households with incomes below 50 per cent of average household income. This compares with 28 per cent in the USA, 14 per cent in Italy, and 4 per cent in Sweden.[54]

Lone parenthood increases the risk of children living in poverty by a factor of between two and eight. For example, the proportion of children living in poor households where the youngest dependent child is less than six years old is 23 per cent in couple and 46 per cent in lone-parent households in the UK, 20 per cent and 66 per cent in the USA.[55] The child poverty risk for children is greatly reduced when there is parental involvement in the labour market: in the UK 25 per cent of children in couple-one-earner households are poor, compared with 7 per cent in couple-two-earner households; 64 per cent of children in no-earner lone-parent households are poor, 28 per cent where these households contain one earner. In the USA the same figures are 32 per cent and 14 per cent for couple households, and 93 per cent and 43 per cent for lone-parent ones.[56] No society can really be child-centred in its values or public policy when so many children are materially disadvantaged. Child poverty is the biggest problem facing The Family in societies such as the UK and the USA today, but nobody would think so from the Family Values debate.

There are other huge gaps in the logic of Family Values discourses: constant slippages between the terms 'feminism', 'mothers' and 'women' and between 'parents' and 'mothers'; strange equations between 'feminism', on the one hand, and women's employment and a principled opposition to children, on the other; and a selective, if not cavalier, use of social facts. It's both 'factually wrong and morally insensitive'[57] to blame modern changes in the family on women and/or on feminism. Then there are the endless recitations of what feminism does, says or means. It *is* very striking that most remarks about feminism in this literature are offered as self-evidently true and are rarely referenced, although they often occur in otherwise liberally referenced academic texts.[58] Feminism is treated differently from other political positions here – socialism, Marxism, environmentalism, communism, communitarianism; only feminism appears as this monolithic thing, scarcely inspected or interrogated face to face, but just there, like Stonehenge, glowering over everything. One wonders what 'feminism', if any, these authors have actually read. Of course, there's no such animal as a feminist Bible with lists of commandments which can be readily consulted to make life easy: 'Thou shalt hate men, children and The Family in equal measure'; 'Thou shalt decant thy children into daycare'; 'Thou shalt work outside the home', etc., etc. If there were, the list of commandments would run into thousands and many would be contradictory.[59]

In the absence of any such biblical authority, it'd be unwise to say authoritatively, 'but feminism said/didn't say this'. The boot's really on the other foot. If people want to argue that feminism said all women should work outside the home or that feminism thinks babies are rubbish, then it's up to them to make the case by pointing to publicly argued positions subscribed to by the majority of those who call themselves feminists. This would be a difficult exercise, because the reality is much more complex: feminism was/is about the claiming of rights and opportunities on a non-gendered, non-discriminatory basis, including the right of entry to, and occupancy of, the educational system and the job market on terms that don't disadvantage women;[60] it was/is about a political analysis of gender which sees particular institutional structures, including families, schools, and legal and healthcare systems, as linked to a more deep-seated and long-lived system of masculine power and privilege, which is itself closely tied in with the economic and moral structures of capitalism;[61] it did/does concern itself with the ways in which the behaviour of men, women and children, including inside families, is influenced by these wider processes of power and economics;[62] it did/does see motherhood as both an experience and an institution,[63] and reproduction as something women deserve control over if they're to have a decent quality of life;[64] and one of its most important springboards was/is the actual experiences of people and families, including women feeling overworked, undervalued, trapped and mistreated, children being poorly looked after and having little control over their lives, and men either feeling marginal to the enterprise, or groaning under the burden of the breadwinning role, or infected by the property-owning germ of capitalism and wanting to possess their wives and children;[65] or various mixtures of these.

Feminism's main target – in so far as it had one – was never The Family in any abstract sense, but rather isolated nuclear families in which mother, father and child/ren are physically and emotionally segregated from other social ties, and therefore likely to become unhealthily and claustrophobically co-dependent.[66] Feminism as a philosophy has never been against men as individual human beings, but against patriarchal social structures and some men's unthinking alignment with these.[67]

■

A key argument of Family Values polemic, which is that feminism led to women en masse threatening The Family by taking employment outside the home, gets the historical processes the wrong way round. Historically, the family wage system – the idea that wages should reflect the costs to men of having families rather than the value of individual labour – was very important in establishing the occupational gender hierarchy which we still have, in diluted form.[68] The family wage system was tied to the breadwinner ethic, but both started to be eroded years before second-wave feminism hit the ground.[69] Some men's resistance to the breadwinner ethic and the flight from family commitment today are products of a moral climate that endorses irresponsibility, self-indulgence and detachment from the claims of others almost as signs of personal health, and which disparages as unfit and overly constraining fixed roles for adults. Similarly, changes in the labour market which have increased opportunities for women's employment were well in train before the onset of feminism. Their roots lie in the technological, economic and legal changes that have occurred since 1945, and which have multiplied the demand for labour in the service industries where women have traditionally been concentrated.

The reasons why mothers take jobs are various and not always to be derived from simple answers to researchers' questions, especially in a climate which has rediscovered 'working mothers' as a social problem. The primary engine driving women's employment in couple families is the need for two incomes to provide materially for children, and it's this motivation which underlies an apparent change in attitudes to traditional gender roles. However, when women are asked that old question, 'why do you work?', the perceived fragility of marriage and the strains of domestic isolation are often just as important as money.[70]

As Barbara Ehrenreich comments in her *The Hearts of Men*, the irony is that both men and women have reacted against similar sets of social pressures by repeating the litany of narcissistic consumerism which has rightly been singled out by critics such as Lasch as socially corrosive. But the sexes have done this in ways that have effectively set them against one another. Men began to disentangle themselves from the claims of family responsibilities first; women next requested similar rights and opportunities; men then complained about women's demands; and through it all The Family both as idealized construct and as actual practice has served as the projected site of many of their discontents.

Family structure is much less important than what happens in families, and the way families interact with the wider social world. Negative personal relationships, not enough money and inadequate social support are much more damaging to the people who live in families than a shortage of traditional Family Values.[71] Children are most influenced by the kinds of relationships they have with their parents and others who care for them, but 'the nurture assumption' – that the parental input is all-important – ignores the ways in which the wider culture is transmitted to children, including through peer relationships.[72]

Men need to take their own responsibility for regarding family life as a tangential asset. The pictures for divorce and the rise in single motherhood are similar. Women petition for divorce about two and a half times more often than men; the most common reason for women to be granted divorces is the 'unreasonable behaviour' of their husbands.[73] An American study of 1,360 mainly white middle-class couples found that women thought about divorce more often than men did, and the strongest correlate of such thoughts was dissatisfaction with husbands' household work: for each of five daily tasks (meal preparation, food shopping, childcare, daily housework and 'meal cleanup') women were 3 per cent less likely to think about divorce if their husbands did it at least half the time.[74] Some studies suggest that men reporting more traditional gender arrangements with respect to childcare and money are more likely to divorce, and that cohabiting women who report traditional gender arrangements with respect to finance are more likely to separate[75] – so the old model may not be the panacea some people would like to think it is.

We all know that the same statistics can be used to prove many different things, but the terrain of Family Values is especially prone to such potholes. Daycare, whether children are 'decanted' into it or parents make informed choices to use it, is a prime example. Lone parenthood and other 'deviations' from the traditional family model are others. In each of these cases research findings are cited selectively and with scant regard for their reliability and generalizability, the point being more to insert them into the rhetoric than to take a clear-sighted look at what's really going on.

Conducting high-quality research and using research data scientifically and without bias are genuinely difficult exercises – but they're even more difficult when researchers don't prioritize science and aren't conscious of the biases they may impart to research 'findings'. 'Science' here means an attitude which respects the clarity and logical coherence of theories, and which confronts these with real-world evidence using systematic and explicit procedures. This is the best method we have of sorting out the facts from the 'factoids'. Social science has a special moral obligation here, and much of it hasn't been nearly moral or scientific enough. The field of family research is especially bedevilled by the problem of how to disentangle correlation from causal association – are the children of lone mothers more prone to psychological problems and low educational achievement because lone motherhood is a pathology and children need fathers, or because lone mothers and their children are more likely to be poor? Are children who live with their fathers better learners than those who don't because fathers are practical and psychological aids to the learning process, or is the input mostly a material one?[76] If we could conduct research experiments with family structure – by randomly assigning some children to have one parent and some to have two – it'd be much easier to answer these questions. But when such research *is* carried out, for example in evaluating the effects on children of daycare by randomly allocating some children to be offered daycare places, the policy 'experts' mostly ignore the evidence in favour of less reliable findings from weaker studies.[77]

Much media attention has recently been given to one particular piece of research – the National Institute of Child Health and Development Study – concerned with the daycare experiences of 1,364 children in ten US cities followed from 1991. The findings of this study were publicized as showing that longer exposure to daycare produces more aggressive children. The loudest 'academic' voice in this public furore was that of Professor Jay Belsky, an American 'expert', now working at London University, who has for years been highly attached to the old idea that daycare ruins the psychologically necessary bond between mother and child; Belsky is well known for propounding the Victorian notion that mothers ought to stay at home.[78] His credibility as an 'expert' on the topic of the NICHD Study is further diminished by the charge of self-aggrandizement made by his co-investigators at some of the other twenty-three institutional sites taking part in the Study; they say he wrongly portrays himself as the Study's lead investigator and broadcasts biased views of the findings; many are no longer on speaking terms with him, and there are rumours of legal action.[79]

The NICHD Study is an example of many that have been used to ring alarm bells about daycare's damaging effects on children. What all these studies have in common is that their design – mainly just observing what happens to children who are in daycare – can't distinguish cause from correlation. The conclusion from well-designed evaluations of daycare as a policy intervention is that children's health and development are promoted by good-quality forms of it, which also produce a positive long-term impact on such current social policy concerns as the incidence of unintended teenage pregnancy, crime and unemployment.[80] One reason may be that daycare promotes socially co-operative forms of behaviour; it's more difficult for children to learn these in one-to-one childcare at home. The finding that children's development is promoted by group care came out of another large study in the USA.[81] But such evidence is replaced in much of the Family Values debate by recycled correlational 'factoids' seemingly proving that daycare damages children, because the children in daycare in countries such as the UK and the USA tend to be poorer than those who aren't, and are thus liable to suffer from the health and educational consequences of poverty. The question in the policy field, and addressed by much of the research, is 'how does daycare harm children?', not 'how might it benefit them?'[82]

■

This may all seem to be dry and academic and off the point, but it couldn't be more central. The social policy challenge is to improve family life, including the experiences of children and parents of both genders, and this means that we need to know what the effects of different social policies and interventions really are.

'Safer births "could cut violent crime"', said a headline in a British newspaper a few years ago.[83] The paper was reporting research presented to a meeting of the American Association for the Advancement of Science which suggested that birth interventions such as instrumental delivery could raise the risk of violent crime among children. If this is so, one likely mediator is the risk of women developing the distress labelled as 'postnatal depression' following such births.[84]

Dominant discourses affect the kinds of topics studied in research, and the prominence given to their findings. Far more research effort has gone into the negative effects of daycare on children than on their vulnerability to poverty; the consequences of lone motherhood for children seem an obvious candidate for endless study, whereas the possible effects on children's behaviour of global rises in obstetric intervention rates is a question that slips on and off the research agenda, leaving no visible impression on the policy discourse at all. In the same vein, we know something about the effects on children of their mass consumption of television violence,[85] but the information available is slight compared to the size of the 'working mothers' literature. There's no joined-up policy thinking capable of placing these different sorts of research evidence next to each other, in order, for example, to judge the relative effects producible by extending daycare versus providing more sex education in schools as strategies for reducing unintended teenage pregnancy; or by providing social and financial support for disadvantaged families compared with introducing crime education programmes for young people 'at risk' of taking up lives of crime. Politicians and policy-makers like answers that confirm what they already 'know'.

■

There's nothing very new in the discussion about Family Values. There were those in the early nineteenth century who warned that the disappearance of authority in the household was a cause of national turbulence.[86] At the end of the nineteenth century across Europe, the falling birth rate, combined with evidence of family poverty, provoked similar policy concerns, which were then addressed with innovative legislation.[87]

Most people still live in families, and family attachments, whether based on law and/or biology or not, remain central in most people's lives. But families have, for a long time, meant different things to men and women. Men have the luxury of seeing them as havens, even when the tie of economic responsibility is broken; women know families as places of unpaid labour, caring and altruism – a moral code which is out of step with that of the wider society, and therefore largely undervalued by it. The negative consequences of this for women's self-esteem and wellbeing become progressively more pronounced as society goes further in the direction of greedy individualism.

The sense in which The Family and the interests of women as citizens are at odds with one another is a real one, even when you subtract the amplification of the Family Values debate. Women's biological responsibilities for bearing and breastfeeding children are a relatively minor part of this conflict; most of it inheres in men's refusal to own The Family as a site of labour and commitment. What men don't do for families inhibits women's ability to claim citizenship. You can't turn the clock back to a world where it's morally right for only men to be citizens. And men's reluctance as individuals and as major players in the policy-making process to prioritize the safety and wellbeing of children reveals the rhetoric of Family Values as just so much hot air.

In the story about two praying mantises talking in the garden, the first says, 'It's tougher than I thought being a single parent.' The second says, 'Yeah. Maybe we shouldn't have eaten our husbands after all.'[88] Today's concerns about how what's happening to families may magnify the narcissism and consumerism of modern society are issues that need to be taken very seriously indeed. But narcissism and its converse, altruism, are deeply gendered activities. Clinging to romanticized images of The Family in the past won't help us to sort out the mess we're in now; neither will the invention of new myths about the power of women to devour men or about the corporate conspiracies of feminism to denigrate men, children and family life, or about the ease with which ordinary women can demolish The Family in a single stroke by taking part-time, low-paid jobs to help pay the bills and get them out of the house. Public policy needs to catch up with the game, which is one about the demise of the breadwinner ethic, the right of both genders to citizenship in the public world and of children to life-enhancing forms of care, and everyone's struggle to negotiate new forms of personal and reproductive life in a world which offers few models aside from competitive self-gratification. 'The question', as Barbara Ehrenreich phrased it in her *The Hearts of Men*, 'is whether we rebels of both sexes have enough in common to work together toward a more generous, dignified and caring society.'[89]

■

In the middle of writing this, I go downstairs to find Tabitha charging up and down the kitchen pushing a wooden duck on wheels. She has a snotty nose and is wearing a wonderfully cheerful multistriped jumper. When she sees me, she lies down on the floor giggling, inviting me to blow raspberries on her tummy. Whoever said that feminists don't love children must have a real talent for ignoring evidence. How could anyone possibly believe that the love and labour of childrearing isn't the most worthwhile of all, and how could we ever build a society that is so dismissive of this most necessary and gratifying human activity? Are we absolutely mad?

7

The Rape of
Mother Earth

The chrome yellow of daffodils shouts from the green edging of country lanes, and from cottage gardens, where the nonchalance of nature is replaced by the artifice of man – or, more likely, woman – and the screams of the daffodils are carefully mixed with the politer notes of pale blue hyacinths, baby pink and yellow primula and the slightly tired remains of winter heathers. Beards of aubretia tumble out of old stone walls, in far more shades of purple than man or woman could possibly have imagined. A blue and white marbled sky is stretched above the rural scene, with a silvery sun responding weakly to the daffodils' brightness, but at least it signals the end of a long winter.

The fields under the shining sky hold clumps of cows, a few horses, and lambs and their mothers, plump off-white shapes arranged picturesquely on the horizon, under trees or curled up by brown fast-running streams. The sheep eat the rich green grass and the lambs nibble at it too, in between rushes to butt their mothers for liquid refreshment. The air is full of the sound of the lambs and sheep calling to one another: the maternal calls rasping and throaty as if from too much smoking, the lambs' high and thin with incipient panic. Then the lambs lie down in pairs, the picture of innocence, white lambs with pink ears: candidates for the slaughterhouse, dinner for human tables, output for the GNP, victims of the biggest industry of all – meat addiction. This natural landscape is grotesque, really, a factory feeding man's bad habits, a nasty arrangement of capitalist artefacts. It's certainly no arcadia of untrammelled rural happiness; time isn't on the lambs' side; in the middle of life there's always death.

The fields and the footpaths all around wear yellow notices the same colour as the daffodils: FOOT AND MOUTH DISEASE KEEP OUT. The notices list a series of relevant laws and regulations and the possibility of a £5,000 fine for transgressions. Yellow and black striped ties across gates and stiles flap crossly in the wind; puzzled walkers make the best of it, cats and rabbits can't read, and in the black trees where the fields dip before rising to the next village, rooks croak menacingly from their perilous nests, not unlike the politicians whose messages of warning about all this have been laughably ill-timed.

Foot and mouth disease is a highly contagious viral disease affecting ungulates or cloven-hoofed animals – cattle, pigs, sheep, goats, deer, buffaloes, elephants, hedgehogs, rats. It produces fluid-filled blisters and erosions in animals' mouths and noses, and on their teats and feet. It causes pain, lameness, loss of appetite and reduced lactation, but it rarely kills, and most affected animals recover. Foot and mouth disease is endemic in many countries outside Europe and North America, including China, Mongolia, Saudi Arabia and Argentina. Because the virus isn't killed by freezing, salting or curing, it survives for long periods in meat intended for human or animal consumption. This current outbreak in Britain probably started in February 2001 at a farm in Heddon-on-the-Wall, Northumberland. A report on this farm some months previously had noted the problem of substandard food being fed to pigs, along with the appalling conditions under which many were living: 'in absolute squalor including rotting carcasses of pigs littering the unit; piglets were literally being eaten alive after being born amongst the rest of the pigs'.[1]

By 7 April 2001 there were 1,105 cases of foot and mouth disease in the UK, and the outbreak had spread to Northern Ireland, France and the Netherlands. In the UK 764,000 animals had been slaughtered and many had been burnt in vast funeral pyres which ruined the first signs of spring by spreading the smell of noxious barbecued meat across the country,[2] and releasing more deadly pollutants than all the country's most dangerous factories combined.[3]

But the number of animals killed by then in the foot and mouth epidemic was only slightly more than the number of pigs, sheep and cattle killed routinely every week in the UK for food.[4] Foot and mouth disease and BSE – bovine spongiform encephalopathy, or mad cow disease – are the latest afflictions to raise searching questions about our cultural dependence on meat, and about the politics, economics and values which drive the meat industry.

The first cases of BSE were identified at the end of 1986, though it probably started in the 1970s. The original cause is unknown. BSE leads to irreversible 'spongy' changes in cows' brains and is always fatal. Both foot and mouth disease and BSE are transmissible to humans, but foot and mouth disease is an inconsequential infection in human beings, whereas the human form of BSE, vCJD – variant Creutzfeldt–Jakob disease – condemns its victims to years of suffering and death. It took ten years for BSE to be recognized in humans; by September 2000 there were eighty known human victims in the UK, most of them, for unknown reasons, young people. The first was probably Vicky Rimmer, who fell ill with an obscure neurodegenerative disease in the summer of 1993 at the age of fifteen; her grandmother said she'd become ill through eating infected beef, though only some medical experts agreed with her at the time. Vicky died in 1997 after four years in a coma.[5]

Humans can catch vCJD from eating infected meat, but there are many other possible pathways. Products derived from cows have an alarming number of points of entry into the food chain. Blood and other waste from slaughterhouses can contaminate sewers or rivers and are ingredients of commonly used agricultural fertilizers; tallow, the fat extracted in the process of rendering bovine 'material', and gelatine, from skin and bones, are used to make a wide variety of foodstuffs; tallow is processed as glycerine, used in jellies and baking, and a constituent of most cosmetic creams, ointments and toiletries applied to the skin, lips and eyelids – the highest-risk cosmetics are those promoted in the anti-ageing industry, which contain processed brain extracts, placental material, spleen and thymus; gelatine appears in food, is used as a coating for tablets, and also to make cosmetics, glue and photographic chemicals; bovine tissues and fluids help to make fire extinguisher foam, buttons, handles, lubricants, racquet strings, paint and cleaning agents, and also many medicines, including vaccines, hormone treatments and protein products, such as heparin; they're found in sutures and medical devices such as heart valves, and collagen used in implants. 'Herbal' products aren't exempt, either; herbal dietary supplements, for example, commonly list 'orchis', which is made from bulls' testicles, and one such product contains seventeen different types of bovine offal including the pituitary, pineal gland, placenta, prostate and thyroid.[6]

BSE became an epidemic because of an intensive farming practice – the recycling of animal protein in animal feed, or feeding cows to cows. The disease was transmitted by means of common practices employed in slaughterhouses and the rendering industry. The processes used to strip the spinal cords and peripheral nerve tissues of cows meant that infected meat was passed on to both animals and humans. The Inquiry set up at a cost of £27 million[7] to investigate the BSE epidemic in the UK described the slaughtering procedures in use at the time in its report, published in 2000:

> In a typical large slaughterhouse animals were unloaded from lorries into the holding area and then moved towards the slaughter hall in single file along special passageways. They were then fed one by one into a pen for stunning. There were two methods of stunning used for adult animals. The captive bolt method involved firing a metal bolt into the animal's brain, leaving a hole in its skull; the non-penetrative concussion method involved firing a mushroom-shaped bolt at the animal's head, thus rendering the animal unconscious without penetrating its brain or skull. It was common practice, following captive bolt stunning, to insert a pithing rod into the hole in the skull in order to cause further damage to the brain and spinal cord, and thus to prevent the animal from kicking due to reflex muscular action.

Once the animal was unconscious, its hind legs were shackled and it was hoisted to an overhead rail, known as the slaughter line. Hanging with its head closest to the floor, the animal could then be moved around the plant to the various stages of the slaughtering process. It would first be moved along until it was directly over the bleeding trough, where it would finally be killed by severing the large blood vessels in its neck . . .

Once bled, the carcass was moved down the line to be dressed. First the forefeet, hind feet, udder or pizzle [penis] were removed with a knife, then the hide would be pulled off with a powered hide puller, and after that the head would be cut off. . . . Then the abdominal wall would be cut open and the internal organs would tumble out onto the inspection table. Organs such as liver and kidneys which would go for human consumption were separated out and sent to the 'offal room' for sorting. The rest of the 'abdominal mass' was sent, either down chutes or in containers, to a different area known as the 'gut room'.

The final stage in the process involved splitting what was left of the carcass and removing the spinal cord.[8]

BSE is a peculiarly British disease; by April 2001 more than 17,000 cows had been affected in the UK, compared to less than 1,500 elsewhere, and there had only been four recognized cases of vCJD outside the UK. One very important factor identified by the BSE Inquiry Report was practices in UK slaughterhouses, which varied 'from the lamentable to the good, with the majority tending towards the former rather than the latter'.[9] Until the 1980s the rendering industry was virtually unregulated in terms of any quality control and production methods.

The practice of feeding animals to animals has been going on for many years. Currently in the UK and other European countries, blood, poultry, offal, feather meal and tallow are all legally permitted animal by-products which can be used to feed farm animals.[10] In the UK, the use of animal protein in animal feed was recognized in the Fertilizers and Feedingstuffs Act of 1926, but it became widespread only after the Second World War, when there was a drive to reduce the reliance on imported food. This was achieved by a combined breeding and feeding programme which produced cows capable of high milk yields when given high-protein food. Farmers supplemented their cows' forage-based diet with protein concentrates bought from animal feed manufacturers. Animal protein was used rather than soya protein because it had similar effects on milk supply but with the added advantage of helping to dispose of animal waste.

'Many have expressed the view that it was not surprising that a practice as unnatural as feeding ruminant protein to ruminants should result in a plague such as BSE', commented the BSE Inquiry Report; 'Objection can be taken to many intensive farming practices on ethical or aesthetic grounds.'[11] BSE and foot and mouth disease aren't simply local problems, temporarily putting the world off British meat and the British countryside. Their spread and

aggressive treatment are signs of a profligate and destructive culture which
has become the paradigm for the 'good' life, while making this literally impossible for most of the world's population, now and in the future.

■

We live in a toxic world which poses a major threat to public and personal
health. It's a world which is intrinsically and perpetually exploitative of human
and natural resources, including entire ecosystems. It turns nature and human
health into commodities that are brokered in the market place just like any
other. Most environmental damage happens because of the earth's domination
by the Western lifestyle, which depends on constantly rising levels of consumption, an addiction to technology, and meat as the basis of the human diet.
Its most toxic aspect is the form of material and social relations which produces the logic that the earth's resources are there to be bought and sold and
to create corporate and individual profit. Some people are far more culpable
than others. The most culpable are men and male-dominated transnational corporations. The major victims are the poor, women and children, and the populations of Third World countries. The script of female nature being tortured
by male culture is also directly inscribed on women's bodies in the medical
management of that most 'natural' of all activities, childbirth. And all of this
is the global background to the more domestic policy concerns of Western
countries: what to do about our roads, our criminals, our men, women, children and The Family.

On planet earth there's virtually no nature unaffected by 'man' any more.[12]
Nature has been replaced by the managed world. For example, almost 80 per
cent of food in the UK is processed in some way, with eight processors holding
60 per cent of the market. This manufactured food culture has homogenized
not just our diet but the countryside, turning it into just another factory.
Farming in the industrialized West has little to do with nature; the countryside
is simply home to an industrial-scale food production, with chemicals making
natural cycles irrelevant, and agricultural 'products' traded on world commodity markets. Wildlife and plantlife have no place in such a landscape:
skylarks, lapwings, corn buntings, barn owls and grey partridges; adonis blue,
marbled white, chequered skipper and pearl-bordered fritillary butterflies once
abundant in British nature, are now disappearing; wild flowers such as corn-
flowers, pheasant's eye and shepherd's needle are increasingly rare. Some
97 per cent of Britain's meadowland has disappeared. The distribution of
twenty-four out of twenty-eight farmland bird species contracted during the
1970s and 1980s, and seven species are thought to have been more than
halved in population numbers.[13] Chemical treatment of the land reduces
nature's 'free' pollination services – a third of the US's agricultural production
is from insect-pollinated plants, which makes the services of the threatened

honeybee 60–100 times more valuable than the honey it produces.[14] Some three-quarters of the world's plant species have been lost since the beginning of the twentieth century. Africa has lost half its tree cover in the same period.[15]

Our food is laden with chemicals, with genetically modified materials and other hidden health risks; our rain is acid; our drinking water harbours pathogens; our bodies soak up radiation from all the electrical technologies – computers, mobile phones, televisions, microwave ovens, electricity transmission lines – that have become an accepted part of modern life; the air we breathe carries lead and dangerous particulates; and the ground is contaminated with chemical spills and hazardous waste. Planet earth is warming up because of 'man's' multiple environmentally damaging activities. The earth's climate is driven by energy from the sun, most of which arrives as visible light. The energy absorbed by the earth's atmosphere must be sent back out to space as infrared radiation, but this process is blocked by the formation of so-called 'greenhouse gases' in the atmosphere. The main greenhouse gases are carbon dioxide, ozone, methane, nitrous oxide, and the chlorofluorocarbons (CFCs). Levels of all of these have been rising. These rises are associated with human activity, specifically our addiction to energy: our inability to get out of our cars and give up the products of an energy-hungry industry and agriculture.

Emissions of carbon dioxide come mainly from burning coal, oil and natural gas; methane and nitrous oxide are produced mainly by agriculture and changes in land use; ozone comes from car exhausts and CFCs derive from industrial products. Cars and cattle, producing carbon dioxide and methane respectively, are the two most significant causes of global warming. In its most recent report, the Intergovernmental Panel on Climate Change doubled the estimate made in its report four years previously, predicting a rise of 5.8°C by the end of this century.[16] The Panel observed that there is now 'strong evidence' that most of this rise is attributable to human activities.[17]

Polar ice shelves are cracking, mountain glaciers around the world are dissolving, temperature-sensitive coral reefs are bleaching under stress, the timing of the seasons has changed, and the geographic range of optimal temperatures for various plants, animals and disease vectors is clearly shifting.[18] The consequences of global warming are likely to include widespread flooding and the disappearance of entire island nations; the destruction of arable land; deaths due directly to higher temperatures and the extension of diseases such as malaria; the loss of many plant and animal species; continuing deforestation and desertification; and the build up of toxic and radioactive wastes.[19] The effects of global warming will be greatest for Third World countries which depend on agriculture, and where even slight changes in climate can ruin rural livelihoods by further depriving already water-stressed regions. Estimates of the scale of the malnutrition likely to result from global warming range from 18 million to 412 million; the people at greatest risk are those in sub-Saharan Africa, south and south-east Asia, tropical areas of Latin America, and some

Pacific Islands.[20] The governments most resistant to implementing the modest targets of the Kyoto treaty for reducing greenhouse gas emissions are the most guilty; the USA, where 'pollution president'[21] George W. Bush declined to sign the agreement, has 4 per cent of the world's population but is responsible for a quarter of its greenhouse gases.[22]

■

Worldwide, passenger cars account for 13 per cent of carbon dioxide emissions.[23] In Europe, the transport sector produces 20 per cent of the total.[24] The average American car driven the average American distance – 10,000 miles – in an average American year releases its own weight in carbon dioxide into the atmosphere.[25] Road traffic creates particulate matter, a form of air pollution associated with respiratory and heart disease and mortality: about 40 per cent of all particulate matter comes from traffic. World Health Organization estimates put the number of deaths every year in Europe from air pollution at some 170,000; the figure for the USA is around 100,000.[26] Diesel engines emit 80 per cent more particulate matter than petrol engines; because some of these particulates are finer (due to the incomplete burning of fuel in diesel engines), they are more dangerous and probably carcinogenic.[27] Lead, which has been added to petrol since the 1920s, finds its way into water, food and human lungs through lead dust in the atmosphere released from car exhausts, and is associated with multiple health problems, including birth defects, high blood pressure, and developmental problems in children.[28] Even with new limits on emissions, vehicle exhausts are responsible for some 20,000 tonnes of lead every year in the air over North America;[29] in 1996 70,000 tonnes of lead were still being added to petrol worldwide.[30] Unleaded petrol can contain up to 2 per cent of benzene, which is both carcinogenic and neurotoxic.[31] The volume of such pollutants has increased enormously: for example, the 25 million gallons of benzene produced worldwide in 1940 had become 2 billion gallons in the USA alone by the early 1980s.[32] Poor households without cars tend to be located in areas where air pollution from vehicle emissions is greatest, thus compounding the disadvantage of not having access to the personal benefit of motorized transport.[33] As many people now die from traffic-caused pollution as from traffic accidents.[34]

Noise pollution is a side effect of car use. Ninety-two per cent of England and Wales is significantly affected by road transport noise; 65 per cent of people in European Union countries are exposed regularly to sound levels that produce serious annoyance, interference with speech and sleep and other health effects.[35] Exposure to even relatively low levels of noise for long periods can raise blood pressure, disrupt children's cognitive development and increase psychiatric disorders.[36] Prolonged exposure to high-intensity noise is associated with increases in cardiovascular disease and cholesterol levels, mental health problems and birth defects.[37] A study of an airport in the Netherlands showed a 'dose effect' relationship between the number of aircraft overflights at night and the use of cardiovascular drugs; the increased incidence of heart trouble and hypertension in the community couldn't be explained by other factors such as age and sex.[38] By 2050, aviation is also likely to become one of the main sources of greenhouse gas emissions, accounting for some 10 per cent of climate change.[39]

■

'The Western image of the good life is one in which there is a slab of steak on every plate and a chicken in every foil bag.'[40] For most of the people interviewed in northern England in a study of gender and food in the early 1980s a 'proper meal' had to have meat at its centre and it had to be cooked by a *woman*. The insistence on meat came mainly from the men; when asked if they would cook differently if they were living on their own, 156 of the 181 women said they would, with the main changes being less meat and fewer 'proper' meals.[41] Nella Last, who kept a diary for Mass Observation during the Second World War, and spent much of it searching for worthwhile bits of meat to cook for her husband, commented, 'I would sooner have fruit and vegetables than meat. If I catered only for myself, I don't think I'd eat 3 d. worth of meat a week.'[42] Surveys of diet today show gender differences in diet, with women in general eating more wholemeal bread, fruit and vegetables than men.[43] In the nineteenth century, wives who were 'delicate' or who didn't go out to work were said never to eat meat at all.[44] When the meat supply is limited, men receive it: meat-eating is a measure of a virile culture, so vegetarianism is equated with emasculation and femininity.[45] This means that stereotypically masculine activities such as violence and war require meat to fuel them: soldiers must eat the blood of red meat in order to be properly warlike. In the Second World War, meat rations for men in the army and navy provided them with two and a half times as much meat as the average citizen.[46] The link between virility and meat explains why nineteenth-century doctors recommended vegetarianism as a cure for young men's self-abuse. The association between vegetables and women links second-class food and second-class citizens: neither vegetables nor women can make it on their own. We talk about 'the meat of the question' and 'beefing up' something, but 'like a vegetable' connotes passivity and dullness.

The true story of how the West was won is a story of ecocide and genocide in the interests of meat addiction.[47] Britain's attachment to beef drove the direction of much colonial policy. The aristocracy and emerging bourgeoisie developed a capacious appetite for fat-laced beef – so much so that in 1283 Edward I issued a decree limiting the number of meat courses that could be served at a single setting.[48] A record of a three-course dinner served in the reign of Richard II a century later included larded boar's head, pottage of liver and kidneys, beef, mutton, pork, roasted rabbit, duck, pheasant, chicken, linnets, sparrows, hares, teals, woodcock and snipe.[49] Enormous, prize-winning cattle served as a metaphor for the wealth and avaricious consumerism of the British ruling classes. New pasturelands were sought in Scotland, Ireland, Argentina, Australia, New Zealand and North America. Ranchers on the American plains killed off the buffalo and drove the Indians away to clear space for cattle-grazing. By the mid-1880s much of the American West belonged to British bankers and business men who insisted on beef artificially fattened with corn. The final chapter of the 'cattlization' of the Americas was a systematic attempt by multinational corporations to create a single world market for the production and distribution of beef: 'the world steer' as the equivalent of 'the world car'.[50]

The huge appetite for beef in industrialized nations is a form of conspicuous consumption that drives us to demand more and more land and resources. Most meat-eaters consume far more protein than their bodies can absorb; the saturated fats and cholesterol in animal flesh are major health risks. Red meat is high-status meat, while items like sausages and beefburgers are low status; 'strong' meat, that is dark meat, is especially suitable for men, and weaker white meat for women. The phrase 'to eat humble pie' is a reference to the habit of giving the poorest cuts of meat, for example entrails or 'umbles' of venison, to the lowest-status people.[51] As Carol Adams put it in her *The Sexual Politics of Meat*, 'People with power have always eaten meat.'[52] In the food diaries kept by the households in the northern England research, men and boys ate more high-status meat than women and girls.[53] It's a pattern that reflects a wider cultural picture of nutritional inequalities between social groups. John Boyd Orr's classic survey of British diet in the 1930s, *Food, Health and Income*, showed an almost linear relationship between social class (defined in terms of income) and meat consumption: the poorest ate 17.0 ounces of meat per week, the richest 29.3 ounces.[54] Around a quarter of the food expenditure of the working poor went on meat, with a dependence on bacon and the cheapest bits of cattle and sheep – heads, tails, kidneys, tongues, hearts, livers and skirt, often taken from the carcasses of diseased animals sold cheaply by farmers to black market butchers.[55] The consumption of livestock products rises with income. World meat consumption has leapt from 44 million to 184 million tons since 1950, and annual consumption per person has doubled – from 17 kilos in 1950 to 33 in 1994.[56] Local epidemics affecting perceptions of meat such as foot and mouth disease or BSE cause a tiny dent in this mountain of meat-eating; in the UK 5,000 people a week are reported to 'go veggie'.[57] Similarly, the organic food market in the UK has grown from £40 million in 1987 to £267 million in 1997,[58] but less than 0.5 per cent of British farmland is farmed organically.[59]

Many vegetarians recall a particular moment of exposure to the reality of animal-eating, usually in childhood, that put them off meat for life. The French romantic poet Alphonse de Lamartine had a pet lamb that the family cook suggested was big enough to be killed one day; his mother then led him through a slaughterhouse:

> I saw some men, their arms naked and besmeared with blood, knocking a bull on the head, others cutting the throats of calves and sheep, and separating their still heaving limbs. Streams of smoking gore ran along the pavement. The thought of these scenes, the necessary preliminaries of one of those dishes of meat which I had so often seen on the table, made me take a disgust to animal food.[60]

But growing and killing animals for pleasure is such an accepted part of our culture that most people never think about it. The first vegetarian social movements were a product of the eighteenth century, when flesh-eating was conceived as injurious to human character and as encouraging insensitivity to all forms of suffering. The reasons for vegetarianism can be ethical, aesthetic or practical. Pythagoras, an early, articulate defender, took the view that the cosmos was made up of interconnected living things; the possible migration of human souls into animals made eating these particularly inadvisable.[61] The vegetarian doctor Anna Kingsford was against meat on moral grounds; people were always asking her to join this or that peace movement, she complained, but if you want people to stop fighting like beasts of prey you must first stop them living *off* beasts of prey: 'universal peace is absolutely impossible to a carnivorous race'.[62] Kingsford also objected to meat-eating because it tied women to slaughterhouses, butchers' shops and dead carcasses, observing that, 'Butchers are the Pariahs of the western world; the very name itself of their trade has become a synonym for barbarity'; she thought that the simple and wholesome cooking required by vegetarianism would directly aid women's emancipation.[63] The poet Percy Bysshe Shelley was a florid vegetarian, believing that vegetables and distilled water would cure all ills; in his *A Vindication of Natural Diet* (1884), a title self-consciously modelled on his mother-in-law, Mary Wollstonecraft's, *A Vindication of the Rights of Woman*, Shelley made a most modern point about the fundamental resource issue of a carnivorous culture: 'The most fertile districts of the habitable globe are now actually cultivated by men for animals at a delay and waste of aliment absolutely incapable of calculation.'[64]

There now three times as many domestic animals as human beings on the planet,[65] including 1.28 billion cattle which graze on 24 per cent of the available landmass.[66] As Jeremy Rifkin phrases it in his *Beyond Beef*:

> The devastating environmental, economic, and human toll of maintaining a worldwide cattle complex is little discussed in public policy circles. Most people are largely unaware of the wide-ranging effects cattle are having on the ecosystems of the planet . . . cattle production and beef consumption now rank

among the gravest threats to the future well-being of the earth and its human population.[67]

Meat and fish production damage the earth in a number of ways: overfishing of the Earth's oceans has nearly eliminated many species of fish – nine of the world's seventeen fisheries are now in serious decline;[68] cattle-grazing requires the cutting down of rainforests, which endangers animal and human populations; intensive grazing methods cause soil erosion and nutrient depletion; chemical fertilizers used on animal feed crops produce nitrous oxide, another greenhouse gas; ammonia from animal waste and agricultural fertilizers contributes to acid rain, which kills aquatic and plant life; and methane-emitting livestock have a significant direct input to the 'greenhouse effect' and global warming. Cattle and other animals reared for meat release some 73 million tonnes of methane – the most potent of the greenhouse gases – into the air each year; this represents some 20 per cent of all the methane released into the atmosphere.[69] Shelley's point about land being given over to animals instead of feeding human beings directly means that millions in the developing world are deprived of the grain and water they need – a pound of wheat takes about 1,000 pounds of water to grow, but a pound of beef takes much more.[70] A third of the world's grain harvest is eaten by cattle.[71] If the world's affluent could reduce their consumption of grain-fed livestock products by 20 per cent, this would release 128 million tons of grain for direct human consumption, enough to serve the needs of world population growth for more than four years.[72]

In the UK alone, 800 million animals are slaughtered for food each year.[73] This institution of butchering is a uniquely human achievement – all other carnivorous animals kill and eat their prey themselves. As investigations following the foot and mouth epidemic revealed, many animals are reared in very poor conditions. For example, about 50 per cent of the 800,000 breeding sows in the UK are kept indoors in cramped stalls, and they give birth in farrowing crates which are barely larger than the sow herself, so that sores and abrasions are caused when she tries to turn round. Broiler chickens are housed in large, windowless sheds in blocks of up to 100,000 birds, with each bird allotted a space equivalent in size to a sheet of A4 paper. The chickens are killed after six to seven weeks (a chicken's natural lifespan is around seven years), during which time the litter on the shed floor isn't changed: by the time of slaughter, 80 per cent of it consists of the birds' faeces.[74]

As the report of the BSE inquiry explained, most cows are killed by throat-cutting, following stunning by a captive bolt pistol which is held to the cow's head. When cows are agitated and struggling, stunning may fail because the bolt isn't positioned correctly, and then the animal is still conscious when its throat is cut. Electrical stunning is used for pigs, sheep and calves, but many are inadequately stunned because of inaccurate positioning, or too brief or too low a voltage. Chickens are killed by hanging them upside down shackled by their feet to a moving line, dragging their heads and necks through an electrically charged water bath, moving them to an automatic neck cutter and bleeding them before putting them in a scalding tank which makes plucking easier. One study found that about 25 per cent of birds were still alive when they got to the scalding tank.[75]

■

All the various polls and surveys conducted show that women are more likely than men to be vegetarian. For example, a National Opinion Poll of 1,004 adults conducted by Dalepak and the Vegetarian Society in May 1998 reported that 10 per cent of women and 4 per cent of men agreed with the statement 'I am a vegetarian and eat no meat at all.'[76] In a nationwide survey in 2000 carried out by the Vegetarian Research Group in the USA, 7 per cent of women and 2 per cent of men said they never ate meat.[77]

There's a strong historical link between feminism and the defence of animal rights because animals, as well as women, are mistreated by patriarchal societies. Early feminists such as Charlotte Perkins Gilman, Anna Kingsford, Mary Wollstonecraft and Susan B. Anthony saw vegetarianism and animal rights as an essential part of the feminist agenda.[78] Women in nineteenth- and early twentieth-century Britain supported animal rights almost as much as they argued for the suffrage; many made connections between the sufferings of animals used in medical experiments and the fates of women at the hands of the medical profession (from which they were then excluded): 'the vivisected animal stood for vivisected woman: the woman strapped to the gynaecologist's table, the woman strapped and bound in the pornographic fiction of the period'.[79]

Feminist defences of animals and attacks on 'corpse-eaters' are tied to the principle of accountability for what we do to others' bodies: 'we are a community of subjects . . . not a collection of otherized objects'.[80] Some 80 per cent of animal rights and environmental campaigners active today are women.[81] Women's defence of the rights of animals not to be tortured and not to be eaten is part of a much broader picture in which they predominate amongst those who campaign on or write about, issues of environmental concern. The simplest explanation for this is that women's social and domestic roles both require and facilitate a greater degree of empathy with other people and other forms of life than do masculine roles. Research on environmentalism suggests that a sense of community with others may be nearly as important as concern over the biosphere in generating environmentalist politics.[82] Caring *about* follows from caring *for*: caring labour and emotional connection are intimately related.[83] Appreciating multiple points of view is also a characteristic of minority groups generally, since making one's way successfully in the world calls for an understanding of power relations.[84] Another way to put this is to suggest that women see through social myths with greater clarity than do men.[85]

In Charlotte Perkins Gilman's novel *Herland*, three men – a playboy, a doctor and a sociologist – chance on an all-female culture where for two thousand years women have given birth to daughters unaided by men. Herland is a meatless place, where fruit- and nut-bearing trees, grains, berries, citrus fruits, olives and figs are carefully cultivated as sources of food. The men are amazed by the absence of cattle, but the women explain they need the land for feeding people, and the absence of meat helps to deal with the problem of war.[86] Vegetarianism is a theme in many feminist utopian visions, where it joins other forms of non-violence, co-operation and lack of hierarchy to construct the framework of a society based on values quite different from those driving our malignant own.[87]

■

In 1966, American astronauts gave us startling new images of our planet as a brilliant blue globe spinning effortlessly in infinite space. These pictures suggested the intense fragility and organic wholeness of the earth, a concept of the earth itself as Other, detached and separate. Although the pictorial image was new, the idea is an ancient one: the ground we tread, the seas we sail, the nature we enjoy or plunder that coats the surface of that spinning Christmas-tree bauble is our first woman, Mother Earth. Mother Earth must be respected: she's her own person, full of wisdom and integrity. She nourishes us, and we are literally starved without her beneficence. But her maternal resources are limited, and if we draw on them too much, there'll be nothing left. Being female, she needs our protection; she can't be relied on to defend herself against the vices of human greed and violence. In the aftermath of that epic moon trip, the advertising industries located in a geographically small, but socially dominant, patch of Mother Earth promoted ecological consciousness as a commodity to end, and sell, all. The appeal to buy 'natural' products precisely played on the theme of the earth as a helpless, beloved woman – a victim to be rescued from degradation by acts of communitarian altruism.[88]

Humans, animals and plants are gendered, but so are entire universes of natural and material objects. Every plumber knows about male and female connections; the eighteenth-century Swedish scientist Carl Linnaeus inscribed the gender of plants using the same raw sexual graphics – and went on most chauvinistically to divide plants into classes according to physical properties of the 'male' botanical organ.[89] In English, ships and hurricanes are traditionally female, while 'man/he/his' are supposed to signal everything human. Other languages make much more of a business about grammatical gender, attaching it to all kinds of inanimate objects.

The twentieth-century reconstruction of Mother Earth is a new twist to an old cultural narrative about the essential links between women and nature. In Latin and the romance languages of medieval and early modern Europe, nature was a feminine noun; in Western history and philosophy, and also in many others, the femaleness of the earth – the earth as the original, idealized nurturing mother – is a critical part of pre-scientific organic cosmology. Nature is, on the whole, beneficent, although she can also be unkempt, wild and chaotic. Roman writers such as Ovid, Seneca and Pliny recited the metaphor of planetary maternity as a defence against the abuses of early deforestation and mining. Mothers are not for mutilating. Mother Earth was alive, and sensitive. It was in her womb that the natural resources of precious minerals and metals were gestated, making mining the ecological equivalent of forced surgical delivery. Interference with the earth's natural processes isn't only unethical, it can lead to catastrophic sterility.[90]

Such beliefs acted as brakes on exploitative environmental behaviour – until the so-called Enlightenment and the Scientific Revolution came along. These resulted in a sadistic twist of the gendered metaphor; while nature retained her female form, this now acquired the status of territory to be interrogated and owned by the male knower – *homo sapiens*, as Linnaeus aptly named him. The first step was taken by Copernican theory, which replaced the female earth with the sun, traditionally regarded as male, as the centre of everything. The womanly earth was transformed into 'just one tiny, externally moved planet circling in an insignificant orbit around the masculine sun'.[91] In Francis Bacon's phrase, 'man's domination over the universe' became the object of intellectual knowledge and scientific understanding.[92] Nature was the place where men intervened, dissected and manipulated in order to know, and masculine science was alone capable of exposing nature's hidden laws. Hence the designation, by the feminist scientist Sandra Harding, of Newton's mechanics as a 'rape manual' because of their characterization of nature as a woman 'indifferent to or even welcoming rape'.[93]

Somewhere between 1500 and 1700 the organic metaphor for the earth was displaced by a very different view of the earth and the cosmos as machines, as assemblages of material parts whose constitution and operation could be mapped and explained by the new religion of science. A feature of this world-view which is still with us today is dualistic thinking and the alignment of paired opposites: culture/nature, man/woman, town/country, science/art, reason/emotion, mind/body, public/private, active/passive, dominant/submissive, adult/child and so forth. Each couplet has its own history, but the total configuration adds up to much more than this. For example, the pairing of man/woman with culture/nature helps to legitimate man's domination of both women *and* nature.[94] Of course it depends where you stand as to whether one couplet features more prominently than the others. The triad of gender, women's naturalness as the Other, and the symbolism of nature as a wayward female whose secrets must actively be penetrated and mastered provides a highly plausible framework of connection and explanation from the viewpoint of the argument of this book.

■

The first pesticide, 4-chloro-2-methylphenoxyacetic acid, or MCPA, was a by-product of the Second World War. It was developed in Britain by the Ministry of Agriculture, aided by the 'War Ags', the War Agricultural Executive Committees which controlled how farms were run, and in conjunction with the chemical company ICI. At the end of the war MCPA was marketed to UK farmers as methoxone or 'cornland cleaner', and before long was being applied to almost all UK cereal crops.[95] Hailed initially as a symptom of progress, of 'man's' ability to master nature through technology, evidence of the harm caused by pesticides was clear by the mid-twentieth century: the development of resistance in insects; long-term persistence in the environment; accumulation in human, animal and plant tissue. Hundreds of billions of tons of pesticide have now been released into the global environment. Some six billion pounds of pesticides are sold annually in global markets, and applied to 'crops, forests, lawns, gardens, parks, highways, rail lines, power lines, lakes, ponds, swimming pools, office buildings, aircraft, shops, hospitals, schools and daycare centers'.[96]

Over 70,000 out of some 4 million 'known' chemicals are now in common commercial use, and 1,000 new ones are produced each year.[97] The US Environmental Protection Agency has registered 30,000 separate pesticide products and permits 325 active pesticide ingredients to be used in some 675 different types of food. In 1995 the US Food and Drug Administration's Total Diet Study found widespread contamination above 'safe' limits of many foods commonly consumed by adults.[98] A third of the active pesticides that are permitted within the US are suspected of causing cancer in animals, another third are thought to disrupt the central nervous system, and others to interfere with the endocrine system.[99] Some 86 per cent of high-volume chemicals in the European Union (those produced at a rate of over 1,000 tonnes per year) lack even the minimum set of basic safety data, and 21 per cent have no safety data at all.[100] About 75 per cent of the 2,500 or so chemicals in large-scale use don't have sufficient toxicity data publicly available for even a preliminary toxicity assessment.[101] The worst environmental toxics, known as 'Pops', or persistent organic pollutants, are extremely toxic in small amounts, and they also travel long distances via air currents, thus endangering people and wildlife all over the world. They have long molecular chains which can't be broken down by sunlight, water, acids etc., and when breakdown does occur, it can create chemicals that are even more hazardous than the original substances – for example dioxin, a by-product of combustion processes involving chlorine.

These chemicals accumulate in humans and wildlife instead of breaking down harmlessly into the environment, a fact which helps to account for the alarming finding of more than 350 chemicals, some of which are banned in most countries, in breastmilk.[102] Corpses today keep much longer than they used to because of all these accumulated chemicals.[103]

The environment has never been poison-free, but until the 1950s, pollution was largely a local problem. Now it's a global one. The charity Oxfam has estimated that there are some 750,000 pesticide poisonings annually, with around 375,000 occurring in the Third World.[104] Herbicides make up 90 per cent of total pesticides in weight and have largely replaced mechanical methods of weed control; rain washes herbicides off crops and into streams and drinking water; in 1995 14 million people in the USA drank water with detectable herbicide residues.[105] Nitrates are the biggest chemical pollutant of Britain's water supply; since the 1950s applications of nitrate fertilizer to crops have increased sixfold.[106] Potassium fertilizers, in widespread use, add some 3,000 curies of radioactive potassium to US farmlands every year.[107]

Chemical companies don't choose the safest chemicals, they choose the cheapest and most saleable. One of the most widely used food additives is sodium nitrate, which forms potent cancer-causing agents (nitrosamines), and is in nearly all processed meat, bacon, ham and sausages. It's used to prevent botulism and other infections, but the same end could be achieved with constant refrigeration, or with ascorbic acid (vitamin C): the companies prefer sodium nitrate because it stops the meat turning unattractively grey with age, which is what would happen naturally.[108]

In 1993, United States industries released 1.3 million tonnes of toxic chemicals into air, land and water.[109] In the UK, 35 per cent of all 'unauthorized' emissions to air, land and water come from the chemical industry.[110] For example, ICI's plant in Runcorn, Cheshire, one of the worst offenders, released over a thousand tonnes of both trichloroethylene and 1,2-dichloromethane into the atmosphere in 1998. The Friends of the Earth factory watch website[111] lists factories in England, Wales and Northern Ireland according to the amounts of recognized pollutants they contribute to air, water or land. In 1999, three of the worst offenders were ICI, which contributed 28 per cent of the national total of known carcinogens to the air; ACORDIS, with 56 per cent of the national total of recognized reproductive system toxics; and AES Drax Power Ltd, which produced 38 per cent of the national total of suspected immune system toxics.

Pollution and poverty go hand in hand. A study by Friends of the Earth linking the location of UK factories with data on area household income found a concentration in poor areas; for example, in the north-east, over 80 per cent of polluting factories are in areas with below average household income: in Teesside, one area has seventeen factories, and an average household income of £6,200 – 64 per cent less than the national average. Overall, 66 per cent of all cancer-causing chemicals emitted into the air come from factories in the most deprived 10 per cent of the country.[112] These findings repeat those of work on 'environmental justice' in the USA, where poorer communities, particularly ethnic minority communities, bear the greatest burden of toxic pollution. 'Environmental racism' leads companies deliberately to site their factories in poor, Black communities, where they expect less opposition to development and also weaker enforcement of environmental regulations.[113] The related practice is chemical industries and other big corporations locating their operations in Third World countries, where environmental regulation is less stringent, and communities are unlikely to organize active opposition. Some 80 per cent of all pesticide production is in the hands of twenty companies with annual sales of $25 billion, and most of this production is in Third World countries, to keep labour costs down and avoid environmental constraints.[114]

Chemicals affect health in known and unknown ways. They enter the body through the nose, mouth or skin, and disturb normal metabolic function. Increasing numbers of chemicals are being shown to disrupt the function of the endocrine, immune and nervous systems of both humans and animals. Most exposures to chemicals occur as mixtures, rather than individual chemicals, but this issue is barely considered in chemical regulation.[115] Children are especially vulnerable to the health effects of chemicals, because they eat a smaller range of foods than adults, they drink more than they eat, they tend to consume types of food and drink which are high in pesticide residues, their bodies are still developing, they have a lower ability to break down chemicals, and they breathe air closer to the ground, which is more contaminated. Monitoring of pesticide effects has been based on the 'norm' of the healthy adult white male body, so the effects on children, pregnant women, women generally, old people, ethnic minorities and the ill are largely unstudied. In his book *Our Children's Toxic Legacy*, John Wargo comments that, 'The global scale and intensity of pesticide use ignite questions of such enormous diversity regarding chemical movement, fate and biological effects that we may never fully understand the consequences of past licensing and use behavior.'[116]

Rachel Carson's thesis in *Silent Spring*[117] was that the chemicals likely to cause the greatest damage to the human reproductive system and which affect the largest number of people are those used to manage crops. The example of Love Canal, described in chapter 3 above, where the Hooker Chemical Company dumped more than 20,000 tons of toxic waste with severe adverse effects on reproductive health, has been duplicated many times in the USA and elsewhere as large areas of ground, turned into waste dumping sites, have been saturated with chemical contaminants.[118]

The developed countries produce 90 per cent of the world's hazardous waste.[119] US industry works with more than 400 highly toxic chemicals, producing more than a ton of hazardous waste per citizen per year.[120] In the UK about 80 per cent of all municipal waste, produced at an average of 4 pounds, per person per day,[121] goes to landfill sites (14 per cent is incinerated, only 6 per cent is recycled).[122] Some 80 per cent of the population live within two kilometres of current or closed landfill sites, so any attributable excess of health risk is extremely important in public health terms.[123] The US General Accounting Office has estimated that there are between 130,000 and 450,000 contaminated commercial and industrial sites in the USA, with a potential clean-up bill of $650 billion.[124] The scale of pollution in some places is phenomenal. For example, in the mid-1980s some 430 billion tonnes of domestic waste were discharged into the Mediterranean every year, with coastal industries contributing some 5,000 tonnes of zinc, 1,400 tonnes of lead, 950 tonnes of chromium, 10 tonnes of mercury, and 90 tonnes of pesticides; a further 500 tonnes of mercury were estimated to be dumped into this enclosed sea by rivers and the atmosphere.[125] All these hazards are sustained by inadequate regulatory systems, dependent mainly on voluntary action from the chemical industry. Efforts at global chemical control have so far been very limited: for example, the Persistent Organic Pollutants treaty covers only 12 chemicals out of the 70,000 in common use.[126]

By the mid-1980s, there were over 500 nuclear power plants globally, producing an increasing proportion – some 20 per cent – of the world's electricity, and some 400 research reactors.[127] Using nuclear fuel to make electricity produces 2,000 times more radiation than burning coal for the same purpose.[128] The average nuclear reactor yields 30 tons of unusable matter a year, mostly spent fuel rods used to hold uranium pellets, which need to be kept safe for 250,000 years.[129] No effective solutions have been found for the long-term storage or use of nuclear waste.[130] Originally hailed as a safe and clean method of generating power, the hazards of nuclear energy have manifested themselves many times over. The accident at the Chernobyl Nuclear Power Station in the Ukraine in 1986 discharged 200 tons of radioactivity into the environment – more than the Hiroshima and Nagasaki bombs put together.[131] Less than four months after the well-publicized Three Mile Island incident in Pennsylvania in 1979, when a nuclear reactor dosed the community round it with 15 curies of radioactive iodine, there was another at Church Rock, New Mexico, when an earth dam holding radioactive uranium tailings burst, releasing 93 million gallons of liquid waste and more than 1,000 tons of solid waste into the Little Puerco river, an important local source of water for washing and watering livestock. Official signs warned people not to drink from the river, but the Navajo herdsmen who lived in the area pointed out that animals can't read. This was the worst incident of radiation contamination in the history of the USA, but it got much less attention than Three Mile Island because it occurred in a relatively isolated place, and affected mainly Navajo Indians.[132]

But by far the worst of the world's nuclear 'accidents' has been the explosion of some five hundred atomic bombs above ground. Atmospheric testing has added to the atmosphere some 27 billion curies of iodine-131, 34 million curies of caesium-137, 22 million curies of strontium-90, and 350,000 curies of plutonium-239 along with other long-lived fission products. Each person on earth is estimated to have received from this fallout a dose of four to five millirems per year – enough to cause 67,500 fatal cancers and more than 43,000 genetic defects.[133] One estimate of the overall cost in human misery and death of total global radiation exposure puts it at 385 million cancers from nuclear bomb production and testing, 9.7 million from bomb and bomb plant accidents, 6.6 million from the 'routine' discharges of nuclear power plants, and 588 million children born with deformities.[134]

Military activity is probably the most serious polluter globally.[135] Emissions from the operations of the armed forces account for 6–10 per cent of global air pollution, and the US military is the largest generator of hazardous waste in the world.[136] One hidden side effect of war is the vast amount of radioactive and otherwise toxic waste generated by the production of chemical, biological and nuclear armaments, even in peacetime.[137] High explosive and blast munitions, incendiary weapons, and accidental detonation of weapons, including landmines, result in widespread, long-lasting destruction of human habitats and the disappearance of entire ecosystems.[138]

■

Forty-nine of the 100 biggest economies in the world today are nation states, and 51 are transnational corporations (TNCs).[139] TNCs are the main institutional agents responsible for the global environmental crisis. The biggest TNCs have annual sales which exceed the output of most developing countries;[140] the UN Centre on TNCs lists 600 with annual sales of more than $1 billion, equal to more than a fifth of the world's total industrial and agricultural production; 74 of these account for more than 50 per cent of total sales.[141] TNCs produce a vast range of goods and services for world and domestic markets. They dominate foreign direct investment, which trebled between 1992 and 1997, while over the same period development aid to Third World countries declined. Six TNCs handle about 85 per cent of the world grain trade; 11 account for 81 per cent of world agrochemical sales; 15 control 85–90 per cent of the world cotton trade; 3 account for 83 per cent of the world trade in cocoa; and 5 are responsible for 70 per cent of the trade in tobacco leaf.[142] Cigarettes are heavily promoted in Third World countries, especially to women, and profits are rising rapidly, as smoking and smoking-related illness are on the increase.[143] Converting the land now used for growing tobacco to grain would provide enough grain to support the entire population of the world for six months, and would substantially reduce mortality rates and healthcare costs.[144]

Supported by the governments of the economically powerful countries, TNCs maintain the North's economic power and the profligate lifestyles of the rich by exporting the environmental costs of resource-hungry and pollution-intensive industries to the Third World, using free trade economics. Economic 'logic' supports this move by citing the lower costs of pollution in the Third World, where there's more illness and death anyway and life is cheaper.[145] Profits are maximized by moving operations into countries with low taxes and labour costs and weak environmental regulations. The repression of labour organizations is a global trend supporting such moves.[146]

The activities of TNCs contribute directly to global climate instability by promoting an energy-intensive, export-oriented model of development. More goods travel more distance as local markets close. The average chicken travels 2,000 kilometres before being eaten; one kilogram of food transported globally generates 10 kilograms of carbon dioxide; non-local food production makes six to twelve times more carbon dioxide than does local production.[147]

One of the main functions of TNCs is to encourage the world's poor to switch to a Western diet – McDonald's beefburgers, Kentucky Fried Chicken, Coca-Cola, Pepsi-Cola and Seven-Up. This is a financially and nutritionally disastrous move for the TNCs' victims, and there's no way the world can (or should) sustain an American diet for everyone. TNCs operate with little government control and usually no sense of accountability to developing countries and peoples. Much of the damage to the world's fisheries is being done by trawlers owned by TNCs based in the West and Asia. Mining, the world's fifth largest industry, is a major area of TNC activity and a significant cause of the displacement of Third World populations.[148] TNCs are also major players in deforestation, clearing land for cattle, using the wood directly for products such as chopsticks and toothpicks, and growing profit-making plantations of eucalyptus trees and oil-palm. Sometimes the links with increasing global climate instability are even more direct; behind 'pollution president' George W. Bush's refusal to co-operate with the Kyoto treaty lay a presidential campaign donation of more than $1 million from the giant oil company Exxon, the third largest company in the world, based in Bush's home state of Texas.[149]

Over a third of maize seed sales in developing countries is now in the hands of TNCs.[150] The first genetically engineered corn crops were harvested by farmers in the USA and Canada in 1996: genetic manipulation of plants has been added to the TNCs' profit sheets. The big chemical companies have restyled themselves as 'life sciences corporations' to buy up seed and biotechnology companies, and form new, even bigger conglomerates, using genetic engineering to establish monopolies on life in the form of what are disturbingly known as 'anti-life modifiers' or 'terminator technologies'. In 1998 the world's largest cotton-seed company, the US Delta and Pine Land Company, together with the US Department of Agriculture, developed a patent on a technique that means seeds can only be planted once; the seed's capacity to germinate if planted again is switched off, so that it becomes sterile. TNCs are patenting seeds that local farmers have used and carefully husbanded for generations. Staple foods and local farming resources are turned into the inventions of Western corporations and Western scientists, a move which threatens the independence and food security of over a billion poor farmers in Third World countries, and will have unknown consequences in terms of the earth's biodiversity.[151]

The expansion of TNCs marks a particular kind of economic power, where corporate capital, a professional and technocratic elite and state functionaries form a monocultural historical block, sharing practices, programmes, rhetoric and a 'manipulative mode of thinking about nature and the social world'.[152] Giant TNCs are run by a small number of key decision-makers, who have ready access to governmental decision-makers and the heads of international agencies, and use their money and power to control government policies and set the rules of the global economy game so that these operate in their favour. Power, worldwide, shows a skewed distribution towards men. In the Third World, women hold 13.5 per cent of administrative/managerial jobs and 6 per cent of Cabinet posts; in the First World the comparable figures are 31 per cent and 5 per cent,[153] and 95 per cent of senior management positions are held by men.[154]

The nuclear industry has traditionally been exclusively masculine territory. A study of 650 nuclear decision-makers in the early 1990s found that 99 per cent were men.[155] In male technostrategic discourse, the death of innocent bystanders is renamed 'collateral damage'.[156] The Manhattan Project in the USA had its own linguistic code: the atom bomb was 'the gadget', plutonium was the 'product'.[157] Such power is experienced as creative, even as reproductive: 'The inventors of the atomic bomb called its first test "Trinity" after the Holy Trinity, the united Father, Son and Holy Spirit, "the male forces of Creation" . . . Scientists at Los Alamos called the atom bomb, "Oppenheimer's baby"; those at Lawrence Livermore [a laboratory in California] called the hydrogen bomb "Teller's baby".'[158] The Hiroshima and Nagasaki bombs were known as 'little boy' and 'fat man'; in the early tests bombs which exploded according to plan were called 'little boys' – the duds were 'little girls'. When the French did nuclear tests in the South Pacific, all the craters gouged out of the earth by the bombs were given female names.[159] President Truman called the Hiroshima bomb 'a harnessing of the basic power of the universe'.[160]

■

The vulnerability of the human reproductive system and the developing fetus to the harmful effects of chemical and other forms of pollution means that issues to do with motherhood are at the heart of many pollution controversies.[161] But the biology of motherhood represents another kind of power which has historically been controlled by a male-dominated medical and scientific establishment. The scenario of colonization marked by 'man's' 1969 moon landing flows seamlessly into the birth of the world's first 'test-tube' baby in 1978: one points to extraterrestrial migration, the other suggests new interventions and 'procedures' for procreation, a process traditionally consigned by Mother Nature to a hidden place frustratingly beyond the scientific gaze.[162]

Investment in in vitro fertilization (IVF) and other reproductive technologies was stimulated by lateral scientific thinking – from cows to women. The Seed (*sic*) brothers, one a physicist, the other a surgeon, ran a cattle-breeding business on a farm outside Chicago. In 1970 they began transferring embryos between cows, and then tried the same manoeuvres in women, setting up a private clinic, Fertility and Genetics Research Inc., which financed the work leading to the first 'flushed-out' embryo in 1983. The baby was born by Caesarean in 1984; the Seed brothers considered that the whole process ought to cost couples at least 'as much as a new car'.[163]

One of Mother Nature's best-kept secrets has been the sex of the unborn child. Since in the cattle industry only females are needed in the dairy industry and only males in the beef sector, cattle breeders had a strong incentive to develop successful sperm separation techniques which would allow for only one sex to be produced. One such technique was patented by an American ranch owner in the late 1970s, who claimed it worked even better in humans.[164] The most common justification offered for researching sex determination in humans is the avoidance of sex-linked diseases (which occur most commonly in males), but there are other important motives to do with controlling both population and nature. When sex determination and selective abortion became technically possible in the early 1980s, physicians in India, 'the heartland of sex-selective abortion',[165] set up businesses to detect and abort girls.[166] A UNICEF Report for Bombay in 1984 on abortions following prenatal sex determination noted that 7,999 of the 8,000 fetuses were female.[167] Worldwide, techniques of sex determination are mainly used to practise what has been called prenatal 'femicide',[168] 'arguably the most brutal and destructive manifestation of the anti-female bias that pervades "patriarchal" societies', and which accounts for the disappearance of hundreds of thousands of girls every year.[169]

'Egg farming'[170] treats the bodies of women as fertile fields to be harvested. Both biotechnology in agriculture – reducing nature to a pool of genetic units – and reproductive technology – reducing women to egg hatcheries and wombs for hire – are justified with the promise of doing better than nature can, despite evidence to the contrary in the form of high failure rates and disabling side effects. For instance, the live birth rate per treatment cycle for IVF in the UK is around 18 per cent.[171] Death rates for babies conceived in this way are some 32 per cent higher than for normal conceptions.[172] Women undergoing 'assisted reproduction' are more likely than other women to suffer from a number of health problems, including 'ovarian hyperstimulation syndrome', significant bone loss and a possibly enhanced risk of breast and ovarian cancer.[173]

Other kinds of profit motive are never very far away. The year Louise Brown, the first test-tube baby, was born in the UK, the doctors 'responsible' for her birth, Patrick Steptoe and Robert Edwards, set up Bourn Hall, a private IVF clinic. They sold the clinic ten years later to Ares-Serono, a multinational pharmaceutical company and a major producer of infertility drugs, which used the UK as a base to develop a world market in assisted conception technology. The company's logo was nothing to do with women at all; instead it portrayed the childhood fable which cuts mothers out of the childbirth drama altogether – a stork carrying a baby in a sling hanging from its beak.[174]

'Reproductive technologies' include 'the full range of biomedical/technical interferences during the process of procreation whether aimed at producing a child or preventing/terminating pregnancy' – hormonal and mechanical contraception; sterilization; abortion; prenatal monitoring; surgical and other techniques used in childbirth; sex selection and determination; artificial in-semination; IVF; embryo 'flushing' and transfer; and other techniques such as cloning, on which scientists are currently working.[175] All these procedures involve the invasion of the female body in a mechanical process of 'dismem-berment' which separates out body parts and the body from its personal and social context.[176] Mechanical mothers don't use their breasts to feed their babies; the artificial feeding of infants, the mark of 'developed' societies, was primarily an invention of male paediatricians interested in building up a pro-fitable scientific business for themselves,[177] and thoroughly frustrated by their inability to penetrate Mother Nature's secrets in order to access accurate quan-titative information about infant nutrition. Early paediatric advice was to breastfeed by the clock for only a few months or weeks, but humans are pri-mates designed to breastfeed 'on demand' for two to seven years.[178] Today, many mothers don't even give birth, either: close to one in four in both the UK and the USA have their babies cut out of their abdomens in a major sur-gical operation which is euphemistically called Caesarean 'section'. In the UK Caesareans were 2 per cent of all births in 1953, and 18 per cent in 1997: in 2001 the rate was 21 per cent.[179] In the USA the 1999 rate was 22 per cent.[180]

Caesarean surgery is life-saving in some circumstances, but no region in the world, according to the World Health Organization, can be justified in having a rate above 10–15 per cent[181] (though the true figure is probably closer to 8 per cent[182]). The risks to mothers from life-threatening complications such as haemorrhage, sepsis and uterine rupture are four times higher following Caesarean birth;[183] it's also a risk factor for reduced fertility and complications in any subsequent pregnancy and birth.[184] Babies born by Caesarean are more likely to be premature and have respiratory distress, and are less likely to be breastfed.[185]

In countries with mixed private and public healthcare, the growing fashion for Caesarean surgery is closely tied to obstetricians' lucrative and demanding work schedules, which require careful management if the doctor is actually to be present at the birth.[186] 'Low-risk' women having private care have significantly higher rates of Caesarean surgery than other 'low-risk' women, and higher rates of other interventions such as induced labour, epidural analgesia, instrumental deliveries and episiotomy.[187] It's impossible to explain the rise in Caesarean surgery by the increase in the average age of mothers and the number of older women having pregnancy problems.[188] But it is highly related to obstetricians' fears of litigation in a context in which, if something goes wrong, they can't be blamed for cutting mothers' bodies open, whereas they can if they 'fail' to do so.

Cutting the baby out through the mother's abdomen is at the extreme end of a continuum of intervention. In the UK, induction of labour by rupturing the membranes or using oxytocic drugs rose from 8 per cent in 1962 to 20 per cent in 1995; 'instrumental' deliveries increased from 4 per cent in 1953 to 11 per cent in 1995.[189] In the USA, 21 per cent of childbearing women had their membranes artificially ruptured in 1999.[190] These practices are part of a style of medicalized childbirth known as 'the active management of labour', but the active agent here is the doctor, not the mother. In a logical expansion of capitalist thinking, medically controlled childbirth commodifies both mothers and fetuses. Prenatal testing and surveillance function as '"quality control" on the assembly line of the products of conception'; mothers become 'the unskilled workers on a reproductive assembly line'.[191] The practices of 'active management' and those of routine, technological prenatal surveillance, like high rates of Caesarean surgery, aren't based on any sound scientific evidence that they help to promote the health of mothers and babies.[192]

At the same time, many women worldwide have babies in unhygienic, life-threatening circumstances, and safe motherhood has rarely been a public policy priority. The range in lifetime risk of maternal death is enormous – from 1 in 7 to 1 in 9,200. The highest rates are in Afghanistan, Guinea, Sierre Leone and Somalia, and the lowest in Hong Kong, Spain, Switzerland and Norway.[193] In 'developed' countries such as the UK, the poorest women are 20 times more likely than the richest to die in childbirth, and 'non-white' women have double the risk of 'white' women.[194]

In the USA one million episiotomies (cuts in the vaginal outlet) were performed on childbearing women in 1999,[195] again despite evidence that routine use of this form of surgery doesn't improve either maternal or infant health.[196] This popular surgical manoeuvre, designed to expedite 'normal' delivery, is developed countries' version of female genital mutilation. In the UK the episiotomy rate in 1995 was 19 per cent, a fall from 52 per cent in 1980 (and from over 90 per cent in some UK hospitals[197]); this fall is largely accounted for by the rise in Caesarean rates.[198] Although often dismissed as a 'minor' procedure, episiotomy can cause haemorrhage, infection and death, interfere with breastfeeding, and be a common cause of severe pain and discomfort lasting long after childbirth.[199]

Episiotomy was first suggested by male doctors in the eighteenth century, and introduced to the USA in 1851.[200] Other forms of female genital mutilation were pioneered in the West in the 1860s, when a Dr Isaac Baker Brown removed women's clitorises as a cure for masturbation, 'nymphomania', depression and marital dissatisfaction, taking as an indication for the operation any sign that a woman wanted to work outside the home.[201] Brown later extended his operation to include removal of the labia. In 1872 a Dr Robert Battey publicized a second operation: removing women's ovaries for such indications as 'troublesomeness' and 'erotic' tendencies.[202] During the latter part of the nineteenth and well into the twentieth century in the USA and the UK, clitoridectomy was a common practice and 'an ideological crusade' in certain medical circles.[203] Later in the twentieth century there were inexplicable fashions for hysterectomy (cutting out uteruses) – in the 1970s the most commonly performed operation in the USA[204] – and for mastectomy (cutting off breasts); 'inexplicable', that is, in terms of sound scientific evidence that these forms of surgery are effective treatments for women's health problems.[205] Rates of surgery on women's reproductive organs soared in the 1970s, as did interventions in childbirth, both at a time when feminist activism was on the increase and in the news.

But what we more commonly think of as female genital mutilation is a surgical operation currently performed in more than forty countries in North and Central Africa, the Middle East and South and Central American countries, as well as by some groups in Malaysia and Indonesia. Up to 140 million women and girls are estimated to have been mutilated in this way – some 6,000 every day.[206] The resulting list of health problems is horrific, including death, shock, haemorrhage, serious infection, retention of urine, kidney damage, reproductive tract infections because of obstructed menstrual flow, cysts, abscesses and tumours, infertility and major childbirth complications. In societies which practise female genital mutilation, this method of induction into womanhood is simply regarded as normal, just as giving birth in hospital – another routine procedure lacking in scientific justification[207] – together with its attendant surgical and medical procedures, is an accepted element in motherhood in the West today. Cleanliness and hygiene feature as cultural justifications for female genital mutilation, just they did for the transfer of childbirth in the West from home to hospital, and just as other routine 'assaults'[208] on the bodies of childbearing women such as pubic shaving and pre-birth enemas did, and continue to do in some places still.

The language of rape and assault features prominently in the large literature on women and childbirth written since the 1960s, much of it protesting about the unwarranted 'medicalization' and 'technologization' of birth.[209]

Female genital mutilation is associated with patriarchal social systems, with the most extreme form, infibulation, being practised in the most strongly patriarchal societies.[210] Although the link between patriarchal ideology and the medical treatment of women's bodies may be less obvious in the developed world, the history of medicine is replete with florid anti-feminism.[211] Conventional medical histories, mainly written by doctors who portray themselves as heroes in the progressive advance of scientific knowledge, are rhetorical devices for concealing the use of obstetrics and gynaecology as instruments for the enslavement of women.[212]

A new justification for assaulting women's bodies is to protect babies. The promotion of embryos and fetuses as independently existing entities whose rights are likely to collide with their mothers' interests is a pronounced theme in the positions of many obstetricians today, especially when it comes to defending the use of Caesarean surgery[213] or denying women abortion rights.[214] The litigation industry makes major profits out of doctors' insistence that motherhood is characterized by a tendency to 'fetal neglect', whether this means drinking alcohol during pregnancy, refusing Caesarean surgery, or deciding that an unplanned pregnancy is better terminated than leading to the birth of a child in health-damaging circumstances. Doctrines of 'fetal personhood' draw heavily on sociobiological theories of determinism to depict as small, helpless people against whom mothers (not fathers) conspire murder what obstetricians are happy in other circumstances to define as 'products of conception'. All of this ignores the symbiotic physical and social relationship existing between women and the children they carry inside them, and care for afterwards. Thus, the physical consequences of interventions in childbirth are inseparable from a long list of 'psychosocial' miseries which affect the way women feel after birth and about their babies, who, aside from being subjects of joy and love, can retain a lingering aura of obstetrical commodification.[215] The concept of two people united as one challenges dominant Western notions of individual identity, and is difficult to square with the model of 'naturally' competitive relationships between people: hence the ease with which conflict between mothers and fetuses suggested itself as a strategy for persuading mothers to do what obstetricians and paediatricians really want.

■

Simone de Beauvoir observed that patriarchy sees women and nature in the same terms.[216] War, environmental destruction, and the denial of women's bodily integrity are products of the same masculine mentality. Patriarchy and capitalism are linked through masculine violence; sexism, racism, classism and the rape of nature all depend on a process of objectification which strips living things of their autonomous vitality and turns them into commodities from which material profit can be made.[217] As Petra Kelly, a West German

Green Party MP, has written, 'There is no essential difference between the rape of a woman, the conquest of a country, and the destruction of the earth. The his/story of the world records the gender of the rapists, conquerors and destroyers.'[218] Historically, rape has been legitimate in marriage and murder in war; the rape of the earth is legitimate if the resource has a market and can be owned.

The metaphor of Mother Earth is the most common form cross-culturally of the widespread association between women and nature.[219] Globally, small farms still produce 75 per cent of the world's food, and 70 per cent of the world's farmers are women. Women's work in gatherer-hunter societies has traditionally provided 90 per cent of human food: meat is the exception, not the rule.[220] Contrary to popular belief, archaeological remains show that the early humans had bodies programmed to eat a vegetarian diet.[221] In his book *The Rise and Fall of the Third Chimpanzee*, Jared Diamond describes going on a hunt with a New Guinea tribe who had preserved their Stone Age culture and technology. The proceeds of the day amounted to two baby birds, a few frogs, and an awful lot of mushrooms. The men boasted about the large animals they killed, but admitted that this happened on only a few occasions in a lifetime.[222]

Throughout much of history, and still in many countries today, the agricultural work of women gives them a particularly close relationship with nature. For instance, since rural women are often in charge of the family water supply and sanitary arrangements, they know how to find local sources of water and monitor its quality.[223] This environmental expertise is drowned by changes in global and national economies.[224] Mining projects have a particular tendency to disturb traditional social systems, with money, alcohol and imported foods increasing the burden on women's agricultural role and producing alcohol abuse and domestic violence.[225]

The 'development' process, as applied to the Third World, downplays these links between women and nature. Their overall effect is to damage women by severing their access to the land, creating more work for them, and increasing their dependency on men. Development programmes themselves have traditionally paid little attention to women's labour, regarding women as a 'problem' because of their adherence to traditional farming methods, treating them as farmers' wives,[226] and institutionalizing a sexist view of the gender division of labour, with men as breadwinners and women as reproducers and home-keepers.[227] Aid planners have invested only 1–4 per cent of their budgets in projects benefiting women, resisting women's empowerment as an explicit goal.[228]

One major effect of the rape of Mother Earth is the disruption of care chains – personal links between people across the globe based on the work (paid or unpaid) of caring, chains consisting largely of women.[229] Care is about tending nature, being concerned for other human beings and for the relations between them. It's no accident that care as a sentiment and a domain of work has historically been closely associated with women, whose labour becomes invisible once the Western economic model is applied.

Like many of the other policy initiatives discussed in this book, development programmes aren't deliberately designed to favour men; they do so because the mindset of those who plan them fails to consider the issue of gender relations. Even broad concepts of development, which take account of self-respect as well as national economic growth as goals, remain fixed on the production of market commodities rather than on the reproduction and maintenance of human resources.[230] The concept of 'development' is itself problematic. Equating development with economic growth empties it of all social implications; like the word 'modernization', it misleadingly implies the superiority of Western industrial practices.

∎

The scale of the problems, and the interconnectedness of the social relations supporting them, suggest that nothing less than a radically new cultural scenario will do to protect our fragile spinning bauble from the ravages some human beings are inflicting on it. It isn't that we don't know how to live in sustainable and non-earth-damaging ways. For much of human history, this is how most of us have lived. In *Ancient Futures*,[231] Helena Norberg-Hodge describes a Tibetan people who, until the 'penetration' of the tourist industry in the 1970s, sustained a way of life in a harsh environment that damaged neither them nor it. Ladakh is a remote region of Kashmir where temperatures in the eight-month-long winter fall to −40°F, and in the short growing season farmers have to be very clever indeed to nudge barley and other hardy crops out of the thin earth. The Ladakh herd domestic cattle, which provide meat, milk, butter, cheese, labour, transport, food and fuel – the latter in the form of dried dung cakes which are burnt in the winter. The Ladakh eat some goat meat in winter but believe animals should never be killed lightly or without asking for forgiveness. This approach is common in 'developing' countries. The Masai farmers of Kenya, for example, were reportedly shocked at the UK's mass slaughter of cattle in the foot and mouth epidemic. Cows are human beings' friends. And foot and mouth disease is so ordinary it shares a name, *oloirobi*, with the common cold; the Masai nurse affected cattle back to health using herbal remedies.[232]

Among the Ladakh, treating nature with respect includes using human waste productively by mixing it with ash and earth for use as a fertilizer. Nothing is wasted or thrown away; the Ladakh provide for all their needs locally. Private property and the hardest work are shared; the people have a lot of leisure (especially in the winter when farming can't be done), and crime is unknown. The status of women is high – a feature of Ladakh life commented on by all early travellers who came into contact with it – and old people and children are treated with respect.

When Western tourists first appeared the Ladakh called them 'people from Mars'. Norberg-Hodge helped set up a project to enable the Ladakh to understand some of the consequences of adopting a Western way of life – for example, the effects of the pesticides the TNCs wanted them to start using on their fields – and to develop new technologies – for example, solar heating – in resource-preserving ways. Such projects involve massive resistance to the increasing cultural imperative asserting Westernization and capitalist technological development as the 'natural' way forward. They call for rethinking the conventional view that the world's main problems are poverty and over-population, and economic development the answer: the causal relationship is really the other way round.

It's easy to romanticize case studies such as the Ladakh, but such examples remind us of how we ourselves, in the West, used to live not so very long ago. In English writer Alison Uttley's fictional reincarnation of her childhood in the 1880s and 1890s on a Derbyshire farm, she 'walked four miles every morning to the village school . . . It was the only school, and to it went the minister's children, the struggling doctor's, the girls from the saw-mill . . . children from remote farms and little manor houses.' When she got home in the evening:

> she played outside in the dusk, running races with herself, skipping up and down the cobbled farmyard, tossing a ball in the air to hit the sycamore tree. . . . Then she met the farm men walking slowly home with the cans of milk, steadying them with both hands as they swayed on the yokes across their shoulders. She collected the eggs from the window ledge in the barn . . . The stars came out and twinkled in the great clean-water trough.[233]

Manami Suzuki, born in Japan in the late 1950s, recalls growing up in the Japanese countryside surrounded by animals and woods:

> My family lived near the coast and I spent a lot of time swimming and fishing. My school was an hour's walk . . . away from our house across some really beautiful countryside and I have vivid memories of making that journey on foot every day, watching the seasons changing the face of the land. Farmers on the way would greet me and sometimes give me fruit and other produce they had just harvested.[234]

■

'Motivated by an obsession with unlimited economic growth, the science of technology has been corrupted and shaped into a tool for the rape of the earth', say two public health experts at the beginning of their book on the hazards of modern technology.[235] The desecration of the earth is the result of a specific masculine consciousness that devalues women's experiences. Globalization is turning life itself into the ultimate commodity: planet earth is being replaced by Life Inc. in the masculine world of free trade and deregulated commerce. The industry of risk assessment produces 'scientific-looking claims' to defend the indefensible: the continuing production of dioxin; the incineration of plastics and nerve gas weapons; genetic engineering for herbicide-resistant crops; feeding cows dead animals.[236] Globalization is the grim, destructive economic reality of untrammelled profit maximization: 'the overriding corporate purpose'.[237] Just as patriarchy has operated to inhibit women's independence, globalization prevents Third World countries from pursuing independent economic and social policies, and it also widens material inequalities between rich and poor.[238] The cause and consequence of the rape of Mother Earth is a global pattern of growing inequalities between the First World and the Third, between classes and ethnicities and between men and women.

If the world consisted of a village of 100 people, there would be 57 Asians, 21 Europeans, 14 from the Western hemisphere (North and South) and 8 Africans. Eighty would live in substandard housing, 70 would be illiterate, 50 would be malnourished, and 6 would own 59 per cent of the world's wealth, and all of the 6 would be from the USA.[239] Some 23 per cent of the world's population – about 1.3 billion people – live in poverty. At least 400 million live in ecologically fragile areas where deforestation, pollution and other forms of environmental degradation are putting increasing numbers of livelihoods at risk.[240] Deregulation of the world's product and financial markets has created a world class of investors and entrepreneurs: in 1996 the United Nations Development Programme reported that the assets of the world's 358 billionaires exceeded the combined incomes of nearly half the world's population.[241] Inequality has now reached 'monstrous proportions', with the richest fifth of the world owning 85 per cent of the world's GNP and the poorest fifth just 1.4 per cent.[242] The First World consumes four times more of earth's resources than the Third World.[243] Masculinist institutions have brought these outcomes about, and women, along with other marginalized groups, have consequently suffered.

Our industrial, technological and capitalist society is a violent society which behaves as though it's at war with nature. Soil, forests, oceans, animals and people are treated as if they had no integrity or meaning. Capital and energy-intensive global growth spawn a volatile monoculture which is insensitive to cultural diversity and in which no one feels connected to place, tradition or the planet. We need a new world order which values all human beings, the right to satisfy all basic human needs, ecological tolerance and a respect for the future. The domination of nature and of women, the eating of animals, the economic goal of unlimited growth (for some), monopolistic corporate power and the pursuit of technology for its own sake are the same side of the same coin. A new relationship with nature and respect for Mother Earth are needed to reverse these malignancies, but these won't come about until we've untangled the links between culture, masculinity and violence against all forms of life.

8

Delusional Systems

In 1749 a boat brought a consignment of leaves from the coca bush, *Erythroxylon*, to Europe from South America, where they had traditionally been chewed for their pleasure-enhancing properties for at least two thousand years. The main active ingredient of coca leaves, an alkaloid, was isolated in pure form in 1844, and later named cocaine by the German chemist Albert Niemann. Cocaine was enthusiastically promoted as a cure for many diseases in a 1859 pamphlet by an Italian physician, Paulo Mantegazza, who had chewed it with the Peruvian Indians. But it was a paper by a German army surgeon, Dr Theodor Aschenbrandt,[1] which set in train a momentous revolution in Western ideas about the human condition. Aschenbrandt had given cocaine to a troop of exhausted Bavarian soldiers during their autumn manoeuvres in 1883, and his paper, which claimed cocaine's efficacy in rejuvenating the tired soldiers, was read by a financially embarrassed 28-year-old Viennese neurologist who, like the soldiers, was suffering from chronic fatigue, as well as depression and other health problems at the time. When he read Aschenbrandt's paper, Sigmund Freud was on a mission not just to cure himself but to make an important scientific discovery and thus also his professional name; a significant side effect would be the generation of enough money to marry his fiancée, the well-connected Martha Bernays.[2]

After reading Aschenbrandt's paper, Freud got hold of one gram of cocaine, took it, felt more cheerful, and then proceeded to take regular doses of 30–50 mg for two to three years, recommending it to colleagues, friends and family, including to his beloved Martha (he thought it would put colour in her cheeks). In 1884 he published a paper, 'Über Coca', in which he described the drug's exhilarating effects on his own depression.[3] Like Mantegazza, he went on to make all kinds of claims about cocaine's therapeutic effectiveness for all sorts of diseases from seasickness and impotence to heart disease, morphine addiction and diabetes. Cocaine enjoyed great popularity in medical and professional circles throughout the 1880s. Its two leading suppliers, Parke Davis and Merck, both of which enthusiastically promoted Freud's claims, were the forerunners of two of the largest pharmaceutical companies operating today.[4] However, as with most 'wonder' drugs, reports of cocaine's adverse effects soon appeared – addiction, mood swings, hyperactivity, cardiac irregularities, fatal poisoning, sexual excitation followed by loss of libido, hallucinations and mental disturbances akin to paranoid psychosis. By 1887, some years before his major work was undertaken, Freud had recanted his original enthusiasm.

But the matter of one Viennese doctor's relationship with cocaine does not end there. From evidence in the form of letters to his friend and colleague Wilhelm Fliess, it seems that Freud resumed his cocaine habit in 1892 and continued it throughout the years of his major 'discoveries' concerning the unconscious, infantile sexuality and the Oedipal drama.[5] The Freud–Fliess letters came to light because Fliess's widow sold them to a Berlin bookseller after her husband's death. They were found in the late 1930s by Marie Bonaparte, a princess of Greece and Denmark and a disciple of Freud's, who saved them from the Nazis and got them shipped to London, where they were translated and substantially edited by Freud's daughter, Anna, and the analyst Ernst Kriss.[6]

Wilhelm Fliess was a Berlin nose and throat specialist who claimed to have discovered something called the 'nasal reflex neurosis' one dull winter's day in 1897. He was lying in the bath when a plumber came to check the gas installation. The man complained of a headache and dizziness, and when Fliess looked up his nose he saw a swelling in the nasal septum. After he'd applied cocaine to it, the plumber's afflictions magically disappeared. Fliess and Freud met in 1887 when Fliess attended Freud's lectures. The focus on noses and cocaine became a shared obsession. Freud allowed Fliess to operate several times on his nose for 'neurotic disturbances', and started dosing himself with cocaine again regularly in 1892, using his nose as the route of entry: both he and Fliess suffered from constant nasal disorders – infections, ulceration, bleeding and necrosis – as a result (though it was another addiction, to tobacco, which eventually killed Freud, in the form of cancer of the jaw).

The most famous 'professional' result of Freud and Fliess's folie à deux was Emma Eckstein, a patient handed over by Freud to Fliess for nasal surgery to treat her masturbation. Emma, a 27-year-old woman from a prominent Viennese family who was active in the women's movement, was complaining of stomach and menstrual problems and difficulty walking. Fliess's theory about the nasal reflex neurosis made it responsible for a variety of symptoms, but especially malfunctions of the reproductive and sexual organs. These were related to a 'genital spot' in the nose which could be treated with cocaine, by cauterization or, in resistant cases, by surgery. Nasal surgery was thus an alternative to the prescription more usual at the time of genital surgery for women as a 'cure' for the 'disease' of masturbation. (Interestingly, the medicalization of masturbation never produced the same conclusion of genital or nasal amputation where men were concerned.) Fliess's operation on Emma, which involved removing a bone, was bungled; he left half a metre of gauze in her nasal cavity, she had a severe infection and nearly bled to death – a response interpreted by Freud as hysterical and designed to bring him to her side.[7] Freud had a hard time coming to terms with Fliess's mistake, and the two men subsequently had a fundamental disagreement about what became known as Freud's 'seduction theory'. Freud thought Emma had been a victim of sexual abuse, and told Fliess so; Fliess's unreceptive response may have been connected to his own possible role as abuser of his own son, Robert, who was also to become a psychoanalyst.[8]

But the origins of psychoanalysis as a major delusional system[9] of the twentieth century are bound up with the 'case histories' of two other women – 'Anna O' and 'Dora'. Freud learnt about the case of Anna O from a high-status Viennese physician called Josef Breuer. Breuer had discovered that his patients' symptoms were often relieved when they talked under hypnosis. Freud was also using, but becoming disillusioned by, hypnosis, a technique he'd learnt from the French doctor Charcot while on a travelling scholarship to Paris. The custom of psychoanalytic patients lying on a couch derives from hypnosis, where patients had to lie down in order to relax – though Freud later admitted to a dislike of being stared at for eight hours a day, and added the rationalization that putting the patient on a couch enabled the analyst to be as shadowy as possible.[10]

Anna O was in real life Bertha Pappenheim, the brilliant 21-year-old daughter of a wealthy Viennese Jewish family. Bertha/Anna watched her younger brother go to university and law school while she, according to the custom of the time, was confined to the home doing charity work and nursing her tubercular father. After her father died, she developed debilitating psychological symptoms (paralysis, hallucinations, anorexia, suicidal thoughts, and a speech disorder in which she became unable to speak her native German, and instead spoke other languages, curiously intermixed). Bertha/Anna saw Breuer almost daily in 1880–2, and it was she who named the practice of therapists listening to their clients 'the talking cure'.[11] Bertha/Anna features as the first case history in Breuer and Freud's *Studies on Hysteria* (1895). This book was iconoclastic for its time in reversing the usual unfriendly portrayal of female hysterics as moral and mental freaks. Instead Breuer and Freud suggested that the origins of female hysteria lay in hostile social conditions which suppressed women's creativity and drive.

Bertha/Anna didn't recover as a result of this attention – a fact which has been 'one of the most closely guarded secrets' in the whole history of psychoanalysis.[12] They didn't recognize what her mother had originally suggested[13] – that she had the symptoms of tubercular meningitis, caught from her father. She nonetheless managed to live an active life as an educationalist and feminist social reformer committed to improving the social and economic position of Jewish women and children in Germany. She wrote fiction, a play about women's rights, translated Mary Wollstonecraft's *Vindication of the Rights of Woman* into German, established an organization, the Jüdischer Frauenbund, which campaigned against the white slave trade in East Europe, and worked to increase legal protection for women. She died shortly after being interrogated by the Gestapo in 1936 for an anti-Hitler remark, and wrote her own obituary: 'The Jews of the entire world – men and women – owe her thanks for this social achievement. But they withhold it. What a pity!'[14]

When Breuer told Freud about Anna O's case, Freud heard, and for a while listened to, the evidence presented by her that her life was unbearably circumscribed and she couldn't tolerate the stress this caused her. When it came to Freud's other most famous case, that of Dora, he heard something else which also captured his attention as evidence about the origins of neurosis, and which, as he interpreted and reinterpreted it, was to have an enormous influence on the development and ultimate fate of psychoanalysis.

Philip Bauer was a Viennese industrialist who made his living from cloth factories in Bohemia. In 1900 he took his 18-year-old daughter, Ida, to Freud, a doctor he trusted because Freud had some years earlier treated him for syphilis. Ida was acting strangely and threatening suicide; her father didn't know what to do with her. At first Freud didn't see the case as very promising, but he took it on to make some money. His brief encounter with Ida Bauer gave birth to his 1905 classic *Fragment of an Analysis of a Case of Hysteria*, in which Ida appears as Dora, the name of Freud's daughter's maid.

The outline of Ida/Dora's case is well known. She told Freud that she had been sexually molested since the age of 14 by Herr K, a man called Hans Zellenka in real life,[15] a friend of her father's and the very person who'd directed him to Freud to seek treatment for venereal disease. To complicate matters, Ida/Dora's father was having an affair with Herr K's wife. Ida/Dora felt that her father, who treated her very much like his possession anyway, had handed her over to Herr K as a kind of guilt payment for his adulterous affair with Frau K. To make matters even worse, Ida/Dora's governess was also in love with her father and fairly indifferent to her charge, who idolized her. When Ida told her mother about Herr K's advances, her mother told her father, and her father accused her of making it up. This is, in the end, more or less what Freud also decided had been going on. Somewhere between 1895 and 1897 Freud gave up what is oddly known as the 'seduction theory' (being molested by one's father as a child is hardly 'seduction') in favour of the view that it's all infantile fantasy. So instead of attending to Ida/Dora's account of events, Freud argued that her hysteria derived from her sexual fantasies about masturbation, incest with her father, and desire for both Herr and Frau K. Not surprisingly, Ida/Dora found this approach unhelpful and broke off her 'treatment' after only a few weeks.

The history of the seduction theory in psychoanalysis has been told in detail by Jeffrey Masson, a North American analyst who worked with Freud's daughter, Anna, at the Freud archives in London. Masson was an accepted member of the psychoanalytic establishment until he published his book *The Assault on Truth: Freud's suppression of the seduction theory*. The book was based on material in the Freud archives, including unpublished letters between Freud and Sándor Ferenczi, a Hungarian doctor and later friend of Freud's, about the reality of childhood sexual abuse and the principles of psychotherapy. Masson also undertook a new edition of the Freud–Fliess letters, with privileged access given him by Anna Freud.[16] From these letters it seemed clear that Freud's initial willingness to take his female patients' accounts of male sexual harassment at face value was later either suppressed or abandoned. Freud's 1896 paper, 'The aetiology of hysteria', which argued this interpretation, was his first major address to professional colleagues.[17] Drawing on eighteen cases of female hysteria, the paper proposed that real sexual assault was responsible for women's hysterical symptoms. His patients' accounts would have resonated with Freud's experiences with Charcot in Paris when he'd been confronted with the violent evidence of childhood abuse in the Paris morgue.[18] But Freud's paper received a chilling reception, and he was urged not to publish it in order to preserve his reputation. In 1905–6, Freud said he had exaggerated the importance of childhood seduction as a cause of hysteria, and argued that he'd reached his conclusion on 'scanty evidence'.[19]

In a letter to Fliess, Freud cited four sources of doubt about the seduction theory: (1) using it, he hadn't cured anyone; (2) the frequency of abusive fathers couldn't possibly be as high as his women patients were suggesting it was; (3) the human unconscious was unable to distinguish true from false events; and (4) this resistance of the unconscious to recalling reality couldn't be overcome by even the worst traumas.[20] Freud's volte-face had been excised from the earlier edition of the correspondence between Freud and Fliess through the omission of 158 letters by Anna Freud in the interests of consistency – her father, she told Masson, had simply been wrong the first time round.[21]

What is certainly true is that Freud's denial of the reality of sexual assault preserved the possibility of a psychoanalysis based on the precepts of childhood sexual fantasy and the Oedipal drama. 'I was driven to recognise in the end', said Freud in 1933 of his female patients' complaints that they had been seduced by their fathers, 'that these reports were untrue and so came to understand that hysterical symptoms are derived from phantasy and not real occurrences. It was only later that I was able to recognise in this phantasy of being seduced by the father the expression of the typical Oedipal complex in women.'[22] Without Freud's dismissal of the testimony of his women patients, it's hard to see how there would have been any psychoanalysis at all.

Masson's account has led to the formulation of the generic question: was Freud a liar? Others, apart from Masson, have noted troubling inconsistencies in Freud's accounts of the genesis and fate of the seduction theory between 1896 and his later writings.[23] A recent re-examination of the debate by Paul Roazen concludes that Freud's rejection of the seduction theory 'makes for a slippery-sounding story. One almost inevitably wonders how regularly Freud cooked his own books.'[24] Freud's need to save face when his colleagues disbelieved his original formulation of the theory must have reminded him of his earlier mistake concerning the wonder-drug cocaine. In this earlier episode of face-saving, Freud had blamed 'addictive personality' for the damage wrought by the drug, rather than cocaine itself, adding a caution about the inherent dangers of the hypodermic syringe; this directly contradicted recommendations he'd published two years before specifically advising the injection route.[25]

The sad outcome for Ida/Dora of Freud's second big 'mistake' determined the whole future development of psychoanalysis. It became a system of thought dedicated, not to the simple therapeutic power of 'the talking cure' – one possible direction it could have taken – but to replacing people's own accounts of reality with a different reality derived from the beliefs and value-systems of psychoanalysts themselves. This decisive turn for psychoanalysis had a deeply gendered aspect. The early psychoanalysts were men. Most of the patients, the veracity of whose accounts had to be set aside in the interests of psychoanalysis as a professional belief system, were women.

Freud's total immersion in his own culture when it came to beliefs about the role and capabilities of women has provided material for countless attacks and counter-attacks; most notably perhaps, in our own time, Kate Millett's capable characterization in her *Sexual Politics* of Freud's mission to set himself up as a new prophet for the old doctrine of separate spheres: 'Freud's doctrine of penis envy is in fact a superbly timed accusation, enabling masculine sentiment to take the offensive . . . The whole weight of responsibility, and even of guilt, is now placed upon any woman unwilling to "stay in her place" . . . Apart from ridicule, the counterrevolutionary period never employed a more withering or destructive weapon against feminist insurgence.'[26]

Freud's theories about human psychology were derived from a cocaine-clouded introspection into his own condition, and from contact with a relatively small number of people, mostly young, upper middle-class women, who came, or were sent, to him for help with conditions labelled as hysteria. Although Freud's published works mention 145 patients in all, only six are discussed in detail.[27] In only one of these cases was there any prolonged successful contact between analyst and analysand. The others were seen by Freud briefly or not at all, and no cure resulted; in one case the patient actually suffered a paranoid breakdown following treatment.[28]

Freudianism is a 'genuine pseudoreligious movement',[29] akin in its cultural impact to that of Christianity.[30] The 'theory of civilization'[31] it offers is a theory, not a science, and what it describes would hardly be regarded as civilized by everyone. The fantasy of the perfect, gender-divided, nuclear family based on compulsory heterosexuality and the oppression of women and children dominates to an impressively unreal degree; the notion, stolen from an old Greek drama, that psychological maturity is achieved only through resolving a neurotic pattern of parent–child relationships, in which children universally love their mothers and hate, desire and/or compete with their fathers, idealizes 'good' separation above connectedness as a sign of maturity and produces the absurd inference that women experience themselves as *biologically* handicapped because men have both power and penises. Psychoanalysis, itself a cultural product, omits culture from its frame of reference, fixating instead on 'a universe of immutable human nature';[32] the social relations of men and women, parents and children, doctors and patients, and the institutions which constrain and support these, are treated as unimportant epiphenomena. The central enterprise is transcribing the masculine psychology of patriarchal society into an ungrounded narrative about universal human conduct. In this sense, psychoanalysis is 'a meditation' on patriarchy.[33] What, in the process, goes missing is most of what happens in real families, including those whose cultural and material practices are very different from those on which psychoanalytic theory was based.

■

Today unknown numbers of people spend unknown amounts of money going to analysts or therapists of one sort or another. The 'extraordinary degree of demographic bias' among the people who use therapists has persisted since Freud's time: the majority are white, relatively young, affluent and educated.[34] Starting in the 1950s and 1960s, the habit of educated, urban professional people seeking a solution to their personal problems in the analyst or therapist's consulting room spread outwards to become a major cultural practice. Therapy, the answer to everything, is also the route to personal growth on a journey that is overwhelmingly obsessed with the self. In his book *How Are We to Live?*, the ethicist Peter Singer tells the story of an American diplomat who visited a Freudian analyst for five years because he felt very dissatisfied with his career, and in particular found it difficult to support the American foreign policy current at the time. The analyst explained to him that the US government and his superiors were father images, that he disliked his work because he unconsciously hated his father, and the solution therefore was to

work on his relationship with his father. Eventually, the diplomat was advised
by someone else that he might have genuine reasons for career dissatisfaction,
and perhaps should change his employment, which he did.[35]

Stuart Sutherland, a professor of experimental psychology, was referred to
a psychoanalyst when he had a severe mental breakdown in his mid-forties
precipitated by his wife's extra-marital affair. The analyst allowed Sutherland 'to ramble on rather incoherently about my problems and my background
and occasionally he made a few interpretations. I had the feeling that he was
slightly bored with the whole proceedings: he seemed to spend most of his
time either examining his wristwatch or gazing into the sunlit garden from
which came the noise of children playing.'[36] Since the bored analyst was too
busy to take Sutherland on as a regular client, he recommended another. This
one diagnosed repressed homosexuality, suggesting that Sutherland wanted his
father 'to fuck you until the shit ran out'.[37] When Sutherland said he thought
this treatment wasn't helping, he was warned of the dangers of leaving it 'prematurely'. However, when the analyst went on holiday, Sutherland didn't go
back and refused to pay the bill on the grounds that he'd been told the therapy
would make him feel better, which it didn't.

When novelist Nina Bawden was seeking help for her son Nikki, a clever,
antisocial young man who'd been arrested for drug taking, in and out of psychiatric care, and eventually diagnosed as a schizophrenic, her GP recommended a clinic run by a disciple of the 'radical' therapist R. D. Laing. Nikki
and his parents were duly invited for a 'family therapy' session: 'The doctor
asked us what we were doing, I said I was finishing a novel. Austen spoke
about his job in the World Service of the BBC. He said he enjoyed it so much
that the prospect of retiring was quite disturbing. The American doctor deliv-
ered his verdict. We were a couple "obsessed with death".'[38] Since the clinic
had been paid in advance £800 a week (at 1970s prices), Nikki stayed there.
Some days later he disappeared. The clinic notified no one, on the grounds
that this would be an invasion of his privacy. Staff told the family that Nikki
had to free himself from them, so even if he killed himself the therapy should
be counted a success. His body was found in the river some months later.

R. D. Laing, whose name was invoked in the treatment of Nina Bawden's
son, was a key figure in the anti-psychiatry movement of the 1960s. This took
the seemingly liberal stance of criticizing institutional psychiatric power, hierarchical relationships between doctors and patients, and the sadistic, but all
too common, 'treatments' of psychosurgery and electric shocks. Instead mental
illness was to be explained by its social context, especially the family, and by
the institution of psychiatry itself, which caused more problems than it solved.
Laing's *The Divided Self* (1960) was the bible of the counterculture; the book
he wrote with Aaron Esterson, *Sanity, Madness and the Family* (1964), seemed
to offer an exposé of just those kinds of constrictive and discriminatory stereotypes of which Bertha/Anna and Ida/Dora would have complained had they

possessed the right words at the time. But the 'therapeutic community' established by Laing and his friends at Kingsley Hall in East London, and his treatment of Mary Barnes, his Dora or Anna O, exemplify exactly the same dissonance with ethical and scientific principles of effectiveness and safety, dependence on the charisma of a male guru, and generalization of theories about the human condition relying on unvalidated precepts – for instance, the supremacy of death anxiety which Nina Bawden found so unhelpful in the case of her son.

Mary Barnes was a middle-aged Catholic with a long career as a psychiatric patient when she picked Laing to help her, having failed to persuade Anna Freud to take her on. Laing told her she needed 'analysis 24 hours out of 24'.[39] Her treatment at Kingsley Hall involved regression to infancy, complete dependence on being cared for by others, and unsociable creative games with her faeces.[40] Whatever Laing did or didn't do with his female patients, David Cooper, another 'radical' psychiatrist who worked at Kingsley Hall and was a close colleague of Laing's, advocated 'bed therapy' (sex) with patients. For Cooper, orgasms were the ultimate in self-expression; non-orgasmic women could always be recognized because they didn't finish their sentences.[41] The practices of the anti-psychiatrists may well have been the most sexist of all, but they weren't alone in having sex with their patients; Phyllis Chesler's book *Women and Madness* achieved notoriety in the 1970s for suggesting that this was a widespread occurrence within many forms of therapy.[42] Surveys put the proportion of therapists engaging in sexual or erotic contact with patients at between 5 per cent and 13 per cent;[43] a survey in 1983 showed that around 15 per cent of therapists had some kind of sexual contact with one or more patients.[44]

■

Academic psychologist Hans Eysenck has called psychoanalysis 'the most stupendous intellectual confidence trick of the twentieth century'.[45] Its claims to effectiveness went largely unchallenged until the early 1950s, when Eysenck published a famous five-page paper which argued, on the basis of 8,053 'cases' included in 24 studies, that many of those who turned to therapy for help would get better on their own simply with time.[46] Moreover, psychoanalysis had the worst recovery rate of all approaches. Eysenck's estimate of a 66 per cent spontaneous recovery rate was halved in a later paper,[47] bringing it in line with the proportion of people who get better in clinical trials when given a supposedly inactive 'placebo' drug.[48] In the early studies it was therapists themselves who decided whether or not a treatment had been effective,[49] and they tended only to include in their estimates of success patients who didn't terminate treatment 'prematurely', that is, before the analysts themselves were willing to concede that the end might have come. Over the years, the length of time analysts think analysis needs to last has risen constantly: from 1–2 years in the 1920s, to 2–4 years in the 1930s and 1940s, to 6–8 years today.[50] In fictitiously constructed and taped therapy sessions, analysts have been shown to be more likely than other kinds of therapists to perceive positive change where none exists.[51] Therapists in general are twice as likely as their patients to claim that treatment has been a success.[52]

One doesn't have to be particularly inventive about the design of experiments to demonstrate the importance of subjective perception ('bias') in psychiatric labelling. A study involving 464 senior psychiatrists divided them into four groups and presented them with identical case histories save for changes in the name and the sex of the patient. When the patient was called Wayne, 37 per cent said he had a personality disorder, was a drug abuser or a malingerer; this figure dropped to 19 per cent when his name was Matthew. A diagnosis of schizophrenia was offered by 77 per cent for Wayne and 57 per cent for Matthew. Changing the names of women patients had no such effect, but women were twice as likely to be diagnosed with a personality disorder.[53]

Any sensible 'scientific' approach to evaluation means comparing the fates of patients receiving therapy with those of other, similar, patients, who don't. It's only by having comparative 'experimental' and 'control' groups that the effects of psychoanalysis can be distinguished from those of time or the many other factors which can aid or impede recovery. Eysenck's criticisms have been supported by many other studies.[54] For example, a 1996 review of the effectiveness of psychotherapy for the English Department of Health demonstrated that 'Many, if not most, of the cherished beliefs of theorists and practitioners of particular methods of psychotherapy remain largely unsupported by the evidence.'[55] The vast majority of the four hundred or so 'brand name' therapies being practised today are totally unevaluated. Psychotherapy research is dominated by small, uncontrolled studies with poorly defined and measured outcomes, many patients dropping out and short periods of follow up. The early claims to effectiveness were based mainly on single case studies; this, plus theoretical discussion, remains the dominant evaluation method today.[56]

The collective findings of these enquiries into the effectiveness of psychoanalysis and psychotherapy suggest no evidence that psychoanalysis or psychotherapy has any positive effect on the course of neurotic disorders over and above the curative effects of time or 'inactive' placebo treatments. Of course, the shortage of sound studies doesn't mean that the different therapies are worthless: no evidence of effect isn't evidence of ineffectiveness. Psychotherapy may also work for some and not for others. In one review of a number of studies, around a third more patients in therapy groups compared to those in untreated groups improved, but twice as many also deteriorated.[57]

'Placebo' treatments occupy a curious role in psychotherapy research. When therapists Gene Glass and Mary Smith examined the findings of over five hundred studies of some form of psychological therapy, they decided that there *was* evidence that therapy worked, although they were unable to find any support for the importance of the therapists' experience or the length of treatment.[58] Glass and Smith regarded 'placebo' treatments (discussion groups, pills, playing with puzzles, relaxation training, arts classes, etc.) as forms of therapy. Subsequent reanalysis of the same data by other researchers[59] comparing therapy patients with those getting 'placebo' treatments found no difference in effectiveness between the two. This suggests that 'the placebo condition contains the necessary, and possibly the sufficient, ingredient for much of the beneficial effect of all forms of psychotherapy'.[60] Put differently, 'belief by psychotherapists in the superiority of their own methods *is for them a placebo of sorts*, in the sense of serving as a self-sustaining, if empirically unjustified, myth'.[61] In one study university professors from unrelated disciplines had just as much 'success' in helping patients to improve as experienced professional psychotherapists.[62]

One definition of psychoanalysis is the attempt to transform 'neurotic misery' into 'ordinary unhappiness'.[63] This is entirely laudable, so long as the neurotic misery comes first, rather than being how analysts have to define unhappiness in order to get people into their consulting rooms in the first place. The medicalization of unhappiness as a disease is a general characteristic of modern medicine: without it, the pharmaceutical industry would be much poorer than it is.[64]

Contrasting with the lack of evidence for the therapeutic effectiveness of psychoanalysis and other forms of psychotherapy is the mass of data establishing the importance to health of ordinary social support and friendship.[65] The British therapist Peter Lomas is a major champion of this view. From orthodox Freudian beginnings, Lomas moved to the position that the major usefulness of psychotherapy is the 'ordinary' support it can offer to distressed human beings.[66] 'What stimulates me, what makes me think and what holds me together,' said Lomas in a recent interview:

> is what in the real world would be the ordinary thing to do to help this person. Would it be to try to understand them, would it be to try to talk to them about their childhood, would it be just to sit with them, would it be to put a rocket under them, would it be to hug them? What would be the decent thing to do?[67]

The abuses of power and dissonances of interpretation which happen in traditional psychotherapeutic encounters would be much less likely to happen were its masculine methods and arcane rituals to be abolished in favour of compassion, spontaneity and humanity.[68]

In the early 1960s I experienced the beginnings of this approach to therapy when I myself saw Peter Lomas as a patient for about eighteen months. I have no doubt that my visits to him helped me to avoid a major breakdown. The feeling he conveyed that here was a person who listened to, and cared about, me was quite unlike all my subsequent encounters with therapists of various kinds.

Lomas's promotion of 'ordinariness' recognizes the value of the reciprocal, informal care that is part of most people's daily experiences.[69] An age of experts, in which we now live, demotes the importance of these networks as 'unprofessional' and they therefore become invisible. A significant element in this is that social support has traditionally been an aspect of women's work in and outside the family.

■

The status of psychoanalysis as a secular religion mimics that of capitalism, with which it has important characteristics in common. The insistence in psychoanalytic encounters on the psychological importance of people paying market rates derives from Freud's observation that the transactions between analyst and analysand must mimic the real world of economic motives in order to work.[70] It's also been pointed out that part of psychotherapy's resistance to research evidence may derive from its status as a business enterprise. In commercial terms, psychotherapy *has* been enormously successful. Maintaining this hold on the market demands the practice of exclusivity, which in turn means rejecting scientific validation as inappropriate whenever there's any danger that its evidence may counter the business claims of success.[71]

The synonymity of psychoanalysis with the personality types required for success in a capitalist economic and social system is one explanation as to why, from such inauspicious and crazy beginnings, Freud's ideas entered into the collective consciousness and cultural slang of such a large part of the industrial world. Capitalism's culture of narcissism provided a fertile ground for Freudian ideas; once introspection had been defined as health-promoting, people could look inwards and backwards to their childhoods as causes of dis-ease. Psychoanalytic thinking fitted the social demand for individualistic, self-actualizing people. The exact carpentry of the fit can be studied. For example, in the years between 1876 and 1907, when psychoanalytic ideas first began to root themselves in American culture, the general ideas of release and individual expansion underlying psychoanalysis were also gaining currency in economics, as the economic system moved from deficit to surplus.[72] In Sherry Turkle's report on how the French intelligentsia eagerly picked up psychoanalysis in the late 1960s, there were clear similarities between the tenets and practices of psychoanalysis, on the one hand, and prevailing cultural ideas about the self and the links between the personal and the political, on the other.[73] This enthusiasm for referring the 'visible back to the invisible' was also in part a response by activists to the apparent failure of 1960s radical movements.

Both psychoanalysis and capitalism are predicated on a model of the human condition which sees individual self-fulfilment as the chief goal of life. 'Man' is out for himself; success, including economic success, is a measure of self-worth, and failure must therefore be due to personal limitations. The compliance of psychoanalysis and psychotherapy with patriarchal and capitalist ideologies means that the primary cast of psychoanalytic 'treatment' is adjustment to the social order: this stress on 'pacification and counterinsurgency'[74] brings with it an unacknowledged dismissal of the brute material causes of human distress. If people make themselves ill, the social causes of illness simply disappear from the frame. Poverty and inequality, as well as discrimination and sexual violence, become hysterical fantasies.

When the feminist psychologist Dorothy Tennov wrote her book *Psychotherapy: The hazardous cure*, it was turned down by the publisher on the grounds that he couldn't possibly publish a book which was so critical of psychoanalysis, since he himself made so much money from it.[75] In America, where analysts' incomes are heavily determined by what insurance companies will pay for, research on cure rates has been strongly resisted as threatening to analysts' economic security.[76] One reason why few sound studies of the effectiveness of psychoanalysis exist is because psychoanalysts and therapists lack much interest in research, seeing it as 'an activity of hostile competition'.[77] Of more than 16,000 experienced therapists invited to take part in a project on the effects of therapy, only 85 (0.5 per cent) even bothered to reply.[78] In a study by the American Psychoanalytic Association of 10,000 patients, only 595 histories were supplied by 'participating' analysts. Of these 595, 289 'did not complete' the treatment; of the remaining 306, details were provided only for 210, and 35 of these were completely cured. This cure rate of 0.4 per cent becomes 'about 97 per cent' in an unscientific burst of confidence in the Association's report.[79]

Since psychoanalysis and psychotherapy are commodities to be bought and sold in the market place, their sellers have a vested interest in retaining control over product information. Over the last decade, when 'Freud-bashing' has become an industry, psychoanalysts have mounted a major publicity campaign, using marketing techniques to promote their wares. They're even resorting to cost-effective electronic mail as a medium of treatment, thus repeating Freud's assertion that the shadowy nature of the analyst's existence is a *sine qua non* of successful therapy.[80]

∎

A physicist, a philosopher and an economist are on a desert island with nothing to eat but a can of beans. But they have no can opener. The philosopher and the physicist debate various unpromising solutions to the problem, while the economist knows immediately what to do: assume a can opener![81] Ergo, the can of beans is opened, but it turns out to be a can of worms.

Economics is replete with such jokes about economists' tendencies to make assumptions rather than confront facts. The reason is that economics, like psychoanalysis, isn't an empirical science. It's an approach, a highly selective way of looking at the world, rather than a separate discipline defined by its subject-matter.[82] What economists specialize in is very similar to the trade of psychoanalysis: models of behaviour based on stories. One of the stories economists tell is that economics is science. But, like psychoanalysis, economics lacks most of the defining features of scientific activity: its theoretical models aren't based on careful observation, its hypotheses aren't tested in controlled experiments, and its predictive power isn't set against the standard of whether what's predicted actually does happen. The accuracy of economic forecasts is appalling: for example, American economists didn't notice the signs of the forthcoming 1930 recession; in 1993–4 they failed to predict the Japanese recession, the American recovery, the collapse of the German economy, and the turmoil in the European exchange rate mechanism;[83] in 1997 there was a further spectacular failure of prediction concerning East Asian economies.[84] In the UK, the average error made by the Treasury on one-year-ahead forecasts of GDP growth is around 1.5 per cent, about the same figure as average actual growth.[85] The Organization for Economic Co-operation and Development (OECD) examined its own forecasting records, those of the International Monetary Fund and those of national governments in 1993. What the OECD study found was that a simple measure of predicting next year's growth as equal to this year's (a procedure requiring no specialist knowledge of economics at all) worked as well as the expert forecasts for the seven major world economies, and slightly better than these when it came to predicting inflation. Recognizing this, the London Business School says that the best way to forecast is often and late.[86]

In his recent book, *Debunking Economics*, economist Steve Keen describes his progressive realization that what most of his colleagues in mainstream economics practise is an esoteric religion, not science. They honestly believe that a world governed by economic theory is a better place, but in this they behave like zealots rather than dispassionate intellectuals, and you can't argue with zealots.[87] There are many features of the modern world that economic theory can't adequately explain. For example, although human beings' predilection for consuming goods and services is crucial to economic theory, we have to look outside this for an explanation of perhaps the most obvious feature of consumption today – what Veblen called 'conspicuous consumption'. Veblen's celebrated *The Theory of the Leisure Class* refers the 'vicarious' buying of miscellaneous goods to the gendering of household roles in which women, essentially men's chattels, act as 'ceremonial consumers'. Where women are not 'allowed' to work for profit outside the household, the economy profits from their 'habitual rendering of vicarious leisure and consumption . . . the abiding mark of the unfree servant'.[88] Neo-classical economics (the 'orthodox' economics still taught to most students today) also can't explain high unemployment rates, and predicts that full employment produces inflation, which it doesn't.[89] Cutting income tax (personal or corporate) and reducing welfare expenditure are widely hailed among economists as promoting productivity and business motivation. But experience doesn't bear this out; the first effect of cutting personal taxes is to increase savings; reduced welfare spending reduces demand.[90] 'Virtually every aspect of conventional economic theory is intellectually unsound', argues Keen; 'virtually every economic policy recommendation is just as likely to do general harm as it is to lead to the general good.'[91]

What most economists do instead of science is mathematics: they produce and refine mathematical models, in a process whose masonic complexity gives the *appearance* of precision and accuracy (it props up economists' beliefs that what they're doing *is* science). Mathematical analysis first became popular in economics in the nineteenth century as a way of raising its prestige by aping the methods of the physical sciences. A further 'tragic turn' was taken around 1940, when econometrics became a new vogue, conveying an 'air of easy mathematical mastery'.[92] In a recent edition of the journal *Econometrica* (July 2001) the contents included such titles as: 'Representing preferences with a unique subjective state space', 'Likelihood inference for discretely observed nonlinear diffusions' and 'Necessity of transversality conditions for infinite horizon problems'. As a substitute for empirical work, mathematics saves labour: the number of papers in economic journals based on actual data about people's behaviour is strikingly small.[93] The dependence of neo-classical economics on mathematics permits an essential further trick, which is the conflation of statistical significance with other forms of significance – social, policy, scientific. In one review of papers in the *American Economic Review* in the 1980s, over two-thirds were guilty of failing to distinguish statistical from other sorts of significance, and didn't give the basic data which would enable readers to decide for themselves.[94]

The main function of neo-classical economics is to provide a logically coherent account of free enterprise capitalism. It's the economics which 'explains' business activity in the non-socialist world – 'a surrogate ideology for the market economy'.[95] The 'classical' theory of the early economists – Adam Smith, Alfred Marshall, David Ricardo, Robert Malthus – became 'neo-classical' when adjustments had to be made in theoretical models to allow for the complex and rather imperfectly competitive way in which capitalist economies developed. In the twentieth century, Keynesian economics built on the tradition of classical economics by idolizing market forces as the best guarantee of economic growth, but adding to this the precept that the public good sometimes requires state intervention in the economy.

The economists' account functions as a *justificatory* model, although its defenders, much like the high priests of psychoanalysis, claim that it has important explanatory capability. Economists enjoy high prestige as government policy advisers, media pundits, and experts on national accounting systems, monetarism and trade behaviour. Some Wall Street economists have clauses in their contracts which stipulate a certain amount of media coverage as a key function of the job.[96] The result is that, as Paul Ormerod says in his book *The Death of Economics*, 'Economics dominates political debate, to the extent that it is scarcely possible to have a serious political career in many Western countries without being able to repeat more or less accurately its current fashionable orthodoxies.'[97] The gravitas of the subject derives in part from its well-heeled masculinity.[98] In this cultural confidence trick, economics is no different from other patriarchal thought systems. The difference lies in the extraordinary cheek with which economics has asserted its central assumption: that of Rational Economic Man, a fictional, overmasculinized being whose sole interest lies in promoting his own happiness through the accumulation of goods and services in a free enterprise market system. This peculiar, non-empirical notion is economics' 'fundamental building block'.[99]

A core textbook for students of economics when I went as an undergraduate to Oxford in 1962 was Samuelson's *Economics*, a heavy, expensive, highly popular tome whose purchase out of our meagre student budgets was with hindsight hardly a rational economic decision. Paul Samuelson led a powerful economics department at the Massachusetts Institute of Technology and was a prolific writer on economics, specializing in the elaboration of various theories in micro- and macro-economics which earned him the Nobel Prize in 1970. Samuelson's definition of economics as 'the study of how men and society . . . choose to employ scarce productive resources to produce various commodities . . . and distribute them for consumption'[100] followed an earlier, much-quoted definition by the British economist Lionel Robbins of economics as 'the science which studies human behaviour as a relationship between ends and scarce means which have alternative uses'.[101] This definition takes the existing market economy as a given; it ignores the dynamic issue of how demand, employment, output and so forth change over time; and it omits social influences as irrelevant to individual market behaviour. The 'votes of consumers' in an isolated, asocial format are seen as the driving force of the entire economic system. Any other way of doing things (socialism, communism) is an 'alternative' economic system (just as, within health care, Chinese medicine or homeopathy, which have perfectly adequate theories and successes of their own, are deemed 'alternative' to the accepted allopathic system of Western medicine).

In Alfred Stonier and Douglas Hague's *A Textbook of Economic Theory*, another obligatory purchase for students of economics in the 1960s, the description is even more stark:

> Economists are most usually concerned with people in two capacities, as con-
> sumers and as business men . . . When economists discuss the actions of con-
> sumers they assume that consumers behave 'rationally'. For example, they
> assume that when a consumer goes into a shop and asks for a newspaper, he
> does not really want a box of chocolates.

What does he want?

> The first question which we need to answer is, 'How does the consumer decide
> which of the various available commodities to buy?' To answer this let us assume
> that the consumer, when he makes his purchases, has the sole aim of obtaining
> the greatest possible satisfaction from his available financial resources. In tech-
> nical language . . . this means that the consumer obeys the principle of 'eco-
> nomic rationality'.[102]

Who was this person? Where did he come from? I puzzled over these
questions in silence at the time, not having the language to communicate
them to anyone else. In fact, the gestation of Rational Economic Man was co-
terminous with the rise of economics as a field of study. No one actually
invented him in exactly this format; rather he sidled into existence as a kind
of corporate fantasy. He was economists' psychic projection: the separated,
autonomous, mechanical self that made all the models work. Rational
Economic Man enabled economists to bypass a much more inchoate and
challenging reality.

Adam Smith's two-volume *An Inquiry into the Nature and Causes of the
Wealth of Nations* was published shortly before the American Declaration of
Independence in 1776, cost £1.16s, and was soon sold out. Smith, an absent-
minded, poorly biographized bachelor,[103] was the son of a local customs col-
lector in a small Scottish port town. After a stint as professor of logic and then
moral philosophy at the University of Glasgow, and a spell tutoring the son
of an aristocratic family on its European travels, Smith spent ten years, to the
frustration of his friends, writing *The Wealth of Nations*. The book provided
economics with its basic structure for the next hundred and fifty years, including the elements which coalesced to form Rational Economic Man. Smith's
schema overturned the old mercantilist view that national economic strength
derived from the accumulation of precious metals; *The Wealth of Nations*
switched the focus instead to an alternative type of gold, the productivity of
the labour force. In Smith's system, 'man' will toil effectively only for pecu-
niary profit; the principle of self-interest leads to maximum productivity and
so assures the public good. The economic wellbeing of nation states is best
guaranteed by unfettered markets in which 'men' are free to act as selfishly as
possible. Rational Economic Man is intrinsically selfish, and a collection of
selfish men is exactly what the system needs.

There are two obvious problems with Smith's model: the markets and the men. In the world in which *The Wealth of Nations* was written, most people worked in agriculture, and the businesses that did exist were small and responsive to changing market prices and production costs; the reality fitted the model. Unlike later economists, in Smith's work empirical observation came first, and theory second. But the development of big business meant that the framework of Rational Economic Man's operations had to be hugely enlarged to accommodate monopolistic and oligopolistic business activity (the domination of the market by a single large business, or a few of these). This brought about a situation of less than perfect competition, which is, of course, much enhanced today by the rise of multinational corporations. Neo-classical economics took over from classical economics to represent this greater complexity, but it incorporated precisely the same principles of free trade as a self-evident good, economic 'growth' as a measure of national wellbeing, the expansion of production as the goal of public economic policy, happiness as consisting of the consumption of goods, and the machine of the economic system as being ultimately powered by Rational Economic Man.

Today our global economy looks much more like this than did the economy of Adam Smith's time. Many barriers to free trade have gone, national currencies are set by the market as well as by governments, and this unfettered free-for-all ought, according to classical economy theory, have brought about a more stable, economically expansionary and fairer world. But it hasn't: 'the world refuses to dance to the expected tune'.[104] This is because the economic theory that social welfare is guaranteed by perfect competition has no empirical base; 'the calculus of hedonism' driving Rational Economic Man isn't a theory of consumer demand which fits the way people actually behave.

The initial gendering of Rational Economic Man was by default rather than design. The division of labour in eighteenth-century Scotland did make men masters in the market place; Alfred Marshall's *Principles of Economics*, another bible of classical economics, was written at a time (1892) when Victorian men's passions for inactive women at home were at their height. But even the giants of economic theory must have noticed, out of the corners of their narrowly focused eyes, that approximately half the human population, including that of their own societies, is involved in forms of labour which are excluded from the classical economic model. In Samuelson's *Economics*, for example, women are listed only under the titles 'discrimination against', 'protective labor legislation for' and 'wages of'. Giving women the 'doubtful privilege' of being embraced within the definition of Rational Economic Man[105] in no way solves the problem that men, in the sense of human beings, are often far from rational, do not behave as autonomous agents isolated from social influence or from considerations of personal relationships, are routinely involved in forms of production which lack market value, do not act as though economics is divorced from politics or from social life, and are altogether fairly powerless against a sea of market forces and a tidal wave of corporate and state-sanctified economic power.

The environmentalist Hazel Henderson produced in 1982 the aptly domestic image of a layered cake (figure 1) in order to demonstrate how much economic activity lies outside the sphere of Rational Economic Man. The icing on the cake is the official market economy, consisting of all cash transactions. Beneath that is the private sector (production, employment, consumption, investment, savings), which rests on the public sector of state and local government spending (defence, roads, education, etc.). Together these make up the GNP. The bottom two layers of the cake are outside the GNP: unpaid domestic and volunteer work, caring work, home-based production, subsistence agriculture; and the natural resource base of mother nature, which absorbs many of the uncalculated costs of GNP-defined activity: pollution, toxic waste and so forth. Environment-damaging activities feature elsewhere in the cake as productive activities; for example, the jobs created by dealing with oil spills and other pollution accidents, and the labour of wars and the military complex. Thus the environment is as much a victim of classical economics as are women.[106] When neither the planet nor women's work are counted as work, the danger is that both will count for nothing at all in the social and economic policies that are chosen and implemented. New Zealand economist Marilyn Waring's book *Counting for Nothing*[107] is a cogent argument for national accounts which value both the ecosystem and domestic and caring work.

Attempts *have* been made to include the unpaid and subsistence work of women in national accounting systems. In 1972, James Tobin and Bill Nordhaus constructed a Measurement of Economic Welfare (MEW) which ascribes value to household work, and also attributes costs to some aspects of urbanization, such as commuting to work. Comparing the results with conventional GNP estimates shows lower growth rates for the adjusted index: annual growth of 1.1 per cent over the period from 1921 to 1965, instead of 1.7 per cent.[108] Another version of an approach which tries to include some non-market factors in national accounts is the Index of Sustainable Economic Welfare (ISEW) created by Herman Daly and Richard Cobb.[109] This deducts from the value of economic activity the costs of environmental damage and depleting non-renewable resources. The result is, as with the MEW, a significant mismatch with GNP estimates of growth. A concrete example of what happens when environmental degradation is included in the growth equation is the value of Indonesia's GNP in 1983; when the depletion of petroleum reserves, forests and soil fertility is taken into account, the GNP falls by 22 per cent.[110]

There's plenty of evidence that neo-classical economics doesn't work any better than its predecessor – in the explanatory, rather than justificatory sense. For example, a major characteristic of the modern economy is its 'irrational' performance. While some things are produced in abundance – cars, chemicals,

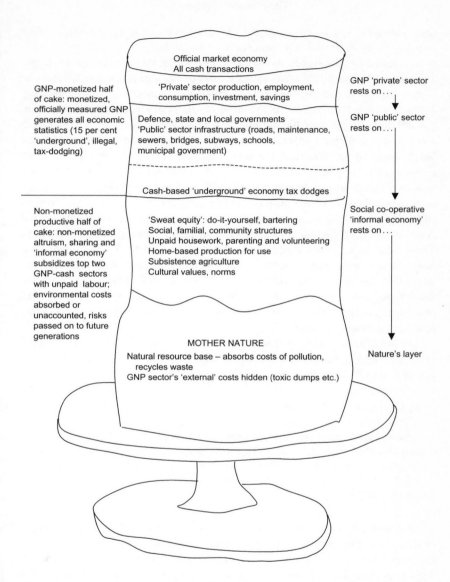

Figure 1 Total productive system of an industrial economy: Hazel Henderson's three-layer cake with icing

drugs, cosmetics, cigarettes, alcohol, luxury food – others – housing, public transport – are in chronically short supply. Money for some things such as military weapons, space travel, atomic tests and industrial research seems amply available, whereas it isn't for education, street cleaning and healthcare: the 'commodities' in which most people most of the time are most interested. Many products have no useful function at all, or fail adequately to perform the one they do have. What explains the rise of one technology rather than another is not inherent superiority in appealing to rational consumer choices, but a whole lot of 'irrational' factors which shape what people decide they ought to like. A trivial example of this is the QWERTY typewriter keyboard, now reproduced on computers worldwide. This was designed in 1873 as a feat of anti-engineering, whose purpose was to make typists type as slowly as possible. To this end, the commonest letters were scattered over all the rows, and concentrated on the left-hand side (an inconvenience for right-handed people). The reason for the anti-design was that the typewriter of 1873 jammed when adjacent keys were struck in quick succession. When this technical problem was solved, trials in 1932 with a more efficient keyboard layout showed that this would double typing speed and reduce typing effort by 95 per cent. But more efficient methods have universally failed to catch on, such is everyone's psychological investment in the old system.[111]

The well-known economist Joan Robinson (who should have got the Nobel prize, but didn't) explains the basic problem of mismatch between production and need in her *Contributions to Modern Economic Philosophy*:

> Capitalism is dazzlingly efficient at producing goods to be sold in the shops, and, directly or indirectly, profits are derived from selling. The services to meet basic human needs do not lend themselves to mass production: they are not an easy field for making profits . . . To supply goods is a source of profit, but to supply services is a 'burden upon industry'. It is for this reason that when, as a nation, 'we have never had it so good', we find that we 'cannot afford' just what we most need.[112]

Oligopoly, the only cause of deficient production in the neo-classical model, can't explain this pattern. In the real world, production is irrational, precisely because it isn't controlled by the super-rational consumer, perfectly in touch with 'his' needs. The market for goods and services is dominated by what the well-known economist and social critic John Kenneth Galbraith calls the 'power' or 'planning system'.[113] This is an alliance between large corporations, the state and the business elite, such that the economy is controlled by these forms of corporate and individual behaviour, rather than by market forces of supply and demand mediated by the will of Rational Economic Man: 'All modern industrial countries are subject to the same tyrannical circumstance. In all, the large corporations, unions and numerous individuals have escaped the discipline of the market and gained power.'[114] As Galbraith notes, this exercise of power carries 'the rich gloss of reputability': 'The men who guide the modern corporation and the outlying financial, legal, legislative, technical, advertising and other sacerdotal services of corporate function are the most respectable, affluent and prestigious members of the national community. They are the Establishment.'[115]

Because neo-classical economics reflects an outdated economic and social system, and is based on theoretical models and not the sociology of economic behaviour, most of what it announces turns out to be just as imaginary:

> The world economy is in crisis . . . The orthodoxy of economics, trapped in an idealised, mechanistic view of the world, is powerless to assist.[116]

> Neo-classical and neo-Keynesian economics, though providing unlimited opportunity for the demanding niceties of refinement, has a decisive flaw. It offers no useful handle for grasping the economic problems that now beset modern society.[117]

> The promotion of the concept that the untrammelled, self-sufficient, competitive individual will maximise human welfare damages deeply the possibility of ever creating a truly affluent, cohesive society in which everyone can participate.[118]

In *Liar's Poker*[119], Michael Lewis, then an investment banker, reflected on the huge rise in the popularity of economics as a university subject, and the growing requirement of an economics degree for a job on Wall Street. But in Lewis' experience, what one learns from such a course is almost entirely irrelevant to a job as a trader on world capital markets or in an investment bank; an economics degree functions purely to demonstrate that its owner subscribes to a belief-system enshrining the principles of self-interest and the primacy of economic life. In experiments conducted at Cornell University in the early 1990s, a group of students was each given some money and asked to divide it into two accounts: a private account, kept by the individual, and a public account, which would then be given more cash by the organizers and divided equally between all the students. The 'best' solution in this situation is a fully co-operative one: everyone puts all their money into the public account. But a self-interested individual will decide to invest solely in the private account, assuming that he or she will still be able to benefit from the greater public spiritedness of others, who will donate all their money to the public account. Whereas 50 per cent of other students gave all their money to the public account, only 20 per cent of economics students were willing to do so.[120]

One of the conclusions of this experiment is that people behave co-operatively far more than the model of self-interested economic man would suggest. This is part of a whole spectrum of evidence that the human species is capable of great altruism. Altruism props up caring labour – the 'non-market' work people, mainly women, do to maintain the survival, health and wellbeing of men, children and families, and those unable to care for themselves. What economist Nancy Folbre calls 'the invisible heart'[121] is as much a principle of economic activity as 'the invisible hand' – Adam Smith's characterization of market behaviour.

'Economism' – discrimination against people for not being part of the economy – is illustrated in the standard undergraduate economics textbook joke about what happens when a man marries his housekeeper. What happens is that her labour, being presumably paid before marriage, but not after, disappears from the GNP. This, of course, happens all the time, although its impact on the GNP these days must be less than it used to be, since there are far fewer housekeepers around. What we have instead is, in J. K. Galbraith's telling phrase, 'a crypto-servant class' of women, whose prime function is to manage and execute within households the activities of consumption which are themselves so necessary to an ever-expanding GNP. This function of women is so effectively concealed in neo-classical economics that it's possible (as happened to me in the 1960s) 'for most women to study economics without discovering how they are being used'.[122] This isn't quite how Joan Robinson would have put it, but she experienced her own disappointments with classical economics when she arrived to study it at Cambridge in the 1920s. Hoping the subject would offer 'scope for rational argument' and help her to understand the problem of world poverty,[123] she found instead the doctrine of free trade imposed as an absolute dogma, within a theoretical schema 'which (with whatever reservations and exceptions) represents the capitalist world as a kibbutz operated in a perfectly enlightened manner to maximise the welfare of all its members'.[124]

Economics did at some point wake up to the fact that the existence of women and children needed to appear somewhere in their models. Enter the economic model of the household. The New Household Economics has its own 'high priest',[125] Gary Becker, another Nobel prize winner who specializes in applying economic models to unlikely areas. Before the household came crime, which Becker portrayed as a rational choice on the part of criminals, who weigh up the costs and benefits of the crime market before deciding to take it up.[126] Becker's line on households conceptualizes marriage (and presumably non-marital heterosexual partnerships) as 'a two person firm':[127] principally a way of maximizing income, since people apparently marry other people with whom they can make the most money. Within marriage a process of economic specialization ensures greater productivity and efficiency. Thus, the gendered division of labour is, like everything else, primarily driven by market interests.

This economic concept of the household isn't at all the same thing as a family composed of different people with different interests and resources; it's a neatly unitary concept, an entourage led by a male Head, a kind of benevolent patriarch, who always considers the interests of all family members, and thus makes the best choices for everyone all the time.[128] The effort required to bring the theory into the real world of gender inequalities (in and outside households) calls for the creative annexing of sociobiology to 'explain' why women's greater 'investment' in children requires both that they do more housework and are paid less for their non-household work. Maximizing the quality of children as the 'commodity' produced by the 'business' of marriage requires that old bogey, task specialization, in the interests of greater efficiency. Another theory is dragged in here – that of 'human capital', which attributes such gender differences to free choice: women, Rational Economic Men as they are, *choose* to be exploited, because this maximizes their personal utility (satisfaction).[129]

The counter-evidence to the economists' portrayal of households as happily functioning, internally specialized economic units includes the widespread physical abuse of women and children by men in families (see chapter 3 above), inequalities in power relations and resource distribution within families,[130] and the rather striking finding that poor children do better when government financial assistance is given to their mothers rather than their fathers.[131] But economists have clung to their own piece of nonsense about benevolent patriarchy in the face of mountains of evidence to the contrary, and have thus further increased their chances of carrying out intellectually and socially useless work.[132]

Donald McCloskey, a distinguished American economist, lived for over half a century as a man. In this guise, he carried out serious and provocative work arguing that much of economics is mere rhetoric, a one-sided conversation full of literary metaphors designed to impress with their scientism, but achieving nothing very much in the way of socially useful explanation or prediction. For example, 'To say that markets can be represented by supply and demand "curves" is no less a metaphor than to say that the west wind is "the breath of autumn's being".'[133] Sometime in the 1990s Donald decided to become Deirdre. The major impact of becoming Deirdre on the critiques of mainstream economics McCloskey had already developed was that he now became Aunt Deirdre watching boys playing in a sandbox:

> The situation is sad. It is sad that economists, mainly men, are confident that their mechanical methods are correct and produce correct results. The men stride round offering advice to governments and criticisms of each other's work as though they were doing real science. They are so happy, and so proud of their masculine achievements. Their business suits are impressive, their reports fluent, their numbers weighty. Lord, Lord, one would like them to be right! . . .
>
> It is the essential sadness of boys' games . . . The sad, unspeakably sad fact about the enterprise of modern economics is that much of what it claims to have accomplished since 1945 is a game in a sandbox.[134]

Feminist economics was the last of the feminist academic challenges to social science to arrive in institutionalized form – not until the late 1980s and early 1990s.[135] The International Association for Feminist Economics was formed in 1991.[136] In 1995 a survey of 400 members of the American Economic Association revealed that only 1 per cent thought that feminist economics had achieved any significant impact on mainstream economic work.[137]

■

Once it was called eugenics, then sociobiology, now it's rebranded as evolutionary psychology,[138] though there are disputes about whether these last two really are the same animal.[139] Close to the beginning of it all, an 'amiable but rather aimless'[140] young man called Charles Darwin spent five years on a ship called HMS *Beagle* studying nature in other places, and scribbling some observations about evolution in a small red notebook. Darwin only actually used the word 'evolution' towards the end of his life, in the last edition of his *The Origin of Species*, a work whose publication he withheld for twenty years because he knew it would be deeply controversial. In presenting his ideas to the world, Darwin realized they would upset the Victorians, wedded as they were to ideas about a divinely ordered and inherently harmonious nature. But his alternative view, of nature as a perpetual selfish struggle, could only have been formed in that self-same social context. Natural selection was 'genetic capitalism',[141] the biological version of economic competition, the representation of the living world – the world of Rational Economic Man – as a capitalist financial balance sheet; Adam Smith's theories about selfish, profiteering men in cities writ large on the landscape of Mother Earth. As Marx observed in a letter to Engels, 'It is remarkable how Darwin recognizes among beasts and plants his English Society with its division of labour, competition, opening up of new markets, "inventions", and the Malthusian "struggle for existence".'[142] One aspect of this English Society was its intransigent sexism: women's domesticity and incapacity to scale masculine heights were features of Darwin's thought that pre-dated, rather than followed from, his observations about evolution.[143]

Like economics and psychoanalysis, sociobiology and evolutionary psychology (SB/EP) form a cultural paradigm for interpreting human behaviour which offers a seemingly logical and scientific framework for thinking about this. Of the three thought systems, SB/EP is the one with the most surface relevance to many of the central arguments of this book. It also underpins the other two: psychoanalysis is renowned for its explicit celebration of the biological origins of social behaviour, and economics, although dealing less explicitly in the coinage of biological explanations, nonetheless rests on an essentialist biological account, which depends heavily on gendered notions of people's private and public behaviour.

Since Freud is in trouble, 'biobabble' has replaced 'psychobabble' as the trendy delusional system today.[144] 'Genomania'[145] or 'geneticism' provide the major ideological support for SB/EP. The gene has become a 'ubiquitous popular image, appearing in newspapers, television programmes, fiction, film, advertising, magazines and childcare books', carrying the resounding, over-simplified message that personhood, behaviour, and human destiny can all be defined in terms of DNA.[146] 'Geneticism', defined as 'the enthusiastic mis-application of not fully understood genetic principles in situations to which they do not apply',[147] means that we're constantly bombarded with messages about our genes making us 'what we are': 'Keep quiet, husband dear, your brain wasn't built for talking';[148] 'Back pain may be inherited';[149] 'Women's green fingers and evolution.'[150] Scarcely a week passes without the announce-ment in the press of a possible genetic cause of some human ill which may produce a cure. What we had previously thought to be messy moral, political and economic issues turn out, after all, to be simply a matter of 'an occasional nucleotide substitution'.[151]

■

Eugenics has its own disreputable, much-written-about history.[152] Sociobiol-ogy, defined as 'the systematic study of the biological basis of all forms of social behavior',[153] started in the late 1940s in the USA. It was driven by new ethological work, such as that by Konrad Lorenz, on the innate bases of animal behaviour, and by the increasing power and success of biology. These coa-lesced in a context of dissatisfaction with prevailing social science under-standings of human behaviour; old ideas about instinct and behaviourist theories didn't seem to work very well any more, so something was needed to replace them. Books such as Robert Ardrey's *African Genesis* (1961) and his *Territorial Imperative* (1966), Lionel Tiger's *Men in Groups* (1969) and (with Robin Fox) *Imperial Animal* (1971), laid the ground for Desmond Morris's hugely successful popularization in books such as *The Naked Ape* (1967), *Intimate Behaviour* (1971), *The Human Zoo* (1979) and *Bodywatch-ing* (1985), of the amusingly uncomfortable notion that human beings can understand their behaviour better by thinking of themselves as animals. One small example is the use of cars as penis symbols (see chapter 2 above).

Sexual selection is a subspecies of natural selection. Natural selection ordains that people with traits that were adaptive during the time humans evolved as a distinct species some 100,000–600,000 years ago stand a better chance of getting their genes into the next generation. Sexual selection says that men's genetic interests are served by having as much sex with as many fertile women as possible, so as to spread their genes as far as possible, while women's reproductive chances are enhanced by finding successful, resource-rich mates with good genes to look after them while they have babies. According to the popularist sociobiology of E. O. Wilson, it thus pays males to be 'aggressive, hasty, fickle and undiscriminating', while it's more profitable for women to 'be coy, to hold back until they can identify males with the best genes'.[154]

Aside from men's promiscuity and women's coyness, two concepts are especially necessary to this chain of reasoning: kin selection and parental investment. We aren't just out to people the world with our genes, but rather to increase the pool of genes derived from ourselves and our kin. Parental investment theory, the progeny of biological anthropologist Robert Trivers, begins with the male and female roles in reproduction. While women only produce some 400 eggs in a lifetime, there are around 100 million sperm in each male ejaculate, so one certainly needs a calculator to work out the likely spillage over an average male lifetime. This 'theoretical' ability of men to inseminate thousands of women gives them much less of an investment than women in each baby. Women, with their miserable 400 eggs, which have, furthermore, to be gestated for a whole nine months, must obviously do their best to find men with good genes, otherwise they're simply wasting their time.[155] It seems that the male sex hormones are associated with something called 'symmetry', which women go for, though it's not clear why, since 'symmetrical' men have sex earlier with more partners[156] and invest less in romantic relationships than their non-symmetrical counterparts.[157] Parental investment theory is also used to 'explain' men's greater interest in sexual variety without commitment, prostitution, pornography, high-status jobs and economic resources: the male animal's overwhelming interest in self-propagation accounts for most of his bad (as well as some of his good) behaviour.

The eloquence with which theorists of SB/EP write about the prodigious quantities of sperm men can produce parallels as a rhetorical device the psychoanalysts' preoccupation with penises: in both cases the early debates were dominated by men, though more recently women have introduced a more balanced view. A good example is Sarah Blaffer Hrdy, who describes herself as an anthropologist, primatologist and evolutionary theorist, and whose book *Mother Nature* focuses instead on what other animals can tell us about the contradictions and conflicts which characterize motherhood.[158]

In mainstream SB/EP the free market enterprise system combines with the gonadal preoccupation to produce the notion of 'sperm competition',[159] and with militarist ideology to give us the aggressively entertaining idea of 'sperm wars'.[160] Robin Baker's book of that name derives a whole evolutionary programme from conjectural collisions deep in a woman's body between sperm from different men. The fundamental questions are quantitative and economic: 'Why do men inseminate enough sperm at each intercourse to fertilize the entire population of the United States – twice over? And why, then, do half of them dribble back down the woman's leg?'[161] One of the answers is that this is a process with seemingly semi-magical qualities: men apparently possess the means unconsciously to adjust the size of their ejaculates according to the threat of insemination of their mates by sexual competitors.[162] And (of course): 'The large size of the human penis and testicles relative to those of many other primates also appears to be an adaptation for sperm competition.'[163] Inspired by such observations as a correlation between testis size and aggression in the quail,[164] the size and secretions of men's gonads have been intensely scrutinized over many years for their potential to 'explain' masculine behaviours such as crime, aggression and rape. The use of anti-androgen drugs to reduce male crime has been enthusiastically promoted on these grounds for more than forty years, despite no evidence that this approach has any effect.[165] No matter: evolutionary psychology has come to the rescue by providing a new biological interpretation of crime: since men are 'naturally' highly competitive, the masculine specialism in crime is simply part of men's achievement more generally – it's just another way of seeking to outbid other men in status and resources.[166]

The nadir of sexual selection fantasies is Randy (*sic*) Thornhill and Craig Palmer's *A Natural History of Rape*, dedicated to 'the women and the girls in our lives'. Thornhill, a biologist, and Palmer, an anthropologist, argue that sexual coercion joins male choice and intrasex competition as evolutionary manoeuvres designed to ensure genetic survival. Rape is a way of circumventing female choice; it only occurs because women aren't willing to have sex with any man at any time; in particular, it's a method used by unsuccessful men to propagate their genes. The evolutionary significance of rape is proved by the rape statistics, which show that most rape involves young men as the perpetrators and young women as the victims, that rape victims suffer most if they are young, married, didn't resist, and were forced to have penile–vaginal contact.[167]

The term 'sociobiology' was initially helped to media fame by the work of Edward O. Wilson, a Harvard entomologist whose book *The Insect Societies* (1971) ended with the suggestion that similar principles of population biology and comparative zoology could profitably be applied to humans. The twenty-fifth anniversary edition of Wilson's *Sociobiology*, issued in 2000, has elephants, chimpanzees, insects and penguins on the cover: the only human image is the face of Wilson himself. Wilson is nothing if not 'deadly ambitious'[168] to swallow all scientific disciplines in one great gulp of sociobiology: chapter 27 of *Sociobiology*, entitled 'Man: from sociobiology to sociology', opens with the following invitation:

> Let us now consider man in the free spirit of natural history, as though we were
> zoologists from another planet completing a catalog of social species on Earth.
> In this macroscopic view, the humanities and social sciences shrink to special-
> ized branches of biology; history, biography, and fiction are the research proto-
> cols of human ethology; and anthropology and sociology together constitute the
> sociobiology of a single primate species.[169]

Wilson was raised as a southern Baptist and had a 'conversion' experience as a biology student at the University of Alabama in 1947. He 'discovered' evolution:

> Suddenly – that is not too strong a word – I saw the world in a wholly new way . . . a door opened to a new world. I was enthralled, couldn't stop thinking about the implications evolution has for classification and for the rest of biology. And for philosophy. And for just about everything . . . I had experienced the Ionian Enchantment . . . a belief in the unity of the sciences – a conviction, far deeper than a mere working proposition, that the world is orderly and *can be explained by a small number of natural laws.*'[170] [my italics]

Wilson's discovery gave him a 'wonderful feeling' of release from the confinements of fundamentalist religion: 'Preferring a search for objective reality over revelation', he admitted, 'is another way of satisfying religious hunger.'[171] In exactly the same way, Francis Galton, Charles Darwin's cousin, the 'father' of eugenics, rejoiced when he saw how Darwin's *The Origin of Species* replaced the religious doctrine of 'man's' fall from grace with the more profane idea of his progressive rise from barbarism to civilization.[172]

In much SB/EP, the study of how non-humans behave is used as a starting point for theories about the origins and functions of human behaviour. In Wilson's sociobiology, for example, the sexual communication of fireflies, colony divisions among army ants, fights between yellow dung-fly males, and the nesting habits of higher termites lead to the question: 'Is aggression in man adaptive? From the biologist's point of view,' Wilson decides, 'it certainly seems to be. It is hard to believe that any characteristic so widespread and easily invoked in a species as aggressive behaviour is in man could be neutral or negative in its effects on individual survival and reproduction.'[173]

On the contrary, the evidence presented in this book suggests that aggression is negative: it destroys people, animals, social systems and the environment. The main problem with SB/EP is exactly the same as the problem exhibited by economics and psychoanalysis. In claiming to be 'real' or 'standard' science, SB/EP, psychoanalysis and economics so distort the rules of the scientific method that the danger is that all we are left with is science fiction. Ethologist Richard Dawkins' book *The Selfish Gene* actually opens with the declaration, 'This book should be read almost as though it *were* science fiction' [my italics]. *The Selfish Gene*, published in 1976, the year after Wilson's *Sociobiology*, imported another modern metaphor into the SB/EP paradigm – that of genes as motivated drivers of human organisms, which are consequently nothing more than 'blindly programmed' 'robot vehicles'.[174] Genes, like diamonds, are forever: they 'swarm in huge colonies . . . sealed off from the outside world, communicating with it by tortuous indirect routes, manipulating it by remote control . . . their preservation is the ultimate rationale for our existence'.[175] The language of conscious motive imputed to genes here is quite extraordinary: genes may have many capacities, but deciding, like Rational Economic Man, to pursue their own self-interest isn't one of them.

It's very easy to portray much SB/EP as facile and offensive nonsense. While some of its practitioners do invite such caricatures through their sloppy logic and hyperbolic writing, there are many sociobiologies, and they aren't all the same. But, according to Ullica Segerstråle in her historical account of the debate, what unites all the different schools is their 'strong commitment' to their own position; critics of SB/EP display an equal tenacity in their attacks on it for its political, moral and scientific failings.[176] The most virulent criticism of Wilson's sociobiology came initially from two of his Harvard colleagues, scientists Stephen Gould and Richard Lewontin, who have maintained their resistance to a genetically determined status quo erected on a foundation of 'bad' science. As Segerstråle shows in her book, arguments about morality and science have been completely intertwined in most arguments about SB/EP. But the essence of most criticism is this point about science. 'Minuscule samples, uncontrolled experiments, exquisite analyses of heterogeneous data, and unsupported speculations'[177] all flower seductively. The SB/EP case is so full of holes it's like a giant sieve. The holes range from the speculative status of 'facts' about 'hunter-gatherer' societies, and the persistent reconstitution of anthropological evidence as uncontroversial,[178] to the misrepresentation of multiple human behaviours as universal[179] and unjustified leaps from animal to human behaviour;[180] from the focus on the characteristics and genetic origins of masculine rather than feminine behaviours (aggression/selfishness rather than pacificism/co-operation) to the stereotyping of what masculine and feminine behaviours really are.

Imputed causes and mechanisms are often obscure. For example, why would women evolve to rely on men's spatial skills rather than develop their own? How do women know whether men have good genes or not? How can theories about gender-differentiated parental investment be squared with the evidence about contemporary women choosing to delay or refrain from childbearing, or arguments about male violence against women as a masculinist genetic strategy explain the frequency of men's violence to their pregnant mates (see chapter 3 above)? How *do* men adjust the volume of their ejaculates according to sexual circumstance? Without a shared instinct for mathematics, how could anyone compute the coefficients of consanguinity needed to support the kin selection theory?[181] How can genetics explain the enormous diversity that exists in the geographical and social patterning of disease,[182] or in the cultural construction of sex 'differences',[183] including huge fluctuations in crime rates,[184] and the systematically patterned differences in values and behaviours existing among people in different modern nations?[185]

Not all SB/EP is guilty of such leaps: the work of Dawkins, in particular, has stressed the primary need for 'gene science'[186] – though, as he himself has admitted, his choice of metaphors for describing genes was unfortunate.[187] The scientificity of SB/EP depends on a set of interlocking fallacies: aspects of human behaviour (for example, aggression) are first reified as abstract forces, then measured quantitatively, then attached to non-human behaviour, and then, finally, there's the leap to the genetic conclusion: given all the previous steps, the behaviour in question has to have a genetic basis. Biologist Steven Rose calls this a 'world of looking glass logic'.[188] In the looking glass world, four standards 'essential to the acceptance of conjectures' about the evolutionary basis of human behaviours are abrogated: the standard that there needs to be a good fit between hypothesis and data; that the evolutionary explanation should be at least as good as alternative explanations; that behaviours should be independently observed or documented; and that the postulated characteristics really do relate to reproductive fitness.[189] Evolutionary psychology adds two more developed conceptual errors to sociobiology's reductionist account: misunderstanding the relationship between enabling and causal mechanisms, and privileging distal (remote) above proximal (closer) causes.

Man is an animal. 'Man' is the apposite term here, as the characterization of men in SB/EP gives them an astonishingly brute-like appearance: men, like (some) other male primates, stride about their territories killing other animals and fighting off other males in order to claim the 'best' (youngest, most fertile) females. It's just the same in Wall Street as it is in the jungle. Surprisingly, these characteristics of 'homo sapiens' are deemed 'the most highly evolved'.[190] If this is what evolution means, it's perhaps no bad thing that, as some critical rejoinders to Darwin have put it, it seems as though the process of evolution has entirely passed women by.[191]

Much popularist SB/EP harks back to the world of 'hunter-gatherer' societies to explain human behaviour. For evolutionary reasons, men are innately better at throwing things, have a genetic preference for large meat meals, and excel at map reading. Conversely, women are more verbal, observant, vegetarian, meticulous and industrious.[192] 'Hunter-gatherer' societies are described as societies in which bands of people lived in large extended kin groups; murder, committed by men mainly in disputes over women, was common; and there was a strong sexual division of labour, with men hunting large game and women looking after children and collecting food closer to home. Although only a small portion of the diets of 'hunter-gatherers' consisted of meat, this was 'the richest, most desired source of proteins and fats'.[193] It was also a good method of population control, since high-protein diets would have increased lactation and delayed the next pregnancy.[194] Men hunted meat to give women in exchange for sex; successful hunters had more affairs. These 'facts' linger on in the 'modern male mind' as an inspiration for their contemporary conduct.[195] Meat-eating, male aggression, agriculture and patriarchy are thus neatly packaged together as biological 'consequences' of our genetic inheritance.

It's difficult to take seriously such claims to 'know' how our human ancestors lived.[196] It's clear that people bring to the study of archaeological sites their own presumptions about gender, lifestyle and technology. For example, when a mortar and pestle are found in the grave of a woman they're said to prove she ground food, but the same objects in a man's grave show that he made them.[197] Archaeological evidence is equally consistent with the theory that human survival has depended more on women's productive work than men's; this is supported by modern descriptions of gatherer-hunter societies.[198]

In 1986 Bruno Latour and Sharon Strum, an anthropologist of science and a primatologist respectively, evaluated common evolutionary theories using nine simple methodological questions, including: what are the units of evolution? What qualities do the units possess? What form do relationships between the units take? What time delays are involved? What method of measurement can be used to assess answers to these questions? All the theories failed miserably.[199]

■

Sociobiology was a 'real menace'[200] and its descendant, evolutionary psychology, is 'culturally pernicious'[201] because of the seductive formulae they provide for understanding and treating complex social problems. Like its predecessor, evolutionary psychology has specifically been used to justify conservative social policies, especially a reduction in state support and intervention for disadvantaged groups.[202] Opposition to 'welfare statism' was a significant motivation for a particularly famous moment in the story of SB/EP – Richard Herrnstein and Charles Murray's *The Bell Curve: Intelligence and class structure in American life* (1994).[203] Murray was renowned for his opinions on the destructive effects of state intervention,[204] and Herrnstein, a disciple of behaviourist psychology, was equally obsessed with the heritability of IQ, convinced that there'd been a liberal conspiracy to obscure its significance.[205] *The Bell Curve*, like Wilson's work on sociobiology, sold enormous numbers and gained huge amounts of publicity for its contention that the IQ dice are loaded against Black people. The book contained no new information, but merely drew together and reinterpreted existing data, like Wilson's and other SB/EP texts.

As applied to the 'problem' of inequality between the sexes, SB/EP offers a magnificently persuasive justification of the status quo: rape and sexual coercion and the entire panoply of male aggression and violence are just nature's ways of getting selfish genes to propagate; the sexual division of labour, which, even (especially?) in 'advanced' societies loads most of the domestic burden on women's shoulders, is driven by neuroendocrinology; labour market differences, caused by 'basic biological sex differences in personality and temperament',[206] are just as much a by-product of natural selection as bipedal locomotion and opposable thumbs. Within such a schema, gendered phenomena as diverse as 'the glass ceiling' and men's refusal to iron become slickly understandable as products of immutable biological constraints. Men are 'neurologically designed' to find housework boring and unrewarding;[207] women will never rise in the labour market beyond a certain point because they lack men's hunting and status-seeking drives, cannot be single-minded, and are unprepared to take risks.[208] We live in a patriarchy which is the effect, not the cause, of sex/gender differences. It's a system run by a genetically driven neuroendocrinological machine which specifies a universal male disposition to dominate everything in sight,[209] and is uncannily characterized by just the kind of gendered division of labour about which women complain and which men find convenient: 'the home life of our own dear nuclear family'.[210] Can it be coincidence that the most popular SB/EP theorists are men? There's an intimate connection between 'the place of women in science and the science of women's place'.[211] An example of this is that when women flooded into the field of primate behaviour in the 1970s, their observations captured a new view of what animals were up to: it seemed female animals could be just as dominant, competitive and sexually aggressive as the males – it simply depends on who's doing the observing.[212]

In 1949 Nicholas Pastore investigated the attitudes to social, political and economic questions of twenty-five British and American scientists prominent in the nature–nurture controversy. He assessed their positions as 'hereditarian' or 'environmental', and their attitudes as 'conservative', 'liberal' or 'radical'. Of the twelve environmentalists, all but one were liberal or radical in their attitudes; of the twelve hereditarians, all except one were conservative. Thus, he concluded, the positions scientists took on the relative influences of nature and nurture were significantly related to 'particular sociopolitical orientations'.[213] These orientations had a marked effect on how hypotheses were formulated, the methods used to verify them, and the conclusions drawn, including about the social implications of 'scientific' evidence. In other words, the science the scientists did was informed by their political values.

The geneticist Richard Lewontin asks people in the audiences for his lectures to put up their hands if they think Blacks are mentally inferior to whites. No one does. But when he asks how many believe that men are biologically superior to women a few hands always sneak up.[214] Using nature to support racist arguments is no longer politically correct, but it's still very much 'within respectable limits' to see women's failure to achieve equality with men as a genetically determined fate.[215]

It's a complex world and innate tendencies are undoubtedly important, whether they really do predispose us to avoid the ironing, practise terrorism, affect coyness or emit unnecessarily large quantities of germinal material. But such innate dispositions – their exact nature, extent, implications and (im)mutability – need to be distinguished from the 'quite unnecessary excrescences' of SB/EP: 'the mindless fatalism; the bad genetics; the casual, distorted slapdash treatment of the psychology of motive'.[216]

Appeals to biological determinism are always most likely to be heard at moments of tension in gender relationships. When women seem to be getting on, men use Mother Nature to pull them back.[217] The central strategy here is collapsing gender into sex.[218] The aversion to culture has a messianic edge; if believing in nature isn't a fundamentalist religion, then what is?[219] 'Neuro-genetic determinism'[220] circumvents the complexity of biology and its fluid, interactive relationship with environment; there's never any absolutely naked way of seeing. Even the two-sexed body is a post-Enlightenment cultural construct.[221]

■

The discovery by the Czech Augustinian monk Gregor Mendel of trait heritability in pea plants gave contemporary eugenists in the early years of the twentieth century a new scientific vocabulary. In the same way, the 'Holy Grail' of modern geneticism is the human genome – finding the 'human biogram',[222] the real 'bible' of man – which offers the promise of identifying all the genes affecting human behaviour.[223] The Human Genome Project originated in initiatives taken in the mid-1980s by Robert Sinsheimer, a molecular biologist, and Charles DeLisi, a physicist. Sinsheimer became chancellor of the Santa Cruz campus of the University of California in 1977 and had just failed in a major ambition to acquire a laser telescope for the university. DeLisi's work on the heritability of mutations had given him the idea of comparing the genomes of children and parents; from there it was a short visionary step to the notion of sequencing the entire human genome.

In the 1980s discoveries about the role of genes in disease were accumulating with a dizzy speed. Physicists and chemists had been migrating into biology for some time, convinced that the kind of big science used to split the atom would push molecular biology into a new age (and provide good career paths as well).[224] The first serious discussions about the Human Genome Project happened at a workshop at Santa Cruz in 1985.[225] Since then, $2,932.5 million has been spent on it in the United States alone.[226] Similar moves were made in the UK, France, Italy, (former) West Germany, the Netherlands, Denmark and the (then) Soviet Union. The ultimate goal of the Human Genome Project is to map the chemical sequence of the three billion nucleotide base pairs that make up the human genome – a search for certainty which is pervaded by religious metaphors about the answers that will be delivered once geneticists have laid bare the genetic blueprint of the human 'race'. The human genome was originally estimated to consist of some 100,000 genes, but the working draft DNA sequence published in February 2001 readjusted this number to '35,000 or so' – 'only twice as many as those of a tiny transparent worm'.[227] The first complete human sequence was expected to be that of a composite person, but 'it would have both an X and a Y sex chromosome, which would formally make it a male'.[228] The number of genes per chromosome as revealed in the draft DNA sequence varied thirteenfold, with the Y-chromosome having the smallest number.[229]

'Screening' for problems lurking beneath the surface of things, for the hidden causes of human fates, is part of our cultural mindset. A *New Yorker* cartoon in the early 1990s showed an advertisement for a 'drive thru' testing centre on a busy highway offering tests for 'emissions, drugs, intelligence, cholesterol, polygraph, blood pressure, soil and water, steering and brakes, stress and loyalty'.[230] The dystopic vision at the end of the Human Genome Project is individualized printouts of our genes and genetic susceptibilities: we will each of us know, finally, what we are made of.

As well as understanding the genetic causes of human behaviour, the second major promised product of the Human Genome Project is an end to disease.[231] However, when the draft human genome sequence was published in early 2001, even its enthusiasts noted that a huge number of questions had not even begun to be tackled. These included: correlating single-base DNA variations (the project's focus) with actual patterns of health and disease; whether disease susceptibility can be predicted at all from gene sequence variation; and mapping the genes involved in 'complex traits and multigene disease'.[232] For the project to deliver what its proponents promise, the major burden of disease has to be genetically determined, the model of single gene disorders such as Huntington's has to be the general rule, and there have to be effective treatments for vulnerable individuals. None of these applies in the current state of knowledge. For example, in most 'genetic' disorders, the disease is modified both by other genes and by environmental and behavioural factors: 'Dissecting the genetic and environmental influences on common diseases presents a huge and longterm challenge.'[233] Understanding genetic susceptibility for diabetes, for instance, might eventually yield improved treatment for some subgroups of diabetics, but a simple change in eating habits, which requires no scientific knowledge beyond what we already have, would achieve much more. The genetic components in disease are often small.[234] While much is made of discoveries of this or that gene for this or that type of cancer, fewer than 10 per cent of all cancers involve inherited mutations.[235] An example is the celebrated 'breast cancer gene'. The two culprit genes, BRCA1 and BRCA2, may raise the lifetime risk of breast cancer between threefold and sevenfold, but 15–60 per cent of women carrying these genes will never develop the disease, and some 90–95 per cent of breast cancer cases are left unexplained by the genetic hypothesis.[236]

A cartoon in the *British Medical Journal* depicts two women enjoying a smoke and a bottle of wine: one says to the other, 'Cancer? Frankly darling I just don't have the gene for it', while the other replies, 'Well actually, darling, I do, but I simply don't care.'[237] The imaginative responses of many human beings to their condition are always liable to mess up the behavioural edicts of genomaniac science.

Most significantly, as Neil Holtzman, the director of genetics and public policy at Johns Hopkins University, put it, 'Exaggerating the importance of genetic factors as determinants of health stops people thinking about the need to clean up the environment and tackle socioeconomic inequity.'[238] The same is true of SB/EP as of psychoanalysis: a fixation on the architecture of our bodies means that we stop looking elsewhere for the sources and remedies of pressing social problems.

We share 99 per cent of our genes with chimpanzees[239] and 35 per cent with daffodils:[240] some of us might prefer the association with flowers to that with apes. The most serious limitation of 'human nature theorizing' is that:

> it fails to capture the very characteristic of humans that, from a broader per-spective, distinguishes them from other species: the human capacity for devis-ing and acting out, from time to time and place to place, radically different modes of life . . . Might it be proper, then, to say it is human nature to be opportune in inventing new ways of life, to possess an open agenda for action, to make different histories?[241]

∎

In 1996 the French physicist Alan Sokal published a paper in the American cultural studies journal *Social Text* called 'Transgressing the boundaries: toward a transformative hermeneutics of quantum gravity'.[242] The paper used recent developments in quantum gravity physics to argue that there's no such thing as an external physical world whose truths await discovery by science. Physical reality is a social construct, and all knowledge is subjective, with its principal role that of encoding dominant ideologies and cultural power rela-tions. The conclusion of Sokal's forty-five-page paper was the need for modern science to refute authoritarianism and elitism and redefine its content, method-ology and institutional base, in order better to serve the political project of the new global world order.

Sokal's argument fits well with the newest delusional system – a frame-work of cultural understanding called postmodernism. This 'puzzling, uppity'[243] term has a number of tantalizingly flexible meanings:

> It may mean . . . a work of imagination that defies the difference between paint-ing and sculpture, styles and genres, gallery and the street, art and everything else. It means a life that looks suspiciously like a TV serial . . . It means licence to do whatever one may fancy and advice not to take anything you or the others do too seriously . . . It means a shopping mall overflowing with goods whose major use is the joy of purchasing them; and existence that feels like a life-long confinement to the shopping mall. It means the exhilarating freedom to pursue

anything and the mind-boggling uncertainty as to what is worth pursuing and in the name of what one should pursue it.[244]

The term 'postmodernism' originated in the work of an Hispanic poet, Federica de Onis, who used it in the 1930s to describe a particular aesthetic style. In the Anglophone world it emerged in the 1950s with the different referent of a historical period, and finally arrived in force in the 1980s in the writings of French philosophers such as Jacques Lacan, Julia Kristeva, Luce Irigaray and Jean Baudrillard.[245] Postmodernity is where the world finds itself after the breakdown of the 'Enlightenment Project', which lasted from the last part of the eighteenth century until well into the twentieth, and was all about believing in facts, rationality and an objectively understandable external world which could accurately be represented in human beings' knowledge.[246] Postmodernity is a set of historical circumstances: the rise of multinationalism, global culture, mass tourism, space travel, pluralistic identities, a consumer society devoted to the production and satisfaction, not of needs, but of desires and longings.[247] It's symbolized by the image of a Bedouin on a camel wearing jeans under his robes, holding a transistor radio and bearing an advertisement for Coca-Cola on the camel's back;[248] 'It is the principle: *anything goes.*'[249]

If anything goes, one thing that definitely must go is the primacy of 'grand narrative': Christianity, Islam, Hinduism, Marxism, feminism, quantum physics, humanism – these are simply different stories which, because they present different versions of the truth, reveal the emptiness of the idea of truth itself. Truth is never *found* but perpetually *made*; theories of communications and games are the *only* devices which can aid our understanding. This goes for such old-fashioned notions as race, class and gender, all of which have no referent beyond constantly shifting personal identities, which is a neat way to dispose of the conceptual tools needed to improve the lives of vulnerable people.[250] This viewpoint is most strongly stated in the bible of postmodernism by the French philosopher Jean-François Lyotard. His *The Postmodern Condition: A report on knowledge*[251] was commissioned by the University Council of the government of Quebec, and is unusual among government-sponsored reports in not presenting any data on what academics are actually *doing* by way of teaching or research: it simply expounds one academic's view.

There are three major problems with postmodernism as the newest delusional system. The first is its obscurity. The language used by postmodernists is dense, imprecise, long-winded, grammatically complex, hugely inaccessible and hence intrinsically undemocratic: the very opposite of the general ethos of universal anything-goes-for-everybody underlying postmodernism's central ambition of demystifying and opening up knowledge to multiple perspectives and realities.[252]

The second problem is that postmodernism wraps intellectuals in sterile debates and isolates them from important social movements. A main function of postmodernism is to support the careers of postmodernists: 'the concept of "postmodernity" has a value entirely of its own in so far as it purports to capture and articulate the novel experience of just one, but one crucial social category of contemporary society: the intellectuals'.[253] Postmodernism usefully replaces other ideas with which intellectuals have got bored. This category of intellectuals may be more unitary than most of the categories postmodernism discusses, consisting mainly of white, male intellectuals 'who speak to and about one another with coded familiarity', using language rooted in significant 'master' narratives.[254]

This point about intellectual pretentiousness is best made by reference to Sokal's paper, which was, in fact, a spoof. Sokal's purpose in spoof-spinning was to defend science as a worthwhile endeavour. The 'scientific attitude' respects the clarity and logical coherence of theories, and believes in confronting theories with real-world evidence; science isn't a text, but a set of systematic and explicit practices, whose emphasis on experiment and verification offers the best safeguard there is against ideological bias.[255]

The third problem of postmodernism is this attack on science. Science as a social institution *is* linked to various forms of power; scientists *do* sometimes behave reprehensibly; and the pursuit of rational understanding of the world *does* embody the two popularly discredited notions of rationality, and the world as objectively real. For these reasons, French philosophy, the first major repository of intellectual postmodernism (often, significantly, combined with psychoanalytic theory), has a lot to say about scientific ideas and terminology. However, most of it misunderstands, confuses, jargonizes or otherwise misrepresents what scientists have done or are trying to do.[256] This isn't because science is inherently incomprehensible to non-scientists, but because the postmodernists who attack it haven't taken the trouble to find out what it is. Lyotard's book, for example, which had as its main focus the epistemological state of the natural sciences, was based on what Lyotard admits was an extremely limited knowledge of science on his part: 'I made up stories, I referred to a quantity of books I'd never read, apparently it impressed people.'[257]

As I write this, the world's media run and rerun the images of the terrorist attacks on New York and Washington. Our screens and newsprint are full of smoke and fire, of burning and collapsing buildings, of anguished cellular phone activity, of people's anxious, sobbing faces. The mantra of the black toyplanes divebombing the World Trade Center is continually flashed across our screens, superseded by the great red sun of the Manhattan dawn hung with a carpet of terrorists' dust. In the aftermath, Americans rush out to buy flags and guns: 'They want to do something, so that's what they're doing – they're buying guns.'[258] Almost certainly those responsible for these acts of violence will all be men. All the experts on terrorism who are invited to air their views in the media are men, bonded in what comes over as a deep-seated fascination with violence. The devastating prospect of war is affirmed in authoritative tones, almost with a smile on the face. When President Bush says this is the first war of the twenty-first century, he doesn't say it with any obvious regret. SB/EP specifies that aggression even at the level of national states is biological in origin.[259] It would thus be a great deal safer for all of us if the world's weapon systems were controlled by women[260] (a point made by UN Secretary Kofi Annan when he argued for girls' education – see chapter 4 above).

Economics would predict – and perhaps the terrorists did too – a direct relationship between the material collapse of buildings and the temporary collapse of world trading markets; a young male reporter speaks enthusiastically of the 'virility' with which the markets are responding to the challenge. Aggression breeds aggression. Peacefulness, of course, might also be a fertile state, given half a chance. The same 'genetic evidence' that SB/EP draws on could easily be reassembled to construct a persuasive argument about the existence of genetically programmed learning rules for co-operative behaviour.[261] Genomania is shaped by culture, just like everything else.

■

All delusional systems have their time and place, their proponents, defenders, users and critics. Power informs who believes what and when, and whose interests are most represented and confirmed by particular belief structures. Hence the shadowy existence of women and other so-called minorities' perspectives and experiences in the language and claims of psychoanalysis, SB/EP and neo-classical economics; hence the enormous and enduring capacity of these belief-systems to legitimate gender divisiveness – masculinity as alienated and aggressive 'rationality', femininity as marginalized and nearly invisible community; hence also some academics' contribution to this debate in the form of the magnificently obscurantist edifice of postmodernist theory, which completely blocks our view of any sensible way forward.

A number of characteristics are shared by the first three of the delusional systems discussed in this chapter. The first is biological determinism: the dangerously fundamentalist idea that our conduct is irretrievably driven by the bodies we inhabit. The second is the invisibility of culture. How human beings construct the way they live is treated, at best, as an irritating artefact of their biology; at worst, it simply isn't on the agenda. Thirdly, the self-serving individual is king of it all: orchestrating social relations in the light of individualized psychical truth, dominating the economy, shaping social structures as means to genetic survival. Finally, we have the subtle, but nonetheless forced, disappearance of power relations. If power corrupts, it's because power explains, and nothing else will do the job nearly as well. Postmodernism adds insult to injury by making us all victims of a constantly moving kaleidoscope with no fixed centre, no common focus for our troubled gaze, and thus no place from which we can collectively plot our escape to a better world.

The problem is that the production of ideas has a life of its own.[262]

9
World-travelling

The American economist Donald McCloskey's transition to Deirdre took three years during his/her early fifties. S/he compares gender-crossing to foreign travel:

> On a trip to New York to see a friend after my own crossing I stood in the hall of photographs of Ellis Island and wept at the courage . . .
> It's strange to have been a man and now to be a woman. But it's no stranger perhaps than having once been a West African and now being an American, or once a priest and now a businessman.[1]

Making the gender transition isn't just a question of getting the surgery, fixing the hair and buying the makeup: women hold beer bottles differently from men, for example, they cross roads differently, they stick to the proper paths across parks rather than going directly, they talk differently, both among themselves and with men. Before he stops being Donald, he goes to a square dance with his wife, where he 'played the manly role but daydreamed at the dance about what it would feel like to be a woman. He watched a woman . . . talking animatedly to other women, with the self-deprecating style women use when charming others of their tribe. *Unlike the boasting of my tribe*, he thought.'[2]

'The social construction of gender is, after all, something a gender crosser comes to know with unusual vividness. She does it for a living.'[3] When he dresses as a woman, Donald talks to his mother about life and relationships, whereas as a man he 'would have been bored or embarrassed once the talk moved beyond exchanges of salient fact and lofty opinion and What I Just Accomplished. He had been puzzled as men are by the endless gossip of women. "Gossip," the male jibe. How do they find things to talk about? I mean, without sports.'[4] He buys Deborah Tannen's book on men and women in conversation, *You Just Don't Understand*, and practises Tannen's 'rules': 'Listen, do not interrupt, support the speaker, maintain eye contact, do not gratuitously change the subject . . . within a few minutes the two other men were treating Donald as a woman. They were going on with their ping-pong of conversation. . . . He was out of it, as women are in men's eyes.'[5]

It's a little awkward, changing gender, in the academic community. For a start, it has an effect on what one means by knowledge. As a male economist, Donald had built a career criticizing the redundant, obfuscating games of many of his colleagues (see chapter 8 above); as Deirdre, these now seem even sillier. 'The notion of love' enters her mindset as a topic which belongs in any serious science of economics; a 'more modest contemplative voice' substitutes for a 'hardhitting' masculine style in her own work, which becomes more open to sociological approaches.[6] 'The notion that we can prove or disprove a great social truth by standing at a blackboard', she decides, 'is a peculiarly masculine delusion.'[7] On an institutional level, the dean tells Deirdre her gender change is great for their affirmative action programme – he's acquired one more woman without actually having to *do* anything. Wait a minute, he says then, as one economist to another, it's better than that – I can cut your salary by 30 per cent! Deirdre publishes a paper attacking economists' uses of statistical significance, but the men don't understand how fundamental a point 'Aunt Deirdre' has made about their sandbox games; they simply send her copies of their own papers on the subject.

As Deirdre, she is less assertive, less confident, less single-minded, more patient and more interested in clothes, cooking and people's stories than Donald was. She cries more, remembers colours better, drives less aggressively, navigates by landmarks rather than maps, and is uninterested in cars, sports and war stories. After a while:

> She had started to forget what it was like to be a man . . . She forgot what it felt like to not understand relationships because you find them boring. Or to feel that you are by rights the local hero. Or to feel that people should serve you. Or most superficially and most fundamentally to think of men as 'we' and women as 'they'.[8]

Once people start treating you as another kind of person, that's the person you become. The writer James Morris became Jan; his/her account of this process notes that:

> The more I was treated as woman, the more woman I became . . . If I was assumed to be incompetent at reversing cars, or opening bottles, oddly incompetent I found myself becoming. If a case was thought too heavy for me, inexplicably I found it so myself . . . Men treated me more and more as a junior . . .

my lawyer, in an unguarded moment one morning, even called me 'my child':
and so, addressed every day of my life as an inferior . . . I accepted the
condition.[9]

(Auto)biographies about sex/gender transitions show that the 'scenario of
gender' is culturally rich, complex and multifaceted; not at all the binary structure described in stories of sociobiology as mapped directly onto a primary
and uncomplicated division of biological sex.[10]

■

Virginia Woolf wrote *Orlando* for her androgynous lover, Vita Sackville-West,
whose son described it as 'the longest and most charming love-letter in literature'.[11] In this audacious, irreverent 'upper class fairy tale',[12] we watch a character shifting gender through three hundred years of European history. Orlando
begins as a young man at the court of Queen Elizabeth I, becomes an ambas-
sador in Constantinople in the reign of King Charles, marries a dancer, falls
into a coma, awakens as a young woman in eighteenth-century England, and
carries us with her/him to the end of the saga, which is when the book was
published in October 1928. Like Donald/Deirdre McCloskey, Orlando understands much more about gender as a woman than she did as a man. For
example, 'She remembered how, as a young man, she had insisted that women
must be obedient, chaste, scented, and exquisitely apparelled. "Now I shall
have to pay in my own person for those desires," she reflected; "for women
are not (judging by my own short experience of the sex) obedient, chaste,
scented, and exquisitely apparelled by nature."'[13] As a woman, Orlando will
never be able to swear, wear a coronet, walk in procession, lead an army, or
prance down Whitehall on a charger. The most she'll be able to do is 'to pour
out tea and ask my lords how they like it. "D'you take sugar? D'you take
cream?" . . . mincing out the words, she was horrified to perceive how low an
opinion she was forming of the other sex, the manly, to which it had once been
her pride to belong.'[14]

■

In Charlotte Perkins Gilman's short story, 'If I were a man', Mollie turns into
her husband Gerald for the day. On the train she discovers how everything *fits*
so well – her back against the seat, her feet on the floor; when the conductor
comes round, she reaches in her pocket for change: 'These pockets came as a
revelation. Of course she had known they were there, had counted them, made
fun of them, mended them, even envied them; but she never had dreamed of
how it *felt* to have pockets.' She looks at the women's hats around her in the
carriage as she never has before; while the men's seem normal and dignified,
the women's seem suddenly 'like the decorations of an insane monkey'.[15]

Since she looks like a man, the other men treat her as one, which includes all kinds of confidences about women: she learns for the first time what men *really* think of women.

■

Evelyn, a university professor, leaves England for a teaching post in the USA. On his last night in London, he watches the famous actress Tristessa de St Ange in a film version of *Wuthering Heights*. His companion, whose name he's forgotten, embarrasses him by crying: 'As far as I can remember, this girl had grey eyes and a certain air of childlike hesitancy. I always liked that particular quality in a woman . . . Sometimes I'd amuse myself by tying a girl to the bed before I copulated with her. Apart from that, I was perfectly normal.'[16] In America, Evelyn finds a scene of civil and social chaos; Black and feminist militants are conducting guerrilla warfare in the cities; elsewhere, groups of religious zealots defend 'freedom'. In New York, Blacks erect a wall round Harlem, and female sharpshooters target men who loiter too long in front of blue movie theatres, and send would-be brides razors through the post. Evelyn takes up with a Black model called Leilah, who gets pregnant by him; but he's bored with her by now, and forces her to have an abortion, which is botched, leaving Leilah without a womb as well as without a baby.

The job falls through; Evelyn decides to take a vacation crossing America in a second-hand car. En route he's captured by a technologically advanced group of matriarchal feminist separatists who castrate him, planning also to impregnate him with his own sperm. The conversion of Evelyn to Eve takes two months, during which s/he's fed female hormones, and is psychologically reprogrammed by being read tales of the old barbarous acts against women (female circumcision, foot-binding, etc.) and made to watch old Hollywood movies.

At the end of the two months, Eve's nurse/carer, Sophia, takes off her/his bandages and leaves her/him alone with a mirror:

> But when I looked in the mirror, I saw Eve; I did not see myself. I saw a young woman who, though she was I, I could in no way acknowledge as myself, for this one was only a lyrical abstraction of femininity to me, a tinted arrangement of curved lines . . .
>
> Let the punishment fit the crime, whatever it had been. They had turned me into the *Playboy* center fold. I was the object of all the unfocused desires that had ever existed in my own head. I had become my own masturbatory fantasy . . .
>
> 'Don't you think,' asked Sophia, 'that the domination of man has caused us all too much pain? Were you ever happy, when you were a man, since you left the womb, unless you were trying to get back into it?' And she gave me a virgin's look of disdain.

'Will I be happy now I am a woman?' I demanded.

'Oh, no!' she said and laughed. 'Of course not! Not until we all live in a happy world!'[17]

Angela Carter's novel *The Passion of New Eve* is a theatrical play on essentialist notions of sex and gender. She lampoons the artificiality of masculine ideas about women, using her hero/ine's conversion from a licentious young man into a confused but fully 'functional' woman as a way of insinuating the point: gender is what we make it.

As Deirdre McCloskey put it: 'Doing gender can be viewed as an accretion of learned habits, learned so well that they feel like external conditions, merely the way things are. It is a shell made by the snail and then confining it . . . *Nature, nurture? One can't be sure. Even I, inside the experiment. Yet what does it matter?*'[18] 'Scientific explanations do not much matter', decides Jan Morris in *Conundrum*. 'What matters is the liberty of us all to live as we wish to live; love however we want to love; and to know ourselves.'[19]

■

Evelyn's confrontation with Eve in the mirror is reminiscent of another, real, world-travelling encounter. In the 1950s, the American journalist John Griffin decided to live like a 'Negro' in order to find out at first hand about living conditions for Blacks in the South. Using medication and ultraviolet rays to dye his skin, shaving his head and rubbing in skin stain, he acquired the identity of an itinerant Negro, staying in cheap rooms in ghetto areas. The first shock was when he saw himself in the mirror:

> Turning off all the lights, I went into the bathroom and closed the door. I stood in the darkness before the mirror, my hand on the light switch. I forced myself to flick it on.
>
> In the flood of light against white tile, the face and shoulders of a stranger – a fierce, bald, very dark Negro – glared at me from the glass. He in no way resembled me . . .
>
> I had expected to see myself disguised, but this was something else. I was imprisoned in the flesh of an utter stranger, an unsympathetic one with whom I felt no kinship . . . The worst of it was that I could feel no companionship with this new person. I did not like the way he looked.[20]

■

On the space freighter *Mindful*, Dr Shevek, a physicist from the cold anarchic-socialist planet of Anarres, set out on a journey to the mother planet, Urras, an altogether different, capitalist kind of place. Shevek was on a mission to promote human solidarity. He also had something to give – the General

Temporal Theory, an invention which permitted the instantaneous transferral of matter across space.

Anarres had been populated some six hundred years before by a revolution started by a syndicate of cooks and waiters and led by Odo, a female communitarian. The bleak moon of Anarres was given to the Odonians by the Council of World Governments to keep them from doing any more mischief on Urras. Since then, the two worlds had proceeded on their own singular trajectories: while Urras was a class- and status-ridden society, driven by the profit motive and disfigured by much crime, hunger and unemployment, the suppression of women and a total disregard for ecology, Anarres was peopled by pacifist vegetarian revolutionaries; there was no crime, sex equality prevailed, and the government was simply a structure for co-ordinating production and distribution and ensuring that the nasty jobs were shared out equally.

After he had his measles vaccine from the freighter medic (like Third World cultures in the twentieth century, the Anarresti were vulnerable to the diseases of 'civilization'), Shevek engaged the doctor in conversation. He asked why there weren't any women on the ship. Dr Kimoe replied that:

> running a space freighter was not women's work. History courses and his knowledge of Odo's writings gave Shevek a context in which to understand this tautological answer, and he said no more. But the doctor asked a question in return, a question about Anarres. 'Is it true, Dr. Shevek, that women in your society are treated exactly like men? . . . Is there really no distinction between men's work and women's work?'
>
> 'Well, no, it seems a very mechanical basis for the division of labour, doesn't it? A person chooses work according to interest, talent, strength – what has the sex to do with that?'
>
> 'Men are physically stronger,' the doctor asserted with professional finality.
>
> 'Yes, often, and larger, but what does that matter when we have machines? . . .'
>
> Kimoe stared at him, shocked out of politeness. 'But the loss of – of everything feminine – of delicacy – and the loss of masculine self-respect – You can't pretend, surely, in *your* work, that women are your *equals*? In physics, in mathematics, in the intellect? . . .'
>
> Shevek sat in the cushioned, comfortable chair . . . On the viewscreen the brilliant curve of Urras hung still against black space, like a blue-green opal. That lovely sight, and the lounge, had become familiar to Shevek these last days, but now . . . all of it seemed as alien as it had the first time he saw it.[21]

The Anarresti missionary's exposure to life on Urras is a mixed experience. He enjoys its luxuries, the beauty of the landscape, the vitality and intelligence of the people he meets. He's upset by the poverty, the media trash, the absence of women from intellectual life – back in Anarres his own partner, Takver, is a fish geneticist, an able 'working mother'. Shevek tries to fit into the culture of Urras by becoming a consumer:

> Perfumes, clocks, lamps, statues, cosmetics, candles, pictures, cameras, games, vases, sofas, kettles, puzzles, pillows, dolls, colanders, hassocks, jewels, carpets, toothpicks, calendars, a baby's teething rattle of platinum with a handle of rock crystal . . . everything either useless to begin with or ornamented so as to disguise its use . . . the strangest thing . . . was that none of the millions of things for sale were made there.[22]

He tries to eat meat, but his stomach rebels. When it comes to his secondary mission, handing over the General Temporal Theory, he's completely stymied by the Urrasti's primary conceptual failure to understand the idea of a gift.

At the end of Ursula Le Guin's *The Dispossessed*, subtitled 'an ambiguous utopia', Shevek goes back to Anarres, to Takver and the children, who are, like women and children in science fiction novels everywhere, waiting for him.

■

As a form of world-travelling, science fiction has, for most of its life, been overwhelmingly constrained by its authors' embeddedness in one culture (for another example, see the beginning of chapter 4 above). Like science, science fiction has tended to repeat, rather than revise, certain of our earthly customs, including, especially, those relating to sex and gender. While spaceships take off for distant worlds and the technology is quite marvellous, their brave male explorers have mainly ventured out into the well-known territory of 'intergalactic suburbia'.[23] Galaxies everywhere are liberally sprinkled with white middle-class nuclear families, and are prone to sprout women whose chief characteristics are weak brains and skimpy underwear.[24]

The standard history of science fiction as a genre dates its birth as 'the fiction of a technological age'[25] to the Industrial Revolution. Its midwife was 19-year-old Mary Shelley, daughter of the feminist Mary Wollstonecraft and soon-to-be wife of the poet Percy Bysshe Shelley. Mary Shelley started to write *Frankenstein*, her own version of *Paradise Lost*, while holed up in a Swiss villa during the wet summer of 1816. She'd lost a newborn child the year before and her own mother had died giving birth to her, leaving a body of writings which others said proved she was a monster.[26]

The core of Mary Shelley's parable about the evils of modern technology is a failed experiment involving a monster. Victor Frankenstein, a scientist – whose idealistic, single-minded character is loosely based on Percy Shelley's own[27] – makes a body from bits of corpses retrieved from graveyards, hospitals and slaughterhouses, and gives it life (the means is unspecified, but it probably had something to do with the wonderful new business of electricity). Having laboured at this task for two years, obsessed by the 'beauty of the dream' of creating life, Frankenstein's dream metamorphoses into a nightmare of horror and disgust at what he's done. The monster escapes, and the book opens with series of letters written by Robert Walton, an explorer, who comes across Frankenstein desperately searching for his lost monster in the Arctic. The monster, endowed with feelings and intelligence, struggles to find a place in human society, but he suffers from the loneliness of never seeing anyone resembling himself. This is a male monster, although most readings of *Frankenstein* view him – nameless, homeless, a male creation – as figuratively female.[28] After Frankenstein refuses to make a female mate for him, the monster exacts revenge by killing Frankenstein's brother, his best friend and Frankenstein's new wife, on their wedding night. Shelley suggests that the monster's real tragedy was not his creation per se, but the failure of his creator to take any kind of responsibility for him. As the monster says, 'Am I to be thought the only criminal, when all humankind sinned against me?'[29]

World-travelling is an essential device of science fiction because it's an act capable of breaking the links between nature and culture which tie us down – both materially and metaphorically – in *this* world. Since the 1970s there's been a flowering of science fiction written by women, and much of this has led into a whole new laboratory of experiments about sex and gender. The female scientists in the new science fiction laboratory have poured the political preoccupation with sexuality and gender as social constructs into the literary test-tube and have created much strangely coloured, combustible material as a result. Science fiction has become 'social science fiction', as the heritage of its writers has annexed to it the inventive possibilities of sociology, anthropology, economics and linguistics, as well as science proper.[30] Le Guin, for example, is the daughter of Alfred Kroeber, the celebrated cultural anthropologist whose work on the primacy of cultural forms in shaping individual personality had an enormous impact on early twentieth-century anthropology.[31]

Most significantly, the genre is one of three places – the others are detective stories and supernatural fiction – to look for the work of 'outsider artists', whose 'unlabeled, disallowed, disavowed, not-even-consciously-perceived experience' can't easily be embodied in other forms of art.[32] Science fiction is a literary form that allows for the writing of new 'myths of human intelligence and human adaptability'.[33] What is sex? What is gender? What kind of society can you have if women don't give birth to babies any more? Where cooperation and community replace competition and The Family, what happens to 'natural' human aggression? Is peace simply dull (a thought Le Guin seems to leave us with at the end of *The Dispossessed*) or does it make people happy? How might our understandings of what people 'are' be reshaped by watching what happens to their behaviour in entirely different circumstances?

Estrangement from one's own culture is a route to denaturalization. Sociobiologists couldn't write science fiction (though what they write is a form of fiction anyway). All stories, both scientific and otherwise, are rooted in experience acquired within a particular political order which reads its own scripts into 'alien' worlds.

■

Our nearest aliens are species with whom we have a lot in common. In the early 1920s a little girl called Alice Hastings Bradley was taken by her parents, an attorney/explorer/naturalist and a writer respectively, on a 2,700-mile trek across Africa in search of the black gorillas of the Ugandan mountains.[34] Alice's mother, Mary Hastings Bradley, wrote a book about this called *Alice in Jungle Land*. Altogether she wrote thirty-five books, including the first observations to be made by a Westerner about the non-aggressive habits of gorillas.[35] When she grew up, little Alice became a successful painter, an art critic, a major in the US army, and the first woman to work in photo-intelligence. Together with her second husband, she founded the CIA. After acquiring a PhD in experimental psychology, she turned into James Tiptree Jr, a famous science fiction writer, renowned for the 'ineluctably masculine', 'lean, muscular' style of his writing.[36] Her writing name was borrowed from a jampot – though she used the alternative 'Racoona Sheldon' for 'overtly feminist' tales.[37] In 1987 at the age of 72 Alice Sheldon shot her blind and bedridden husband and then herself; they were found dead in bed together, holding hands.[38]

Alice Sheldon's writing is much preoccupied with 'alien conversations' of many kinds.[39] Her science fiction was, she said, a response to the 'sky-darkening presence of patriarchy'.[40] She talked of feeling wounded by what men do to the planet and other humans, appalled by wars, aggression, competition and dominance. Her reputation for masculine writing was earned through an authentic authorial misogyny, though notes of ridicule were always discernible somewhere. In 'Houston, Houston, do you read?',[41] three male survivors of an earthly disaster are accidentally precipitated by solar flare activity 300 years into the future on an American spacecraft. They're rescued just before their air supply runs out by another craft with an all-female crew who tell the men that the holocaust from which they've just fled resulted in near-universal sterility; the women in this future world are therefore all cloned. In an oft-quoted line, the women explain about the exclusion of men from their world: 'We simply have no facilities for people with your emotional problems.'[42] One of the three men gets high on the prospects for him in this situation of male scarcity, and tries to rape one of the female astronauts. But rape in zero gravity is an awkward feat, and he's also quite unaware it's a set-up job and the women are simply after his sperm.

The lead character in 'Houston, Houston' is Orren Lorimer, a scientist, the least macho of the three men, but even he finds himself defending patriarchy just a little bit – men's invaluable contribution to history, the sacrifices they've made to defend women, and so forth. The ship's captain is unimpressed: 'As I understand it, what you protected people from was largely other males, wasn't it?' In the transmissions between base and the female spacecraft the men hear the women saying, ' "I think they're aliens". Are we not? Lorimer thinks.' At the end of the story, after an outbreak of male violence has led to his colleagues' death, Lorimer wearily asks the women what they call themselves. ' "Women's World? Liberation? Amazonia?" "Why, we call ourselves human beings" ', they say.[43]

The cultural estrangement required by science fiction enabled Sheldon to see the links between masculinity, violence and death (of life forms and planets): to answer the question asked by Donna Haraway at the beginning of her own mammoth work on the 'science' of primatology, the question about how love, power and science are intertwined in modern constructions of nature.[44] 'The problem', says Sheldon, 'is to try to understand real people, and to determine whether a handful of genes on one chromosome has any identifiable effects on their way of being human.'[45]

As Orren Lorimer in Tiptree's 'Houston, Houston' observed, the real aliens in much science fiction are actually representatives from our own culture. Aliens reproduce hierarchical divisions of race, class and gender;[46] they personify difference, a way of defining men in relation to women and women in relation to men; but aliens also stand for the divided selves forced on women by the attempt to survive the distortions of patriarchy.[47] Le Guin's Anarresti, and the cloned all-female survivors of the ravaged earth in 'Houston, Houston', iterate common themes of 'utopias' where the old rules of alienation no longer apply.[48] These are quasi-tribal worlds with a real sense of community (rarely based on biological kinship) which lack any need for government; there's no competition, profit motive, crime or war, and very little violence; ecologically minded, altruistic people live, often literally, in harmony with nature; there's no class, hierarchy or organized religion; technology is put to democratic, social uses; women are sexually and physically free; and flexible, often communal childrearing arrangements obtain, creating a different, non-possessive psychology for adults and children alike: 'There are no words more obscene than "I can't live without you".'[49] In all these respects, stories such as Joanna Russ's *The Female Man*, Charlotte Perkins Gilman's *Herland*, Suzy McKee Charnos's *Motherlines*, Monique Wittig's *Les Guérillères*, Marge Piercy's *Woman on the Edge of Time*, Sally Gearhart's *The Wanderground* and Ursula Le Guin's *The Left Hand of Darkness* offer people displeased with contemporary gender arrangements an alternative, less alienated vision.

■

Playing around with gender is one way to do it; the other is to do without gender altogether.

Le Guin's *The Left Hand of Darkness* is set on another icy planet, Gethen or Winter, where the inhabitants are human but neither male nor female.

They're all capable of bearing or fathering children during periods of sexual receptiveness called kemmer, when each partner takes on female or male characteristics at random to form a female–male pair. As an early investigator of Gethenian culture explained:

> Consider: Anyone can turn his hand to anything. This sounds very simple, but its psychological effects are incalculable. The fact that everyone between seventeen and thirty-five or so is liable to be . . . 'tied down to childbearing' implies that no one is quite so thoroughly 'tied down' here as women, elsewhere, are likely to be – psychologically or physically. Burden and privilege are shared out pretty equally; everybody has the same risk to run or choice to make. Therefore nobody here is quite so free as a free male anywhere else.
>   Consider: A child has no psycho-sexual relationship to his mother and father. There is no myth of Oedipus on Winter.
>   Consider: There is no unconsenting sex, no rape . . .
>   Consider: There is no division of humanity into strong and weak halves, protective/protected, dominant/submissive, owner/chattel, active/passive. In fact the whole tendency to dualism that pervades human thinking may be found to be lessened or changed on Winter.[50]

Earth envoy Genly Ai has a difficult time as an alien on Winter. After two years there, he still can't see the people of the planet through their own eyes; he can only see them as men or women, categories so irrelevant to the Gethenians but so essential to his own culture.

'I eliminated gender to find out what was left', explained Le Guin in an essay some years later. In fact, her first intention had been to write a novel about a society that had never had war; that came first, the genderlessness second.[51] It's hard to eliminate gender when you come from a gendered place. 'When we look at what we can't see, what we do see is the stuff inside our heads.'[52] The inhabitants of Gethen are referred to as male, a practice which earned Le Guin a certain amount of criticism. She did it originally because she enjoyed writing the sentence, 'the king was pregnant', and because she refused to mangle the English language by using non-sexist pronouns.[53] Later she regretted this decision and changed it (in the screenplay and other versions of the novel).

The Left Hand of Darkness was published around the same time as Joanna Russ started to write *The Female Man*, a classic of contemporary science fiction: indeed, it was Russ's speculations about what would happen if you changed Le Guin's masculine pronouns that brought her own all-female world of Whileaway into being.[54] But Whileaway is only one of the worlds in *The Female Man*. The book is the sociobiologist's anti-text, a racy treatise on the intersections of nature and nurture, and, as Russ has argued, 'the truest, most complete account available of what it feels like to be alienated as a woman and a feminist'.[55] *The Female Man* is about a completely successful experiment in which four genetically identical women are raised in four parallel universes. Janet Evason ('Evason is not "son", but "daughter". This is *your* translation'[56]) comes from Whileaway, another serene, safe place without any discernible government, where a plague killed all the men and the women learnt how to merge ova, giving each child a 'body mother' and an 'other mother'. Everyone has a child when they're about thirty, enjoying a five-year vacation from everything else while doing so. Russ once said that she brought Janet to earth in order to reconcile her to a two-sexed world, where the alienation of the sexes from the future of human possibilities is almost complete.[57] Jeannine, a timid New York librarian with shapeless clothes and an impotent boyfriend, belongs to the USA of the 1960s, except that the Second World War never happened, and the Great Depression never ended. Joanna is a modern woman, too, but, despite bearing the author's name, she's a prickly fictional character. The fourth woman, Jael, has silver eyes and nails and works for the Bureau of Comparative Ethnology, specializing in disguises. She's a cybernetically enhanced creature of the future: a trained killer from a universe locked in perpetual sexual combat.

Towards the end of *The Female Man*, Jael arrives in New York to seek out her three other selves. 'If you discount the wombs that bore us,' she pronounces:

> our pre-natal nourishment, and our deliveries (none of which differ essentially) we ought to have started out with the same autonomic nervous system, the same adrenals, the same hair and teeth and eyes, the same circulatory system, and the same innocence. We ought to think alike and feel alike and act alike, but of course we don't. So plastic is humankind . . .
>
> Between our dress, and our opinions, and our habits, and our beliefs, and our values, and our mannerisms, and our manners, and our expressions, and our ages, and our experience, even I can hardly believe that I am looking at three other myselves. No layman would entertain for a moment the notion that he beheld four versions of the same woman. Did I say a moment? Not for an age of moments, particularly if the layman were indeed *a man*.[58]

Janet persistently misreads American culture, especially when it comes to the courtship rituals of New York parties. Unlike the portrayal of Anarres, Russ is careful to show that Whileaway is *fun*:

> there is too, under it all, the incredible explosive energy, the gaiety of high intelligence, the obliquities of wit, the cast of mind that makes industrial areas into gardens and ha-has . . . that strews across a planet sceneries, mountains, glider preserves, culs-de-sac, comic nude statuary, artistic lists of tautologies and circular mathematical proofs (over which aficionadas are moved to tears), and the best graffiti in this or any other world.[59]

Russ's contestation of sociobiology takes a different form in another modern classic: Marge Piercy's *Woman on the Edge of Time*. In this novel, the scripts of gender are simply rewritten to become random matters of individual personality. In the novel's 'utopia' – the New England community of Mattapoisett in 2137 – there *are* men and women, but it's extremely hard to tell the difference between them; they're the same kinds of people and they do the same sorts of things. In Mattapoisett Le Guin's linguistic dilemma is solved with the sex neutral pronoun 'per' (for person). The cultural achievement of eradicating gender in Mattapoisett is built on a momentous sacrifice on the part of women; in a famous passage in the novel, a member of the community explains:

> It was part of women's long revolution. When we were breaking all the old hierarchies. Finally there was that one thing we had to give up too, the only power we ever had, in return for no more power for anyone. The original production: the power to give birth. Cause as long as we were biologically enchained, we'd never be equal. And males never would be humanized to be loving and tender. So we all became mothers.[60]

Babies are conceived and gestated in a brooder; each baby enters a family of three co-mothers of both sexes who share responsibility for its welfare. Even 'the last refuge of women'[61] – breastfeeding – has been given up, and men do it as well, though the psychological dangers of exclusive breastfeeding are avoided by at least two of a child's co-mothers sharing this role.

This explanation of the human possibilities of technology is given to Connie Ramos, the novel's world-traveller, a poor Mexican woman from our own time (New York City in the mid-1970s). Connie's life has been scarred by the injustices typically meted out to those at the bottom of the class, gender and ethnic heap. She's been raped, suffered a dangerous illegal abortion, had her daughter taken into care, become a drug and alcohol addict, been labelled 'socially disorganized' and a paranoid schizophrenic, and kept drugged in a mental hospital. To Connie, aspects of the quaintly rural, gender-muted world of Mattapoisett seem at first a repeat of the grindingly poor rural Mexico she knew as a child. But then she begins to see that the village-based, economically self-sufficient society of Mattapoisett preserves the best of the old way of life while using modern technology to promote the human values of equality, harmony and solidarity. Mattapoisett is a rural society (living in cities 'didn't work'[62]); it's run by consensus and without violence either to other human beings or to nature; windmills generate power, and although the people have learnt how to manipulate the weather they rarely do so because of the unknown biosystem effects; they've also learnt how to communicate with animals, though they do eat them as a necessary way of culling the herd.

Like Genly Ai, the capitalists of Urras, and the three men in Tiptree's spacecraft, Connie Ramos has trouble coming to terms with the implosion of the sex/sexuality/gender triad; strong, well-muscled women who 'love' other women and speak with 'that air of brisk unselfconscious authority . . . associated with men'[63] must surely be dykes; people who carry babies on their backs must be women. It's just tremendously disconcerting to be in a place where gender is no longer the primary characterization of social relations.

■

In Charlotte Perkins Gilman's *Herland*, there've been no men for two thousand years: again, some dreadful war killed all of them. In Herland there aren't any wars, aggression, competition, kings, aristocracies, smoke, dirt, noise, meat-eating or dogs. The narrator of *Herland* is a sociologist, Vandyck Jennings, one of (another) three men – the others are a doctor and a playboy – who set out to find a fabled all-female country. 'Van' is prefigured in Gilman's *Woman and Economics*, where Gilman imagines 'an extraterrestrial sociologist, studying human life and hearing for the first time of our so-called "maternal sacrifice" as a means of benefiting the species'.[64]

Van and his friends search by plane and power boat, armed with camera, binoculars and guns, for the land of women they have only heard about. When they first glimpse it, Herland looks like a country in a state of 'perfect cultivation . . . an enormous garden'. Putting the plane down, they're amazed to see only women and children running out of their houses: ' "Only women there – and children," Jeff urged excitedly.

"But they look – why, this is a *civilized* country!" I protested. "There must be men." '[65]

Later, when the men meet the women of Herland face to face, Van notes his own reactions:

> They were not young. They were not old. They were not, in the girl sense, beautiful. They were not in the least ferocious. And yet, as I looked from face to face, calm, grave, wise, wholly unafraid, evidently assured and determined, I had the funniest feeling . . . It was that sense of being hopelessly in the wrong. . . . We felt like small boys, very small boys, caught doing mischief in some gracious lady's house.[66]

Much of the book consists of the men trying to find out from the women of Herland how their society works; in turn, the men attempt to explain and justify their own. They have particular trouble with economics: 'We rather spread ourselves,' explains Van:

> telling of the advantages of competition: how it developed fine qualities; that without it there would be 'no stimulus to industry'. Terry was very strong on that point.

'No stimulus to industry,' they repeated, with that puzzled look we had learned
to know so well. '*Stimulus? To Industry?* But don't you *like* to work?'
'No man would work unless he had to,' Terry declared.
'Oh, no *man*? You mean that is one of your sex distinctions?'
'No, indeed!' he said hastily. 'No one, I mean, man or woman, would work
without incentive. Competition is the – the motor power, you see.'

The women explain it isn't like that for them. Is it really true that in the
men's country no mother would work for her children *without* the stimulus of
competition? No, of course Terry didn't mean that:

Mothers, he supposed, would of course work for their children in the home; but
the world's work was different – that had to be done by men, and required the
competitive element.
. . . 'Tell us – what is the work of the world, that men do – which we have
not here?'
'Oh, everything,' Terry said grandly. 'The men do everything with us.' He
squared his broad shoulders and lifted his chest. 'We do not allow our women
to work. Women are loved – idolized – honored – kept in the home to care for
the children.'
'What is "the home"?' asked [one of the women] a little wistfully.'[67]

Quite the most disconcerting aspect for all three men of their exposure to
the culture of Herland is that the women are perfectly indifferent to what the
men think of them. This is because in the men's own country, culture is male:
'When we say *men, man, manly, manhood*, and all the other masculine deriva-
tives, we have in the background of our minds a huge vague crowded picture
of the world and all its activities', whereas 'when we say *women*, we think
female – the sex'. But in Herland, with the great sweep of their two-thousand-
year all-female civilisation, *man* means the sex, and women are 'the world'.[68]

■

The apotheosis of the harmony-with-nature theme, present in such worlds as
Herland and Mattapoisett, is *The Wanderground* of Sally Miller Gearhart's
novel. This is another post-Holocaust, multiple mothering world. Set in North
America sometime in the reasonably near future, its culture is described by
'Hill women', the rural descendants of women who, some eighty years before,
escaped from a right-wing dystopia of witch-hunts and the legal and military
suppression of women. The Hill women have developed extraordinary tele-
kinetic and telepathic powers. They can fly and make objects move through
space; they're able to communicate with each other without speaking, and can
also reach out to trees, water, fish and the whole of the natural world. They
'have sex' with trees and bushes, and group sex with the moon. It's a vision
of the unity of mind and body, which transcends in a unique way traditional

sex/gender dualisms. *The Wanderground* uses the same literary device to bring out the contrasts between the old and new worlds as many other science fiction novels which speculate about gender: the old and the new co-exist. While the Hill women commune with nature, in the City live the men. They live there because Mother Earth has colluded with the women's revolt: nothing about masculinity works outside the City. The men are impotent when they try to leave, animals no longer obey them, and all their technology gives up. Between the City men and the Hill women are the Gentles, men who occupy the symbolic space of a third sex/gender, and who help the outlaw women to monitor what the remnants of the patriarchy might be up to. The Gentles know that the women are the only hope for the survival of the planet. They are simply not the same species: 'Men and women can do nothing but violence to one another.'[69]

■

'We are only one possible future', says Luciente of Mattapoisett to Connie Ramos: 'Yours is a crux time. Alternate universes co-exist. Probabilities clash and possibilities wink out forever.'[70] The business of imagining other worlds is a way of considering the future for our own highly disorganized one.

The future projected by Zoe Fairbairns in her novel *Benefits* is the formation of a 'family party' dedicated to the preservation of women's traditional roles in post-Orwellian Britain. The only benefits that the new right-wing government doesn't cancel are the social welfare payments made to mothers:

> And the dying welfare state brought its own newspeak as well: governments' failure to link child benefit, unemployment pay and so on to the cost of living was *the fight against inflation*; putting children on half-time schooling was referred to as *giving parents a free hand*; closing hospitals and dumping dying patients on the doorsteps of unwarned and distant relatives was *community care*.[71]

The Family movement is led by David Laing, a 'shrivelled and ageless, anxious and ill'[72] young man, who is dangerously addicted to coffee, and who once had a relationship with a feminist activist, another of the novel's leading characters. Laing's rise to power as head of a new Department for Family Welfare is assured after an election resulting in a left–right deadlock. He and his colleagues urge women to give up their jobs and return to the home, thus simultaneously solving the problem of unemployment; they introduce the Protection of Women Act, which forbids feminist meetings and makes lesbianism illegal.

All these national policies develop at the same time as a Europe-wide population policy in which only certain white middle-class women are regarded as fit for motherhood; the 'benefits' of the title thus come to be used selectively as an old-fashioned eugenic strategy. The scientists invent a contraceptive chemical which can be added to the water supply; the antidote's provided by government centres only to ideologically sound women. The new contraceptive technology is part of an extensive research programme which includes the rearing of many identical twins in order to study the relationship between nature and nurture. But what happens when the chemical, the water and the antidote coincide in women's bodies is that they are rendered unfit for their primary purpose. Grossly deformed babies are stillborn. There's absolutely no future in pro-family, anti-women eugenics.

In Margaret Atwood's uncomfortable parable, *The Handmaid's Tale*, women's fertility literally means their silencing: the women who are assigned the duty of reproduction are separated from the power of words by being forbidden to read and write and to speak freely: they have 'learned to whisper almost without a sound'.[73] Gilead is located somewhere in a near-future USA, in which the forces of moral conservatism, which gathered strength in the closing years of the twentieth century, have created a military religious state. All women's bank accounts and credit cards have been deactivated, the university has been closed, and people are routinely hung for Gender Treachery. The regime was designed by politicians in the aftermath of the superpower arms stalemate, which recognized the need for nations to deal unimpeded with their own internal rebellions. Its design drew heavily on the work of sociobiologists who cited the theory of natural polygamy as a scientific justification for the regime's treatment of women.

Women in Gilead are divided into three classes: wives; Marthas, who cook and clean; and handmaids, who do the grocery shopping and reproduce, being held down for this purpose ceremonially every month by the wives of the Commanders to whom they've been assigned. The puzzling of twentieth-century sociobiologists over the unnecessary female orgasm is solved; it's disappeared as 'a symptom of frivolity merely, like jazz garters or beauty spots'.[74] Handmaids who don't conceive are banished to 'the colonies'. But dish-towels are the same as they always were, as are football games.

Atwood's narrator, Offred, is the handmaid of Commander Fred, and he instigates an unusual relationship with her. The commander is an ex-market researcher, one of Gilead's original designers; the relationship he develops with Offred centres on Scrabble (the power of the word) and hand lotion (the balm of Gilead). After a few drinks at one such illicit meeting, Commander Fred becomes loquacious on the subject of the old order:

> The problem wasn't only with the women, he says. The main problem was with the men. There was nothing for them any more.
> Nothing? I say. But they had . . .
> There was nothing for them to do, he says.
> They could make money, I say, a little nastily . . .

It's not enough, he says. It's too abstract. I mean there was nothing for them to do with women.

What do you mean? I say . . .

I'm not talking about sex, he says. That was part of it, the sex was too easy. Anyone could just buy it. There was nothing to work for, nothing to fight for. We have the stats from that time. You know what they were complaining about the most? Inability to feel . . .

Do they feel now? I say.

Yes, he says, looking at me. They do. He stands up, comes around the desk to the chair where I'm sitting. He puts his hands on my shoulders, from behind. I can't see him.[75]

■

Most dystopias described by women science fiction writers are uncomfortable exaggerations of the sex/gender divisions prevailing in turn of the century Euro-American culture. Many present their dystopic worlds as emanating directly from present trends: the realignment of women with The Family; the technological control of reproduction; the disabilities of men in a culture which has opened at least some of its opportunities to women; religious fundamentalism and its displacement onto other areas of belief and human activity.

The Wasting which is the setting for Suzy McKee Charnos's *Walk to the End of the World* was caused by devastating war, pollution and cultural exhaustion. The men blamed it on the women, many of whom had resisted the rightwing politics which produced the Wasting, and had consequently been pushed out as idealists or hysterics. But the women blame the Wasting on the men's combined stupidity and cleverness. This is a recognizable sex war, the backlash against feminism of the late twentieth and early twenty-first centuries.

Nothing much survives in Charnos's bleak post-Holocaust world, except for a few scattered mutants and wild weeds. But a handful of high-ranking male officials had hidden in shelters, taking some women with them for breeding purposes. When the men emerge, they lay claim to a strip of land which they call the Holdfast, and where they use as much ingenuity as they can and as much technology as they can remember in order to survive:

> What else do they remember? They remember the evil races whose red skins, brown skins, yellow skins, black skins, skins all the colors of fresh-turned earth marked them as mere treacherous imitations of men, who are white; youths who repudiated their fathers' ways; animals that raided men's crops and waylaid and killed men in the wild places of the world; and most of all the men's own cunning, greedy females. Those were the rebels who caused the downfall of men's righteous rule: men call them 'unmen'. Of all the unmen, only females and their young remain, still the enemies of men.'[76]

The men of the Holdfast maintain a corral of slave women who do all the hard work, including producing human milk, which is turned into curdcake

for the women's own nourishment, since the men don't give them enough
to eat. The women use 'soft' speech, which the men can't understand.
'Bra-burner' is remembered as a term of abuse indicating a woman who stole
and destroyed her master's weapons; the women's own weapon is witchery,
for which they themselves are burnt and eaten. Spectator blood sports flourish, but women, not other animals, are the hunted. Increasingly the men turn
to cannibalism, as it's difficult to harvest food successfully on the ravaged
land. The over-riding cast of Holdfast culture – if it can be called that – is
men's hatred of women: every man is pure and honourable, and every woman
is foul and dangerous. But men need women to make sons. Girl children are
abandoned; boys are consigned to the Boyhouse, where their primary lesson
is in woman-loathing.

Like oppressed groups everywhere, the women resist. One of them, Alldera,
a skilled long-distance runner, escapes to find the free women who are reputed
to live in the wilderness beyond the Holdfast. At the time (1972–3) she was
writing *Walk to the End of the World*, Charnos was reading the literature of
the women's movement: Shulamith Firestone's *Dialectic of Sex*, Robin
Morgan's *Sisterhood is Powerful*. This political reading enlarged her own
consciousness about being trapped in women's powerlessness; consequently,
Alldera, a minor character in *Walk to the End of the World*, ran out of it to
become a major one in the book's sequel, *Motherlines*.

Publishers initially turned down *Motherlines* because there aren't any male
characters in it.[77] There are two sorts of women in the book: the 'free fems'
who hid out in the wilderness beyond the Holdfast in *Walk to the Edge of the
World*, and the Riding Women. The Riding Women are *Motherlines*' utopia,
descendants of a group of women who, during the Wasting, took control of a
government laboratory which was conducting experiments on parthenogen-
esis. The original aim of the experiments was to provide the scientists with a
way of increasing women's fertility. But in the women's hands this technology means that they know how to give each daughter a double set of genes
from the same mother. Despite this technological trick, ties of blood are not
socially privileged, and every child has a number of 'sharemothers'. The
Riding Women live like nomads, close to the land and to their specially bred
horses, on whom they depend for transport and food – and also semen to kick-
start human reproduction. This carefully orchestrated process is perceived by
Alldera – herself horribly raped in the Holdfast – as quite the most repugnant
act of all.

∎

Cross-dressing, a habit in which 6 per cent of contemporary Americans are
said to indulge,[78] can be an attempt to discover vicariously how the other
gender lives,[79] though there's usually another serious purpose to it. And it

certainly provides another kind of challenge to binary notions of identity. There's nothing stable or literal about this: for instance, in the early twentieth century, boy babies wore pink and girls blue;[80] today when we look for sex/gender appropriate toilets, we'd get into a lot of trouble if we interpreted trousered figures literally.

When the jazz musician Billy Tipton died in 1989, it was the funeral director who broke the news of his real sex to his family. His current wife (he'd had four previous ones) explained she'd never seen him naked: Billy had told her he had an abdominal injury which required the constant wearing of bandages. Jazz musicians in the 1930s and 1940s were almost all male. So Dorothy became Billy to further her chances of musical success.[81]

Nadezha Durova is one of hundreds of Russian women disguised as men who've fought in wars. She did a ten-year stint in the Russian light cavalry during the Napoleonic wars, having begun her army career at twenty-two, when she ran away from home in the Ural mountains in order to escape the confined role of women – not, she explained, the biological side of woman-hood (she'd married and had a son before she went into the army).[82]

The fact that women cross-dress, as far as we can tell, much more than men suggests a different set of motives for this form of gender world-travelling among women and men. During the Middle Ages, cross-dressing was sanc-tioned in certain circumstances as a legitimate way for women to gain higher status – though they had to get it right, or they ran the risk of being executed for it, like Joan of Arc.[83]

One of the most famous feminist literary cross-dressers was Amandine-Aurore Lucile Dupin, baronne Dudevant. George Sand had cross-dressed as a child and a young woman in order to be able to do things girls couldn't. But the formal adoption of masculine attire came when she realized how tremen-dously limiting femininity could be to one who wanted fully to enter the literary and political world. Her mother also pointed out that dressing as a man would be cheaper.[84] During her life, George Sand moved between the mascu-line and the feminine; Flaubert called her the third sex. On her death, Henry James, a great admirer, commented that the beauty of what George Sand did for us was not 'the extension she gives to the feminine nature, but the richness that she adds to the masculine'.[85]

The English writer Marian Evans called herself George Eliot – the George after Sand, and after George Henry Lewes, with whom she lived.[86] Many female writers have adopted the same strategy, though the Brontë sisters protested that their pseudonyms of Acton, Currer and Ellis Bell were chosen for their androgynous neutrality.[87] Women have written under assumed male names far more than men have chosen to masquerade as women writers.[88] Alice Sheldon thought James Tiptree 'would be a good camouflage', though she 'couldn't have avoided having the thought . . . that the editor would take my stories more seriously'.[89] It's a matter of convenience – a way of sidestepping the prejudices meted out to 'authoresses'.[90] Thus, for example, reviews of the Brontës' work after their true sex became known were considerably less laudatory than before the secret was out:[91] the nature of 'female genius' is a special product, since the standard model is male.

■

Travelling to other worlds, whether through name-changing, cross-dressing, swapping ethnic and gender categories, or using the wonderful power of the human imagination to invest other places with some of the comforts that seem missing in one's own, is a method of discovering the undiscoverable: of finding out what it's like to be someone else. It's a way of gaining the experience, but also of extracting that meaning which can be so elusive in the ordinary, non-travelling routines of life. We really do need to know how the other half lives; it helps to understand what it's like to leave our own skins and have other-worldly experiences.

Many people in everyday non-fictional life are world-travellers from necessity and for survival. These experiences of inhabiting different worlds typically belong to minority groups. In the cultural setting of *Gender on Planet Earth*, people 'of colour', poor people, the homeless, the less able-bodied, homosexuals, vegetarians, pacifists and cyclists are some of the groups who practise world-hopping on a grand scale as an everyday habit, though often without being aware that this is what they're doing. But the most experienced world-hoppers are women living in patriarchal social systems.

In other, fictional worlds, aliens are re-created as insiders, and the true horrors of living with monsters become palpable, breathable reality. Outsiders, grabbing the freedom of their imaginations while denied other sorts, weave stories out of the desert they inhabit about worlds in which they could feasibly live.

It's easy to ridicule such fantasies, which include warning projections about the science (fiction) places towards which our own culture might be heading. But these are elegantly authentic fables, rooted in hard studies of life on earth. We should take them seriously.

10
Civic Rituals and Real Futures

A newspaper lies on the floor. Like the one Virginia Woolf picked up in a restaurant near the British Museum in 1928, its text can be decoded to yield a picture of the difficult world in which we live. There are two headlines on the front page: 'Relief for Josie Russell as man who killed her mother and sister is jailed for life'; and 'Terror as plane is "shot down"'.[1] The first story is one about a man on trial for beating a mother and one of her daughters to death in a quiet lane in rural England five years ago, leaving her other daughter barely alive with a fractured skull. The second headline refers to a flight from Israel to Siberia which exploded into the Black Sea, killing everyone on board, possibly because it was hit by a 'rogue missile' fired by the Ukraine army during 'exercises' in the Crimea. Other prominent stories in this newspaper are about the unremarkable antics of 2-year-old Brooklyn Beckham, son of a famous footballer and a 'Spice girl'; the capture by the Taliban government in Afghanistan of a female journalist, and the dossier of information placed on the 10 Downing Street website about Osama Bin Laden and the 11 September terrorist attacks on the USA; scientists' analysis of the speech patterns of eight of Britain's top (male) football commentators; Spice Girl Mel C's loss of 20 pounds due to her Mum's home cooking; a reduction in the bank rate, boosting the stock market and the fortunes of home-owners; and 'ex-wife loses college fees row', about a woman who claimed her husband forced her to sell property to pay for her stepsons' education.

These are our preoccupations: war, crime, violence, money, sports, vacant commercialized glamour. Woolf concluded from her newspaper that even an alien from another galaxy would see that we lived in a patriarchy.

And so do we. Patriarchy isn't simply a colourful political term used by feminists to attack men. It doesn't belong to the past, it's 'an important dimension of the structuring of modern societies . . . a living reality'.[2] We need the concept of patriarchy to understand the social problems described in this book: not only (most obviously) the enduring problem of gender inequality, but the domination of our planet by individual and corporate masculine violence towards women, children, animals, nature and other men, and the fashion for forms of transport and food that damage human beings and entire ecosystems.

But one of many problems about the term 'patriarchy' is that it belongs to the very same compost heap which is home to the festering remains of gender and feminism. This is all rubbish, we cry, rinsing our hands with the anti-bacterial properties of postmodernism. In the West's brave new world, there are surely just a few remaining vestiges of discrimination to root out, some cosmetic improvement to be hoped for in how laws and other mechanisms shaping public policy support the principle of human rights. The behaviour of some – organizations as well as individuals – does still leave something to be desired. But there are bound to be stragglers, even on the road to paradise.

It's true that in the West the old forms of patriarchy have disappeared: husbands and fathers can't, by and large, any longer tell women what to do and expect the law to agree with them; women's bodies are not, on the whole, objects to be exploited and owned by others; the wages paid to employed women can't just be set according to the whims of (benevolently?) sexist bosses. But this doesn't mean that patriarchy has been eliminated. According to sociologist Sylvia Walby, in her book *Theorizing Patriarchy*, it's merely changed its form. In countries such as the UK and the USA, the twentieth century saw a shift from a private to a public form of patriarchy. Patriarchy has become less a matter of individual imposition, and more one of collective discrimination. The household has ceased to be the main site of women's oppression, and has been replaced by public sectors, for example employment and the state. This means that women in these societies 'are no longer restricted to the domestic hearth, but have the whole society in which to roam and be exploited'.[3]

There are many different definitions of patriarchy. According to three of the most authoritative, offered by a sociologist, a historian and an economist respectively, patriarchy:

> is a system of social structures and practices in which men dominate, oppress and exploit women.[4]
>
> means the manifestation and institutionalization of male dominance over women and children in the family and the extension of male dominance over women in society in general. It implies that men hold power in all the important institutions of society.[5]
>
> is a set of social relations between men, which have a material base, and which, though hierarchical, establish or create interdependence and solidarity among

men that enable them to dominate women. The material base upon which patriarchy rests lies most fundamentally in men's control over women's labour
power.[6]

∎

Patterns of domination extend to other groups as well: thus both working-class
people and Black people are 'feminized' in their relations with the dominant
group.[7] In their book *Aliens and Alienists*, the psychiatrists Roland Littlewood
and Maurice Lipsedge write of their experience of trying to understand the
mental health problems of ethnic minority groups in East London: 'Outsiders
always pose a threat to the status quo . . . Their apartness is different . . . We
forget that the outsiders are part of our definition of ourselves. To confirm our
identity we push the outsiders even further away. By reducing their humanity
we emphasize our own . . . They are nature: we are culture.'[8] The 'racializa-
tion' of patriarchy[9] means that the privileging of white people is intertwined
with that of men. But within every 'racial' category, women are the procre-
ators, not the citizens; nationalism, the brotherhood of man, assigns 'sisters'
to motherhood, and to a conspiracy of silence about how this is actually experienced. 'Women become metaphors for what they represent, rather than
what they are.'[10] Books about the pains and difficulties of having and bringing up children[11] continue to hit unharmonious notes as 'the exclusionary
nature of the master script'[12] thunders on. Meanwhile, two Barbie dolls are
sold every second.[13]

∎

'Women feel hemmed in by Space-Invading Men', shouted a headline in the
New York Times, reporting on experiments conducted by lawyer Gillian
Costello on how men and women use the space inside subway systems: 'Men
take up a lot more room on the subway than women. They stretch out. They
lean. They do the Ward Cleaver ankle-on-knee leg cross. But mostly, and most
damnably, they tend to sit with their legs splayed out.'[14] 'One day in my early
twenties in Manhattan,' observed Joanna Russ, in her recent (non-fictional)
book about patriarchy:

> I formed a hypothesis that the reason men did not bump into me in the street
> was that I made way for them so habitually that I had ceased to notice that I did
> so. I decided to test this notion by walking in a straight line. Three collisions
> and two 'why don't you look where you're going's later, I abandoned the project.
> Twenty years later I found similar observations in *Body Politics*.[15] In Eugene,
> Oregon, researcher Fox observed people passing on the sidewalk and noted who
> got out of whose way. In twelve out of nineteen mixed-sex encounters she
> observed, it was the woman who moved, in four cases both moved, and in three
> cases the man did.[16]

When I swim in a crowded swimming bath, exactly the same thing happens. There am I, politely plunging my way through the chlorinated water, and there is he, advancing towards me with no intention of deviating from his path. If I don't get out of the way, I'll be hit – and so I have been, often, when I haven't moved quickly enough. Another manifestation of this is he-who-tries-to-over-take-me, assuming that old(ish) women don't swim fast. It's only a three-lane highway, so whoever's in the middle needs to get out of the way quickly. But the only way this can happen, given our relative speeds, is if I slow down. Once, when I didn't do this (just to test the hypothesis), he stopped and angrily demanded, 'What's your problem?'

Male-centredness is another symptom of patriarchy. It's related to another of patriarchy's tricks: its invisibility. Actually, what's invisible here is the male gender. It's this that really perpetuates patriarchy:

> just as the invisibility of whiteness as a race perpetuates racism. The more invis-
> ible male gender is, the more gender problems like violence and discrimination
> are identified with women and the less likely we are to notice that patriarchy
> even exists as an oppressive system. . . . men can rest behind the comforting illu-
> sion that violence and other oppressive patterns have nothing to do with them.[17]

The notion of patriarchy gives us a theoretical framework for understanding the nuanced experiences of our everyday lives. It describes the tone of the culture, its internal structure of power relations. While it's about material reality, it's also about the psychic representations in our heads. In the interplay between these two, human beings are always in danger of finding themselves locked in the defining embrace of their gender, either as people (men) who are alienated from a sensitivity and connectedness to others, including the planet, or as people (women) who loiter on the margins, struggling with their consciences, and often against the idea that institutionalized social exclusion has anything to do with the way they feel.

The Nordic theorist Anna Jónasdottir has a particular angle on this. She argues that the combination of patriarchy and capitalism produces social norms which:

> say that men not only have the right to women's love, care and devotion, but
> also that they have . . . the freedom to *take* for themselves. Women, on the other
> hand, have the right to freely *give* of themselves, but a very limited legitimate
> freedom to *take* for themselves. Thus men . . . can build themselves up as
> powerful social beings and continue to dominate women through their constant
> accumulation of the existential forces taken and received from women. If capital
> is accumulated alienated labor, male authority is accumulated alienated love.[18]
> [my italics]

As a method for accumulating alienated love, patriarchy doesn't depend on a *biological* definition of gender relations (although this doesn't stop, and may actually foster, the invention of 'scientific' theories of biological determination – see chapter 8 above). Secondly, patriarchy operates *systematically* through social institutions. The idea of a social system, or an institution, as 'a pattern of expected action or individuals or groups enforced by social sanctions, both positive and negative'[19] is one many people find hard to grasp. Similarly, they have difficulty with the notion that institutions can be 'substantively, as well as metaphorically' gendered.[20] But it is only this perspective which can explain the phenomena described in this book.

'Planetary environmental degradation is rarely understood as connected with human poverty and hunger. Why is it that it is easier to think about the whole planetary ecosphere than to understand the social effects of our everyday relationships?', ask Richard Bellah and his colleagues in *The Good Society*.[21] *Gender on Planet Earth* has argued that exactly the same principles of analysis can be applied to a wide range of problems facing the world today. What we in the West think of as domestic policy concerns – transport, crime, the unhygienic meat industry, disintegrating families, troubled children, marginalized men, the poisoned and decaying urban and rural environment – are linked to global problems of food scarcity, poverty, inequality, environmental destruction and the exploitation of women and children. Planet earth is dominated by a violent, aggressive, competitive, commodified, selfish way of life. Behind this lies an historical alliance between a capitalist economic system and a patriarchal social system which has produced masculinity in the form of living creatures called men. Men walk the earth shouldering this burden and perpetuating its evils. Women collude in this: femininity, also socially constructed, fits women for the role of accepting, and even emulating, what men do.

Glimpses of the multiple damages caused by the 'sex/gender system' *are* more likely among feminists. What sociologist Cynthia Cockburn calls the 'sustained anathematization of feminism'[22] which surrounds us is an enormous deterrent to taking the argument seriously. The greatest sadness is the caricature of feminism as 'a card-carrying nutsy little sect', which prevents us from seeing it for what it really is – 'an inherently radical and profound vision of what can save the planet', as American feminist Robin Morgan has termed it.[23]

The ideas of patriarchy and male oppression are peculiarly uncomfortable to many people today, even those who recognize elements of both in their values and daily lives. American sociologist Allan Johnson in his book *The Gender Knot* talks about the need to get past many people's 'defensive reactions' to the term 'patriarchy'. It's routinely interpreted to mean men, whereas (he repeats the point others have made), 'Patriarchy is a kind of society, and a society is more than a collection of people. As such, "patriarchy" doesn't refer to me or any other man or collection of men, but to a kind of society in which men *and* women participate.'[24] In so far as men do oppress women, most of them do it 'in spite of themselves'.[25] 'At the interpersonal level,' says sociologist Dorothy Smith in her *The Everyday World as Problematic*, 'it is not a conspiracy among men that they impose on women. It is a complementary social process between men and women.'[26] There aren't any 'Patriarch Headquarters, with flags and limousines, where all the strategies are worked out', observes R. W. Connell in his *Masculinities*;[27] there's no central control room where, particularly at times of feminist challenge, the operations of the anti-feminist brigades are planned with military precision. We can't blame it on the generals this time. It isn't a sex war: it's a place in which we're all stuck, together.

Without a 'systems' perspective we retreat into the mindless laddism of the sex war: the bad lads versus the good girls. Men aren't inherently bad and women aren't redeemingly good. If on balance research shows, as it does, that women are more egalitarian than men, that they are less warlike and more interested in peace, and that they are more aware of environmental issues, this is mostly because their experiences of life on earth remain qualitatively different from men's; they're still more rooted in caring labour and personal relations.

Patricia Williams, an American professor of law, talks of racism and other 'isms' as 'public secrets'. Such secrets – accepted and well-known understandings of what's really going on – mean it's only a 'civil ritual' that makes us say 'in the face of all our differences, we are all one, we are the world'.[28] Pretending inclusiveness is no way to a real future.

Imagine what would happen if the standard human being ceased to be a white male and became instead a Black, pregnant female. This might just 'destabilize the unity of rights discourse'; it would certainly threaten ideas about bodily integrity; the abstracted male would retreat to the outside of the social circle.[29] This, of course, is not what we'd want to happen. What we want to happen is that people should *think* about the way they think, and about the way they behave.

And take responsibility for what they are. To paraphrase a famous saying, men have nothing to lose but their chains. For this is inescapable: the position of men as a group in the maintenance of destructive gender divisions on planet earth isn't the same as that of women; it's men who need to take the initiative in changing these.

Virginia Woolf would have found solace in the words of the British psychiatrist, Anthony Clare, in his recent book, *On Men*:

> But all men, myself included, do not just love women. We do not see them only as colleagues, friends, lovers; as sexually desirable, physically attractive, mentally stimulating. We fear them, hate them, marginalise them, denigrate them and categorise them. And we continually strive to control and dominate them. The call to us men, at the beginning of the twenty first century, to turn away from violence, to get in touch with our feelings, to express our fears and admit our

inadequacies, is a doomed call if it is made, as it tends to be made, predominantly by women. Men, apart from a minority, seem fearful of making the changes that the death of patriarchy demands. Yet that is the scale of the challenge. *Men can only save themselves. They cannot rely on women to save them.*[30] [my italics]

Clare is restating a point of view rehearsed some years ago by John Stoltenberg in his *Refusing to be a Man*. After fifteen years' exposure to feminist politics, Stoltenberg reached the position that 'There cannot be both gender polarity and justice on earth.' 'Penis privilege', as he terms it, must be actively disavowed by men. 'The pride to which we aspire', he comments:

> is not in being *men*, but in being *men who* . . . men who are living their lives in a way that will make a difference.
>
> We must be transformers of selfhood – our own and others'. If we are not, we will have betrayed women's lives utterly, and we will have lost a part of ourselves that is precious and rare on this earth.[31]

■

People who analyse the nature of a problem are often called upon to say what should be done about it. This is strange, since analytic skills don't necessarily qualify one as an expert in practical policy. Many years ago I wrote a book about the history and situation of housewives,[32] and I was asked by the publisher to say in the last chapter what I proposed should be done about it. So I wrote an impassioned plea for the liberation of housewives through abolishing the housewife role, dismantling The Family, and abandoning traditional gender roles. My plea fell largely on deaf ears, like many proposals for radical change. This isn't surprising, given that closure to the desirability of change is what generates the need for radicalism in the first place.

Some of what I said in the last chapter of *Housewife* would still be relevant to a 'what to do about it all?' section in *Gender on Planet Earth*. But, as I've argued throughout the book, gender inequality *isn't the main problem*. The main problem is the personal, social and environmental destructiveness produced by a society predicated on an institutionalized system of gender inequality which makes men, unless they're very careful, into alienated beasts, and women, if they're honest, into scared outsiders. There's only one way to break this, and that's slowly and together. In between capitulating to 'inevitable doom' and believing in the unbelievable 'quick fix'[33] is another way. But this needs deep thought and a sense of serious engagement with the issues, not just a facile exchange of aphorisms about them, or a shopping list of instant remedies.

The scale of the problem that confronts us makes it inane to suggest specific policy options for addressing gender issues. In an increasingly globalized world, it generally 'makes less and less sense to think about social policy in a simply national context'.[34] Having said that, some 'solutions' on the domestic front are blindingly obvious. These include: the reorganization of 'work' to value unpaid labour and recognize the rights of part-time workers; the strengthening of laws against discrimination; and attention to the needs of little children for good quality daycare in a world where it's unlikely that mothers (or fathers) can stay at home full-time. It *is* often forgotten that the fates of women and children are closely linked; societies that treat women unfairly have high rates of disadvantage among children. In the league table of child poverty in the developed world, the bottom four places out of twenty-three are occupied by the UK, Italy, the USA and Mexico. Children and women do best in the Nordic countries, which have focused on family-oriented social policies (using 'family' in a practical rather than ideological sense).[35]

What we don't need is a patriarchal rehearsal of the importance of family life, or a mystical invocation of the notion of 'community'. Women, the coalface domestic labourers, have always known that caring for, and about, little children and vulnerable adults is a central, perhaps *the* central, human task. It's they who've invisibly practised, while academics have endlessly written about it, that sense of community which goes beyond gender and all the 'isms' because it's about recognizing what all human beings have together, rather than what may in different cultures, times and places be said to divide them. It isn't helpful to move from seeing women as victims to a new pity for men as the innocent oppressed. No-one is innocent in this; but we're not all equally guilty; some of us have much more power to act than others.

Figure 2 is a revised version of the Earth Charter. The original draft was produced for the 1992 Earth Summit in Rio and has subsequently been worked on by a collection of NGOs round the world. The Charter is now going through an official review process, with the goal of ratification by UN national states in December 2002. My revisions have reordered the priorities and amended the one relating to gender equality. The content of figure 2 is more of a vision than a policy agenda. But the problem with most policy agendas is that they lack a vision.

■

As political scientist Irene Diamond puts it in her book *Fertile Ground*, 'The hope that the earth might be reclaimed for all grows from the basic wisdom that to reclaim the earth we need to recreate ourselves. We must reimagine who we are as persons and create an appropriate politics.'[36] Or as anthropologist Mary Catherine Bateson says: 'The fundamental problem of our society and our species today is to discover a way to flourish that will not be at the expense of some other community or of the biosphere, to replace competition with creative independence.'[37] Those who reflect on the discomforts of our daily life, such as diarist and writer May Sarton, put it more simply: 'We are

TOGETHER IN HOPE WE PLEDGE TO:

1. Strive to build free, just, participatory, sustainable and peaceful societies.
2. Care for the community of life in all of its diversity.
3. Respect Earth and all life.
4. Secure Earth's abundance and beauty for present and future generations.

IN PURSUIT OF THESE GOALS, WE WILL:

5. Affirm and promote equality between men and women as a prerequisite to sustainable development, and abandon our collusion with oppressive gender beliefs and practices.
6. Create a culture of peace and cooperation.
7. Eradicate poverty, as an ethical, social, economic and ecological imperative.
8. Treat all living beings with compassion, and protect them from cruelty and wanton destruction.
9. Honor and defend the right of all persons, without discrimination, to an environment supportive of their dignity, bodily health, and spiritual well being.
10. Adopt patterns of consumption, production, and reproduction that respect and safeguard Earth's regenerative capacities, human rights and community well being.
11. Ensure that economic activities support and promote human development in an equitable and sustainable manner.
12. Establish access to information, inclusive democratic participation in decision making, and transparency, truthfulness, and accountability in governance.
13. Make the knowledge, values and skills needed to build just and sustainable communities an integral part of formal education and life long learning for all.
14. Protect and restore the integrity of Earth's ecological systems, with special concern for biological diversity and the natural processes that sustain and renew life.
15. Prevent harm to the environment as the best method of ecological protection and, when knowledge is limited, take the path of caution.
16. Advance worldwide the cooperative study of ecological systems, the dissemination and application of knowledge, and the development, adoption and transfer of clean technologies.

Figure 2 The Earth Charter

Source: Adapted from R. Bertell (2000) *Planet Earth: The latest weapon of war.* London: Women's Press, p. 198

all in the same boat and the boat is commanded by thugs.'[38] And men, such as clinical psychologist Paul Gilbert, who have thought about male violence have no doubt about the potential terrors ahead: 'If our planet ends up with the nightmare scenarios of increasing environmental destruction, poverty and violence . . . then in part it will be because of our trivialisation of the trainable qualities of compassion, empathy and sharing.'[39]

■

Suriya, a woman from northern Afghanistan, was stoned to death in February 2001 at a sports stadium in Mazar-e-Sharif, watched by a crowd of several thousand. She was allegedly guilty of adultery. No punishment was reported for the man involved.[40]

Public punishments of women in Afghanistan, commonly held on Fridays, have become a new form of spectator sports. A leather cricket bat is often used to carry out beatings.

Zarneena, an Afghan mother of seven, who is said to have killed her husband, was shot by a Taliban fighter in 1999 in a packed football stadium in Kabul. The film clip on the website of the Revolutionary Association of Women of Afghanistan (RAWA) is there because a member of RAWA smuggled a video camera into the stadium under her burqa, the uncompromising head-to-toe garment with a gauzy slit for the eyes which the ruling Taliban had demanded that all Afghan women wear. They'd also ordered all women to refrain from paid work and stay at home, paint their windows black, and walk quietly with a male relative at the side of the road if they have to go out, and they'd closed all schools to girls over the age of eight, emptied the universities of female students, removed women's passports, and limited healthcare by closing hospitals and refusing treatment to any woman not accompanied by a close male relative.

In 1997 a UN report on Violence Against Women described widespread and systematic violation of women's rights in Afghanistan: violations in the areas of physical security, education, health, employment, freedom of association, and protection from trafficking and prostitution. A report by Physicians for Human Rights in 1998 on the situation of Afghan women found 97 per cent suffering from major depression, and a quarter frequently considering suicide – if poverty, malnutrition, disease or the Talibans didn't get them first.

'When radical Muslim movements are on the rise, women are the canaries in the mines.'[41] Discrimination against women exists throughout the world; Afghanistan was unusual because such discrimination was official government policy. The motivation was the religious 'authority' of the Koran, but the edicts of male Gods have always been a matter of interpretation. Equally important was the anti-women male solidarity of Taliban politicians and fighters, who vented their misogyny by requiring women to stay at home while at the same time abusing them in acts of rape, forced prostitution and marriage, and pursuing a cult of homosexuality reminiscent of that of the ancient Athenians, who locked women up in a part of the house called the gynaeceum, where they raised children and did household tasks.[42]

The fate of Afghan women was put under the spotlight by the events of 11 September 2001, but fundamentalist crimes against women have been committed in Afghanistan since the fall of the Soviet regime in 1978. In 1989 Arab militants working with the Afghan resistance to the post-Soviet 'puppet' regime issued a fatwa stating that Afghan women would be killed if they worked for humanitarian groups. After the fatwa, Afghan women going to work were shot and murdered. A second fatwa in 1990 decreed that women should be deprived of education: the fatwa document held the signatures of about two hundred prominent members of the seven main mujahedeen parties.[43] The United Front/Northern Alliance regime of 1992–6 led by Rabbani and his 'brothers in arms', like that of the Taliban, had 'a Kalashnikov in one hand and the Quran in the other'. The so-called minister of information and culture of the Rabbani administration personally supervised major book-burning ceremonies. It was this administration which first forced women out of media and government jobs and into the burqa.

Male MPs laughed when a British woman MP raised the need to ensure that a post-Taliban government in Afghanistan should enable women's voices to be heard. A newspaper joked about 'all women shortlists in Kabul'.[44] Defending women's human rights may be a useful war cry, but sustained commitment to changing this situation is another matter altogether.

The inhuman treatment of women in Afghanistan resembles the dystopia of a science fiction novel. It's paralleled elsewhere by similar ideologies and practices justified in the name of religious fundamentalism. For example, a report by Amnesty International in 2001 about the situation of women in Saudi Arabia demanded to know why the kingdom's authorities should be subjecting women to arbitrary detention, arrest, flogging and execution.[45]

■

'We see through an elaborate system of screens. And this seeing has only become more complicated with CNN coverage and the global communications network, which broadcast immediate and continual pictures of violence and hate. So we *think* we know; and yet we know only what is screened for us and what we allow ourselves to see.'[46]

Media institutions are themselves caught up in the diseases of transnationalism and global concentrations of power which silence the voices of diversity and dissidence. Some seventy to eighty firms control the world's media system, with eight transnational media conglomerates taking the lion's share of $10 billion–$30 billion per year each in media-related revenues. 'As the power of the largest firms grows, they use that power to commercialize content to the greatest extent possible and, if necessary, to protect their political interests, and they denigrate any notion of public service that might interfere with either of those aims.'[47]

■

In 1920, before she went to look up women in the British Museum, Virginia Woolf wrote a piece called 'A Society of Outsiders'. She wrote it in response to the publication of a book by 'Mr Bennett' about women's inferiority.

'A Society of Outsiders' is about a group of young women who make themselves into a society for asking questions. Its instigator is Poll, whose father left her a fortune on condition she read all the books in the London Library (including presumably all those interminable volumes about women). Poll gets depressed by the task and wonders why her father taught her to read at all. Clorinda, another member of the society, points out the nature of the division of labour they've all been brought up to accept; men write the books and civilize the world, while women bear the babies. But since we can read, she urges excitedly, what's to prevent us, before we agree to have any more children, from judging the results of the men's side of the bargain?

The young women divide up the tasks between them: 'One of us was to visit a man-of-war; another was to hide herself in a scholar's study; another was to attend a meeting of business men; while all were to read books, look at pictures, go to concerts, keep our eyes open in the streets, and ask questions perpetually.'[48]

They meet to share their reports. There is, for example, Fanny's visit to the law courts: 'At her first visit she had come to the conclusion that the Judges were either made of wood or were impersonated by large animals resembling man who had been trained to move with extreme dignity, mumble and nod their heads . . . from the evidence she brought we voted that it is unfair to suppose that the Judges are men.'[49]

Then one of the group breaks the agreement and gets pregnant by a 'divinely beautiful' young man. War breaks out; the women abandon their deliberations, which is probably just as well, since they were drowning in statistics. Five years later they meet and try to work out what it all meant. Castalia, the one who gave in to motherhood, decides that the greatest fallacy is woman's belief in man's intellect; but that's women's doing, since women have bred and fed men and kept them in comfort all these years. She concludes that she must try to stop *her* daughter learning to read, and rushes home to keep her away from Cook's *Evening News*. Cassandra, the narrator of the story, points out that this is ridiculous:

'It's no good – not a bit of good,' I said. 'Once she knows how to read there's only one thing you can teach her to believe in – and that is herself.'
'Well, that would be a change,' said Castalia.[50]

The Society of Outsiders give all their papers to Castalia's little girl and make her president of the Society of the future, at which point she bursts into tears.

A Society of Outsiders is mentioned in a much more famous essay of Woolf's, *Three Guineas*. Published in 1938, this was originally conceived as a sequel to *A Room of One's Own*, to be called *On Being Despised*.[51] *Three Guineas* builds on ten years' research on the social and cultural role of women carried out by Woolf during a time of great upheaval in Europe: Hitler came to power in 1933, the Spanish Civil War happened in 1936–9; in Britain there was economic recession and mass unemployment. The task Woolf set herself in *Three Guineas* was to identify the social forces that produce fascism. The 'three guineas' of the title refer to three begging letters she imagines receiving asking for support for different causes: a petition for a society promoting peace run by a prominent barrister; an appeal from the treasurer of a women's college for a donation to the rebuilding fund; a request for money to help a society supporting women's entry into the professions. Three guineas was also the standard gynaecological fee at the time.[52]

Woolf eventually decides to give a guinea to each of her petitioners, but first she discusses the complex reasons for her decision. These involve many of the connecting themes that are the subject of this book: the masculinist values dominating public institutions; the dangerous pseudo-knowledge traded by professionals; the link between war and masculinity; rituals of inclusion, hiding realities of exclusion; inequalities of money and power in the private world of marriage and the family. Woolf argues that masculinity as a socially produced category and the pursuit of war, violence and political authoritarianism are bound up with the patriarchal state. The gender-divided nuclear family is also implicated, because of the psychological disposition this generates in men and women. Women are afraid and men are angry: these positions prevent real freedom from happening anywhere, and their coalition has a positive role in causing war.

The arguments of *Three Guineas* were so much ahead of their time that most people just ignored them or condemned the book as a nasty aberration, hoping Woolf would quickly return to the calmer reaches of her more usual fictional prose.[53] What readers expected from *Three Guineas* was a protest about the atrocities in Spain: what they got instead was 'a harsh, angry polemic denouncing capitalism, imperialism, anti-feminism and patriarchal culture in general'.[54] Particularly shocking were the photographs Woolf included with the essay: not, as expected, of Spanish atrocities, but of ceremonially dressed British men – a general, a judge, an archbishop, university dignitaries, and heralds blowing trumpets. *This* was the establishment Woolf held responsible for war and violence, not foreigners somewhere else on the planet.

The Society of Outsiders enters *Three Guineas* as the form of radical political action needed to challenge the masculine establishment. Women, says Woolf, should establish such a society in order to challenge militarism and promote pacificism, and agitate for a generally more equitable, less hierarchical and more co-operative society, based on values capable of recognizing women's experiences and unpaid work.

■

During the year it's taken me to write this book, millions of people worldwide have died of poverty and hunger, and millions more from the private and public violence of individuals and the weapon-hungry policies of nation states; the self-justifying crimes of capitalism as a social and economic system have further colonized the globe; the exploitation of Mother Nature, of our blue spinning planet's friable ecosystem, has lost none of its frighteningly 'penetrative' power; more and more babies have entered the world in a spirit of violence – either the intercession of the surgeon's knife, or the mud and garbage of a place too poor to afford even elementary hygiene; and everywhere people continue to be prevented through lack of resources and through inhumane laws from caring for others with the strength and compassion they know is a measure of our humanity. All of this is perpetually justified in the name of interlinked delusional systems – God-given authority, the free market, the machinery of our genes, the inevitable psychological projects of human beings who haven't worked out a way of living that doesn't depend on damaging others. Who we are is what we are; and what we are is simply monstrous.

Most of us accept most of this, like everything else, as just what happens. While epidemics of violence against people and the planet go on raging in all their refulgent un-necessity, we in our little corner of it go implacably about our ordinary business. We go to work and complain about the traffic on the roads. The weather (particularly in Britain) seems a personal affront to our liberty. We feed our children and our pets, water our plants, have our teeth and hair fixed. We cook, eat, read, have sex, go shopping – some of us more than others, especially now when it's our national duty to drag the economy out of recession.

■

Planet earth is only one small cosmic body circling one star in a galaxy of some 300,000 million, which is itself only one among several million galaxies. Man – and woman – have been on planet earth for only a few seconds of galactic time. At some known point in the future, planet earth's fiery sun will grow cold, and life as we know it, whatever we do with it from now on, will be over.[55]

Tonight is cold, though not as cold as that. It's 5 November, bonfire night, an occasion on which we English obscurely celebrate the failure of one Guy Fawkes, a mercenary Catholic soldier, to blow up the Houses of Parliament. What is terrorism to one man is heroism to another.

Out in the village the stone cottages cluster under a navy-blue sky streaked with gauzy clouds. Rockets scream and soar into the air, detonating into sparkling colours. Everywhere on the horizon are bursts of orange and green and purple, electric blue and pink. The whole night sky is painted with gunpowder effects, the clouds are underlit by rainbows, the face of the moon is scarred by explosions. The trees and the fields drip with the smell of gunpowder: inside the cottages the women wonder what's burning in the kitchen.

Across the valleys and the hills there are sounds of detonation as in a war zone. Children cry, dogs bark, and trees rustle in a sharp north-easterly wind; desiccated leaves scamper across the roads with a sound quite like the patter of disobedient women's feet. Is bonfire night, dressed up as a harmless aesthetic display, yet another celebration of male violence?

Light from cottage windows streams out across the blackness of fields and trees. I stand at the edge of a field leading out of the village, where a footpath stretches straight to the line between sky and planet earth, out there into the future. Tonight the horizon even seems faintly curved, as though the scale of everything has been altered to remind us of our delicate suspension in the dwarfing hugeness of space. The line between earth and sky posits a question about the future. Whose future will it be? What will it look like? A world without gender might be one without genesis, because we'd be deprived of some of our most cherished myths, but it might also be one without end – in the sense, that is, that we human beings do have an opportunity, if we choose to grasp it, to make our next few billion years' inhabitation of planet earth a better time both for the planet and for us.

Notes

Chapter 1 The Self and Other Dramas

1   H. Rosen (1998) *Speaking from Memory*. Stoke-on-Trent: Trentham Books, p. 30.
2   L. Caldecott and S. Ireland (eds) (1983) *Reclaim the Earth: Women speak out for life on earth*. London: Women's Press.
3   B. McKibben (1990) *The End of Nature*. London: Penguin.
4   B. Brandt (1995) *Whole Life Economics: Revaluing daily life*. Philadelphia: New Society Publishers.
5   See, e.g., H. Rose and S. Rose (eds) (2000) *Alas, Poor Darwin: Arguments against evolutionary psychology*. London: Jonathan Cape; J. Masson (1990) *Against Therapy*. London: Fontana; S. Keen (2001) *Debunking Economics: The naked emperor of the social sciences*. London: Zed Books.
6   C. G. Heilbrun (1989) *Writing a Woman's Life*. London: Women's Press, p. 126.
7   M. Sarton (1973) *Journal of a Solitude*. New York: W. W. Norton, p. 77.
8   Thanks to Joanna Russ, who reviewed her own book in *The Female Man* (1985, originally published 1975, London: Women's Press).
9   V. Woolf (1977, originally published 1929) *A Room of One's Own*. St Albans: Granada, pp. 33–4.
10 Woolf, *A Room of One's Own*, p. 35.
11 Q. Bell (1976) *Virginia Woolf 1912–1941*. St Albans: Paladin.
12 P. J. Williams (1977) *Seeing a Colour-Blind Future*. London: Virago, p. 71.
13 G. Myrdal (1944) *An American Dilemma: The Negro problem and modern democracy*. New York: Harper, p. 1073.
14 Myrdal, *An American Dilemma*, p. 1078.
15 A. Myrdal (1945) *Nation and Family*. London: Kegan Paul, Trench, Trubner, p. 398.
16 R. Blauner (1972) *Racial Oppression in America*. New York: Harper and Row, p. 125.

17   H. M. Hacker (1951) Women as a minority group. *Social Forces*, 50: 60–9.
18   J. B. Miller (1976) *Toward a New Psychology of Women*. Boston: Beacon Press.
19   A. Mahler (1990) *Gustav Mahler: Memories and letters*. Eds D. Mitchell and K. Martner. London: Sphere.
20   Cited in P. Rose (1985) *Writing of Women: Essays in a renaissance*. Middletown, Conn.: Wesleyan University Press, p. 55.
21   K. Blaukopf (trans. I. Goodwin) (1974) *Mahler*. London: Futura.

Chapter 2 On the Problem of Women and Bicycles

1   M. Gullestad (1992) *The Art of Social Relations*. Oslo: Scandinavian University Press.
2   Department of the Environment, Transport and the Regions (2000) *Road Accident Statistics*. www.transdat.detr.gov.uk/facts/accident/bicycle.cycle98.htm, accessed November 2000.
3   British Medical Association (1992) *Cycling Towards Health and Safety*. Oxford: Oxford University Press, p. 120.
4   OECD (2000) *International Road Traffic and Accident Database*. http:/www.bast.de/irtad/english/we33.html, accessed November 2000.
5   D. Morris (1969) *The Human Zoo*. London: Jonathan Cape, p. 108.
6   When the railway came to King's Cross, her body was removed to Bournemouth.
7   J. Legget (1988) *Local Heroines*. London: Pandora.
8   N. White (1998) *Isaac Newton: The last sorcerer*. London: Fourth Estate.
9   V. Woolf (1977, originally published 1929) *A Room of One's Own*. St Albans: Granada, p. 27.
10   An unpleasant military metaphor.
11   Q. Bell (1976) *Virginia Woolf 1882–1912* and *Virginia Woolf 1912–1941*. St Albans: Paladin.
12   Bell, *Virginia Woolf 1882–1912*, p. 55.
13   C. Seymour-Jones (1993) *Beatrice Webb: Woman of conflict*. London: Pandora, p. 230.
14   F. Ashton, *Bicycling: A history*. Newton Abbott: David and Charles.
15   D. Mathew (1993) Pedal power. *Oxford*, 6(1): 11–13.
16   H. G. Wells (1901) *The Wheels of Chance: A holiday adventure*. London: Dent.
17   F. Thompson (1957, originally published as *Lark Rise* (1939), *Over to Candleford* (1941) and *Candleford Green* (1943)) *Lark Rise to Candleford*. Oxford: Oxford University Press, p. 544.
18   G. Lindsay (1990) *Flora Thompson: The story of the Lark Rise writer*. London: Robert Hale.
19   R. Reid (1978) *Marie Curie*. St Albans: Paladin.
20   Ashton, *Bicycling*.
21   L. H. Porter (1895) *Cycling for Health and Pleasure*. New York: Dodd, Mead.
22   Quoted in Ashton, *Bicycling*, p. 85.
23   Quoted in Porter, *Cycling for Health and Pleasure*, p. 21.

24   Thompson, *Lark Rise to Candleford*, p. 546.

25   Wells, *The Wheels of Chance*, p. 42.

26   O. Jennings (1889) *Cycling and Health*. London: Iliffe and Sons.

27   M. E. Ward (1896) *Bicycling for Ladies*. New York: Brentano's.

28   J. Beresford Ryley (1899) *The Dangers of Cycling for Women and Children*. London: Henry Renshaw, p. 18.

29   Jennings, *Cycling and Health*.

30   Ryley, *The Dangers of Cycling for Women and Children*.

31   Jennings, *Cycling and Health*.

32   Porter, *Cycling for Health and Pleasure*, p. 140.

33   Virtuous cycle. *The Times*, 9 August 1996.

34   East London and The City Health Authority (1996) *Transport in London and the Implications for Health*. London: East London and The City Health Authority, Department of Public Health.

35   British Medical Association, *Cycling Towards Health and Safety*, p. 117.

36   http://www.bts.gov/btsprod/nts/, accessed October 2001.

37   H. Finch and J. M. Morgan (1985) *Attitudes to Cycling*. Transport and Road Research Laboratory, Research Report RR19. Crowthorne: Transport and Road Research Laboratory.

38   *Independent*, 12 June 1993.

39   British Medical Association, *Cycling Towards Health and Safety*.

40   C. Dora (1999) A different route to health: implications of transport policies. *British Medical Journal*, 318: 1686–9.

41   W. Tuxworth, A. M. Nevill, C. White and C. Jenkins (1986) Health, fitness, physical activity and morbidity of middle-aged male factory workers. *British Journal of Industrial Medicine*, 43(11): 733–53.

42   British Medical Association, *Cycling Towards Health and Safety*, pp. 115, 118.

43   R. S. Paffenbarger, R. T. Hyde, A. L. Wing and C. C. Hsieh (1986) Physical activity, all-cause mortality and longevity of college alumni. *New England Journal of Medicine*, 314(10): 605–13.

44   British Medical Association, *Cycling Towards Health and Safety*, p. 25.

45   Quoted in D. Davies (1999) Pressure point. *London Cyclist*, February/March, p. 32.

46   Mountain bike enthusiasts prone to faulty equipment. *The Times*, 20 October 2000.

47   G. M. Hammond (1895) Appendix: The influence of the bicycle on health and disease. In Porter, *Cycling for Health and Pleasure*.

48   East London and The City Health Authority, *Transport in London*, p. 19.

49   International Obesity Task Force (1998) *Obesity: Preventing and managing the global epidemic*. Geneva: World Health Organization.

50   Mrs Aria (1906) *Woman and the Motor-Car: Being the Autobiography of an Automobilist*. London: Sidney Appleton, p. 1.

51   Nationwide Personal Transportation Survey (1995) *Our Nation's Travel*. NPTS Early Results Report. http://www.bts.gov/ntda/npts/, accessed October 2001.

52   M. Wachs (1998) The automobile and gender. *Women's Travel Issues: Proceedings of the 2nd National Conference, FHWA-PL-97-024*, July.

53 Central Statistical Office (1995) *Social Focus on Women*. London: CSO, pp. 58–9.

54 Dora, A different route to health.

55 Nationwide Personal Transportation Survey, *Our Nation's Travel*.

56 Department of the Environment, Transport and the Regions, *Road Accident Statistics*.

57 B. Hanratty and W. Patterson (1998) Three quarters of delegates drove to conference on impact of environment on health (letter). *British Medical Journal*, 316: 775.

58 Aria, *Woman and the Motor-Car*, p. 182.

59 A. Porter (1998) First fatal car crash in Britain occurred in 1898 (letter). *British Medical Journal*, 317: 212.

60 D. Mohan and I. Roberts (2001) Global road safety and the contribution of big business. *British Medical Journal*, 323: 648.

61 Department of the Environment, Transport and the Regions, *Road Accident Statistics*.

62 Dora, A different route to health.

63 I. Roberts (1995) China takes to the roads. *British Medical Journal*, 310: 1311–14.

64 Road crashes in deadly top three by 2020 (1998). *AA Magazine*, autumn, p. 13.

65 Roadpeace (2001). *Leaflet*.

66 Department of Health Committee on the Medical Effects of Air Pollutants (1998) *Quantification of the Effects of Air Pollution on Health in the UK*. London: Stationery Office.

67 Environmental Transport Association (1997) *Road Users' Exposure to Air Pollution*. London: ETA.

68 *Independent Inquiry into Inequalities in Health* (The Acheson Report) (1998) London: Stationery Office, p. 58.

69 Department of the Environment, Transport and the Regions, *Road Accident Statistics*.

70 East London and The City Health Authority, *Transport in London*.

71 Department of the Environment, Transport and the Regions, *Road Accident Statistics*.

72 British Medical Association, *Cycling Towards Health and Safety*, p. 120.

73 British Medical Association, *Cycling Towards Health and Safety*, ch. 10.

74 M. J. Wardlaw (2000) Three lessons for a better cycling future. *British Medical Journal*, 321: 1582–5.

75 British Medical Association, *Cycling Towards Health and Safety*, p. 56.

76 E. Showalter (1987) *The Female Malady: Women, madness and English culture 1830–1980*. London: Virago.

77 Gullestad, *The Art of Social Relations*, pp. 8, 3.

78 B. Wootton (1967) *In a World I Never Made*. London: Allen and Unwin, p. 132.

79 H. Miller (1965) *Sexus*. New York: Grove Press, p. 180.

80 K. Millett (1971) *Sexual Politics*. London: Rupert Hart-Davis, p. 24.

81 Millett, *Sexual Politics*, p. 58.

82 J. Smith (1996) *Misogynies*. London: Vintage, p. viii.

Chapter 3 Manslaughter

1   M. Sarton (1997) *Recovering: A journal*. London: Women's Press, p. 19.
2   P. Gilbert (1994) Male violence: towards an integration, p. 352. In J. Archer (ed.) *Male Violence*. London: Routledge.
3   Home Office (2000) *Recorded Crime Statistics 1898–1997*. http://www. homeoffice.gov.uk/rds/publf.htm. The time of access has not always been noted for references in the early part of this book.
4   Home Office, *Recorded Crime Statistics*.
5   This argument is put in S. Brownmiller (1976) *Against Our Will: Men, women and rape*. Harmondsworth: Penguin.
6   D. Povey, J. Cotton and S. Sisson (2000) *Recorded Crime Statistics, England and Wales, April 1999 to March 2000*. Issue 12/00.
7   G. C. Barclay and C. Tavares (2000) *International Comparisons of Criminal Justice Statistics 1998*. Issue 04/00.
     http://www.homeoffice.gov.uk/rds/publf.htm.
8   Barclay and Tavares, *International Comparisons of Criminal Justice Statistics*.
9   A. G. Johnson (1980) On the prevalence of rape in the United States. *SIGNS: Journal of Women in Culture and Society*, 6: 136–46.
10   M. P. Koss, T. E. Dinero, C. A. Seibel and S. L. Cox (1988) Stranger and acquaintance rape: are there differences in the victim's experience? *Psychology of Women Quarterly*, 12: 1–24.
11   P. Pollard (1994) Sexual violence against women. In Archer, *Male Violence*; L. L. Heise, A. Raikes, C. H. Watts and A. B. Zwi (1994) Violence against women: a neglected public health issue in less developed countries. *Social Science and Medicine*, 39(9): 1165–79.
12   E. Stark and A. Flitcraft (1996) *Women at Risk: Domestic violence and women's health*. Thousand Oaks, Calif.: Sage, pp. 121, 125.
13   L. Vogelman and G. Eagle (1991) Overcoming endemic violence against women in South Africa. *Social Justice*, 18(1–2): 209–29.
14   A. Godenzi (1994) What's the big deal? We are men and they are women. In T. Newburn and E. A. Stanko (eds) *Just Boys Doing Business? Men, masculinities and crime*. London: Routledge, p. 136.
15   Hidden toll of rape victims. *Guardian*, 18 February 2000.
16   One in five young women falling victim to stalkers. *Independent*, 7 October 2000.
17   International Medical Advisory Panel (2000) *Statement on Gender-based Violence*. London: IPPF.
18   F. van Velden (1984) *Environment and Sexual Violence*. University of Technology, Faculty of Architecture, Eindhoven, Netherlands: Turtle Edition, p. 43.
19   Home Office (2000) *Domestic Violence: Statistics*. www.crimereduction.gov.uk/domesticviolence3.htm.
20   Home Office, *Domestic Violence*.
21   Five million cases of domestic abuse every year. *Guardian*, 26 October 2000.
22   G. Mezey and S. Bewley (1997) Domestic violence and pregnancy. *British Medical Journal*, 314: 1295.

23   World Bank (1993) *World Development Report: Investing in health*. Oxford: Oxford University Press; Heise et al., Violence against women; J. P. Grant (1995) *The State of the World's Children*. Oxford: Oxford University Press, p. 26.

24   Heise et al., Violence against women, p. 1167.

25   A. Clare (2000) *On Men: Masculinity in crisis*. London: Chatto and Windus, p. 42.

26   Stark and Flitcraft, *Women at Risk*.

27   Stark and Flitcraft, *Women at Risk*, p. 14; W. J. Rudman and D. Davey (2000) Identifying domestic violence within inpatient hospital admissions using medical records. *Women and Health*, 30(4): 1–13, p. 3.

28   Mezey and Bewley, Domestic violence and pregnancy.

29   J. Laurance (2001) Murder is the biggest cause of death in pregnancy. *Independent*, 21 March.

30   K. Abbasi (1998) Obstetricians must ask about domestic violence. *British Medical Journal*, 316: 9.

31   J. Fitzpatrick (1994) The use of international human rights norms to combat violence against women. In R. J. Cook (ed.) *Human Rights of Women: National and international perspectives*. Philadelphia: University of Pennsylvania Press; Heise et al., Violence against women.

32   A. Campbell and S. Muncer (1994) Men and the meaning of violence, p. 332. In Archer, *Male Violence*.

33   J. Smith (1996) *Misogynies*. London: Vintage, p. viii.

34   R. B. Brannon and S. J. Juni (1984) A scale for measuring attitudes about masculinity. *Psychological Documents*, 14: 6–7; E. H. Thompson and J. H. Pleck (1987) The structure of male role norms. In M. S. Kimmel (ed.) *Changing Men: New directions in research on men and masculinity*. Newbury Park, Calif.: Sage.

35   P. Spierenburg (1998) Knife fighting and popular codes of honor in early modern Amsterdam; S. Hughes (1998) Men of steel: duelling, honor and political-liberal Italy. Both in P. Spierenburg (ed.) *Men and Violence: Gender, honor and rituals in modern Europe and America*. Columbus: Ohio State University Press.

36   Hughes, Men of steel, p. 77.

37   J. Bourke (1999) *An Intimate History of Killing*. London: Granta Books, p. 6.

38   B. McCarthy (1994) Warrior values: a socio-historical survey. In Archer, *Male Violence*.

39   U. Mellström (1995) Engineering Lives: technology, time and space in a male-centred world. PhD dissertation, Linköping Studies in Art and Science, Sweden.

40   Quoted in B. Parbring (2000) Men and their machines – a love story. *Genus* (Swedish Secretariat for Gender Research), 1: 12–13.

41   Computer games linked to violence. *Guardian*, 24 April 2000.

42   T. McVeigh (2000) Official: video games really are linked to child violence. *Observer*, 23 April.

43   J. R. Lott (1998) *More Guns, Less Crime*. Chicago: University of Chicago Press, p. 1.

44   W. LaPierre (1995) *Guns, Crime and Freedom*. London: HarperCollins, pp. 218, xiv.

45   A. L. Kellerman and D. T. Reay (1986) Protection or peril? An analysis of

firearm-related deaths in the home. *New England Journal of Medicine*, 314(24): 1557–60.

46 J. Sugarmann (2000) *Every Handgun is Aimed at You*. New York: New Press, p. xi.

47 R. W. Connell (1995) *Masculinities*. Cambridge: Polity, p. 212.

48 Sugarmann, *Every Handgun is Aimed at You*, ch. 6.

49 See J. B. Elshtain (1987) *Women and War*. Brighton: Harvester.

50 Stark and Flitcraft, *Women at Risk*, p. 127.

51 Gender gap revealed on resort to arms. *Guardian*, 16 January 1991; see J. J. Pettman (1996) *Worlding Women: A feminist international politics*. London: Routledge.

52 C. Cockburn (1998) *The Space Between Us: Negotiating gender and national identities in conflict*. London: Zed Books.

53 Bourke, *An Intimate History of Killing*.

54 Cited in Bourke, *An Intimate History of Killing*, pp. 14–15.

55 Bourke, *An Intimate History of Killing*, p. 248.

56 See P. Allatt (1983) Men and war: status, class and the social reproduction of masculinity. In E. Gamarnikow, D. Morgan, J. Purvis and D. Taylorson (eds) *The Public and the Private*. London: Heinemann.

57 Bourke, *An Intimate History of Killing*, pp. 150–1.

58 Bourke, *An Intimate History of Killing*, pp. 37–42.

59 L. Kelly (2000) Wars against women: sexual violence, sexual politics and the militarized state. In S. Jacobs, R. Jacobsen and J. Marchbank (eds) *States of Conflict: Gender, violence and resistance*. London: Zed Books.

60 Kelly, Wars against women, p. 59.

61 A. Comfort (1972) *The Joy of Sex*. New York: Crown.

62 Man jailed for luring girl in Net 'chat room'. *The Times*, 25 October 2000.

63 JANET harassed by computer porn. *Times Higher Education Supplement*, 5 March 1993.

64 C. A. MacKinnon (1979) *Sexual Harassment of Working Women: A case of sex discrimination*. New Haven, Conn., and London: Yale University Press.

65 Sacked airline pilot 'caressed' by captain. *Independent*, 14 January 1995.

66 City dealer 'subjected to sexist behaviour'. *Independent*, 4 August 1995.

67 Survey by J. Brown, Portsmouth University, reported in, When the force is against you. *Independent*, 22 May 1996.

68 C. Cockburn (1991) *In the Way of Women: Men's resistance to sex equality in organizations*. Basingstoke: Macmillan, p. 144.

69 R. Sipes (1973) War, sports and aggression: an empirical test of two rival theories. *American Anthropologist*, 75: 64–86.

70 *Radio Times*, 1–7 September 2001, p. 32.

71 L. B. Iglitzen (1978) War, sex, sports and masculinity. In L. L. Farrar (ed.) *War: A historical, political and social study*. Santa Barbara, Calif.: American Bibliographic Center–Ohio Press.

72 V. Duke and L. Crolley (1996) *Football, Nationality and the State*. Harlow: Addison Wesley Longman, p. 1.

73 Duke and Crolley, *Football, Nationality and the State*, pp. 128, 131.

74 M. Mac an Ghaill (1994) *The Making of Men: Masculinities, sexualities and schooling.* Buckingham: Open University Press.

75 Duke and Crolley, *Football, Nationality and the State*, p. 131.

76 J. Williams and R. Taylor (1994) Boys keep swinging: masculinity and football culture in England, p. 227. In Newburn and Stanko, *Just Boys Doing Business?*

77 Williams and Taylor, Boys keep swinging, pp. 132–6.

78 D. Spender (1980) *Man-made Language.* London: Routledge and Kegan Paul.

79 A. Whitney and K. Marks (2002) The hot question in women's sport: how much is baring too much? *Independent*, 21 January.

80 Cricket club in 'sex bias' row. *Metro*, 31 October 2000.

81 A. Tomlinson (1994) FIFA and the World Cup. In J. Sugden and A. Tomlinson (eds) *Hosts and Champions*. Aldershot: Arena.

82 A. Oakley (1981) *Subject Women*. London: Fontana, p. 255.

83 A. MacMahon (1999) *Taking Care of Men: Sexual politics in the public mind.* Cambridge: Cambridge University Press, p. 30.

84 Football chief assault charge. *The Times*, 20 October 2000.

85 S. Jeffords (1989) *The Remasculinization of America: Gender and the Vietnam War.* Bloomington: Indiana University Press, p. xii.

86 Heise et al., Violence against women; P. Spierenburg (1998) Masculinity: violence and honor; an introduction. In Spierenburg, *Men and Violence*.

87 McCarthy, Warrior values.

88 Connell, *Masculinities*.

89 J. Archer (1994) Power and male violence, pp. 312–3. In Archer, *Male Violence*.

90 K. A. Yllo and M. A. Straus (1984) The impact of structural inequality and existing family norms on rates of wife-beating. *Journal of International and Comparative Social Welfare*, 1: 16–29.

91 Stark and Flitcraft, *Women at Risk*, p. 31.

92 J. W. Messerschmidt (1986) *Capitalism, Patriarchy and Crime: Toward a socialist feminist criminology.* Totowa, N.J.: Rowman and Littlefield.

93 S. Box (1983) *Power, Crime and Mystification.* London: Tavistock, p. 2.

94 Box, *Power, Crime and Mystification*, p. 52.

95 Anger grows as the US jails its two millionth inmate – 25 per cent of world's prison population. *Guardian*, 15 February 2000.

96 Home Office (1997–8) *Offenders as a Percentage of the Population: By gender and age, 1997–98: Social Trends Dataset.* http://www.statistics.gov.uk/statbase/xdataset.asp?vlnk=1454.

97 Boys, 5 and 9, mug pensioner. *Guardian*, 26 April 2000.

98 Fatal rail crash in Belgium was boys 'having fun'. *Observer*, 23 April 2000.

99 Clare, *On Men*, p. 48.

100 Box, *Power, Crime and Mystification*, p. 192.

101 Stark and Flitcraft, *Women at Risk*, p. 130.

102 Five million cases of domestic abuse every year. *Guardian*, 26 October 2000.

103 S. Walby and A. Myhill (2000) *Reducing Domestic Violence . . . What Works?* http://www.homeoffice.gov.uk/violenceagainstwomen/accman.pdf, accessed September 2001.

104 Smith, There's only one Yorkshire Ripper. In *Misogynies*, pp. 163–205.

105 Stark and Flitcraft, *Women at Risk*, p. 34.

106 See K. Pollitt (1995) Violence in a man's world. In *Reasonable Creatures: Essays on women and feminism*. London: Vintage, pp. 26–30.

107 H. Arendt (1970) *On Violence*. New York: Harcourt Brace and World, p. 56.

108 Archer, *Male Violence*, p. 322.

109 Godenzi, What's the big deal, p. 152.

110 Messerschmidt, *Capitalism, Patriarchy and Crime*, p. 150.

111 M. J. Wiener (1998) The Victorian criminalisation of men. In Spierenburg, *Men and Violence*.

112 Box, *Power, Crime and Mystification*, p. 10.

113 D. R. Simon and D. S. Eitzen (1982) *Elite Deviance*. Boston: Allyn and Bacon, p. viii.

114 Box, *Power, Crime and Mystification*, p. 25.

115 Box, *Power, Crime and Mystification*, p. 31.

116 Equal Opportunities Commission (2000) *Women in Senior Management in Wales*. http://www.eoc.org.uk.

117 Box, *Power, Crime and Mystification*, pp. 116–20.

118 M. Savage and A. Witz (eds) (1992) *Gender and Bureaucracy*. Oxford: Blackwell.

119 Cockburn, *In the Way of Women*.

120 Cited in Box, *Power, Crime and Mystification*, p. 42.

121 Privatization linked to rail crash. *Guardian*, 25 February 2000. The cost-cutting strategies introduced after the privatization of the British rail network included the loss of some 6,000 track maintenance workers. Railtrack 'has shed 6,000 repairmen'. *The Times*, 20 October 2000.

122 E. M. Gramlich and P. P. Koshel (1975) *Educational Performance Contracting*. Washington, D.C.: Brookings Institution.

123 R. Nader and W. J. Smith (1994) *Collision Course: The truth about airline safety*. Blue Ridge Summit, Pa.: TAB Books.

124 Simon and Eitzen, *Elite Deviance*, p. 99.

125 Messerschmidt, *Capitalism, Patriarchy and Crime*, p. 105.

126 The Dalkon disaster. *Guardian*, 28 May 1985.

127 K. Yanoshik and J. Norsigian (1989) Contraception, control and choice: international perspectives. In K. S. Ratcliff (ed.) *Healing Technology: Feminist perspectives*. Ann Arbor: University of Michigan Press.

128 Messerschmidt, *Capitalism, Patriarchy and Crime*, pp. 104, 112; Simon and Eitzen, *Elite Deviance*, p. 157.

129 Simon and Eitzen, *Elite Deviance*.

130 Messerschmidt, *Capitalism, Patriarchy and Crime*, p. 105.

131 M. H. Best and W. E. Connolly (1978) Nature and its largest parasite. In R. C. Edwards, M. Reich and T. E. Weisskopf (eds) *The Capitalist System*. Englewood Cliffs, N.J.: Prentice-Hall.

132 B. Commoner (1971) The economic meaning of ecology. In J. Skolnick and E. Currie (eds) *Crisis in American Institutions*. New York: Alfred A. Knopf.

133 I. Gately (2001) *La Diva Nicotina: The story of how tobacco seduced the world*. New York: Simon and Schuster.

134 P. Taylor (1985) *The Smoke Ring: Tobacco, money and multinational politics*. London: Sphere, p. 21.

135   P. Jha and F. J. Chalouka (2000) The economics of global tobacco control. *British Medical Journal*, 321: 358–61.

136   For Peto's sake give up. *Times Higher Education Supplement*, 8 January 1999.

137   £2 m plot to discredit smoking study exposed. *Guardian*, 7 April 2000.

138   Department of Health (1998) *Our Healthier Nation*. London: Stationery Office, p. 20; The truth about tobacco in its own words (2000) (Editorial) *British Medical Journal*, 321: 313–14.

139   Kelly, Wars against women.

140   J. P. Grant (1997) War, children and the responsibility of the international community. In B. S. Levy and V. W. Sidel (eds) *War and Public Health*. New York: Oxford University Press, p. 12; B. S. Levy and V. W. Sidel, The impact of military activities on civilian populations, p. 149. In Levy and Sidel, *War and Public Health*.

141   N. Chomsky (2000) *Rogue States: The rule of force in world affairs*. London: Pluto Press.

142   V. W. Sidel (1988) The arms race as a threat to health. *Lancet*, 20 August: 442–4.

143   S. Woolhander and D. U. Himmelstein (1985) Militarism and mortality: an international analysis of arms spending and infant death rates. *Lancet*, 15 June: 1375–8.

144   Levy and Sidel, The impact of military activities on civilian populations, p. 151.

145   W. H. Foege (1997) Arms and public health: a global perspective, p. 7. In Levy and Sidel, *War and Public Health*.

146   Connell, *Masculinities*, pp. 73, 77.

147   C. Griffin (1991) Experiencing power: dimensions of gender, race and class. British Psychological Society, *Psychology of Women Section Newsletter*, 8: 43–58.

148   A. Campbell (1993) *Out of Control: Men, women and aggression*. London: Pandora, p. 55.

149   B. Campbell (2000) Men are the problem. *Guardian*, 25 October.

150   D. Hall and A. M. Lynch (1998) Violence begins at home. *British Medical Journal*, 316: 1551.

151   Clare, *On Men*, p. 63.

152   Messerschmidt, *Capitalism, Patriarchy and Crime*, p. 51.

153   Department of the Environment, Transport and the Regions (1998) *Transport Statistics*, 18 September.

154   World Bank, *World Development Report*, p. 50.

155   Hall and Lynch, Violence begins at home, p. 1551.

156   S. McNeill (1987) Flashing: its effect on women, p. 94. In J. Hanmer and M. Maynard (eds) *Women, Violence and Social Control*. Basingstoke: Macmillan.

157   McNeill, Flashing.

158   McNeill, Flashing, p. 101.

159   British Crime Survey (1998) *Feelings of Insecurity by Gender.* http://www. statistics.gov.uk/statbase/xsdataset.asp.

160   L. Olson (2000) Fear limits women's mobility. *Genus* (Swedish Secretariat for Gender Research), 1/2000: 5–7.

161   M. Warr (1985) Fear of rape among urban women. *Social Problems*, 32: 238–50.

162 S. Griffin (1981) *Pornography and Silence: Culture's revenge against nature.* London: Women's Press, p. 157.

163 N. Walter (2000) When nothing shocks us any more. *Independent,* 9 October.

Chapter 4 Sick to Death of Women

1 M. Tripp (ed.) (1974) *Woman in the Year 2000.* New York: Dell Publishing. See especially C. Rinzler, Femininity: 2000; L. C. Pogrebin, Born free: a feminist fable; R. Cherry, The end of the medicine man; J. Trahey, The female facade: fierce, fragile and fading.

2 L. Segal (1994) *Straight Sex: The politics of pleasure.* London: Virago, p. 8.

3 B. Friedan (1963) *The Feminine Mystique.* London: Victor Gollancz.

4 F. Lundberg and M. Farnham (1947) *Modern Woman: The lost sex.* New York: Harper, p. 47.

5 Lundberg and Farnham, *Modern Woman,* p. 6.

6 S. Brownmiller (2000) *In Our Time: Memoir of a revolution.* London: Aurum Press, p. 204.

7 Lundberg and Farnham, *Modern Woman,* pp. 173, 357.

8 K. Millett (1971) *Sexual Politics.* London: Rupert Hart-Davis, p. 271; see ch. 8 below.

9 B. Friedan (1977) *It Changed My Life.* New York: Dell Publishing, pp. 33–4.

10 D. Horowitz (1998) *Betty Friedan and the Making of the Feminist Mystique.* Amherst, Mass.: University of Massachusetts Press.

11 Friedan, *The Feminine Mystique,* pp. 82, 102.

12 G. Greer (1970) *The Female Eunuch.* London: MacGibbon and Kee, p. 249.

13 Brownmiller, *In Our Time,* p. 158.

14 The dress sense of feminists was a topic of frequent media comment. See e.g., N. Davidson (1988) *The Failure of Feminism.* New York: Prometheus Books, p. 18 on Kate Millett; Horowitz, *Betty Friedan,* p. 57, on Betty Friedan.

15 D. Spender (1986) What is feminism: a personal answer, p. 214. In J. Mitchell and A. Oakley (eds) *What is Feminism?.* Oxford: Blackwell.

16 P. Wylie (1942) *Generation of Vipers.* New York: Farrar and Rinehart.

17 H. Kramer and J. Sprenger (1971, originally published 1486) *The Malleus Maleficarum.* Trans. M. Summers. New York: Dover Publications.

18 E. Hawes (1943) *Why Women Cry: Or wenches with wrenches.* New York: Cornwall Press, p. 159.

19 E. Hawes (1948) *Anything But Love: A complete digest of the rules for feminine behaviour from birth to death; given out in print, on film, and over the air; read, seen, listened to monthly by some 340,000,000 women.* New York: Rinehart, pp. 30–2.

20 A. Coote and B. Campbell (1982) *Sweet Freedom: The struggle for women's liberation.* London: Pan Books, p. 22.

21 R. Morgan (ed.) (1970) *Sisterhood is Powerful.* New York: Vintage.

22 R. Morgan (1978) *Going Too Far: The personal chronicle of a feminist.* New York: Vintage, pp. 4–5.

23 S. Rowbowtham (2000) *Promise of a Dream.* London: Allen Lane, Penguin Press, p. 117.

24 J. Mitchell (1966) Women: the longest revolution. *New Left Review*, no. 40.

25 Rowbotham, *Promise of a Dream*, p. 116.

26 S. Rowbotham (1997) *Century of Women*. London: Viking, p. 289.

27 See L. Berg (1988) All we had was a voice. In S. Maitland (ed.) *Very Heaven: Looking back at the 1960s*. London: Virago.

28 Rowbotham, *Promise of a Dream*.

29 A. Oakley (1974) *The Sociology of Housework*. London: Martin Robertson, pp. 190–1.

30 S. M. Evans (1998) American women in a new millennium. In C. B. Costello, S. E. Miles and A. J. Stone (eds) *The American Woman 1999–2000*. New York: W. W. Norton.

31 Friedan, *It Changed My Life*, p. 119.

32 Rowbotham, *Century of Women*, pp. 370–1.

33 Evans, American women in a new millennium. Implementation of the 1970 Equal Pay Act in Britain was delayed until 1975.

34 Coote and Campbell, *Sweet Freedom*, p. 26.

35 Friedan, *It Changed My Life*, p. 127.

36 Brownmiller, *In Our Time*, p. 243.

37 Redstockings Manifesto, pp. 109–11. Reprinted in L. B. Tanner (ed.) (1970) *Voices from Women's Liberation*. New York: Signet Books.

38 Morgan, *Sisterhood is Powerful*, p. 72; D. Purkiss (1996) *The Witch in History*. London: Routledge, p. 9.

39 Morgan, *Sisterhood is Powerful*, p. 76.

40 S. Rowbotham (1973) The beginnings of women's liberation in Britain, p. 94. In M. Wandor (ed.) *The Body Politic: Women's Liberation in Britain 1969–1972*. London: Stage One.

41 Reprinted as N. Weisstein, Psychology constructs the female. In V. Gornick and B. K. Moran (eds) (1971) *Woman in Sexist Society*. New York: Basic Books.

42 Brownmiller, *In Our Time*, p. 52.

43 A. Koedt (1970) The myth of the vaginal orgasm, p. 165. Reprinted in Tanner, *Voices from Women's Liberation*.

44 C. Cockburn (1991) *In the Way of Women: Men's resistance to sex equality in organizations*. Basingstoke: Macmillan, p. 1.

45 Morgan, *Sisterhood is Powerful*, p. 64.

46 Brownmiller, *In Our Time*, pp. 38–9; Morgan, *Sisterhood is Powerful*, p. 65.

47 S. Faludi (1992) *Backlash: The undeclared war against women*. London: Chatto and Windus, p. 99.

48 Miss World, p. 250, in Wandor, *The Body Politic*.

49 Miss World, p. 251, in Wandor, *The Body Politic*.

50 Miss World, Channel 5, UK television, 8 p.m., 30 November 2000.

51 Faludi, *Backlash*, p. 100.

52 Morgan, *Sisterhood is Powerful*, p. 10.

53 S. Bashevkin (1998) *Women on the Defensive*. Chicago: University of Chicago Press.

54 V. Woolf (1977, originally published 1929) *A Room of One's Own*. St Albans: Paladin Books, p. 105.

55 Woolf, *A Room of One's Own*, p. 94.

56 J. Marcus (1987) *Virginia Woolf and the Languages of Patriarchy.* Bloomington: Indiana University Press, p. 165.

57 S. Troubley (1982) *All That Summer She Was Mad: Virginia Woolf: Female victim of male medicine.* New York: Continuum, p. 191.

58 C. P. Gilman (1935) *The Living of Charlotte Perkins Gilman: An autobiography.* New York: Appleton-Century.

59 G. Greer (1999) *The Whole Woman.* London: Doubleday, p. 4.

60 V. Woolf (1932) *The Second Common Reader.* Harmondsworth: Penguin, p. 201.

61 N. Wolf (1993) *Fire with Fire.* London: Chatto and Windus, p. 14.

62 M. French (1992) *The War Against Women.* London: Penguin.

63 Equal Opportunities Commission (2000) *Pay and Income.* www.eoc.org.uk, accessed October 2001.

64 Equal Opportunities Commission, *Pay and Income.*

65 Equal Opportunities Commission, *Pay and Income.*

66 Equal Opportunities Commission, *Pay and Income.*

67 Equal Opportunities Commission, *Gender Equality in Pay Practices: Research findings.* http://www/eoc.org.uk, accessed October 2001.

68 Costello et al., *The American Woman,* p. 314.

69 Fawcett Society (2000) *Annual Report 1999–2000.* London, p. 4.

70 Fawcett Society, *Annual Report,* p. 5.

71 H. Joshi and P. Paci (1998) *Unequal Pay for Women and Men: Evidence from the British Birth Cohort Studies.* Cambridge, Mass.: MIT Press, p. 70.

72 Equal Opportunities Commission (2000) New figures show women are not catching up on pay. *Press Release.* http://www.eoc.org.uk/html/press_releases_2000_43.html, accessed December 2000.

73 R. Anker (2001) Theories of occupational segregation by sex: an overview, p. 145. In M. F. Loutfi (ed.) *Women, Gender and Work.* Geneva: International Labour Office.

74 Costello et al., *The American Woman,* p. 303.

75 L. Wirth (2001) *Breaking Through the Glass Ceiling.* Geneva: International Labour Office, p. 16.

76 Costello et al., *The American Woman,* p. 313.

77 Joshi and Paci, *Unequal Pay for Women and Men,* p. 15.

78 Equal Opportunities Commission (2000) *Undervaluing Women.* http://www.eoc.org.uk, accessed December 2000.

79 Equal Opportunities Commission, *Pay and Income.*

80 J. Humphries and J. Rubery (1995) Introduction, p. 6. In J. Humphries and J. Rubery (eds) *The Economics of Equal Opportunities.* Manchester: Equal Opportunities Commission.

81 Anker, Theories of occupational segregation by sex, p. 129.

82 Wirth, *Breaking Through the Glass Ceiling,* p. 10.

83 Equal Opportunities Commission, *Pay and Income.*

84 Costello et al., *The American Woman,* p. 307.

85 Equal Opportunities Commission (2001) *The Gender Pay Gap: A research review.* http://www.eoc.org.uk, accessed October 2001.

86 Equal Opportunities Commission, *Gender Equality in Pay Practices.*

87 Cockburn, *In the Way of Women.*

88   K. Kiernan and M. Wicks (1990) *Family Change and Future Policy.* London: Family Policy Study Centre, p. 30.
89   J. Brannen, G. Mészáros, P. Moss and G. Poland (1994) *Employment and Family Life: A review of research in the UK (1980–1994).* London: Institute of Education, p. 68.
90   Fawcett Society, *Annual Report*, p. 8.
91   Wirth, *Breaking Through the Glass Ceiling*, p. 16.
92   R. M. Kanter (1993) *Men and Women of the Corporation.* New York: Basic Books.
93   J. P. Spradly and B. J. Mann (1975) *Cocktail Waitresses: Women's work in a man's world.* New York: McGraw-Hill.
94   J. L. Pierce (1995) *Gender Trials: Emotional lives in contemporary law firms.* Berkeley: University of California Press.
95   A. R. Hochschild (1983) *The Managed Heart: The commercialization of human feeling.* Berkeley: University of California Press.
96   J. Millar and C. Glendinning (1987) Invisible women, invisible poverty, pp. 13–14. In C. Glendinning and J. Millar (eds) *Women and Poverty in Britain.* Brighton: Wheatsheaf Books.
97   Equal Opportunities Commission (1995) *The Life Cycle of Inequality: Women and men in Britain 1995.* Manchester: Equal Opportunities Commission, p. 2.
98   Costello et al., *The American Woman*, pp. 332, 336.
99   Fawcett Society, *Annual Report*, p. 8.
100 *Human Development Report* (1995) New York: United Nations Development Programme.
101 Costello et al., *The American Woman*, pp. 231, 239.
102 Fawcett Society (2000) *Towards Equality*, December.
103 Equal Opportunities Commission (2000) *Facts about Women and Men in Great Britain 1999.* http://www.eoc.org.uk, accessed December 2000.
104 Fawcett Society (2000) *Towards Equality*, December.
105 Fawcett Society, *Annual Report*, p. 11.
106 J. Judd (2001) Boys pull ahead of girls in maths tests. *Independent*, 1 February.
107 Equal Opportunities Commission, *Facts about Women and Men in Great Britain 1999.*
108 Equal Opportunities Commission, *Facts about Women and Men in Great Britain 1999.*
109 *Population Reports, Series M* (2001). no. 12.
110 J. Vidal (2000) Annan demands action on girls' schooling. *Guardian*, 27 April.
111 Costello et al., *The American Woman*, p. 264.
112 Equal Opportunities Commission (1978–9) *Research Bulletin*, 1(1) (winter), 44.
113 Equal Opportunities Commission, *Facts about Women and Men in Great Britain 1999.*
114 Equal Opportunities Commission, *Research Bulletin*, 1(1) (winter), 44.
115 Equal Opportunities Commission, *Facts About Women and Men in Great Britain 1999.*
116 Costello et al., *The American Woman*, p. 272.
117 Equal Opportunities Commission, *The Life Cycle of Inequality*, p. 2.

118 Costello et al., *The American Woman*, p. 275 (1996 figure).
119 N. Walter (1998) *The New Feminism*. London: Little, Brown, p. 3.
120 C. Hakim (1979) Occupational Segregation. *Research Paper* no. 9, Department of Employment. London: HMSO, p. 23.
121 Equal Opportunities Commission, *Facts about Women and Men in Great Britain 1999*.
122 Costello et al., *The American Woman*, p. 285.
123 Costello et al., *The American Woman*, p. 287.
124 Wirth, *Breaking Through the Glass Ceiling*, p. 29.
125 Fawcett Society, *Annual Report*, p. 5.
126 K. Watson-Smyth (2000) Women hit FTSE glass ceiling. *Independent*, 8 November.
127 Fawcett Society (2000) *Towards Equality*, spring.
128 Wirth, *Breaking Through the Glass Ceiling*, pp. 37–9.
129 Fawcett Society (2000) *Towards Equality*, spring.
130 Fawcett Society (2000) *Towards Equality*, December.
131 Costello et al., *The American Woman*, p. 361.
132 J. P. Fernandez and J. Davis (1999) *Race, Gender and Rhetoric: The true state of race and gender relations in corporate America*. New York: McGraw-Hill, pp. 49, 61.
133 N. Walter (2000) From top jobs to the shop floor, women lose out. *Independent*, 24 August.
134 T. Luckhurst (2001) How Auntie treated Sue. *Independent*, 25 September.
135 S. Rimington (2001) *Open Secret*. London: Hutchinson.
136 M. Freely (2001) Equality? We still have a long way to go. *Independent*, 17 January.
137 Equal Opportunities Commission, *Facts about Women and Men in Great Britain 1999*.
138 Costello et al., *The American Woman*, p. 361.
139 Constitution Unit (2000) *Women's Representation in UK Politics: What can be done within the law*. June. School of Public Policy, University College, London.
140 Wirth, *Breaking Through the Glass Ceiling*, p. 47.
141 Equal Opportunities Commission, *Facts about Women and Men in Great Britain 1999*.
142 A. Macfarlane, M. Mugford, J. Henderson, A. Furtado, J. Stevens and A. Dunn (2000) *Birth Counts: Statistics of pregnancy and childbirth*, vol. 2. London: Stationery Office, p. 478.
143 A. Coote, H. Harman and P. Hewitt (1990) *The Family Way*. London: Institute for Public Policy Research, p. 19.
144 Coote et al., *The Family Way*, p. 18.
145 Fawcett Society (1999) *Towards Equality*, autumn; Rural Development Commission (1994) *Survey of Rural Services*: Rural Development Commission.
146 Department for Education and Employment (1997) *Family and Working Lives Survey*.
147 Joshi and Paci, *Unequal Pay for Women and Men*, p. 10.
148 Costello et al., *The American Woman*, p. 299.

149 N. Stockman, N. Bonney and S. Xuewen (1995) *Women's Work in East and West.* London: UCL Press, p. 90.
150 Costello et al., *The American Woman*, p. 299.
151 H. Meltzer (1994) *Day Care Services for Children: A survey carried out on behalf of the Department of Health in 1990.* London: OPCS.
152 Day Care Trust (1997) *Sharing the Costs of Childcare.* Briefing Paper no. 4.
153 Costello et al., *The American Woman*, pp. 299–300.
154 Evans, American women in a new millennium, p. 68.
155 S. Cassidy (2001) British childcare 'is the most expensive in Europe'. *Independent*, 31 July.
156 Office of Population Censuses and Surveys (1976) *General Household Survey.* London: HMSO, table 6.26.
157 Department for Education and Employment, *Family and Working Lives Survey.*
158 Stockman et al., *Women's Work in East and West*, p. 91.
159 Parents Expect More from Employers but Few Provide Help with Childcare (2001) http://www.mori.com/polls/2001/daycare03.shtml, accessed October 2001.
160 N. Folbre (2001) *The Invisible Heart: Economics and family values.* New York: New Press, p. 62.
161 S. A. Hewlett (1986) *A Lesser Life: The myth of women's liberation in America.* New York: Warner Books, p. 74.
162 H. Wilkinson and I. Briscoe (1996) *Parental Leave: The price of family values?.* London: Demos.
163 J. Ditch, H. Barnes, J. Bradshaw and M. Kilkey (1998) *A Synthesis of National Family Policies 1996.* European Commission, European Observatory on National Family Policies. University of York, p. 62.
164 Wilkinson and Briscoe, *Parental Leave*; Wirth, *Breaking Through the Glass Ceiling*, p. 116.
165 R. Thomas (1996) Business wakes up to problems of young fathers. *Guardian*, 31 October.
166 L. Harding and E. Sheffield (1998) Mothers almost welcome as Britain warms to children. *Guardian*, 12 March.
167 Safe Motherhood (2001) http://www/safemotherhood.org, accessed October 2001.
168 Safe Motherhood (2001) http://www.safemotherhood.org/facts_and_figures/unsafe_abortion_fact.htm, accessed October 2001.
169 Safe Motherhood (2001) http://www.safemotherhood.org/facts_and_figures/unwanted_pregnancy.htm, accessed October 2001.
170 Z. Kmietowicz (2000) New standards set for abortion care. *British Medical Journal*, 320: 733.
171 A. Weyman and J. Walsh (1998) Family planning: programmes and people. *British Journal of Family Planning*, 23: 111.
172 P. Selman and J. Calder (1998) Women's choices. *Nursing Times*, 90(40): 48–50.
173 M. Garg (1998) Uptake of family planning services aiming at an ethnically mixed population in a general practice setting. *British Journal of Family Planning*, 24: 82–3.

174 E. Hemminki, S. Sihvo, P. Koponen and E. Kosunen (1997) Quality of contraceptive services in Finland. *Quality in Health Care*, 6: 62–8.
175 Safe motherhood (2001) http://www.safemotherhood.org/facts_and_figures/unwanted_pregnancy.htm, accessed October 2001.
176 Abortion Surveillance-United States (1997) http://www.cdc.gov/nccdphp/drh/surv_abort.htm, accessed October 2001.
177 *Morbidity and Mortality Weekly Report* (2000), 49(SS-11). http://www.cdc.gov, accessed October 2001.
178 Kaiser Family Foundation (2001) Abortion in the US. http://www.kff.org/content/archive/1431/ru486_fs.html, accessed October 2001.
179 Royal College of Obstetricians and Gynaecologists (2001) *The Care of Women Requesting Induced Abortion*. http://www.rcog.org.uk/guidelines/_induced_abortion.html, accessed October 2001.
180 Safe Motherhood (2001) http://www/safemotherhood.org, accessed October 2001.
181 Coote et al., *The Family Way*, p. 46.
182 A. Bridgwood, G. Malbon, D. Lader and J. Matheson (1996*) Health in England 1995*. London: Office for National Statistics, pp. 75, 223.
183 D. L. Bennett and A. Bauman (2000) Adolescent mental health and risky sexual behaviour. *British Medical Journal*, 321: 251–2.
184 Counseling to prevent unintended pregnancy (1996) JAMA Women's Health. http://www.ama-assn.org/special/contra/treatmnt/guide/cps/unpreg/unpreg4.htm, accessed October 2001.
185 Coote et al., *The Family Way*, p. 47.
186 Royal College of Obstetricians and Gynaecologists (2001) *National Audit of Induced Abortion 2000*. London: Royal College of Obstetricians and Gynaecologists, p. 2.
187 *Proceedings: Abortion Matters, International Conference on Reducing the Need and Improving the Quality of Abortion Services* (1997) Utrecht: Stimezo Nederland.
188 Kaiser Family Foundation, Abortion in the US.
189 I. Allen (1981) *Report on Family Planning, Sterilisation and Abortion Services*. London: Policy Studies Institute; Kmietowicz, New standards set for abortion care.
190 Kaiser Family Foundation, Abortion in the US.
191 F. Charatan (2001) US government limits abortion pill for poor women. *British Medical Journal*, 322: 1015.
192 K. Gardner and L. Davidson (1993) Unwanted pregnancy and abortion, pp. 124–5. In A. McPherson (ed.) *Women's Problems in General Practice*. Oxford: Oxford University Press.
193 Macfarlane et al., *Birth Counts*, p. 228.
194 Royal College of Obstetricians and Gynaecologists, *National Audit of Induced Abortion 2000*, p. 18.
195 Safe Motherhood (2001) http://www.safemotherhood.org/facts_and_figures/unsafe_abortion_fact.htm, accessed October 2001.
196 P. A. O'Brien (1999) The third generation oral contraceptive controversy. *British Medical Journal*, 319: 795–6.

197 A. Bigrigg, M. Evans, B. Gbolade, J. Newton, L. Pollard, A. Szarewski, C. Thomas and M. Walling (1999) Depo Provera: position paper on clinical use, effectiveness and side effects. *British Journal of Family Planning*, 25: 69–76.

198 P. Foster (1995) *Women and the Health Care Industry: An unhealthy relationship?*. Buckingham: Open University Press, ch. 1.

199 *Population Reports, Series M* (2001) no. 12. http://www.jhuccp.org/pr/m12m12/m12boxes.stm, accessed October 2001.

200 Safe Motherhood (2001) http://www.safemotherhood.org/facts_and_figures/unwanted_pregnancy.htm, accessed October 2001.

201 See e.g., French, *The War Against Women*; Greer, *The Whole Woman*; K. Figes (1994) *Because of Her Sex: The myth of equality for women in Britain*. London: Pan Books; Hewlett, *A Lesser Life*; J. Russ (1998) *What Are We Fighting For? Sex, race, class, and the future of feminism*. New York: St Martin's Press.

202 Wirth, *Breaking Through the Glass Ceiling*, pp. 183–6.

203 *Population Reports, Series M*, no. 12.

204 R. Dunbar (2000) Human errors add to natural burden. *Times Higher Education Supplement*, 25 August.

205 G. H. Espinosa (2000) No Mother's Day for women workers: sex discrimination in Mexico, pp. 213, 216–17. In J. Mirsky and M. Radlett (eds) *No Paradise Yet: The world's women face the new century*. London: Zed Books.

206 P. Made (2000) A field of her own: women and land rights in Zimbabwe, pp. 81–3. In Mirsky and Radlett, *No Paradise Yet*.

207 See e.g., E. Fox-Genovese (1996) *'Feminism is Not the Story of My Life'*. New York: Anchor Books; M. Freely (1995) *What About Us? An open letter to the mothers feminism forgot*. London: Bloomsbury.

208 Organization of Women of Afro-Caribbean and Asian Descent (1982) Black women together. In M. Rowe (ed.) *Spare Rib Reader*. Harmondsworth: Penguin. See also N. Yuval-Davis (1997) Women, ethnicity and empowerment. In A. Oakley and J. Mitchell (eds) *Who's Afraid of Feminism?*. London: Hamish Hamilton.

209 Brownmiller, *In Our Time*, p. 70.

210 B. Friedan (1982) *The Second Stage*. London: Michael Joseph, p. 46.

211 S. Firestone (1972) *Dialectic of Sex: The case for feminist revolution*. London: Paladin.

212 Brownmiller, *In Our Time*, p. 52.

213 K. Millett (1974) The pain of public scrutiny. *Ms*, June.

214 G. Greer (1984) *Sex and Destiny*. London: Secker and Warburg.

215 R. Coward (1992) *Our Treacherous Hearts: Why women let men get their way*. London: Faber and Faber.

216 L. Segal (1987) *Is the Future Female? Troubled thoughts on contemporary feminism*. London: Virago.

217 Morgan, *Going Too Far*.

218 K. Millett (1975) *Flying*. London: Hart-Davis, MacGibbon.

219 G. Steinem (1992) *Revolution from Within*. London: Bloomsbury.

220 C. Heilbrun (1988) *Writing a Woman's Life*. London: Women's Press, p. 68;

C. Lasch (1980, originally published 1979) *The Culture of Narcissism*. London: Sphere, p. 19.

221 G. Greer (1991) *The Change: Women, ageing and the menopause*. London: Hamish Hamilton.

222 B. Friedan (1993) *The Fountain of Age*. New York: Simon and Schuster.

223 G. Steinem (1994) *Moving Beyond Words*. London: Bloomsbury.

224 A. Dworkin (1988) *Intercourse*. London: Arrow Books.

225 M. Daly (1993) *Outercourse*. London: Women's Press.

226 B. Ehrenreich (1983) *The Hearts of Men*. London: Pluto Press, p. 122.

227 Brownmiller, *In Our Time*, p. 259.

228 E. Pizzey and J. Shapiro (1982) *Prone to Violence*. London: Hamlyn.

229 J. Kelly (1996) Feminism has been such a disaster for women. *Daily Mail*, 5 February.

230 E. Figes (1970) *Patriarchal Attitudes*. London: Faber and Faber.

231 Figes, *Because of Her Sex*, pp. 217–18.

232 A. R. Roiphe (1972) *Up the Sandbox*. London: Secker and Warburg.

233 K. Roiphe (1994) *The Morning After*. London: Hamish Hamilton.

234 B. Findlen (1995) Introduction. In B. Findlen (ed.) *Listen Up: Voices from the next feminist generation*. Seattle, Wash.: Seal Press.

235 C. H. Sommers (1994) *Who Stole Feminism?*. New York: Simon and Schuster.

236 Wolf, *Fire with Fire*.

237 C. Paglia (1991) *Sexual Personae*. New York: Vintage; C. Paglia (1992) *Sex, Art and American Culture*. Harmondsworth: Penguin.

238 D. MacLeod (1995) Men teachers 'are species in danger'. *Guardian*, 13 January.

239 T. Mooney (1995) Time we heard it for the boys. *Guardian*, 2 August.

240 M. Bright (1998) Boys performing badly. *Observer*, 4 January.

241 D. Hill (1997) Men in crisis. *Guardian*, 29 February.

242 P. Ghazi (1996) Fatherhood at crisis point. *Observer*, 21 April.

243 K. Sengupta (1997) Fathers seen as a nuisance at births. *Independent*, 15 September.

244 P. Lashma (1995) The descent of man. *Independent*, 17 June.

245 *Independent*, 3 March 1999.

246 G. Hinsliff (2000) Official: men are the victims now. *Observer*, 17 December.

247 J. Adams (1993) US male wilts in charge of the in-your-face feminists. *Sunday Times*, 24 October.

248 Lashma, The descent of man.

249 Cynthia Cockburn draws this analogy. Cockburn, *In the Way of Women*, p. 8.

250 Davidson, *The Failure of Feminism*, p. 65.

251 Faludi, *Backlash*, p. 339.

252 S. Keen (1991) *Fire in the Belly: On being a man*. New York: Bantam Books, p. 70.

253 G. Gilder (1995) *Men and Marriage*. Gretna, La.: Pelican Publishing, p. 171.

254 Faludi, *Backlash*, pp. 317–23.

255 Faludi, *Backlash*, pp. 334–9.

256 Greer, *The Whole Woman*, p. 14.

257   M. O'Donnell and S. Sharpe (2000) *Uncertain Masculinities: Youth, ethnicity and class in contemporary Britain*. London: Routledge, p. 192.

258   Cockburn, *In the Way of Women*, p. 157.

259   S. Jeffords (1989) *The Remasculinization of America: Gender and the Vietnam War*. Bloomington: Indiana University Press.

260   R. McKie and E. Ferguson (1997) A matter of life. *Observer*, 5 January.

261   E. Carlsen, A. Giwercman, N. Keiding and N. E. Skakkebaek (1992) Evidence for decreasing quality of semen during past 50 years. *British Medical Journal*, 305: 609–12.

262   S. Irvine, E. Cawood, D. Richardson, E. MacDonald and J. Aitken (1996) Evidence of deteriorating semen quality in the United Kingdom: birth cohort study in 577 men in Scotland over 11 years. *British Medical Journal*, 312: 467–71.

263   Carlsen et al., Evidence for decreasing quality of semen.

264   O. Dyer (1995) Studies highlight chemical threats to reproduction. *British Medical Journal*, 311: 347.

265   Segal, *Straight Sex*, p. 274.

266   Segal, *Straight Sex*, p. 271.

267   Lasch, *The Culture of Narcissism*.

268   Faludi, *Backlash*, p. 12.

269   S. M. Lipset and E. Raab (1978) *The Politics of Unreason: Right-wing extremism in America 1790–1977*. Chicago: University of Chicago Press, p. 132.

270   S. Bashevkin (1998) *Women on the Defensive: Living through conservative times*. Chicago: University of Chicago Press.

271   See A. Oakley (1997) A brief history of gender. In Oakley and Mitchell, *Who's Afraid of Feminism?*.

272   I. Whelehan (2000) Overloaded: popular culture and the future of feminism. *Towards Equality*, 12–13 (September): 12.

273   I Whelehan (2000) *Overloaded: Popular culture and the future of feminism*. London: Women's Press.

274   Greer, *The Whole Woman*, p. 2.

275   Greer, *The Whole Woman*, p. 330.

276   40 years have passed since women set about burning their bras en masse (2000) *The Times*, 25 November.

Chapter 5 Angels in the House

1   G. Cobb (1980) *English Cathedrals: The forgotten centuries*. London: Thames and Hudson.

2   P. Harris (2000) Nation to spend £12.5b on festive gifts, food and drink. *Observer*, 24 December.

3   Office for National Statistics (1997) *Social Focus on Families*. London: Stationery Office, p. 63.

4   E. Caston (1997) Entertaining Angels Unawares. Draft PhD thesis.

5   L. Holcombe (1973) *Victorian Ladies at Work*. Newton Abbot: David and Charles, p. 219.

6   D. Patmore (1949) *The Life and Times of Coventry Patmore.* London: Constable.
7   V. Woolf (1931) Professions for women, p. 59. Reprinted in M. Barrett (ed.) *Virginia Woolf: Women and writing.* London: Women's Press.
8   M. C. Bateson (1990) *Composing a Life.* Harmondsworth: Penguin, p. 40.
9   P. S. Buck (1941) *Of Men and Women.* New York: John Day, p. 126.
10 D. Davies (1966) *A History of Shopping.* London: Routledge and Kegan Paul, pp. 252, 55, 109.
11 C. Beecher (1873) *Miss Beecher's Housekeeper and Healthkeeper.* New York: Harper and Brothers.
12 S. Strasser (1982) *Never Done: A history of American housework.* New York: Pantheon, p. 243.
13 M. Andrews and M. M. Talbot (2000) Introduction: women in consumer culture, p. 1. In M. Andrews and M. M. Talbot (eds) *All the World and Her Husband: Women in twentieth-century consumer culture.* New York: Cassell.
14 G. Greer (1999) *The Whole Woman.* London: Doubleday, p. 136.
15 N. Stockman, N. Bonney and S. Xuewen (1995) *Women's Work in East and West.* London: UCL Press, pp. 105, 126.
16 N. Charles and M. Kerr (1988) *Women, Food and Families.* Manchester: Manchester University Press, p. 56.
17 P. Underhill (1999) *Why We Buy: The science of shopping.* New York: Simon and Schuster, p. 99.
18 Underhill, *Why We Buy*, pp. 98–9, 116.
19 P. Brooker (1999) *A Concise Glossary of Cultural Theory.* London: Arnold.
20 H. Matthews, M. Taylor, B. Percy-Smith and M. Limb (2000) The unacceptable flâneur: the shopping mall as a teenage hangout. In H. Matthews and F. Smith (eds) *Spaces of Childhood.* Special issue of *Childhood: A global journal of child research*, 7(3), August: 279–94.
21 A. M. Scott (1994) Gender segregation in the retail industry, p. 240. In A. M. Scott (ed.) *Gender Segregation and Social Change.* Oxford: Oxford University Press.
22 C. Delphy and D. Leonard (1992) *Familiar Exploitation.* Cambridge: Polity, p. 77.
23 E. Malos (1977) *Housework and the Politics of Women's Liberation.* Bristol: RSM Publications.
24 P. Mainardi (1970) The politics of housework. In R. Morgan (ed.) *Sisterhood is Powerful.* New York: Vintage, p. 451.
25 M. Waring (1988) *Counting for Nothing: What men value and what women are worth.* London: Allen and Unwin with Port Nicholson Press, p. 17.
26 Waring, *Counting for Nothing.*
27 J. K. Galbraith (1980) *Annals of an Abiding Liberal.* London: André Deutsch, p. 38.
28 J. K. Galbraith (1974) *Economics and the Public Purpose.* London: André Deutsch, pp. 29, 157.
29 C. P. Gilman (1903) *The Home: Its work and influence.* London and New York: McClure, Phillips, pp. 72–3.
30 L. Leghorn and B. Warrior (1973) *Houseworker's Handbook.* Cambridge, Mass.: Women's Centre; see also Waring, *Counting for Nothing*, p. 225.

31 L. Leghorn and K. Parker (1981) *Woman's Worth*. London: Routledge and Kegan Paul.

32 T*oronto Star*, 20 June 1978.

33 Cited in P. Kome (1982) *Somebody Has to Do It*. Toronto: McClelland and Stewart, p. 145.

34 D. Piachaud (1987) *Around about Fifty Hours a Week*. London: Child Poverty Action Group.

35 L. Goldschmidt-Clermont (1982) *Unpaid Work in the Household*. Geneva: International Labour Organization.

36 C. Oulton (1993) £18,000 price tag on working wife. *Guardian*, 3 February.

37 S. Federici (1975) *Wages Against Housework*. London: Power of Women Collective and Falling Wall Press, p. 3.

38 S. James (1990) in M. Wandor (ed.) *Once a Feminist*. London: Virago.

39 S. James (1972) *Women, the Unions and Work*. London: Crest Press.

40 M. Palm (2001) Sweden best at gender equality? *Genus* (Swedish Secretariat for Gender Research). Special issue on Gender Equality Research.

41 The question . . . (2001) *Guardian*, 14 February.

42 M. Leidig (2001) Therapist teaches messy Viennese houseproud ways. *Sunday Telegraph*, 16 September.

43 Stockman et al., *Women's Work in East and West*, p. 125.

44 A. M. Berg (1983) Love and power: the division of household labour. In A. Leira (ed.) *Work and Womanhood: Norwegian studies*. Oslo: Institute for Social Research, pp. 220–1.

45 Mass Observation Bulletin (1952) *Shopping*, January/February.

46 S. Bowlby (1988) From corner shop to hypermarket: women and food retailing, p. 77. In J. Little, L. Peake and P. Richardson (eds) *Women in Cities*. London: Macmillan.

47 Office for National Statistics, *Social Focus on Families*, p. 52.

48 S. Coverman and J. Sheley (1986) Changes in men's housework and child-care time, 1965–1975. *Journal of Marriage and the Family*, 48, May: 413–22.

49 S. Witherspoon (1988) Interim report: a woman's work. In R. Jowell, S. Witherspoon and L. Brook (eds) *British Social Attitudes: The 5th report*. London: Social and Community Planning Research, p. 182.

50 A. Oakley (1974) *The Sociology of Housework*. London: Martin Robertson.

51 J. S. Tellis (2000) Mothers' Attitudes Towards Housework and Their Management of Basic Household Tasks. Undergraduate dissertation, Cheltenham and Gloucester College of Higher Education.

52 J. Gershuny and S. Jones (1987) The changing work/leisure balance in Britain 1961–84. *Sociological Review Monograph*, 33: 9–50; J. Brannen, G. Mészáros, P. Moss and G. Poland (1994) *Employment and Family Life: A review of research in the UK (1980–1994)*. London: Institute of Education, p. 40.

53 A. McMahon (1999) *Taking Care of Men: Sexual politics in the public mind*. Cambridge: Cambridge University Press, p. 67.

54 B. B. Manke, A. Seery, A. Crouter and S. McHale (1994) The three corners of domestic labor: mothers', fathers' and children's weekday and weekend housework. *Journal of Marriage and the Family*, 56: 657–68.

55 S. F. Berk (1985) *The Gender Factory: The apportionment of work in American households*. New York: Plenum Press, pp. 7–8.

56 J. Brannen and P. Moss (1991) *Managing Mothers: Dual earner households after maternity leave*. London: Unwin Hyman, p. 39.

57 J. Kunzler (1994) Why men do (no) housework. Explaining male participation in domestic labour: a meta-analysis. Conference Presentation, International Sociological Association, Madrid.

58 J. Gershuny (1997) Sexual divisions and the distribution of work in the household. In G. Dench (ed.) *Rewriting the Sexual Contract*. London: Institute of Community Studies.

59 J. Vasagar (2001) Men still leave the housework to women. *Guardian*, 6 July.

60 G. Cooper and B. Clement (1997) New man debunked by women's dual burden. *Guardian*, 8 September.

61 Cited in C. Mihill (1997) New men still shunning equal share of chores. *Independent*, 8 September.

62 Brannen and Moss, *Managing Mothers*.

63 L. Morris (1990) *The Workings of the Household*. Cambridge: Polity.

64 N. Gregson and M. Lowe (1994) *Servicing the Middle Classes*. London: Routledge.

65 J. Gershuny, M. Godwin and S. Jones (1994) The domestic labour revolution: a process of lagged adaptation?, p. 161. In M. Anderson, F. Bechhofer and J. Gershuny (eds) *The Social and Political Economy of the Household*. Oxford: Oxford University Press.

66 A. Giddens (1992) *The Transformation of Intimacy*. Cambridge: Polity.

67 Fawcett Society (1999) Balancing work and home life. *Towards Equality*, autumn.

68 A. Oakley (1996) Gender matters: man the hunter, p. 26. In H. Roberts and D. Sachdev (eds) *Young People's Social Attitudes*. Ilford: Barnardo's.

69 Pas de deux (1983) *Guardian*, 6 April.

70 S. F. Berk and A. Shih (1980) Contributions to household labor: comparing wives' and husbands' reports. In S. F. Berk (ed.) *Women and Household Labor*. Beverly Hills: Sage.

71 J. Pleck (1985) *Working Wives, Working Husbands*. Beverly Hills: Sage.

72 R. Coward (1992) *Our Treacherous Hearts: Why women let men get their way*. London: Faber and Faber, p. 120.

73 A. R. Hochschild (1989) *The Second Shift: Working parents and the revolution at home*. New York: Viking.

74 C. Hardyment (1988) *From Mangle to Microwave*. Cambridge: Polity, pp. 56, 62.

75 C. Thomas (1995) Domestic labour and health: bringing it all back home. *Sociology of Health and Illness*, 17(3): 328–52, p. 343.

76 Hardyment, *From Mangle to Microwave*, p. 65.

77 E. B. Silva (1995) *Household Technologies and Domestic Labour*. Research Working Paper no. 11. Leeds: University of Leeds, Gender Analysis and Policy Unit, p. 32.

78 Hardyment, *From Mangle to Microwave*, p. 86.

79 S. Strasser (1982) *Never Done: A history of American housework*. New York: Pantheon.

80   C. Cockburn and S. Ormrod (1993) *Gender and Technology in the Making.* London: Sage, p. 16.

81   A. Oakley (1984) *The Captured Womb: A history of the medical care of pregnant women.* Oxford: Blackwell.

82   Hardyment, *From Mangle to Microwave*, pp. 143–4.

83   H. Joshi (1987) The cost of caring. In C. Glendinning and J. Millar (eds) *Women and Poverty in Britain.* Brighton: Wheatsheaf Books.

84   H. Hartmann (1981) The family as the locus of gender, class and political struggle: the example of housework. *SIGNS: Journal of Women in Culture and Society*, 6(3): 366–94.

85   J. P. Robinson (1980) Housework technology and household work. In Berk, *Women and Household Labor*, p. 62.

86   Silva, *Household Technologies and Domestic Labour*, p. 31.

87   Gilman, *The Home*, p. 37.

88   M. Luxton (1980) *More than a Labour of Love.* Toronto: Women's Educational Press.

89   R. Smeds, O. Huida, E. Haavio-Mannila and K. Kauppinen-Toropainen (1994) Sweeping away the dust of tradition: vacuum cleaning as a site of technical and social innovation. In C. Cockburn and R. Fûrst Dilic (eds) *Bringing Technology Home: Gender and technology in a changing Europe.* Buckingham: Open University Press.

90   Cockburn and Ormrod, *Gender and Technology in the Making*, p. 15.

91   A. Oakley (1981) *From Here to Maternity: Becoming a mother.* Harmondsworth: Penguin; M. Wagner (1994) *Pursuing the Birth Machine.* Camperdown, NSW: ACE Books.

92   M. Martin (1991) *'Hello, Central?': Gender, technology and culture in the formation of telephone systems.* Montreal and Kingston: McGill-Queens University Press.

93   Cockburn and Ormrod, *Gender and Technology in the Making.*

94   Gershuny et al., The domestic labour revolution, p. 159.

95   A. R. Melrose (2000) Preface. In A. R. Melrose (ed.) *Beyond the World of Pooh: Selections from the memoirs of Christopher Milne.* London: Methuen, p. vii.

96   Melrose, *Beyond the World of Pooh*, p. 32.

97   Melrose, *Beyond the World of Pooh*, p. 25.

98   Melrose, *Beyond the World of Pooh*, p. 49.

99   H. Penn (1999) Children in the majority world: is Outer Mongolia really so far away? In S. Hood, B. Mayall and S. Oliver (eds) *Critical Issues in Social Research.* Buckingham: Open University Press.

100 J. Wullschläger (1995) *Inventing Wonderland: The lives and fantasies of Lewis Carroll, Edward Lear, J. M. Barrie, Kenneth Grahame, A. A. Milne.* London: Methuen.

101 A. Prince (1994) *Kenneth Grahame: An innocent in the Wild Wood.* London: Allison and Busby, p. 307.

102 I. Smallwood (1989) *A Childhood at Green Hedges.* London: Methuen.

103 D. Oldman (1994) Childhood as a mode of production. In B. Mayall (ed.) *Children's Childhoods: Observed and experienced.* London: Falmer Press.

104 McMahon, *Taking Care of Men*, p. 116.
105 Coverman and Sheley, Changes in men's housework and child-care time.
106 Office for National Statistics, *Social Focus on Families*, p. 52.
107 A. Oakley and A. S. Rigby (1998) Are men good for the welfare of women and children?, p. 114. In J. Popay, J. Hearn and J. Edwards (eds) *Men, Gender Divisions and Welfare*. London: Routledge.
108 See e.g., K. Kiernan and M. Wicks (1990) *Family Change and Future Policy*. London: Family Policy Studies Centre, p. 30; McMahon, *Taking Care of Men*, p. 87.
109 M. Luxton (1986) Two hands for the clock: changing patterns in the gendered division of labour in the home, p. 45. In R. Hamilton and M. Barrett (eds) *The Politics of Diversity*. London: Verso.
110 Brannen and Moss, *Managing Mothers*, p. 168.
111 D. Hiller and W. Philliber (1986) The division of labour in contemporary marriage: expectations, perceptions and performance. *Social Problems*, 33(3): 191–201.
112 A. Booth and J. Edwards (1980) Fathers: the invisible parent. *Sex Roles*, 6(3): 445–6.
113 G. Russell (1983) *The Changing Role of Fathers?*. St Lucia: UQP.
114 C. Lewis (1986) *Becoming a Father*. Milton Keynes: Open University Press.
115 Family Policy Studies Centre (1996) *Parenting in the 1990s*. London: Family Policy Studies Centre.
116 J. Waldfogel (1997) The effects of children on women's wages. *American Sociological Review*, 62(2): 209–17.
117 C. Norton (2000) A son means father's pay also rises. *The Times*, 19 June.
118 Office for National Statistics, *Social Focus on Families*, p. 25.
119 Government Statistical Service (1999) *Social Trends*, 29, p. 42.
120 Economic and Social Research Council (1999) *Research Results*, no. 14, October.
121 J. Bradshaw, C. Stimson, C. Skinner and J. Williams (1999) Non-resident fathers in Britain, pp. 416–17. In S. McRae (ed.) *Changing Britain: Families and households in the 1990s*. Oxford: Oxford University Press.
122 J. A. Selzer (1991) Relationships between fathers and children who live apart: the father's role after separation. *Journal of Marriage and the Family*, 53: 79–102.
123 M. Ingham (1984) *Men*. London: Century; K. Funder, M. Harrison and R. Weston (1993) *Settling Down: Pathways of parents after divorce*. Melbourne: Australian Institute of Family Studies.
124 M. Gallagher (1999) The importance of being married. In W. F. Horn, D. Blankenhorn and M. B. Pearlstein (eds) *The Fatherhood Movement*. New York: Lexington Books.
125 A. Clare (2000) *On Men: Masculinity in crisis*. London: Chatto and Windus, p. 186.
126 H. Graham (1986) *Women, Health and the Family*. Brighton: Harvester Press.
127 M. Bartley, J. Popay and C. Owen (1992) Domestic conditions, paid employment and women's experience of ill-health. *Sociology of Health and Illness*, 14(3): 313–43.

128 J. Y. Avotri and V. Walters (1999) 'You just look at our work and see if you have any freedom on earth': Ghanaian women's accounts of their work and their health. *Social Science and Medicine*, 48: 1123–33, p. 1127.

129 J. Popay (1991) 'My health is alright, I'm just tired all the time': women's experience of illhealth. In H. Roberts (ed.) *Women's Health Matters*. London: Routledge.

130 Bartley et al., Domestic conditions, paid employment and women's experience of ill-health.

131 V. Woolf (1938) *Three Guineas*. London: Hogarth Press.

132 C. Heilbrun (1979) *Reinventing Womanhood*. New York: W. W. Norton, p. 196.

Chapter 6 Family Values

1   P. Singer (1997) *How Are We to Live? Ethics in an age of self-interest*. Oxford: Oxford University Press, p. 109.

2   P. Farmer (2000) *The Virago Book of Grandmothers*. London: Virago, p. 16.

3   A. Kornhaber (1996) *Contemporary Grandparenting*. Thousand Oaks, Calif.: Sage.

4   P. Uhlenberg and J. B. Kerby (1998) Grandparenthood over time: historical and demographic trends, p. 38. In M. E. Szinovacz (ed.) *Handbook on Grandparenthood*. Westport, Conn.: Greenwood Press.

5   G. Spitze and R. A. Ward (1998) Gender variations. In Szinovacz, *Handbook on Grandparenthood*.

6   See Farmer, *The Virago Book of Grandmothers*, p. 112.

7   Quoted in Farmer, *The Virago Book of Grandmothers*, pp. 213–14.

8   S. Faludi (1992) *Backlash: The undeclared war against women*. London: Chatto and Windus, pp. 150–1.

9   I. Whelehan (2000) *Overloaded: Popular culture and the future of feminism*. London: Women's Press, pp. 18–19.

10 A. Etzioni (1995, originally published 1993) *The Spirit of Community*. London: Fontana, p. 72.

11 L. Davidoff, J. L'Esperance and H. Newby (1976) Landscape with figures: home and community in English society. In J. Mitchell and A. Oakley (eds) *The Rights and Wrongs of Women*. Harmondsworth: Penguin.

12 J. Finch (1989) *Family Obligations and Social Change*. Oxford: Blackwell.

13 C. P. Gilman (1935) *The Living of Charlotte Perkins Gilman: An autobiography*. New York: Appleton-Century, p. 286.

14 C. Lasch (1991) *The True and Only Heaven: Progress and its critics*. New York: W. W. Norton, p. 32.

15 C. Lasch (1995, originally published 1977) *Haven in a Heartless World: The family besieged*. New York: W. W. Norton, pp. xvi–xvii.

16 J. Doane and D. Hodges (1987) *Nostalgia and Sexual Difference*. New York: Methuen, p. 60.

17 C. Lasch (1980, originally published 1979) *The Culture of Narcissism*. London: Sphere, pp. 175–6.

18 F. Fukuyama (1999) *The Great Disruption: Human nature and the reconstitution of social order*. London: Profile Books.

19 C. Murray (1990) *The Emerging British Underclass*. London: Institute of Economic Affairs Health and Welfare Unit, Choice in Welfare Series no. 2.

20 Etzioni, *The Spirit of Community*, p. 56.

21 Etzioni, *The Spirit of Community*, p. 69.

22 A. H. Halsey (1992) Foreword to N. Dennis and G. Erdos, *Families Without Fatherhood*. London: Institute of Economic Affairs.

23 Faludi, *Backlash*, pp. 270–1.

24 S. A. Hewlett (1986) *A Lesser Life: The myth of women's liberation in America*. New York: Warner Books, pp. 179–80.

25 See e.g., A. Oakley (1979) *Becoming a Mother*. Oxford: Martin Robertson.

26 R. Coward (1992) *Our Treacherous Hearts: Why women let men get their way*. London: Faber and Faber, p. 10.

27 R. Coward (1999) *Sacred Cows: Is feminism relevant to the new millennium?*. London: HarperCollins.

28 C. Hakim (1996) 'Mummy, I *want* to be a housewife.' *Times Higher Education Supplement*, 26 April.

29 C. Hakim (1995) Five feminist myths about women's employment. *British Journal of Sociology*, 46(3): 429–55.

30 See M. Benn (1999) *Towards a New Politics of Motherhood*. London: Vintage, p. 13.

31 M. Freely (1995) *What About Us? An open letter to the mothers feminism forgot*. London: Bloomsbury.

32 L. Segal (1994) *Straight Sex: The politics of pleasure*. London: Virago.

33 E. Fox-Genovese (1996) *'Feminism is Not the Story of My Life'*. New York: Anchor Books.

34 M. Phillips (1999) *The Sex-Change Society*. London: Social Market Foundation, p. xv.

35 Phillips, *The Sex-Change Society*, p. xvii.

36 K. Pollitt (1995) *Reasonable Creatures: Essays on women and feminism*. London: Vintage, p. 34.

37 U. Bjornberg and C. Gardberg (1998) Issues concerning the family in Sweden in 1996. In J. Ditch, H. Barnes and J. Bradshaw (eds) *Developments in National Family Policies in 1996*: The University of York and The European Commission.

38 P. Toynbee (1997) Scaring mothers? It's Panorama's bit of fun. *Independent*, 4 February.

39 Benn, *Towards a New Politics of Motherhood*, p. 13.

40 Office for National Statistics (1997) *Social Focus on Families*. London: Stationery Office, p. 24.

41 C. B. Costello, S. Miles and A. J. Stone (eds) (1998) *The American Woman 1999–2000*. Section I, Demographics, p. 222. New York: W. W. Norton.

42 Office for National Statistics, *Social Focus on Families*, p. 25.

43 J. Ditch, H. Barnes, J. Bradshaw and M. Kilkey (1998) *A Synthesis of National Family Policies 1996*: The University of York and The European Commission, p. 22.

44 Office for National Statistics, *Social Focus on Families*, pp. 25–6.

45 Ditch et al., *A Synthesis of National Family Policies*, p. 15.

46   Ditch et al., *A Synthesis of National Family Policies*, p. 10.
47   Office for National Statistics, *Social Focus on Families*, pp. 19–20.
48   Ditch et al., *A Synthesis of National Family Policies*, pp. 5–6.
49   Ditch et al., *A Synthesis of National Family Policies*.
50   P. Romito (1997) 'Damned if you do and damned if you don't': psychological and social constraints on motherhood in contemporary Europe. In A. Oakley and J. Mitchell (eds) *Who's Afraid of Feminism?*. London: Hamish Hamilton.
51   Anthropologist Ida Magli quoted in: Italy's fertility rate falls as women reject childbearing. *British Medical Journal*, 1996, 312: 530.
52   B. Hume (1993) Time to examine the nation's soul. *Independent*, 8 March.
53   H. Harris (1993) Letter. *Independent*, 10 March.
54   Ditch et al., *A Synthesis of National Family Policies*, p. 36.
55   Ditch et al., *A Synthesis of National Family Policies*, p. 39.
56   Ditch et al., *A Synthesis of National Family Policies*, p. 40.
57   R. N. Bellah, R. Madsen, W. M. Sullivan, A. Swidler and S. M. Tipton (1992) *The Good Society*. New York: Alfred A. Knopf, p. 46.
58   See e.g., Lasch, *Haven in a Heartless World*; Etzioni, *The Spirit of Community*.
59   A point made by Whelehan, *Overloaded*, p. 35.
60   See e.g., R. Morgan (ed.) (1970) *Sisterhood is Powerful*. New York: Vintage.
61   See e.g., A. Davis (1982) *Women, Race and Class*. London: Women's Press.
62   See e.g., The Bristol Women's Studies Group (1979) *Half the Sky: An introduction to Women's Studies*. London: Virago.
63   See e.g., A. Rich (1977) *Of Woman Born*. London: Virago.
64   See e.g., E. Frankfort (1973) *Vaginal Politics*. New York: Bantam Books.
65   See e.g., M. Wandor (ed.) (1973) *The Body Politic: Women's liberation in Britain 1969–1972*. London: Stage One.
66   See e.g., Section 3: Society – Steps in analysis. In Wandor, *The Body Politic*; A. Oakley (1974) *Housewife*. London: Allen Lane, ch. 9.
67   S. Walby (1990) *Theorizing Patriarchy*. Oxford: Blackwell.
68   H. I. Hartmann (1981) The unhappy marriage of Marxism and Feminism: towards a more progressive union. In L. Sargent (ed.) *Women and Revolution*. London: Pluto Press.
69   B. Ehrenreich (1983) *The Hearts of Men*. London: Pluto Press.
70   K. Gerson (1985) *Hard Choices: How women decide about work, career and motherhood*. Berkeley and Los Angeles: University of California Press.
71   S. Golombok (2000) *Parenting: What really counts?*. London: Routledge.
72   J. R. Harris (1998) *The Nurture Assumption: Why children turn out the way they do*. London: Bloomsbury.
73   Office for National Statistics, *Social Focus on Families*, p. 19.
74   J. Huber and G. Spitze (1983) *Sex Stratification: Children, housework and jobs*. New York: Academic Press.
75   K. Kiernan and G. Mueller (1999) Who divorces? In S. McRae (ed.), *Changing Britain: Families and households in the 1990s*. Oxford: Oxford University Press.
76   R. Dobson (2000) Children with fathers in family have a head start in life. *Sunday Times*, 21 May.

77 See e.g., G. Cleveland and M. Krashinsky (1998) *The Benefits and Costs of Good Childcare: The economic rationale for public investment in young children*. University of Toronto, Centre for Urban and Community Studies, Monograph no. 1.

78 Radio National (1998) Life matters. Dr Jay Belsky, 21 December. http://www.abc.net.au/rn/talks/lm/stories.S11066.htm, accessed October 2001.

79 Jay Belsky doesn't play well with others. http://www.salon/com/mwt/feature/2001/04/26/belsky/, accessed November 2001.

80 B. Zoritch, I. Roberts and A. Oakley (1998) The health and welfare effects of day-care: a systematic review of randomised controlled trials. *Social Science and Medicine*, 47(3): 317–27.

81 B. N. Vobejdal (1998) Children fare better brought up in groups. *Guardian*, 4 April.

82 Golombok, *Parenting*, p. 88.

83 S. Connor (1994) Safer births 'could cut violent crime'. *Guardian*, 24 February.

84 H. Mills (1997) 'Bad' boys linked to mothers' depression. *Observer*, 19 October.

85 See e.g., W. L. Josephson (1995) *Television Violence: A review of the effects on children of different ages*. Ottawa: Ministry of Supply and Services.

86 Davidoff et al., Landscape with figures, p. 152.

87 Ditch et al., *A Synthesis of National Family Policies*, p. 69.

88 N. Folbre (2001) *The Invisible Heart: Economics and family values*. New York: New Press, p. 17.

89 Ehrenreich, *The Hearts of Men*, p. 13.

Chapter 7 The Rape of Mother Earth

1 Quoted in C. Blackhurst (2001) Slaughter, misery and now traces of a cover-up at the farm where it all began. *Independent*, 27 March.

2 http://www.maff.gov.uk/animalh/diseases/fmd/default.htm.

3 G. Lean (2001) Pyres create more pollution than worst factories in UK. *Independent on Sunday*, 22 April.

4 Radio 4, *PM*, 6 April 2001.

5 *The BSE Inquiry: The Report* (2001). Crown Copyright. http://www.bseinquiry.gov.uk/report. This is the source for the other information about BSE in this chapter, unless otherwise indicated.

6 Minerva (2000) *British Medical Journal*, 321: 392.

7 K. Abbasi (2000) BSE Inquiry plays down errors. *British Medical Journal*, 321: 1097.

8 *The BSE Inquiry: The Report*, vol. 1, 2, paras 128–31.

9 *The BSE Inquiry: The Report*, vol. 1, 5, para. 389.

10 Animal cannibals (2000–1) *Ecologist*, December–January, 30(9): 14.

11 *The BSE Inquiry: The Report*, vol. 1, Introduction, paras 107 and 13, para. 1142.

12 P. Singer (1997) *How Are We to Live? Ethics in an age of self-interest*. Oxford: Oxford University Press.

13 H. Harvey (1998) *The Killing of the Countryside*. London: Vintage, pp. 2, 24.

14 J. N. Abramovitz (1998) Nature's 'free' services, p. 16. In E. Ayres and L. R. Brown (eds) *The World Watch Reader on Global Environmental Issues*. New York: W. W. Norton.

15   J. Madeley (1999) *Big Business, Poor Peoples.* London: Zed Books, pp. 28, 78.

16   M. McCarthy, S. Connor, R. L. Parry and S. Castle (2001) Global warming much worse than predicted, say scientists. *Independent,* 12 July.

17   Intergovernmental Panel on Climate Change (2001) *Climate Change 2001* (3 vols). Cambridge: Cambridge University Press.

18   M. O'Meara (1998) The risks of disrupting climate. In Ayres and Brown, *The World Watch Reader.*

19   R. Smith (2001) Death through selfishness and failure of imagination. (Editorial). *British Medical Journal,* 322: 690.

20   O'Meara, The risks of disrupting climate, p. 38.

21   A. Gumbel (2001) George W. Bush, polluter of the free world. *Independent,* 30 March.

22   M. McCarthy (2000) Heat is on the US as it claims that planting trees will stop global warming. *Independent,* 14 November.

23   I. Roberts (1995) China takes to the roads. *British Medical Journal,* 310: 1311–13.

24   A. Haines, T. McMichael, R. Anderson and J. Houghton (2000) Fossil fuels, transport and public health. *British Medical Journal,* 321: 1168–9.

25   B. McKibben (1990) *The End of Nature.* London: Penguin.

26   World Health Organization (1999) Overview of the environment and health in the 1990s. WHO Regional Office for Europe. *Executive Summary from the Third European Conference on Environment and Health,* London. http://www.who.dk/london99/WelcomeE.htm.

27   R. Edwards (1996) Drivers risk cancer in the cab. *New Scientist,* 26 October: 8.

28   R. A. Goyer (1993) Lead toxicity: current concerns. *Environmental Health Perspectives,* 100: 177–87.

29   A. Motluk (1996) Lead blights the future of Africa's children. *New Scientist,* 23 March: 6.

30   F. Pearce (1996) A heavy responsibility. *New Scientist,* 27 July: 12–13.

31   G. K. Raabe (1993) Review of the carcinogenic potential of gasoline. *Environmental Health Perspectives Supplements,* 101(suppl. 6): 35–8.

32   M. H. Brown (1980) *Laying Waste: The poisoning of America by toxic chemicals.* New York: Pantheon, p. 225.

33   *Independent Inquiry into Inequalities in Health* (The Acheson Report) (1998) London: Stationery Office, p. 58.

34   The full cost of motoring (2000) *Environment and Health News,* 5.1(17): 20.

35   NOPHER (2001) *Noise Pollution and Health.* http://www.ucl.ac.uk/noiseandhealth/NOPHER%202001/NOPHER%202001.htm, accessed October 2001.

36   M. Bond (1996) Plagued by noise. *New Scientist,* 16 November: 14–15.

37   J. Ashton and R. Laura (1998) *Perils of Progress.* London: Zed Books, ch. 16.

38   S. Cohen, D. S. Krantz, G. W. Evans and D. Stokols (1981) Cardiovascular and behavioral effects of community noise. *American Scientist,* 69(5): 528–35.

39   B. Clement and T. Judd (2001) Air fares should rise to combat pollution. *Independent,* 25 January.

40   Singer, *How Are We to Live?,* p. 52.

41 N. Charles and M. Kerr (1988) *Women, Food and Families*. Manchester: Manchester University Press, pp. 73–4.

42 R. Broad and S. Fleming (eds) (1981) *Nella Last's War: A mother's diary 1939–45*. London: Falling Wall Press, p. 51.

43 A. Bridgwood, G. Malbon, D. Lader and J. Matheson (1996) *Health in England 1995: What people know, what people think, what people do*. London: HMSO.

44 F. B. Smith (1979) *The People's Health 1839–1910*. London: Croom Helm, p. 204.

45 C. J. Adams (1990) *The Sexual Politics of Meat*. Cambridge: Polity, p. 15.

46 Adams, *The Sexual Politics of Meat*, p. 32; J. Rifkin (1992) *Beyond Beef: The rise and fall of the cattle culture*. London: HarperCollins, p. 249.

47 Rifkin, *Beyond Beef*.

48 Rifkin, *Beyond Beef*, p. 53.

49 B. Humphries (2001) The diet of early humans: what did our ancestors eat? http://www.ivu.org/history/early/ancestors.html, accessed March 2001.

50 S. E. Sanderson (1986) The emergence of the world steer. In F. L. Tullis and W. L. Hollist (eds) *Food, State and International Political Economy*. Lincoln: University of Nebraska, p. 124.

51 Rifkin, *Beyond Beef*, p. 54.

52 Adams, *The Sexual Politics of Meat*, p. 26.

53 Charles and Kerr, *Women, Food and Families*, pp. 77–8.

54 J. Morris (1994) Cited in J. Ashton (ed.) *The Epidemiological Imagination*. Buckingham: Open University Press, p. 152.

55 Smith, *The People's Health*, p. 205.

56 L. R. Brown (1998) Facing food scarcity, pp. 227–8. In Ayres and Brown, *The World Watch Reader*.

57 http:/news.bbc.co.uk/hi/english/uk/newsid_1246000/1246817.htm, accessed March 2001.

58 H. Norberg-Hodge (2000) *Ancient Futures: Learning from Ladakh*. London: Rider Press, p. xxxi.

59 Harvey, *The Killing of the Countryside*, p. 171.

60 Quoted in K. S. Walters and L. Portness (eds) (1999) *Ethical Vegetarianism: From Pythagoras to Peter Singer*. Albany, N.Y.: State University of New York Press, p. 79.

61 Walters and Portness, *Ethical Vegetarianism*.

62 A. B. Kingsford and E. Maitland (1912) *Addresses and Essays on Vegetarianism*. London: John M. Watkins, p. 7.

63 Kingsford and Maitland, *Addresses and Essays on Vegetarianism*, pp. 61, 136.

64 Cited in Walters and Portness, *Ethical Vegetarianism*, p. 73.

65 Singer, *How Are We to Live?*, p. 53.

66 Rifkin, *Beyond Beef*, p. 1.

67 Rifkin, *Beyond Beef*, p. 2.

68 Madeley, *Big Business, Poor Peoples*, p. 80.

69 McKibben, *The End of Nature*, p. 14.

70 Brown, Facing food scarcity, p. 221.

71 Rifkin, *Beyond Beef*, p. 1.

72 Brown, Facing food scarcity, p. 238.

73 http://www.vegsoc.org/animals, accessed March 2001.
74 http:/www.vegsoc.org/info/pigs.html;   http:/www.vegsoc.org/info/broiler.html, accessed March 2001.
75 http:/www.vegsoc.org/info/broiler.html; http:/www/vegsoc/org/info/cattle.html; http:/www.vegsoc.org/info/pigs.html; http:/www.vegsoc.org/info/sheep.html, accessed March 2001.
76 http:/www.vegsoc.org/info/statveg.html, accessed March 2001.
77 http://www.vrg.org/journal/vj2000may/2000maypoll.htm,   accessed   October 2001.
78 J. Donovan (1990) Animal rights and feminist theory. *SIGNS: Journal of Women in Culture and Society*, 15(2): 350–75.
79 C. Lansbury (1985) *The Old Brown Dog: Women, workers and anti-vivisection in Edwardian England*. Madison, Wis.: University of Wisconsin Press, p. x.
80 C. J. Adams (1994) *Neither Man Nor Beast: Feminism and the defense of animals*. New York: Continuum, pp. 26, 13.
81 Singer, *How Are We to Live?*, pp. 210–11; D. T. Suzuki (1992) *Inventing the Future: Reflections on science, technology and nature*. London: Adamantine.
82 S. Witherspoon, The greening of Britain: romance and nationality, p. 123. In R. Jowell, J. Curtice, L. Brook and D. Arendt (eds) *British Social Attitudes: The eleventh report*. Aldershot: Gower.
83 S. Ruddick (1989) *Maternal Thinking: Towards a politics of peace*. London: Women's Press.
84 J. B. Miller (1976) *Toward a New Psychology of Women*. Boston: Beacon Press.
85 Suzuki, *Inventing the Future*.
86 C. P. Gilman (1979, first published 1915) *Herland*. New York: Pantheon.
87 Donovan, Animal rights and feminist theory; see ch. 9.
88 R. Anderson (2000) Selling 'Mother Earth': advertising and the myth of the natural. In R. Hofrichter (ed.) *Reclaiming the Environmental Debate: The politics of health in a toxic culture*. Cambridge, Mass.: MIT Press.
89 L. Schiebinger (1993) *Nature's Body*. London: HarperCollins.
90 C. Merchant (1980) *The Death of Nature*. London: Wildwood House.
91 S. Harding (1986) *The Science Question in Feminism*. Milton Keynes: Open University Press, p. 114.
92 L. Jordanova (1989) *Sexual Visions*. Hemel Hempstead: Harvester Wheatsheaf, p. 24.
93 Harding, *The Science Question in Feminism*, p. 113.
94 E. F. Keller (1985) *Reflections on Gender and Science*. New Haven, Conn.: Yale University Press.
95 Harvey, *The Killing of the Countryside*, p. 23.
96 J. Wargo (1996) *Our Children's Toxic Legacy: How science and law fail to protect us from pesticides*. New Haven, Conn.: Yale University Press, pp. 131–2.
97 http:/www.wen.org.uk/envfac1.htm, accessed March 2001.
98 E. L. Gunderson (1995) FDA total diet study, July 1986–April 1991, dietary intakes of pesticides, selected elements and other chemicals. *Journal of AOAC International*, 78(6): 1353–63.
99 Wargo, *Our Children's Toxic Legacy*, p. 5.

100   Friends of the Earth (2000) *Crisis in Chemicals*. London: Friends of the Earth [http://www.foe.co.uk], p. 35.

101   Friends of the Earth, *Crisis in Chemicals*, p. 53.

102   G. Lyons (1999) *Toxic Trespass*. WWF. Executive summary available at http://www.wwf-uk.org/news/chem4.pdf, accessed March 2001.

103   Politics of Health Group (n.d.) *Food and Profit*. London: The Politics of Health Group, p. 13.

104   J. Elkington (1985) *The Poisoned Womb*. Harmondsworth: Penguin, p. 231.

105   Wargo, *Our Children's Toxic Legacy*, p. 133.

106   Harvey, *The Killing of the Countryside*, p. 147.

107   C. Caulfield (1989) *Multiple Exposures: Chronicles of the radiation age*. London: Secker and Warburg, p. 196.

108   Politics of Health Group, *Food and Profit*, p. 13.

109   D. Hanson (1995) Toxics release inventory: chemical industry again cuts emissions. *Chemical and Engineering News*, 24 July: 23–4.

110   F. Pearce and S. Tombs (1998) *Toxic Capitalism: Corporate crime and the chemical industry*. Aldershot: Dartsmouth Publishing, p. 177.

111   http://www.foe.co.uk/factorywatch, accessed March 2001.

112   http://www.foe.co.uk/campaigns/industry_and_pollution/factorywatch/pollution/indepth.htm, accessed March 2001.

113   R. D. Bullard (1999) Dismantling environmental racism in the USA. *Local Environment*, 4(1): 5–20.

114   Wargo, *Our Children's Toxic Legacy*, p. 3.

115   Friends of the Earth, *Crisis in Chemicals*, p. 53.

116   Wargo, *Our Children's Toxic Legacy*, p. 289.

117   R. L. Carson (1963) *Silent Spring*. London: Hamish Hamilton.

118   Brown, *Laying Waste*.

119   V. Shiva (2000) The world on the edge, p. 116. In W. Hutton and A. Giddens (eds) *Global Capitalism*. New York: Pantheon.

120   M. Waring (1988) *Counting for Nothing*. London: Allen and Unwin with Port Nicholson Press, p. 128.

121   Brown, *Laying Waste*, p. 268.

122   http://www.doh.gov.uk/landh.htm, accessed March 2001.

123   P. Elliot, T. K. Jensen, I. Maitland, S. Richardson, J. Wakefield and L. Jarup (2001) Risk of adverse birth outcomes in populations living near landfill sites. *British Medical Journal*, 323: 363–8.

124   W. Shutkin and R. Mares (2000) Brownfields and the redevelopment of communities: linking health, economy and justice, p. 59. In Hofrichter, *Reclaiming the Environmental Debate*.

125   Elkington, *The Poisoned Womb*, pp. 207–8.

126   Friends of the Earth, *Crisis in Chemicals*, p. 51.

127   Waring, *Counting for Nothing*, p. 218.

128   Caulfield, *Multiple Exposures*, p. 197.

129   Sellafield safety 'only just tolerable' (2000) *Guardian*, 19 February.

130   P. Brown (2001) The fallout. *Guardian*, 26 September.

131   R. Edwards (1995) Will it get any worse? *New Scientist*, 9 December: 14–15.

132 Caulfield, *Multiple Exposures*, pp. 240–1.
133 Caulfield, *Multiple Exposures*, p. 237.
134 R. Bertell (2000) *Ecologist*, 1 April: 33.
135 A. Rodda (1991) *Women and the Environment*. London: Zed Books, p. 36.
136 K. Yokoro and N. Kamada (1997) The public health effects of the use of nuclear weapons, pp. 121–3. In B. S. Levy and V. W. Sidel (eds) *War and Public Health*. New York: Oxford University Press.
137 M. Renner (1997) Environmental and health effects of weapons production, testing and maintenance. In Levy and Sidel, *War and Public Health*.
138 B. S. Levy, G. S. Shaki and C. Lee (1997) The environmental consequences of war. In Levy and Sidel, *War and Public Health*.
139 Norberg-Hodge, *Ancient Futures*, p. xxi.
140 Madeley, *Big Business, Poor Peoples*, p. 2.
141 P. Dicken (1992) *Global Shift: The internationalisation of economic activity*. London: Paul Chapman, p. 49.
142 Madeley, *Big Business, Poor Peoples*, pp. 36–40.
143 Madeley, *Big Business, Poor Peoples*, p. 50.
144 Brown, Facing food scarcity, p. 236.
145 Shiva, The world on the edge, pp. 113–14.
146 N. Chomsky (2000) *Rogue States*. London: Pluto Press.
147 Shiva, The world on the edge, p. 115.
148 Madeley, *Big Business, Poor Peoples*, p. 87.
149 A. Browne and B. Summerskill (2001) Drivers urged: Boycott Esso and help to save the planet. *Observer*, 6 May.
150 Madeley, *Big Business, Poor Peoples*, p. 27.
151 Shiva, The world on the edge, p. 120.
152 Pearce and Tombs, *Toxic Capitalism*, p. 37.
153 Independent Commission on Population and Quality of Life (1996) *Caring for the Future*. Oxford: Oxford University Press, p. 236.
154 J. Briles (1996) *Gendertraps: Conquering confrontophobia, toxic bosses and other land mines at work*. New York: McGraw-Hill, p. 29.
155 J. Vickers (1993) *Women and War*. London: Zed Books.
156 C. Cohn (1988) Sex and death and the rational world of defense intellectuals. In D. Gioseffi (ed.) *Women and War: Essential voices for the nuclear age*. New York: Touchstar Books.
157 Caulfield, *Multiple Exposures*, p. 47.
158 M. French (1992) *The War Against Women*. London: Penguin, p. 160.
159 French, *The War Against Women*, p. 163.
160 Caulfield, *Multiple Exposures*, p. 62.
161 Elkington, *The Poisoned Womb*, p. 211.
162 G. Corea (1985) *The Mother Machine: Reproductive technologies from artificial insemination to artificial wombs*. New York: Harper and Row, p. 116.
163 Corea, *The Mother Machine*, p. 84.
164 H. B. Holmes and B. B. Hoskins (1985) Prenatal and preconception sex choice technologies: a path to femicide?, p. 16. In G. Corea, R. D. Klein, J. Hanmer, H. B. Holmes, B. Hoskins, M. Kishwar, J. Raymond, R. Rowland and R.

Notes to pp. 144–5

Steinbacher. *Man-Made Women: How new reproductive technologies affect women*. London: Hutchinson.
165 Gendercide Watch (2001) *Female Infanticide*, p. 3. http://www.gendercide.org/case_infanticide.html, accessed October 2001.
166 Corea, *The Mother Machine*, p. 195.
167 Gendercide Watch, *Female Infanticide*.
168 B. B. Hoskins and H. B. Holmes (1984) Techology and prenatal femicide. In R. Arditti, R. Duelli Klein and S. Minden (eds) *Test-Tube Women: What future for motherhood?*. London: Pandora.
169 Gendercide Watch, *Female Infanticide*, p. 6.
170 J. Murphy (1984) Egg farming and women's future. In Arditti et al., *Test-Tube Women*.
171 Human Fertilization and Embryology Authority (2000) *Ninth Annual Report and Accounts*. London: HFEA.
172 T. Hurst and P. Lancaster (2001) *Assisted Conception in Australia and New Zealand, 1998 and 1999*. Sydney: AIHW Perinatal Statistics Unit.
173 A. Venn, L. Watson, F. Bruinsma, G. Giles and D. Healy (1999) Risk of cancer after use of fertility drugs with in-vitro fertilisation. *Lancet*, 354: 1586–90; J. Shelley, A. Venn and J. Lumley (1999) Long-term effects on women of assisted reproduction. *International Journal of Technology Assessment in Health Care*, 15(1): 36–51.
174 N. Pfeffer (1993) *The Stork and the Syringe: A political history of reproductive medicine*. Cambridge: Polity, pp. 166–7.
175 R. D. Klein (1985) What's 'new' about the 'new' reproductive technologies?, p. 64. In Corea et al., *Man-Made Women*.
176 Klein, What's 'new' about the 'new' reproductive technologies?, p. 66.
177 R. D. Apple (1987) *Mothers and Medicine: A social history of infant feeding 1890–1950*. Madison, Wis.: University of Wisconsin Press.
178 K. A. Dettwyler (2001) Humans are primates, designed to breastfeed for years not months (letter). *British Medical Journal*, 323: 689–90.
179 The 1953 figure is for England and Wales, the latter two for England. A. Macfarlane, M. Mugford, J. Henderson, A. Furtado, K. Stevens and A. Dunn (2000) *Birth Counts: Statistics of pregnancy and childbirth*. London: Stationery Office. Vol. 2 tables, p. 530; Royal College of Obstetricians Clinical Effectiveness Support Unit (2001) *The National Sentinel Caesarean Section Audit Report*. London: RCOG.
180 Centers for Disease Control, National Center for Health Statistics (2001). http:/www.cdc.gov/nchs/fastats/delivery.htm, accessed October 2001.
181 Cesarean Fact Sheet (2001). http://www.childbirth.org/section/CSFact.html, accessed October 2001.
182 S. Boseley (2001) Caesarean births soar to one in five. *Guardian*, 26 October.
183 J. Laurance (2001) Caesarean risks 'four times those of natural birth'. *Independent*, 5 May.
184 E. Hemminki (1997) Impact of Caesarean section on future pregnancy – a review of cohort studies. *Paediatric and Perinatal Epidemiology*, 10: 366–79.
185 O. Hjalmarson (1991) Epidemiology of neonatal disorders of respiration. *International Journal of Technology Assessment in Health Care*, 7(suppl. 1).

186   S. F. Murray (2000) Relation between private health insurance and high rates of caesarean section in Chile: qualitative and quantitative study. *British Medical Journal*, 321: 1501–5.

187   C. I. Robert, S. Tracy and B. Peat (2000) Rates for obstetric intervention among private and public patients in Australia: population based descriptive study. *British Medical Journal*, 321: 137–41.

188   J. S. Bell, D. M. Campbell, W. J. Graham, G. C. Penney, M. Ryan and M. H. Hall (2001) Do obstetric complications explain high caesarean section rates among women over 30? A retrospective analysis. *British Medical Journal*, 322: 894–5.

189   Macfarlane et al., *Birth Counts*, vol. 2, pp. 529–30. The earlier figures are for England and Wales, the later ones for England only.

190   Centers for Disease Control, National Center for Health Statistics.

191   B. K. Rothman (1989) *Recreating Motherhood: Ideology and technology in a patriarchal society*. New York: Harper and Row, p. 21.

192   J. G. Thornton and R. J. Lilford (1994) Active management of labour: current knowledge and research issues. *British Medical Journal*, 309: 366–9; L. Bricker, J. Garcia, J. Henderson, M. Mugford, J. Neilson, T. Roberts and M.-A. Martin (2000) Ultrasound screening in pregnancy: a systematic review of the clinical effectiveness, cost-effectiveness and women's views. *Health Technology Assessment*, 4(16).

193   Macfarlane et al., *Birth Counts*, vol. 2, pp. 644–51.

194   S. Mayor (2001) Poorest women 20 times more likely to die in childbirth. *British Medical Journal*, 323: 1324.

195   Centers for Disease Control, National Center for Health Statistics.

196   G. Carroli and J. Belizan (2001) Episiotomy for vaginal birth (Cochrane Review). *Cochrane Library*, Issue 4. Oxford: Update Software.

197   E. Alberman (1977) Facts and figures. In T. Chard and M. Richards (eds) *Benefits and Hazards of the New Obstetrics*. Lavenham: Lavenham Press.

198   Macfarlane et al., *Birth Counts*, vol. 2, p. 532.

199   S. B. Thacker and H. D. Banta (1983) Benefits and risks of episiotomy: an interpretative review of the English language literature, 1860–1980. *Obstetrical and Gynecological Survey*, 38(6): 322–38.

200   Thacker and Banta, Benefits and risks of episiotomy.

201   J. Astbury (1996) *Crazy for You: The making of women's madness*. Auckland: Oxford University Press, pp. 6–7; E. Showalter (1987) *The Female Malady: Women, madness and English culture 1930–1980*. London: Virago, p. 76.

202   A. Dally (1991) *Women Under the Knife: A history of surgery*. London: Hutchinson Radius, pp. 147–50.

203   Dally, *Women Under the Knife*, p. 160.

204   Corea, *The Mother Machine*, p. 308.

205   K. McPherson, J. E. Wennberg, O. B. Hovind and P. Clifford (1982) Small-area variations in the use of common surgical procedures: an international comparison of New England, England and Norway. *New England Journal of Medicine*, 307: 1310–14.

206   J. Jones (2000) Concern mounts over female genital mutilation. *British Medical Journal*, 321: 262.

207   O. Olsen and M. D. Jewell (2001) Home versus hospital birth (Cochrane Review). *Cochrane Library*, Issue 4. Oxford: Update Software.

208   M. L. Romney (1980) Predelivery shaving: an unjustified assault? *Journal of Obstetrics and Gynaecology*, 1: 33–5; M. L. Romney and H. Gordon (1981) Is your enema really necessary? *British Medical Journal*, 282: 1269–71.

209   See e.g., S. Arms (1975) *Immaculate Deception*. New York: Bantam Books; A. Oakley (1984) *The Captured Womb: A history of the medical care of pregnant women*. Oxford: Blackwell, ch. 10; B. K. Rothman (1982) *In Labor: Women and power in the birthplace*. New York: W. W. Norton, ch. 3.

210   Female genital mutilation – a human rights information pack. http://www.amnesty.org/ailib/intcam/femgen/fgm1.htm, accessed October 2001.

211   See e.g., G. J. Barker-Benfield (1976) *The Horrors of the Half-Known Life*. New York: Harper and Row.

212   Dally, *Women Under the Knife*, pp. 1–2.

213   P. Spallone (1989) *Beyond Conception: The new politics of reproduction*. London: Macmillan, ch. 2.

214   R. P. Petchesky (1985) *Abortion and Woman's Choice*. London: Verso, ch. 9.

215   See e.g., P. Romito (1989) Unhappiness after childbirth. In I. Chalmers, M. Enkin and M. J. N. C. Keirse (eds) *Effective Care in Pregnancy and Childbirth*. Oxford: Oxford University Press; S. Brown, J. Lumley, R. Small and J. Astbury (1994) *Missing Voices: The experience of motherhood*. Melbourne: Oxford University Press; A. Oakley (1980) *Women Confined: Towards a sociology of childbirth*. Oxford: Martin Robertson; A. Oakley and M. Richards (1990) Women's experiences of Caesarean delivery. In J. Garcia, R. Kilpatrick and M. Richards (eds) *The Politics of Maternity Care*. Oxford: Clarendon Press.

216   Simone de Beauvoir (1953, originally published 1949) *The Second Sex*. London: Cape.

217   L. Caldecott and S. Leland (1983) Introduction. In L. Caldecott and S. Leland (eds) *Reclaim the Earth*. London: Women's Press.

218   Cited in Waring, *Counting for Nothing*, p. 204.

219   C. E. Sachs (1996) *Gendered Fields: Rural women, agriculture and environment*. Boulder, Col.: Westview Press, p. 30.

220   D. Wall (1988) The diet of early humans: vegetarianism and archaeology. *Vegetarian*, September/October. Available on http://www.ivu.org/history/early/archaeology.html, accessed March 2001.

221   Adams, *The Sexual Politics of Meat*, pp. 147–8.

222   J. Diamond (1991) *The Rise and Fall of the Third Chimpanzee*. London: Vintage, p. 34.

223   Rodda, *Women and the Environment*.

224   Sachs, *Gendered Fields*.

225   Madeley, *Big Business, Poor Peoples*, p. 92.

226   G. McRobie (1981) *Small is Possible*. London: Jonathan Cape, pp. 60–1.

227   N. Kardam (1990) The adaptability of international development agencies: the response of the World Bank to women in development; A. Carloni (1990) Women in FAO projects: cases from Asia, the Near East and Africa; S. W. Yudelman (1990) The inter-American Foundation and gender issues: a feminist view. All

in K. Staudt (ed.) *Women, International Development and Politics*. Philadelphia: Temple University Press.

228   K. E. Ferguson (1990) Women, feminism and development, p. 293. In Staudt, *Women, International Development and Politics*.

229   A. R. Hochschild (2000) Global care chains and emotional surplus value. In Hutton and Giddens, *Global Capitalism*.

230   D. Elson (1995) Rethinking strategies for development: from male-biased to human-centred development. In D. Elson (ed.) *Male Bias in the Development Process*. Manchester: Manchester University Press.

231   Norberg-Hodge, *Ancient Futures*.

232   D. Walsh (2001) Why slaughter all those animals when you can cure the disease with cold ash and dung? *Independent*, 6 April.

233   A. Uttley (1931) *The Country Child*. London: Thomas Nelson and Sons, pp. 7, 11.

234   M. Suzuki (1983) A Japanese woman speaks. In Caldecott and Leland, *Reclaim the Earth*, p. 86.

235   Ashton and Laura, *Perils of Progress*, p. 1.

236   M. H. O'Brien (2000) When harm is not necessary: risk assessment as diversion. In Hofrichter, *Reclaiming the Environmental Debate*.

237   J. Karliner (2000) The globalization of corporate culture and its role in the environmental crisis, p. 178. In Hofrichter, *Reclaiming the Environmental Debate*.

238   World Bank (1996) *Global Economic Prospects and the Developing Countries*. Washington, D.C.: World Bank.

239   *Guardian Society*, 14 February 2001.

240   M. Renner (1998) Chiapas: the fruits of despair, p. 268. In Ayres and Brown, *The World Watch Reader*.

241   J. Faux and L. Mishel (2000) Inequality and the global economy, p. 93. In Hutton and Giddens, *Global Capitalism*.

242   J. P. Grant (1995) *The State of the World's Children*. New York: Oxford University Press for UNICEF, p. 44.

243   Anderson, Selling 'Mother Earth', p. 207.

Chapter 8 Delusional Systems

1   T. Aschenbrandt (1883) Die physiologische Wirkung und die Bedeutung des Cocains. *Deutsche Medizinische Wochenschrift*, 12 December.

2   E. M. Thornton (1983) *Freud and Cocaine: The Freudian fallacy*. London: Blond and Briggs.

3   S. Freud (1884) Über Coca. *Centralblatt für die gesammte Therapie*, 2: 289. See R. Byck (ed.) (1974) *Cocaine Papers: Sigmund Freud*. New York: Stonehill.

4   Byck, *Cocaine Papers*.

5   Thornton, *Freud and Cocaine*.

6   M. Bonaparte, A. Freud and E. Kriss (eds) *The Origins of Psychoanalysis: Letters to Wilhelm Fliess, drafts and notes 1887–1902*. New York: Basic Books.

7   J. C. Smith (1990) *Psychoanalytic Roots of Patriarchy*. New York: New York University Press, p. 35.

8   R. Fliess (1956) *Erogeneity and Libido*. New York: International Universities Press.

9   This is a term used by S. Sutherland (1987) *Breakdown*. Oxford: Oxford University Press, p. 153.

10 Sutherland, *Breakdown*, pp. 115–16.

11 L. Freeman (1972) *The Story of Anna O.: The woman who led Freud to psychoanalysis*. Northvale, N.J.: Jason Aronson, p. 30.

12 Thornton, *Freud and Cocaine*, p. 4.

13 M. Rosenbaum (1984) Anna O (Bertha Pappenheim): her history, p. 12. In M. Rosenbaum and M. Murof (eds) *Anna O: 14 contemporary reinterpretations*. New York: Free Press.

14 D. Edinger (1968) *Bertha Pappenheim: Freud's Anna O*. Highland Park, Ill.: Congregation Solel.

15 H. S. Decker (1991) *Dora, Freud and Vienna 1900*. New York: Free Press, p. 65.

16 J. Masson (trans. and ed.) (1985) *The Complete Letters of Sigmund Freud to Wilhelm Fliess 1887–1904*. Cambridge, Mass.: Belknap Press of Harvard University Press.

17 S. Freud (1896) *The Aetiology of Hysteria*. Standard edition. London: Hogarth Press, vol. III, pp. 189–221.

18 J. M. Masson (1984) *The Assault on Truth: Freud's suppression of the seduction theory*. London: Faber and Faber, p. 15.

19 S. Freud (1905) *Three Essays on the Theory of Sexuality*. Standard edition. London: Hogarth Press, vol. III, pp. 123–45; S. Freud (1906) *My Views on the Part Played by Sexuality in the Aetiology of the Neuroses*. Standard edition. London: Hogarth Press, vol. VII, pp. 269–79.

20 J. Brenkman (1993) *Straight Male Modern: A cultural critique of psychoanalysis*. New York: Routledge, p. 90.

21 J. M. Masson (1991) *Final Analysis*. London: HarperCollins, pp. 177–8, 210–14.

22 S. Freud (1933) *New Introductory Lectures on Psychoanalysis*. Standard edition. London: Hogarth Press, vol. XXII, p. 120.

23 M. Borch-Jacobsen (1996) Neurotica: Freud and the seduction theory. October 76, spring: 15–43; H. Israels and M. Schatzman (1933) The seduction theory. *History of Psychiatry*, 4: 23–59; J. G. Schimck (1987) Fact and fantasy in the seduction theory: a historical review. *Journal of the American Psychoanalytic Association*, 35: 937–65.

24 P. Roazen (1999) Freud in perspective: the problem of seduction. In L. King (ed.) *Committed Uncertainty in Psychotherapy: Essays in honour of Peter Lomas*. London: Whurr Publishing, p. 118.

25 C. Medawar (1992) *Power and Dependence: Social Audit on the safety of medicines*. London: Social Audit, pp. 32–4.

26 K. Millett (1971) *Sexual Politics*. London: Rupert Hart-Davis, p. 189.

27 D. E. Stannard (1980) *Shrinking History: Freud and the failure of psychohistory*. Oxford: Oxford University Press, p. 39.

28 K. Obholzer (1982) *The Wolf Man Sixty Years Later: Conversations with Freud's controversial patient*. London: Routledge and Kegan Paul.

29 R. M. Jurjevich (1974) *The Hoax of Freudianism: A study of brainwashing of the American professionals and laymen*. Philadelphia: Dorrance, p. 7.

30 J. Malcolm (1982) *Psychoanalysis: The impossible profession*. London: Pan Books, p. 22.

31 Smith, *Psychoanalytic Roots of Patriarchy*, p. 39.
32 P. Brown (1973) Male supremacy in Freud. In P. Brown (ed.) *Radical Psychology*. London: Tavistock, p. 448.
33 Brenkman, *Straight Male Modern*, p. 247.
34 Stannard, *Shrinking History*, p. 37.
35 P. Singer (1997) *How Are We to Live? Ethics in an age of self-interest*. Oxford: Oxford University Press, p. 246.
36 Sutherland, *Breakdown*, p. 17.
37 Sutherland, *Breakdown*, p. 20.
38 N. Bawden (1995) *In My Own Time*. London: Virago, p. 120.
39 M. Barnes (1973) Flection/Reflection, p. 176. In Brown, *Radical Psychology*.
40 E. Showalter (1987) *The Female Malady: Women, madness and English culture 1830–1980*. London: Virago, p. 232.
41 Showalter, *The Female Malady*, ch. 9.
42 P. Chesler (1972) *Women and Madness*. London: Allen Lane.
43 S. H. Kardener (1974) Sex and the physician–patient relationship. *American Journal of Psychiatry*, 131: 1134–6; J. C. Holroyd and A. M. Brodsky (1977) Psychologists' attitudes and practices regarding erotic and nonerotic physical contact with patients. *American Psychologist*, 32: 843–9.
44 J. Bouhoutsos (1984) Sexual intimacy between psychotherapists and clients: policy implications for the future. In L. E. Walker (ed.) *Women and Mental Health Policy*. Beverly Hills: Sage.
45 P. B. Medawar (1975) Victims of psychiatry. *New York Review of Books*, 21: 23 January.
46 H. J. Eysenck (1952) The effects of psychotherapy: an evaluation. *Journal of Consulting Psychology*, 16: 319–24.
47 H. J. Eysenck (1973) *The Experimental Study of Freudian Theories*. London: Methuen, pp. 374–5.
48 R. Crow, H. Gage, S. Hampson, J. Hart, A. Kimker and H. Thomas (1999) The role of expectancies in the placebo effect and their use in the delivery of health care: a systematic review. *Health Technology Assessment*, 3(3): 1–96.
49 H. M. Bachrach, R. Galatzer-Levy, A. Skolnikoff and S. Waldron (1991) On the efficacy of psychoanalysis. *Journal of the American Psychoanalytic Association*, 39: 871–916.
50 Malcolm, *Psychoanalysis*, p. 151.
51 S. L. Weiss (1972) Perceived effectiveness of psychotherapy: a function of suggestion? *Journal of Consulting and Clinical Psychology*, 39: 156–9.
52 H. Feifel and J. Eells (1963) Patients and therapists assess the same psychotherapy. *Journal of Consulting Psychology*, 27: 310–18.
53 J. Laurance (2000) Therapists take a dim view of Waynes' world. *Independent*, 5 July.
54 See the references cited in H. J. Eysenck (1985) *Decline and Fall of the Freudian Empire*, p. 80. Harmondsworth: Viking; see also W. M. Epstein (1995) *The Illusion of Psychotherapy*. New Brunswick, N.J., and London: Transaction.
55 D. A. Shapiro (1996) Foreword, p. ix. In A. Roth and P. Fonagy. *What Works for Whom? A critical review of psychotherapy research*. New York: Guildford Press.

56 O. Denman (1995) Questions to be answered in the evaluation of long-term therapy. In M. Aveline and D. A. Shapiro (eds) *Research Foundations for Psychotherapy Practice*. Chichester: John Wiley.

57 A. E. Bergin (1975) Psychotherapy can be dangerous. *Psychology Today*, 9: 96–105.

58 M. L. Smith and G. V. Glass (1977) Meta-analysis of psychotherapy outcome studies. *American Psychologist*, 32(9): 752–60.

59 L. Prioleau, M. Murdock and N. Brody (1983) An analysis of psychotherapy versus placebo studies. *Behavioral and Brain Sciences*, 6: 275–310.

60 J. D. Frank (1983) The placebo is psychotherapy. Commentary, Prioleau et al., *Behavioral and Brain Sciences*, 2: 291.

61 H. W. Simons (1989) Distinguishing the rhetorical from the real: the case of psychotherapeutic placebos. In H. W. Simons (ed.) *Rhetoric in the Human Sciences*. London: Sage, p. 114.

62 H. Strupp (1979) Specific vs. non-specific factors in psychotherapy: a controlled study of outcome. *Archives of General Psychiatry*, 36: 1125–36.

63 Malcolm, *Psychoanalysis*, p. 72.

64 Medawar, *Power and Dependence*.

65 See e.g., L. F. Berkman (1984) Assessing the physical health effects of social networks and social support. *American Review of Public Health*, 5: 413–32; S. Duck (1991) *Friends, for Life: The psychology of personal relationships*. Hemel Hempstead: Harvester Wheatsheaf; A. Oakley (1992) *Social Support and Motherhood*. Oxford: Blackwell.

66 P. Lomas (1993) *Cultivating Intuition: An introduction to psychotherapy*. Northvale, N.J.: Jason Aronson.

67 S. Morgan (1999) Interview with Peter Lomas, p. 22. In King, *Committed Uncertainty in Psychotherapy*.

68 P. Lomas (1987) *The Limits of Interpretation: What's wrong with psychoanalysis?*. Harmondsworth: Penguin.

69 S. Duck (ed.) (1990) *Personal Relationships and Social Support*. London: Sage.

70 Cited in Malcolm, *Psychoanalysis*, p. 25.

71 D. Smail (1999) A century of psychotherapy. In King, *Committed Uncertainty in Psychoanalysis*.

72 N. G. Hale (1971) *Freud and the Americans: The beginnings of psychoanalysis in the USA 1876–1907*. New York: Oxford University Press.

73 S. Turkle (1979) *Psychoanalytic Politics: Freud's French revolution*. London: Deutsch.

74 M. Glenn and R. Kunnes (1973) *Repression or Revolution?*. New York: Harper and Row, p. 50.

75 D. Tennov (1975) *Psychotherapy: The hazardous cure*. New York: Anchor Books, p. 13.

76 Glenn and Kunnes, *Repression or Revolution?*

77 Denman, Questions to be answered, p. 178.

78 R. L. Bednar and J. G. Shapiro (1970) Professional research commitment: a symptom or a syndrome? *Journal of Consulting and Clinical Psychology*, 34(3): 323–6.

79 M. Brody (1962) Prognosis and results of psychotherapy. In J. Nodine and J.

Moyer (eds) *Psychosomatic Medicine*. Philadelphia: Lea and Fobiger; Stannard, *Shrinking History*, pp. 38–9.

80   D. Smith (2000) Analysts turn to P.R. to market themselves. *New York Times on the Web*, 9 December, http://www.psychoanalysis.org.uk/media.htm.

81   D. Strassman (1993) Not a free market: the rhetoric of disciplinary authority in economics, p. 55. In M. A. Ferber and J. A. Nelson (eds) *Beyond Economic Man: Feminist theory and economics*. Chicago: University of Chicago Press.

82   J. Humphries (2000) Rational economic families? Economics, the family and the economy. In J. Cook, J. Roberts and G. Waylen (eds) *Towards a Gendered Political Economy*. Basingstoke: Macmillan.

83   P. Ormerod (1994) *The Death of Economics*. London: Faber and Faber, p. 3

84   P. Ormerod (1998) *Butterfly Economics*. London: Faber and Faber, p. 79.

85   Ormerod, *Butterfly Economics*, p. 80.

86   Ormerod, *The Death of Economics*, p. 106; see S. Keen (2001) *Debunking Economics: The naked emperor of the social sciences*. London: Zed Books, ch. 10.

87   Keen, *Debunking Economics*.

88   T. Veblen (1994, originally published 1899) *The Theory of the Leisure Class*. Mineola, N.Y.: Dove Publications.

89   Ormerod, *The Death of Economics*, p. 116.

90   J. K. Galbraith (1980) *Annals of an Abiding Liberal*. London: André Deutsch, pp. 29–30.

91   Keen, *Debunking Economics*, p. 4.

92   D. N. McCloskey (1998) *The Rhetoric of Economics*. 2nd edition. Madison, Wis.: University of Wisconsin Press, p. 36.

93   D. N. McCloskey (1993) Some consequences of a conjective economics, p. 81. In Ferber and Nelson, *Beyond Economic Man*.

94   D. N. McCloskey and S. Ziliak (1996) The standard error of regression. *Journal of Economic Literature*, 34(March): 97–114.

95   Keen, *Debunking Economics*, p. 312.

96   Ormerod, *The Death of Economics*, p. 67.

97   Ormerod, *The Death of Economics*, p. 4.

98   M. A. Ferber and J. A. Nelson (1993) Introduction: the social construction of economics and the social construction of gender. In Ferber and Nelson, *Beyond Economic Man*.

99   Ormerod, *Butterfly Economics*, p. 3.

100   P. Samuelson (1961) *Economics: An introductory analysis*. New York: McGraw-Hill, p. 6.

101   L. Robbins (1932) *An Essay on the Nature and Significance of Economic Science*. London: Macmillan, p. 15.

102   A. W. Stonier and D. C. Hague (1957) *A Textbook of Economic Theory*. 2nd edition. London: Longmans, Green, pp. 2, 34.

103   Galbraith, *Annals of an Abiding Liberal*, p. 88.

104   Keen, *Debunking Economics*, p. 2.

105   Ormerod, *The Death of Economics*, p. 34.

106   B. Brandt (1995) *Whole Life Economics: Revaluing daily life*. Philadelphia: New Society Publishers.

107 M. Waring (1988) *Counting for Nothing: What men value and what women are worth.* London: Allen and Unwin with Port Nicholson Press.

108 Ormerod, *The Death of Economics*, p. 31; Waring, *Counting for Nothing*, p. 236.

109 H. E. Daly and J. B. Cobb, with contributions by C. W. Cobb (1994) *For the Common Good: Redirecting the economy toward community, the environment, and a sustainable future.* Boston: Beacon Press.

110 Independent Commission on Population and the Quality of Life (1996) *Caring for the Future.* Oxford: Oxford University Press, p. 91.

111 J. Diamond (1997) *Guns, Germs and Steel.* New York: W. W. Norton, p. 248.

112 J. Robinson (1978) *Contributions to Modern Economic Philosophy.* Oxford: Blackwell, p. 239.

113 Galbraith, *Annals of an Abiding Liberal*, p. 359.

114 Galbraith, *Annals of an Abiding Liberal*, p. 34.

115 Galbraith, *Annals of an Abiding Liberal*, p. 361.

116 Ormerod, *The Death of Economics*, p. 3.

117 Galbraith, *Annals of an Abiding Liberal*, p. 354.

118 Ormerod, *The Death of Economics*, p. 211.

119 M. Lewis (1990) *Liar's Poker.* London: Coronet Books.

120 Cited in Ormerod, *The Death of Economics*, pp. 34–5.

121 N. Folbre (2001) *The Invisible Heart: Economics and family values.* New York: New Press.

122 J. K. Galbraith (1974) *Economics and the Public Purpose.* London: André Deutsch, p. 233.

123 J. Robinson (1978) *Contributions to Modern Economics.* Oxford: Blackwell, p. ix.

124 J. Robinson (1971) *Economic Heresies: Some old-fashioned questions in economic theory.* London: Macmillan, p. 144.

125 Waring, *Counting for Nothing*, p. 30.

126 See Ormerod, *Butterfly Economics*, ch. 3.

127 G. S. Becker (1974) A theory of marriage: Part II. *Journal of Political Economy*, 82(2): S11–12.

128 Strassman, Not a free market.

129 See B. G. Birnbaum and M. A. Ferber (1977) The 'New Home Economics': retrospects and prospects. *Journal of Consumer Research*, 4(June): 19–28; Humphries, Rational economic families?

130 A. Sen (1984) *Resources, Values and Development.* Cambridge, Mass.: Harvard University Press.

131 S. Kumar (1979) *Impact of Subsidized Rice on Food Consumption and Nutrition in Kerala.* Washington, D.C.: International Food Policy Research Institute.

132 A. Oakley (2000) *Experiments in Knowing: Gender and method in the social sciences.* Cambridge: Polity, pp. 240–3.

133 McCloskey, *The Rhetoric of Economics*, p. 40.

134 D. N. McCloskey (1996) *The Vices of Economists – The Virtues of the Bourgeoisie.* Amsterdam: Amsterdam University Press, pp. 13–14.

135 J. Cook and J. Roberts (2000) Towards a gendered political economy. In Cook et al., *Towards a Gendered Political Economy*.

136 See G. J. Hewitson (1999) *Feminist Economics: Interrogating the masculinity of Rational Economic Man*. Cheltenham: Edward Elgar.

137 R. Albelda (1995) The impact of feminism in economics – beyond the pale? A discussion and survey results. *Journal of Economic Education*, 26(3): 253–73.

138 On the similarities and differences between sociobiology and evolutionary psychology, see H. Rose and S. Rose (2000) Introduction. In H. Rose and S. Rose (eds) *Alas, Poor Darwin: Arguments against evolutionary psychology*. London: Jonathan Cape.

139 J. H. Barkow, L. Cosmides and J. Tooby (1992) *The Adapted Mind*. Oxford: Oxford University Press, ch. 1. See also U. Segerstråle (2000) *Defenders of the Truth: The sociobiology debate*. Oxford: Oxford University Press.

140 J. Browne (1995) *Charles Darwin: Voyaging*. London: Jonathan Cape, p. xiii.

141 M. Sahlins (1977) *The Use and Abuse of Biology: An anthropological critique of sociobiology*. London: Tavistock, p. 72.

142 Cited in A. Schmidt (1971) *The Concept of Nature in Marx*. London: NLB, p. 46.

143 C. Degler (1991) *In Search of Human Nature*. Oxford: Oxford University Press, p. 27.

144 D. Nelkin and L. Tancredi (1994, originally published 1989) *Dangerous Diagnostics: The social power of biological information*. Chicago: Chicago University Press, p. xiv.

145 R. Lewontin (2000) *It Ain't Necessarily So*. London: Granta Books, p. 193.

146 Nelkin and Tancredi, *Dangerous Diagnostics*, p. xiv.

147 P. B. Medawar and J. S. Medawar (1977) *The Life Science – Current ideas of biology*. New York: Harper and Row, p. 38.

148 *Daily Mail*, 18 May 1996.

149 *Metro*, 12 April 2001.

150 *Guardian*, 14 April 2000.

151 Lewontin, *It Ain't Necessarily So*, pp. 159–60.

152 D. J. Kevles (1985) *In the Name of Eugenics: Genetics and the uses of human heredity*. New York: Alfred A. Knopf.

153 E. O. Wilson (1978) *On Human Nature*. Cambridge, Mass.: Harvard University Press, p. 16.

154 Wilson, *On Human Nature*, p. 125.

155 See A. Fausto-Sterling (2000) Beyond difference: feminism and evolutionary psychology. In Rose and Rose, *Alas, Poor Darwin*.

156 S. B. Hrdy (2000) *Mother Nature*. New York: Vintage, p. 39.

157 R. Thornhill and C. T. Palmer (2000) *A Natural History of Rape: Biological bases of sexual coercion*. Cambridge, Mass.: MIT Press, pp. 48–50.

158 Hrdy, *Mother Nature*.

159 R. Baker and M. A. Bellis (1995) *Human Sperm Competition: Copulation, masturbation and infidelity*. London: Chapman and Hall.

160 R. Baker (1996) *Sperm Wars*. London: Fourth Estate.

161 Baker, *Sperm Wars*, p. xi.

162 Thornhill and Palmer, *A Natural History of Rape*, pp. 44–5.

163 Thornhill and Palmer, *A Natural History of Rape*, p. 45.

164   J. Archer (1988) *The Behavioural Basis of Aggression*. Cambridge: Cambridge University Press, p. 9.
165   R. Prentky (1985) The neurochemistry and neuroendocrinology of sexual aggression, p. 13. In D. P. Farrington and J. Gunn (eds) *Aggression and Dangerousness*. Chichester: John Wiley.
166   Getting human nature right. A talk with Helena Cronin. *Edge*, 73. 30 August 2000, http://www.edge.org/documents/archive/edge73.html.
167   Thornhill and Palmer, *A Natural History of Rape*, p. 113.
168   Segerstråle, *Defenders of the Truth*, p. 49.
169   E. O. Wilson (2000) *Sociobiology: The new synthesis*. 25th anniversary edition. Cambridge, Mass.: Belknap Press of Harvard University Press, p. 597.
170   E. O. Wilson (1998) *Consilience: The unity of knowledge*. London: Abacus, pp. 2–3.
171   Wilson, *Consilience*, p. 4.
172   Kevles, *In the Name of Eugenics*, p. 12.
173   Wilson, *Sociobiology*, p. 254.
174   R. Dawkins (1989, originally published 1976) *The Selfish Gene*. Oxford: Oxford University Press, p. ix.
175   Dawkins, *The Selfish Gene*, p. 19.
176   Segerstråle, *Defenders of the Truth*, p. 1.
177   S. Rose, L. J. Kamin and R. Lewontin (1984) *Not in Our Genes: Biology, ideology and human nature*. Harmondsworth: Penguin, p. 35.
178   M. Midgley (1980) Rival fatalisms: the hollowness of the sociobiological debate, p. 31. In A. Montagu (ed.) *Sociobiology Examined*. Oxford: Oxford University Press.
179   M. Harris (1980) Sociobiology and biological reductionism, p. 320. In Montagu, *Sociobiology Examined*.
180   Prentky, The neurochemistry and neuroendocrinology of sexual aggression, p. 19.
181   J. H. Barkow (1980) Sociobiology: is this the new theory of human nature? p. 172. In Montagu, *Sociobiology Examined*.
182   See e.g., D. A. Lawler, S. Ebrahim and G. Davey-Smith (2001) Sex matters: secular and geographical trends in sex differences in coronary heart disease mortality. *British Medical Journal*, 323: 541–5.
183   See e.g., C. P. MacCormack and M. Strathern (eds) (1980) *Nature, Culture and Gender*. Cambridge: Cambridge University Press; H. C. Triandis (1994) *Culture and Social Behavior*. New York: McGraw-Hill.
184   S. Rose (1995) An inside job or a set up? *Times Higher Education Supplement*, 10 February.
185   G. Hofstede (2001) *Culture's Consequences: Comparing values, behaviors, institutions, and organizations across nations*. Thousand Oaks, Calif.: Sage.
186   Dawkins, *The Selfish Gene*, p. 3.
187   R. Dawkins (1982) *The Extended Phenotype: The gene as unit of selection*. Oxford and San Francisco: Freeman, p. 16.
188   S. Rose (1980) It's only human nature: the sociobiologist's fairyland, p. 165. In Montagu, *Sociobiology Examined*.
189   Fausto-Sterling, Beyond difference, p. 181.

190 L. Tiger (1990) The cerebral bridge from family to foe, p. 101. In J. van der Dennen and V. Folger, *Sociobiology and Conflict: Evolutionary perspectives on competition, cooperation, violence and warfare*. London: Chapman and Hall.

191 See e.g., A. B. Blackwell (1976, originally published 1875) *The Sexes Throughout Nature*. Westport, Conn.: Hyperion Press; S. B. Hrdy (1981) *The Woman That Never Evolved*. Cambridge, Mass.: Harvard University Press; R. Hubbard (1990) *The Politics of Women's Biology*. New Brunswick, N.J.: Rutgers University Press, ch. 7.

192 M. Ridley (1996) *The Origins of Virtue*. Harmondsworth: Penguin, p. 95.

193 Wilson, *On Human Nature*, pp. 82–6.

194 M. Harris (1978) *Cannibals and Kings*. London: Collins, pp. 16–17.

195 Ridley, *The Origins of Virtue*, p. 91.

196 See H. Rose (2000) Colonising the social sciences. In Rose and Rose, *Alas, Poor Darwin*.

197 B. Parbing (2001) Man or woman? *Genus* (Swedish Secretariat for Gender Research), 1, pp. 28–9.

198 S. Slocum (1975) Woman the gatherer: male bias in anthropology. In R. Reiter (ed.) *Toward an Anthropology of Women*. New York: Monthly Review Press. See also J. M. Gero and M. W. Conkey (1991) *Engendering Archeology: Women and prehistory*. Oxford: Blackwell.

199 B. Latour and S. C. Strum (1986) Human social origins: oh please, tell us another story. *Journal of Social and Biological Structures*, 9: 169–87.

200 Midgley, Rival fatalisms, p. 26.

201 Rose and Rose, Introduction, p. 3.

202 Ridley, *The Origins of Virtue*.

203 R. Herrnstein and C. Murray (1984) *The Bell Curve: Intelligence and class structure in American life*. New York: Free Press.

204 C. Murray (1984) *Losing Ground: American social policy 1950–1980*. New York: Basic Books.

205 R. Jacoby and N. Glauberman (eds) (1995) *The Bell Curve: History, documents, opinions*. New York: Random House.

206 K. Browne (1998) *Divided Labours: An evolutionary view of women at work*. London: Weidenfeld and Nicolson, p. 5.

207 A. Moir and B. Moir (1999) *Why Men Don't Iron: The new reality of gender differences*. London: HarperCollins, p. 275.

208 Browne, *Divided Labours*, p. 60.

209 S. Goldberg (1977) *The Inevitability of Patriarchy*. London: Temple Smith.

210 Rose et al., *Not in Our Genes*, p. 149.

211 Lewontin, *It Ain't Necessarily So*, p. 210.

212 M. Small (ed.) (1984) *Female Primates: Studies by women primatologists*. New York: Allan Liss.

213 N. Pastore (1949) *The Nature–Nurture Controversy*. New York: King's Crown Press, p. 176.

214 Lewontin, *It Ain't Necessarily So*, p. 198.

215 Lewontin, *It Ain't Necessarily So*, p. 34.

216 Midgley, Rival fatalisms, p. 132.

217 Degler, *In Search of Human Nature*.

218 A. Oakley (1997) A brief history of gender. In A. Oakley and J. Mitchell (eds) *Who's Afraid of Feminism?*. London: Hamish Hamilton.

219 D. Nelkin (2000) Less selfish than sacred? Genes and the religious impulse in evolutionary psychology. In Rose and Rose, *Alas, Poor Darwin*.

220 S. Rose (1997) *Lifelines: Biology, freedom, determinism*. London: Penguin, p. 277.

221 T. Laqueur (1990) *Making Sex: Body and gender from the Greeks to Freud*. Cambridge, Mass.: Harvard University Press.

222 Wilson, *Sociobiology*, p. 548.

223 Wilson, *On Human Nature*, p. 46.

224 Lewontin, *It Ain't Necessarily So*, p. xiii.

225 R. L. Sinsheimer (1989) The Santa Cruz Workshop, May 1985. *Genomics*, 5(4): 954–6.

226 *Human Genome Project Fact Sheet May 2001*. Excerpts from vol. II (1–2). US Department of Energy Office of Biological and Environmental Research. Available at www.ornl.gov/hgmis/project/about.html.

227 Human Genome Working Draft: First-Edition Travel Guides. *Human Genome News*, 11(3–4), July 2001 (http://www.ornl.gov/hgmis/publicat/hgm/v11n3/03draft.html).

228 D. J. Kevles and L. Hood (1992) *The Code of Codes: Scientific and social issues in the human genome project*. Cambridge, Mass.: Harvard University Press, p. 36.

229 *Human Genome News*.

230 D. Nelkin (1992) The social power of genetic information, p. 177. In Kevles and Hood, *The Code of Codes*.

231 J. D. Watson (1992) A personal view of the project. In Kevles and Hood, *The Code of Codes*.

232 *Human Genome Project Fact Sheet*, p. 3.

233 R. Zimmern, J. Emery and T. Richards (2001) Putting genetics in perspective. (Editorial). *British Medical Journal*, 322: 1005–6, p. 1005.

234 S. Jones (2001) *Genetics in Medicine: Real promises, unreal expectations. One scientist's advice to policymakers in the United Kingdom and the United States*. Milbank Memorial Fund (available at www.milbank.org/000712genetics.html).

235 S. Steingraber (2000) The social production of cancer: a walk upstream, p. 23. In R. Hofrichter (ed.) *Reclaiming the Environmental Debate: The politics of health in a toxic culture*. Cambridge, Mass.: MIT Press.

236 S. Sherwin and C. Simpson (1999) Ethical questions in the pursuit of genetic information: geneticization and BRCA1. In A. K. Thompson and R. F. Chadwick (eds) *Genetic Information: Acquisition, access and control*. New York: Kluwer Academic/Plenum Publishing.

237 T. M. Marteau and C. Lerman (2001) Genetic risk and behavioural change. *British Medical Journal*, 322: 1056–9, p. 1057.

238 N. Holtzman (2001) The cautious view. *British Medical Journal*, 322: 1017.

239 S. L. Washburn (1980) Human behavior and the behavior of other animals, p. 276. In Montagu, *Sociobiology Examined*.

240 Rose and Rose, Introduction, p. 4.

241   K. Bock (1994) *Human Nature Mythology*. Urbana: University of Illinois Press, pp. 102–3.

242   A. Sokal (1996) Transgressing the boundaries: toward a transformative hermeneutics of quantum gravity. *Social Text*, 46/47: 217–52. Reprinted as Appendix A in A. Sokal and J. Bricmont (1998) *Intellectual Impostures*. London: Profile Books.

243   W. T. Anderson (1996) Introduction: what's going on here?, p. 2. In W. T. Anderson (ed.) *The Fontana Postmodernism Reader*. London: HarperCollins.

244   Z. Bauman (1992) *Intimations of Postmodernity*. London: Routledge, p. vii.

245   P. Anderson (1998) *The Origins of Postmodernity*. London: Verso, p. 4

246   D. Harvey (1989) *The Condition of Postmodernity: An enquiry into the origins of cultural change*. Oxford: Blackwell.

247   E. Sternberg (1996) The economy of icons. In Anderson, *The Fontana Postmodernism Reader*.

248   V. Havel (1996) The search for meaning in a global civilization, p. 209. In Anderson, *The Fontana Postmodernism Reader*.

249   P. Feyerabend (1996) Anything goes, p. 196. In Anderson, *The Fontana Postmodernism Reader*.

250   P. Taylor-Gooby (1994) Postmodernism and social policy: a great leap backwards. *Journal of Social Policy*, 23(3): 385–404.

251   J.-F. Lyotard (1984, originally published 1979) *The Postmodern Condition: A report on knowledge*. Trans. G. Bennington and B. Massumi. Manchester: Manchester University Press.

252   S. Katz (1996) How to speak and write postmodern. In Anderson, *The Fontana Postmodernism Reader*.

253   Bauman, *Intimations of Postmodernity*, pp. 93–4.

254   b. hooks (1996) Postmodern blackness, p. 114. In Anderson, *The Fontana Postmodernism Reader*.

255   Sokal and Bricmont, *Intellectual Impostures*, pp. 180–2.

256   See Sokal and Bricmont, *Intellectual Impostures*.

257   Cited in Anderson, *The Origins of Postmodernity*, p. 26.

258   Release from ANANOVA, 13 September 2001, http://www.ananova.com/news/story/sm 397678.html, accessed September 2001.

259   Tiger, The cerebral bridge, p. 105.

260   M. Konner (1982) *The Tangled Wing: Biological constraints on the human spirit*. New York: Holt, Rinehart and Winston, p. 126.

261   D. Layzer (1980) On the evolution of intelligence and social behaviour, p. 221. In Montagu, *Sociobiology Examined*.

262   Rose et al., *Not in Our Genes*, p. 23.

Chapter 9 World-travelling

1   D. N. McCloskey (1999) *Crossing: A memoir*. Chicago: University of Chicago Press, p. xii.

2   McCloskey, *Crossing*, p. 53.

3   McCloskey, *Crossing*, p. xv.
4   McCloskey, *Crossing*, p. 58.
5   McCloskey, *Crossing*, p. 80.
6   D. N. McCloskey (1998) *The Rhetoric of Economics*. 2nd edition. Madison, Wis.: University of Wisconsin Press, p. 192.
7   D. N. McCloskey (1993) Some consequences of a conjective economics, p. 86. In M. A. Ferber and J. A. Nelson (eds) *Beyond Economic Man: Feminist theory and economics*. Chicago: University of Chicago Press.
8   McCloskey, *Crossing*, p. 209.
9   J. Morris (1997, originally published 1974) *Conundrum*. London: Penguin, p. 140.
10 B. L. Hausman (1995) *Changing Sex: Transsexualism, technology and the idea of gender*. Durham, N.C., and London: Duke University Press.
11 N. Nicholson (1973) *Portrait of a Marriage*. London: Futura, p. 209.
12 M. Garber (1993) *Vested Interests: Cross-dressing and cultural anxiety*. London: Penguin, p. 134.
13 V. Woolf (1993, originally published 1928) *Orlando: A biography*. London: Virago, p. 99.
14 Woolf, *Orlando*, p. 100.
15 C. P. Gilman (1914) If I were a man. Reprinted in A. J. Lane (ed.) (1981) *The Charlotte Perkins Gilman Reader*. London: Women's Press, p. 35.
16 A. Carter (1982, originally published 1977) *The Passion of New Eve*. London: Virago, p. 9.
17 Carter, *The Passion of New Eve*, pp. 74–6.
18 McCloskey, *Crossing*, pp. 83–4.
19 Morris, *Conundrum*, p. 8.
20 J. H. Griffin (1960) *Black Like Me*. New York: Signet Books, pp. 15–16.
21 U. K. Le Guin (1974) *The Dispossessed: An ambiguous utopia*. New York: Harper and Row, pp. 14–15.
22 Le Guin, *The Dispossessed*, p. 117.
23 J. Russ (1972) The image of women in science fiction. In S. K. Cornillon (ed.) *Images of Women in Fiction: Feminist perspectives*. Bowling Green, Ohio: Bowling Green University Popular Press, p. 81.
24 A. S. Williams (1992) Introduction. In A. S. Williams (ed.) *The Penguin Book of Classic Fantasy by Women*. London: Penguin, p. xi.
25 B. W. Aldiss (1986) *The Trillion Year Spree: The history of science fiction*. London: Victor Gollancz, p. 14.
26 S. M. Gilbert and S. Gubar (1979) *The Madwoman in the Attic: The woman writer and the nineteenth century literary imagination*. New Haven, Conn.: Yale University Press, p. 221.
27 J. Newman (1991) Mary and the monster: Mary Shelley's *Frankenstein* and Maureen Duffy's *Gor Saga*. In L. Armitt (ed.) *Where No Man Has Gone Before: Women and science fiction*. London: Routledge.
28 See J. Wolmark (1994) *Aliens and Others: Science fiction, feminism and post-modernism*. Hemel Hempstead.: Harvester Wheatsheaf, p. 87.
29 M. Shelley, *Frankenstein or the Modern Prometheus: The 1818 text*. Ed. M. Butler. Oxford: Oxford University Press, p. 189.

30 N. M. Rosinsky (1984) *Feminist Futures: Contemporary women's speculative fiction*. Ann Arbor, Mich.: UMI Research Press.

31 See M. Harris (1969) *The Rise of Anthropological Theory*. London: Routledge and Kegan Paul, ch. 12.

32 J. Russ (1995) *To Write Like a Woman: Essays in feminism and science fiction*. Bloomington: Indiana University Press, p. 90.

33 Russ, *To Write Like a Woman*, p. 91.

34 D. Haraway (1992) *Primate Visions*. London: Verso, p. 378; Aldiss, *The Trillion Year Spree*, p. 365.

35 S. Lefanu (1988) *In the Chinks of the World Machine: Feminism and science fiction*. London: Women's Press, p. 116.

36 Lefanu, *In the Chinks of the World Machine*, p. 122; Williams, Introduction, p. x.

37 Lefanu, *In the Chinks of the World Machine*, p. 122.

38 A. James Tiptree, Jr, Bibliography. http://www.mtsu.edu/~lavery/Tiptree/, accessed September 2001.

39 Haraway, *Primate Visions*, p. 431.

40 D. du Pont (ed.) (1988) *Women of Vision*. New York: St Martin's Press, pp. 43–6.

41 J. Tiptree (1990) Houston, Houston, do you read? In *Her Smoke Rose up Forever: The great years of James Tiptree Jnr*. Intro. John Clute. Sauk City, Wis.: Arkham.

42 Tiptree, Houston, Houston, do you read?, p. 221.

43 Tiptree, Houston, Houston, do you read?, pp. 221–2, 182.

44 Haraway, *Primate Visions*, p. 1.

45 Quoted in Lefanu, *In the Chinks of the World Machine*, p. 112.

46 See Wolmark, *Aliens and Others*.

47 J. Hanna (1985) The Greenskins are here: women, men and aliens. In J. Blackford (ed.) *Contrary Modes: Proceedings of the World Science Fiction Conference, Melbourne, Australia*. Melbourne: Ebony Books.

48 See N. B. Albinski (1988) *Women's Utopias in British and American Fiction*. London: Routledge, ch. 6; Russ, *To Write Like a Woman*, pp. 133–46; Lefanu, *In the Chinks of the World Machine*, ch. 6.

49 S. M. Gearhart (1985) *The Wanderground*. London: Women's Press, p. 4.

50 U. K. Le Guin (1973) *The Left Hand of Darkness*. London: Panther, p. 69.

51 U. K. Le Guin (1989) *Dancing at the Edge of the World: Thoughts on words, women, places*. New York: Harper and Row, pp. 10–11.

52 Le Guin, *Dancing at the Edge of the World*, p. 143.

53 Le Guin, *Dancing at the Edge of the World*, p. 9.

54 Russ, cited in M. Hacker (1977) Science fiction and feminism: the world of Joanna Russ. *Chrysalis*, 4: 67–79, p. 73.

55 Russ, cited in Rosinky, *Feminist Futures*, p. 67.

56 J. Russ (1985, originally published 1975) *The Female Man*. London: Women's Press, p. 18.

57 M. Hacker (1977) Introduction to J. Russ, *The Female Man*. Boston: Gregg Press, p. xix.

58 Russ, *The Female Man*, pp. 162–3.

59 Russ, *The Female Man*, p. 54.

60 M. Piercy (1979) *Woman on the Edge of Time*. London: Women's Press, p. 105.

61   Piercy, *Woman on the Edge of Time*, p. 62.
62   Piercy, *Woman on the Edge of Time*, p. 68.
63   Piercy, *Woman on the Edge of Time*, p. 67.
64   C. P. Gilman (1998, originally published 1898) *Woman and Economics.* Berkeley: University of California Press, p. 191.
65   C. P. Gilman (1979, originally published 1915) *Herland.* New York: Pantheon, p. 11.
66   Gilman, *Herland*, p. 19.
67   Gilman, *Herland*, pp. 60–1.
68   Gilman, *Herland*, p. 137.
69   Gearhart, *The Wanderground*, p. 187.
70   Piercy, *Woman on the Edge of Time*, p. 177.
71   Z. Fairbairns (1979) *Benefits.* London: Virago, pp. 38–9.
72   Fairbairns, *Benefits*, p. 46.
73   M. Atwood (1986) *The Handmaid's Tale.* London: Jonathan Cape, p. 14.
74   Atwood, *The Handmaid's Tale*, p. 105.
75   Atwood, *The Handmaid's Tale*, pp. 221–2.
76   S. M. Charnos (1978) *Walk to the Edge of the World and Motherlines.* London: Women's Press, pp. 4–5.
77   Rosinsky, *Feminist Futures*, p. 111.
78   Garber, *Vested Interests*, p. 4.
79   V. L. Bullough and B. Bullough (1993) *Cross Dressing, Sex, and Gender.* Philadelphia: University of Pennsylvania Press, p. x.
80   Garber, *Vested Interests*, p. 1.
81   Garber, *Vested Interests*, p. 68.
82   Bullough and Bullough, *Cross Dressing, Sex, and Gender*, p. 160.
83   Bullough and Bullough, *Cross Dressing, Sex, and Gender*, pp. 53, 57.
84   C. G. Heilbrun (1989) *Writing a Woman's Life.* London: Women's Press, p. 34.
85   Quoted in Heilbrun, *Writing a Woman's Life*, p. 36.
86   J. Uglow (1987) *George Eliot.* London: Virago, p. 84.
87   Gilbert and Gubar, *Madwoman in the Attic*, p. 65.
88   Heilbrun, *Writing a Woman's Life*, ch. 6.
89   Quoted in Lefanu, *In the Chinks of the World Machine*, pp. 121–2.
90   C. G. Heilbrun (1964) *Towards a Recognition of Androgyny.* New York: W. W. Norton, p. 72.
91   C. Ohmann (1971) Emily Brontë in the hands of male critics. *College English*, 32: 906–13.

Chapter 10 Civic Rituals and Real Futures

1   *Daily Express*, 5 October 2001.
2   C. Cockburn (1991) *In the Way of Women: Men's resistance to sex equality in organizations.* Basingstoke: Macmillan, p. 18.
3   S. Walby (1990) *Theorizing Patriarchy.* Oxford: Blackwell, p. 201.
4   Walby, *Theorizing Patriarchy*, p. 20.
5   G. Lerner (1986) *The Creation of Patriarchy.* Oxford: Oxford University Press, p. 239.

6   H. Hartmann (1981) The unhappy marriage of Marxism and feminism: towards a more progressive union. In L. Sargent (ed.) *Women and Revolution*. London: Pluto Press, pp. 14–15.

7   S. Jeffords (1989) *The Remasculinization of America: Gender and the Vietnam War.* Bloomington: Indiana University Press, p. xii.

8   R. Littlewood and M. Lipsedge (1982) *Aliens and Alienists: Ethnic minorities and psychiatry.* Harmondsworth: Penguin, pp. 37–8.

9   Z. R. Eisenstein (1994) *The Color of Gender: Reimaging democracy.* Berkeley: University of California Press, p. 1.

10 Z. R. Eisenstein (1996) *Hatreds: Racialized and sexualized conflicts in the twenty-first century.* London: Routledge, p. 53.

11 N. Wolf (2001) *Misconceptions: Truth, lies and the unexpected on the journey to motherhood.* New York: Doubleday; R. Cusk (2001) *A Life's Work.* London: Fourth Estate.

12 C. Romany (1993) Women as aliens: a feminist critique of the public/private distinction in international human rights law. *Harvard Human Rights Journal*, 1(6): 87–125, p. 125.

13 Eisenstein, *Hatreds*, p. 54.

14 R. Kennedy (2000) Women feel hemmed in by space-invading men. *New York Times*, 14 November.

15 N. M. Henley (1977) *Body Politics: Power, sex, and non-verbal communication.* Englewood Cliffs, N.J.: Prentice-Hall.

16 J. Russ (1998) *What Are We Fighting For? Sex, race, class, and the future of feminism.* New York: St Martin's Press, pp. 44–5.

17 A. G. Johnson (1997) *The Gender Knot: Unravelling our patriarchal legacy.* Philadelphia: Temple University Press, p. 159.

18 A. C. Jónasdottir (1991) *Love, Power and Political Interests: Towards a theory of patriarchy in contemporary Western societies.* Örebro Studies no. 7. Sweden: University of Örebro.

19 R. N. Bellah, R. Madsen, W. M. Sullivan, A. Swidler and S. M. Tipton (1992) *The Good Society.* New York: Alfred A. Knopf, p. 10.

20 R. W. Connell (1995) *Masculinities.* Cambridge: Polity, p. 73.

21 Bellah et al., *The Good Society*, pp. 14–15.

22 Cockburn, *In the Way of Women*, p. 165.

23 R. Morgan (1978) *Going Too Far: The personal chronicle of a feminist.* New York: Vintage, p. 17.

24 Johnson, *The Gender Knot*, pp. 4–5.

25 Cockburn, *In the Way of Women*, p. 219.

26 D. E. Smith (1988) *The Everyday World as Problematic.* Milton Keynes: Open University Press, p. 34.

27 Connell, *Masculinities*, p. 215.

28 P. J. Williams (1977) *Seeing a Colour-Blind Future.* London: Virago, p. 10.

29 Eisenstein, *The Color of Gender*, p. 218.

30 A. Clare (2000) *On Men: Masculinity in crisis.* London: Chatto and Windus, p. 194.

31 J. Stoltenberg (2000, originally published 1989) *Refusing to be a Man: Essays on sex and justice.* London: UCL Press, p. xiv, p. 175.

32   A. Oakley (1974) *Housewife.* London: Allen Lane.

33   Williams, *Seeing a Colour-Blind Future*, p. 62.

34   S. Watson (1999) Introduction. In S. Watson and L. Doyal (eds) *Engendering Social Policy.* Buckingham: Open University Press, p. 9.

35   J. O'Neale (2000) One in six children live in relative poverty. *British Medical Journal*, 320: 1621.

36   I. Diamond (1994) *Fertile Ground.* Boston: Beacon Press, p. 9.

37   M. C. Bateson (1990) *Composing a Life.* Harmondsworth: Penguin, p. 239.

38   M. Sarton (1995, originally published 1977) *The House by the Sea: A journal.* London: Women's Press, p. 35.

39   P. Gilbert (1994) Male violence: Towards an integration, p. 383. In J. Archer (ed.) *Male Violence.* London: Routledge.

40   http://rawa.fancymarketing.net/stoning.htm, accessed November 2001. Unless otherwise indicated, all information about women in Afghanistan is from the RAWA website.

41   J. Goodwin and J. Neuwirth (2001) The rifle and the veil. *New York Times*, 29 October.

42   J. Smith (1998) *Different for Girls: How culture creates women.* London: Vintage, p. 156.

43   Goodwin and Neuwirth, The rifle and the veil.

44   M.-A. Stevenson (2001) Women in Afghanistan. *Towards Equality: the magazine of the Fawcett Society*, December, p. 3.

45   R. Fisk (2000) Saudi torture of women rampant, says Amnesty. *Independent*, 29 September.

46   Eisenstein, *Hatreds*, p. 25.

47   J. Nichols and R. W. McChesney (2000) *It's the Media, Stupid.* New York: Seven Stories Press, p. 59.

48   V. Woolf (1989) A Society. In S. Dick (ed.) *The Complete Shorter Fiction of Virginia Woolf.* London: Hogarth Press, p. 125.

49   Woolf, A Society, p. 127.

50   Woolf, A Society, p. 136.

51   M. Shiach (1992) Introduction, p. xviii. In M. Shiach (ed.) *Virginia Woolf, A Room of One's Own and Three Guineas.* Oxford: Oxford University Press.

52   J. Marcus (1987) *Virginia Woolf and the Languages of Patriarchy.* Bloomington: Indiana University Press, p. 53.

53   Marcus, *Virginia Woolf and the Languages of Patriarchy*; Shiach, Introduction.

54   Marcus, *Virginia Woolf and the Languages of Patriarchy*, p. 78.

55   B. Russell (1961) The expanding mental universe, pp. 392–3. In R. Egner and L. Dononn (eds) *The Basic Writings of Bertrand Russell.* London: Allen and Unwin.

Index

Index compiled by Jennifer Speake